English
Grammar
in Steps

English grammar presented,

explained and practised in context

by David Bolton & Noel Goodey

Contents

Introduction   5

Verb forms

1   The present simple: *She works*   6
2   The present continuous: *It's raining*   9
3   The present continuous: *He's smoking* OR the present simple: *He smokes?*   13
4   The present continuous and the present simple with future meaning   16
5   The past simple: *He was/He arrived*   18
6   The past continuous: *He was working*   22
7   The present perfect: *I've lost my job*   25
8   The present perfect with *just, yet, ever*, etc.   27
9   The present perfect: other uses   30
10   The past simple: *He came* OR the present perfect: *He's come*   32
11   The present perfect continuous: *He's been waiting for hours*   36
12   The present perfect: continuous or simple?   39
13   The past perfect: *He had come*   42
14   The future: *will/won't, shall/shan't*   45
15   *Going to* OR *will?*   48
16   The future continuous: *I'll be waiting* and the future perfect: *He'll have left*   50

Passives

17   The passive 1: *He was sacked*   Forms and main uses   53
18   The passive 2: other constructions   56
19   *Have/get something done*   60

Questions and answers

20   Questions   62
21   Question tags: *You're English, aren't you?*   65
22   The question words *Who? What? Which?   Do you know who/what/if*, etc?   69
23   *I think so, I hope so*, etc.   *So do I, Neither do I*, etc.   72
24   Auxiliary verbs used alone: *Will you come? – I might*   75

Modals and auxiliary verbs

25   *Can, could, be able to*   79
26   *Can, could, may, would* in requests, offers and invitations   82
27   *Must/mustn't   Have to/don't have to*   85
28   *Must, can't   Must have done, can't have done*   89
29   *May (have), might (have), could (have)*   92
30   *Should/ought to, had better   Should have/ought to have*   95

Other verb constructions

31   *Have got/have*   99
32   Phrasal verbs: *He took off his coat*   102
33   *Look, feel*, etc. + adjective or *like/as if*   105
34   *Used to*   108
35   *Get used to   Be used to*   111
36   The verb *need*   114
37   Verb + direct object/indirect object: *I sent him a letter*   117

If clauses and other conditionals

38 *If* sentences: 1st and 2nd conditional   120
39 *If* in past situations: 3rd conditional   124
40 *Unless, provided (that) As long as, in case*   127
41 *I wish .../If only ...*   130

The infinitive and the *-ing* form

42 The infinitive of purpose *In order to So that, so*   133
43 Verb + infinitive with *to: I want to go*   136
44 Verb + object + infinitive: *I want you to listen*   140
45 Adjective + infinitive: *It's difficult to say*   143
46 Verb + *-ing: I enjoy swimming*   146
47 Preposition + *-ing: I'm tired of waiting*   148
48 *Do you mind + -ing? I don't mind + -ing It's no use, there's no point*, etc. + *-ing*   151
49 *-ing* clauses: *He sat listening*   154
50 *Like, love, hate* + infinitive with *to* or *-ing*   157
51 *I prefer to do/I prefer doing I'd prefer to/I'd rather*   161
52 Verb + infinitive with *to* or + *-ing: Remember to do* or *remember doing*   164

Reported speech

53 Reported speech: *He said it was a good car*   168
54 Reported questions, commands, etc.: *She asked me where I was from*   173

Articles

55 The definite article: *the* (1)   177
56 The definite article: *the* (2)   182
57 *A, an, some*   184

Nouns

58 Nouns: singular and plural: *book/books, child/children*   187
59 Countable and uncountable nouns: *cars, traffic, pollution*   190

Quantifiers

60 *Much, many, a lot, plenty, (very) little, (very) few A little, a few*   194
61 *Some, any, no, none*   197
62 *All/everything, everybody All/every/each whole*   200
63 *All (of), most (of), some (of)*, etc. *Both (of), neither (of), either (of)*   204

Pronouns

64 Demonstratives: *this, that, these, those*   207
65 Reflexive and emphatic pronouns: *myself, himself, themselves*, etc.   210
66 *Someone, something, somewhere, anyone, anything, anywhere*, etc.   214
67 Possessive forms: *The man's children, the door of the room, a friend of mine*   217
68 Possessive adjectives and pronouns: *my, mine*, etc. *My own ... Whose ...?*   221
69 *One/ones*   224

Adjectives

70 The use and position of adjectives   227
71 Comparatives and superlatives (1)   230
72 Comparatives and superlatives (2)   235
73 Adjectives ending in *-ed* and *-ing*: *interested/interesting*   239

Adverbs

74 Adverbs of manner and degree: *slowly, very*   241
75 Adverbs of frequency, time and place: *often, today, there*   246
76 Adverbs of degree: *quite, fairly, pretty, rather So, such*   250
77 Adverbs of degree: *a lot, a bit, much*, etc. *More, most, better, best*, etc.   254
78 *Still, yet Any more/any longer/no longer*   257
79 *Too* and *enough*   260

Prepositions

80 Time prepositions: *in, at, on*   263
81 Prepositions of place: *in, on, at*   266
82 Prepositions of place: *under, opposite*, etc.   270
83 Prepositions of movement: *up, down*, etc.   274
84 Prepositions used for travel and transport: *by bus, go to, arrive at*   277

Prepositions/Link words

85 *For, since, ago*   280
86 *For, during, while*   283
87 *When, as soon as*, etc. in future sentences   286
88 *By/by the time, till/until*   288
89 *Like* and *as As if/as though*   290
90 *Although, though, even though In spite of Because, since, so*   293

Relative clauses

91 Relative clauses with *who, which, that*   296
92 The relative pronouns *where, whose, what*   299
93 Defining and non-defining relative clauses   302
94 Clauses with *-ing* or a past participle *With* in identifying phrases   305

Appendices

1 American English – British English   308
2 Contractions or short forms (*I'm, they're, can't*, etc.)   310
3 Spelling   311
4 Phrasal verbs   313
5 Adjectives with prepositions   315
6 Verbs with prepositions   316
7 Irregular verbs   317
8 Glossary of grammatical terms   318

Index   320

Answers to Practice Exercises   329

Introduction

English Grammar in Steps is for pre-intermediate and intermediate students. It covers the grammar needed by students studying for the Cambridge First Certificate examination. More advanced students will find it useful for revision and consolidation. The book covers the most important grammar topics and grammatical structures.

For the student

How to use the book

A If you want to learn or revise a grammar point:
- Look at the *Contents* or *Index* to find the grammar point you want to work on.
- Each *Unit* is divided into *Steps*, so you can work on the grammar in easy stages, bit by bit.
- The unit and many of the Steps begin with a short presentation text where you will find several examples of the grammar point used in a clear context. Read the text two or three times and note these examples.
- The grammar is then explained in stages, each stage marked with a bullet (●). Study these explanations and the specific examples of the grammar point (which are taken from the presentation text that you have already read).
- At the end of each Step there are some *Check questions*. Write your answers, then check them by looking at *Answers to check questions* at the end of the final Step. The questions confirm that you have understood the explanations given in the Step. If your answers are not correct, read the step again and re-do the *Check questions*.
- At the end of each unit there is a page of exercises (*Practice*) that will test your understanding of the grammar point you have just studied. Each exercise has its own context, so you can use your knowledge of a grammar point in a number of realistic situations. The box at the top of the Practice page will help you to remember what you have just learned. Write your answers in the space provided in the book.

B If you think you know the grammar of the unit, you can go straight to the *Practice* page, look at the box at the top and then do the exercises. But if your answers are not correct, then it would be a good idea to work through the unit Step by Step. (See **A**.)

For the teacher

- *English Grammar in Steps* teaches and practises form, meaning and use.
- It concentrates on those areas which students find most difficult.
- The language of explanation is clear and simple, and, as far as possible, non-technical. To help students to understand the meaning of some grammatical terms, there is a *Glossary* on page 318.
- The book presents each grammatical structure in context. Examples are not random. The context helps students to understand the meaning and use of the structure and gives them several examples of it in the same situation. The contexts are down-to-earth and relevant.
- The style used in the presentation texts and the explanations is informal and everyday. We have frequently used contracted forms in *English Grammar in Steps*. Nowadays contractions are normally used in spoken English and in informal written English.
- *English Grammar in Steps* can be used in class, along with the students' course book. Students can use it for quick reference to consolidate their understanding of a grammar topic. Alternatively, it can be used as a variant to their course book. The class can be asked to spend a few minutes studying a particular grammar point and doing the *Practice* exercises. Or the teacher can use it to present a new grammar topic, taking advantage of the presentation texts in each unit.

The present simple: *She works*

Paul Hart and Sarah Ford live in the same block of flats in Avonmouth. Paul's a postman. He gets up at 5.30 a.m. and goes to work at 6. He usually catches the bus. Sarah lives in the next flat. She's a nurse. She works nights. She gets home from work at 6 a.m., at the same time as Paul leaves for work! They meet on the stairs and say hello, but that's all. He sometimes tries to arrange a date with her, but he doesn't find it easy. And they don't see each other at weekends because Sarah works most weekends. Nurses don't have an easy life. But she says she likes nursing and she doesn't want to change her job. 'I enjoy my job, but I don't have a very good social life. Paul and I don't spend any time together. We often try to arrange a date, but we're never free at the same time.'

Step 1 | Uses of the present simple

We use the present simple to talk about:

- habits or regular activities and situations.
  *Paul **gets up** at 5.30 a.m.   They **meet** on the stairs.*
  *Paul and Sarah **live** in Avonmouth.*

- facts and attitudes that are generally or always true.
  *Nurses **don't have** an easy life.   Sarah **likes** nursing.*

- We don't use the present simple to talk about things that are in progress now, that are temporary. We don't say: Look! It rains. We have to use the present continuous: *Look! It's raining.*
  (For the present continuous, see Unit 2. For the present simple used with a future meaning, see Unit 4 Step 2.)

CHECK QUESTIONS 1   **Which sentences describe a regular activity or an attitude?**
1 Paul has a shower every morning.   2 He went to bed late last night.
3 Sarah's going to Spain next summer.   4 She loves the sun.

Step 2 | The present simple: affirmative/positive forms

To work	I work	You work	He/she/it works
	We work	You work	They work

- In the affirmative, the present simple has the same form as the infinitive in all persons except the 3rd person singular (*he, it, Paul, the flat*, etc.). We add -*s* in the 3rd person singular.
  *Paul **gets** up at 5.30 a.m.   Sarah **likes** nursing.*

- With verbs that end in -*o*, -*ch*, -*sh*, -*ss* (*go, catch, watch, wash, kiss*, etc.), we add -*es* and not just -*s* in the 3rd person singular.
  *Paul go**es** to work at 6.   He usually catch**es** the bus.*

- With some verbs that end in -y (*cry, fly, hurry, try*, etc.) the -y changes to *-ies* in the 3rd person singular.
  *Paul often **tries** to arrange a date with her.*
- But with verbs with a vowel before -y (*buy, play, say*, etc.) we simply add -s.
  *But she **says** she likes nursing.*

CHECK QUESTIONS 2 **Complete the sentences, using the present simple.**
1 Paul (play) football. 2 Sarah (study) Spanish in her spare time.
3 Paul sometimes (miss) the bus to work. 4 Sarah (do) her shopping on Thursdays.

Step 3 | The present simple: negative and question forms

Negative	**Questions**
I don't work	Do I work?
You don't work	Do you work?
He/she/it doesn't work	Does he/she/it work?
We don't work	Do we work?
You don't work	Do you work?
They don't work	Do they work?

- To form the negative we use *don't* (*do not*) for all persons except the 3rd person singular.
  *They **don't see** each other at weekends. I **don't have** a very good social life.*
  *Paul and I **don't spend** much time together.*

- In the 3rd person singular we use *doesn't* (*does not*). We don't add -s to the verb that follows *doesn't*.
  *She **doesn't want** to change her job.* (NOT She doesn't wants)
  *He **doesn't find** it easy.* (NOT He doesn't finds it easy.)

- To form questions we use *do* for all persons except the 3rd person singular.

	Do	+	**subject**	+	**infinitive without** *to*
	Do		*you*		*know any nurses?*
	Do		*Paul and Sarah*		*live together?*
When	*do*		*they*		*see each other?*

- In the 3rd person singular we form the question with *does*.

	Does	*Paul*	*work at weekends?*
When	*does*	*Sarah*	*get home from work?*
	Does	*she*	*like nursing?*

- Note the short answers.
  *Does Sarah work nights? Yes, she **does**.*
  *Does Paul work nights? No, he **doesn't**.*
  *Do they live in the same block of flats? Yes, they **do**.*
  *Do they spend much time together? No, they **don't**.*

CHECK QUESTIONS 3 **Complete the sentences, using the present simple.**
1 Where (live) Paul? 2 Paul (not work) at weekends.
3 Sarah (not want) to change her job. 4 (have) nurses a good social life?

ANSWERS TO CHECK QUESTIONS 1, 2 AND 3

1 1 Paul has a shower every morning. She loves the sun.

2 1 Paul plays football. 2 Sarah studies Spanish in her spare time. 3 Paul sometimes misses the bus to work. 4 Sarah does her shopping on Thursdays.

3 1 Where does Paul live? 2 Paul doesn't work at weekends. 3 Sarah doesn't want to change her job. 4 Do nurses have a good social life?

Practice

We use the present simple to talk about:
- regular, repeated activities or situations
- things that are generally or always true

In the 3rd person singular affirmative the verb has a final -s.
We form the negative with *don't* (*doesn't* in the 3rd person singular).
We form questions with *Do ... ?* (*Does ... ?* in the 3rd person singular).

1 Complete these sentences with the correct form of the verbs in the present simple.

1 I (get up) at 7.30.

....

2 My sister (get up) at 7.45.

....

3 We (watch) TV every evening.

....

4 My father (watch) a lot of films.

....

5 He sometimes (cry) if the film's sad.

....

6 My sister and her friends often (go) to clubs.

....

7 She always (wash) her hair before she (go out).

....

8 She often (get) home very late.

....

2 These facts are not correct. Correct the sentences by changing the form of the verb.

1 Spain doesn't belong to the European Union.

....

2 Russia and Switzerland belong to the EU.

....

3 They drive on the right in Britain.

....

4 You don't see a lot of Japanese cars in Europe.

....

5 Britain has a president.

....

6 The US president lives in New York.

....

7 They don't speak Spanish in Argentina.

....

8 They speak Spanish in Brazil.

....

3 A Spanish boy and a German girl are standing at a drinks machine on a cross-Channel ferry. Complete their conversation.

Katrina: (1) .... English?

Luis: Yes, a little.

Katrina: Where (2) .... come .... ?

Luis: Córdoba in Spain. ¡Bella ciudad!

Katrina: What (3) .... that .... ?

Luis: It (4) .... *beautiful city.*

Katrina: How much (5) .... a cola .... ?

Luis: 80p.

Katrina: (6) .... this machine ....
German money?

Luis: No, it (7) .... , it only takes English money.

4 Personal questions. Complete each question, using the correct form of the present simple, and give your short answer.

1 you/watch/much TV?

....

....

2 TV in your country/have/many American programmes?

....

....

3 you and your friends/play/much sport?

....

....

4 the place where you live/have/a sports centre?

....

....

2

The present continuous: *It's raining*

We're playing on the computer. We're just finishing this game.

I'm having a shower and I'm washing my hair.

What are you all doing? Why aren't you helping me?

I'm watching the end of this programme.

I'm talking to a friend on the phone. She's helping me with my homework.

Jessie

Tim and James

Father

Mother

Helen

We are
we're

Step 1 | The present continuous for actions in progress

● We use the present continuous to talk about something that's in progress now, at this moment.
  Dad's making supper. His wife isn't helping him.
  She's watching television. The children aren't helping him either.

CHECK QUESTIONS 1

Are these things happening now in the situation above? Answer *Yes* or *No*.
1 They're having supper. 2 Tim's playing a computer game.
3 Helen's doing her homework. 4 Jessie's going out.

Step 2 | Forms of the present continuous

● We form the present continuous with the present of *be* + the *-ing* form of the verb. Note: The negative has two possible forms.

Affirmative
I'm (I am) working
You're (You are) working
He's (He is) working
She's (She is) working
It's (It is) working
We're (We are) working
You're (You are) working
They're (They are) working

Negative
I'm not working
You aren't/You're not working
He isn't/He's not working
She isn't/She's not working
It isn't/It's not working
We aren't/We're not working
You aren't/You're not working
They aren't/They're not working

Questions	Short answers
Am I working?	Yes, I am. OR No, I'm not.
Are you working?	Yes, you are. OR No, you aren't/you're not.
Is he/she/it working?	Yes, he is. OR No, he's not/he isn't.
Are we working?	Yes, we are. OR No, we're not/we aren't.
Are you working?	Yes, we are. OR No, we're not/we aren't.
Are they working?	Yes, they are. OR No, they're not/they aren't.

● Note the spelling changes before -*ing*.

Words ending in:

e	have	having
m	swim	swimming
n	run	running
p	stop	stopping
t	get	getting

(See also Appendix 3.)

CHECK QUESTIONS 2 **Put the verb into the present continuous.**
1 Dad (make) supper. 2 Jessie (help) her father? No, she ...
3 She (get) ready to go out. 4 The boys (not help) their father.

Step 3 | Verbs not used in the present continuous

Dad: Tim, I know you're busy, but I want some help.
Tim: But Dad, I'm doing something important.
Dad: Important? What do you mean? I don't believe you!

● Some verbs (most of them verbs of thinking and feeling) are almost never used in the present continuous. The most common are: *agree, be, believe, belong, care, forget, hate, hear, know, like, love, mean, mind, notice, own, remember, seem, suppose, understand, want, wish.*
(See also Unit 3, Step 3.)

CHECK QUESTIONS 3 **Which sentences are incorrect?**
1 James is being in his bedroom at the moment.   2 He's playing a computer game.
3 He's loving computer games.   4 His father's hating computer games.
5 He's thinking they're a waste of money.   6 James isn't agreeing.

Step 4 | Other uses of the present continuous

It's 8.30 p.m. Jessie's doing her maths homework. This year she's studying maths, physics and economics. She's going out with a boy in her class called Carl. At the moment they're spending a lot of time together. Jessie's Dad doesn't think she's doing enough school work. He's also worried about Tim. Tim's always playing games on his computer.
Dad: You're always wasting your time. Why don't you do something useful?
Tim: Oh, you're always saying that, Dad. You're always complaining.

- We often use the present continuous to talk about a temporary activity or situation. It may not be in progress at the moment of speaking.
    This year she's studying maths, physics and economics.
    Carl and Jessie are going out together.
  Note: The only thing that is happening now (at 8.30) is that Jessie is doing her maths homework. The other things are not happening at this moment.

- We sometimes use the present continuous with *always* to talk about things that happen frequently and are irritating.
    Tim's always playing games on his computer.
    You're always complaining.

CHECK QUESTIONS 4

In these sentences, are we talking about what is happening at this moment (A), or about a temporary situation which may not be happening now (B)? Write A or B.
1 Carl's also studying maths, physics and economics.
2 Jessie's sitting at her desk in her bedroom.
3 She's waiting for Carl to phone.
4 She's finding physics quite difficult.

Write sentences using *always* and the present continuous.
5 You (go) out in the evening!
6 She (use) the phone!

Step 5 | The present continuous with future meaning

> Dad: What are you doing tonight, Jessie?
> Jessie: I'm going out. I'm meeting Carl and we're going to a club.

- We often use the present continuous to talk about arrangements we've made for the future. (See also Unit 4.)
    I'm going out. I'm meeting Carl.
    (These are her arrangements for the future. She isn't going out at the moment.)

CHECK QUESTIONS 5

Complete the conversation.
Dad: Where you (1 meet) Carl tonight? And what time you (2 come) home?
Jessie: We (3 meet) at the town hall. I don't know what time I (4 come) home, but not late.

ANSWERS TO
CHECK QUESTIONS
1, 2, 3, 4 AND 5

1 1 No. 2 Yes. 3 No. 4 No.
2 1 Dad's making supper. 2 Is Jessie helping her father? No, she isn't/No, she's not. 3 She's getting ready to go out. 4 The boys aren't helping their father.

3 1, 3, 4, 5, 6
4 1B 2A 3A 4B 5 You're always going out in the evening. 6 She's always using the phone.
5 1 are you meeting 2 are you coming 3 We're meeting 4 I'm coming

Practice

> You can use the present continuous:
> - A for something happening now, at this moment.
> - B for a temporary activity or situation (which may not be happening now).
> - C for arrangements you've made for the future.
> - D with *always* to complain or express irritation about something or someone.
>
> BUT some verbs are almost never used in the present continuous.

1 Here are examples of four different uses of the present continuous. Look at the list in the box above and write A, B, C or D after each sentence.

1 He's writing three books about architecture. [   ]
2 It's raining. [   ]
3 You're always looking at yourself in the mirror! [   ]
4 The phone's ringing. [   ]
5 I'm having German lessons at the moment. [   ]
6 We're leaving on Saturday. [   ]
7 I'm saving up to buy a new computer. [   ]
8 They're arriving at 8.30. [   ]
9 What are you doing with that knife? [   ]
10 She's doing a lot of overtime this week. [   ]

2 Complete the dialogue using the present continuous where possible.

A: Who (1 speak) .... ?

B: It's me. Matthew.

A: Where you (2 phone) .... from?

B: From Australia. I'm here on holiday, remember? I (3 stay) .... in a hotel just by the beach. The sun (4 shine) .... I (5 have) .... a great time. But you (6 not seem) .... very pleased.

A: Matthew, you (7 know) .... what time it is here in England? It's 3 o'clock in the morning! Why you (8 phone) .... me now?

B: Because I (9 want) .... to speak to you.

A: Yes, I (10 understand) .... that. But what you (11 want) .... to tell me?

B: Nothing special. I just (12 wish) .... you were here with me, that's all.

A: I'm glad you (13 enjoy) .... yourself. But I (14 not care) .... really. I (15 try) .... to sleep because I (16 get up) .... early tomorrow. So, if you (17 not mind) .... , I (18 go back) .... to sleep. Goodnight!

3 Use the present continuous where possible to complete what the captain is saying.

Good morning. This is your captain speaking. At the moment we (1 fly) .... at a height of 12,000 metres. If you look out of the windows on your right you can see that we (2 cross) .... the French coast just west of Cherbourg. Unfortunately a strong southerly wind (3 blow) .... and this (4 slow) .... us down. So right now I (5 not think) .... we'll be in Barcelona until 14.30. The weather in Barcelona (6 be) .... fine. The sun (7 shine) .... and the temperature (8 be) .... 28° . I hope you (9 enjoy) .... your flight with us, and the cabin crew (10 look after) .... you.

3 The present continuous: *He's smoking* OR the present simple: *He smokes*?

Liz Rix is working for a year on a Greenpeace ship in the Mediterranean. They're checking pollution levels. Liz is writing a letter to her mother. '... I'm writing this letter in my cabin. The sea's quite rough at the moment and I'm finding it difficult to write! I usually get about two hours' free time a day, and I often write letters or read a book (or I sometimes don't do anything at all - I just sleep!). I'm reading a book about the history of Greenpeace at the moment. Greenpeace workers come from all over the world, but, fortunately, everybody on this ship speaks English ... '

Step 1 | Things happening now OR things happening repeatedly?

- We use the present continuous to talk about something that's in progress at the moment of speaking.
  I'm writing this letter in my cabin.   I'm finding it difficult to write.
- We also use the present continuous to talk about a present activity or situation that may not be in progress at the moment of speaking.
  I'm reading a book about Greenpeace at the moment. (NOT I read a book)
  (Liz hasn't finished her book; she's still reading it, but not at this moment. At this moment she's writing her letter.)
- We use the present simple to talk about repeated actions and regular situations. We often use words like *always, often, usually, sometimes, never* with the present simple. (For *always* with the present continuous, see Unit 2, Step 4.)
  I usually get two hours' free time a day. (NOT I'm getting)
  I often write letters or read.   I sometimes don't do anything at all.
- We also use it to talk about a situation or a general fact.
  Everybody on the ship speaks English. (NOT is speaking)
  Greenpeace workers come from all over the world.

CHECK QUESTIONS 1   **Choose the correct verb form.**
  1 Liz (writes/is writing) a letter.
  2 In her free time she (reads/is reading) a lot.
  3 Greenpeace workers (come/are coming) from all over the world.

Step 2 | Temporary situations OR more permanent situations?

' ... At the moment, I'm working with Thor Svensen, a Norwegian marine biologist. We're taking water samples and analysing them. Thor works at Oslo University, but he's working for Greenpeace for a year ...'

- We use the present continuous to talk about temporary actions or situations.
  At the moment, I'm working with Thor Svensen.
  (Liz will probably have a different job on the ship soon.)

- We use the present simple to talk about more permanent situations. Compare:
  *Thor **works** at Oslo University.* (present simple)   (That's his permanent job.)
  *He's **working** for Greenpeace for a year.* (present continuous)
  (This is a temporary job, for only a year.)

CHECK QUESTIONS 2 **Answer the questions.**
1 What's Thor's permanent job? He ... at Oslo University.
2 What's Liz's present job on the ship? She ... Thor Svensen.

Step 3 | Verbs not used in the continuous form

'... I think this is the best job I've ever had. I want to do it for another year. I like the people on the ship and I know we're doing a useful job. I love life at sea. I'm looking really healthy. The ship has very little fresh water and I'm being extravagant at the moment - washing three times a day! I'd like a shower, but the ship doesn't have showers. But I'm having a great time. I'll finish my letter now because I don't feel very well. The ship's rolling a lot. In fact, I'm feeling a bit sick. I'm thinking of you. Love, Liz.'

- Some verbs describe a state (a situation that stays the same) and not an action. We don't normally use these verbs in the continuous form: *believe, belong, contain, exist, forget, hate, hear, know, like, love, mean, need, own, prefer, realise, remember, seem, suppose, understand, want.*
  *I **want** to stay for another year.* (NOT I'm wanting)
  *I **like** the people.* (NOT I'm liking the people.)
  *I **know** we're doing a useful job.* (NOT I'm knowing)
- Some verbs (*think, have, be, see, smell, taste*) can describe a state or an action. When the verb is an action we can use the continuous form.
  *I **think** this is a great job.* (I think = I believe = a state)
  *I'm **thinking** of you.* (Thoughts of you are going through my mind. = an action)
  *The ship **doesn't have** showers.* (= a state. NOT isn't having)
  *I'm **having** a great time.* (= an action. I'm doing a lot of great things.)
  *I'm **extravagant**.* (= a state, describing the person's character.)
  *I'm **being** extravagant.* (= an action. I'm doing an extravagant thing.)
- The verbs *look* (= someone's appearance), *feel* (= sensations), *hurt* can be used in the simple or the continuous form. The meaning is the same.
  *I'm **looking** really healthy.* (OR I **look** really healthy.)
  *I **don't feel** well at the moment.* (OR I'm **not feeling** well.)

CHECK QUESTIONS 3 **Complete the sentences.**
1 Liz (know) she's doing a useful job.
2 The ship (not have) a lot of fresh water.
3 Liz (feel) a bit sick at the moment.

ANSWERS TO CHECK QUESTIONS 1, 2 AND 3
1 1 is writing   2 reads   3 come
2 1 He works at Oslo university.   2 She's working with Thor Svensen.
3 1 knows   2 doesn't have   3 feels/is feeling

Practice

Present continuous:	For things that are happening at the moment.	*It's raining.*
	For temporary situations and actions.	*I'm having Spanish lessons.*
Present simple:	For things that happen repeatedly.	*I get up at 7.00 every morning.*
	For states, general facts and permanent situations.	*The River Thames flows through London.*

1 Put the verbs into the present continuous or the present simple.

1 The Wheeltech company (make) .... bicycles and mopeds. They (be) .... very successful and at the moment they (build) .... a bigger factory in Nottingham.

2 Normally they (produce) .... more mopeds than bicycles, but this year they (produce) .... 20% more bicycles than mopeds.

3 Customers (buy) .... more bicycles than mopeds at the moment. People (become) .... more and more interested in the kind of exercise you (get) .... on a bicycle. And bicycles (be) .... better for the environment.

4 They always (pay) .... their workers well. Most of the workers (stay) .... with the company for years. On average their pay (rise) .... by 8% every year.

5 All over Britain companies that (make) .... environmentally friendly products (expand) .... at the moment.

2 Complete the dialogue, using the present continuous or the present simple.

'Hi, Sam. What you (1 do) .... ?'

'I (2 write) .... to Sarah.'

'What she (3 do) .... at the moment? She (4 be) .... still

at college?'

'No, she (5 spend) .... six months in Israel.'

'What she (6 do) .... in Israel? She (7 be) .... on holiday?'

'No. At the moment she (8 work) .... on a chicken farm for a couple of months.'

'How much they (9 pay) .... her every week?'

'They (10 give) .... her enough money to live on, and she (11 get) .... her food and accommodation free.'

3 Complete the dialogue, using the present continuous or the present simple.

'you (1 know) .... that girl over there? The one who (2 wear) .... the red sweater?'

'Yes, I (3 know) .... her, but I (4 not remember) .... her name. I (5 think) .... it's Joanne, but I (6 not be) .... sure.'

'She (7 talk) .... to Adam Bird. I (8 think) .... he (9 like) .... her.'

'Well, he (10 be) .... a bit stupid at the moment.'

'Why? What you (11 mean) .... ?'

'Well, he (12 realise) .... that her boyfriend (13 stand) .... behind him?'

'No, I (14 not think) .... he (15 know) .... !'

4 The present continuous and the present simple with future meaning

'What are you doing for your birthday, Jake?'
'I'm having a party on a boat on the Thames. About fifty people are coming. My father, who lives in Germany, is coming over specially for the party. The boat company's providing the food, and everybody's bringing their own drink. I'm not having a disco. I prefer live music, so we're having a reggae band on the boat.'

Step 1 | The present continuous for arrangements for the future

- We use the present continuous to talk about things that we've already arranged to do in the future. We don't use the present simple here.
  What **are you doing** for your birthday? (NOT What do you do for your birthday?)
  I'm **having** a party on a boat on the Thames. (NOT I have)
  I'm **not having** a disco. (NOT I don't have a disco.)
- It's possible to use *be going to* here. We could say:
  What **are you going to** do for your birthday?
  I'm **going to** have a party on a boat on the Thames.
  BUT *be going to* suggests an intention more than an arrangement.
  (For the use of *be going to* see Unit 15.)

CHECK QUESTIONS 1 ▶ **Look at the text. Complete the questions.**
1 How many ... ? About fifty. 2 Who ... ? The boat company.
3 ... you ...? No, I prefer live music.

Step 2 | The present simple for programmes and timetables

This is the timetable for Jake's party:
'The boat leaves Henley at 8 p.m. Then we go down river to Sonning. We stop there for an hour. Then, at 10.30, the boat turns round and comes back to Henley. We get back at about midnight.'

- We often use the present simple when we talk about a programme of future events or a timetable. The time is often given.
  The boat **leaves** at 8 p.m.   We **get back** to Henley at about midnight.

CHECK QUESTIONS 2 ▶ **Complete the questions.**
1 What time ... the boat ... Henley? About eight o'clock.
2 What time ... it ... to Sonning? At 9.30. 3 When ... they ... to Henley? At about 12.

ANSWERS TO
CHECK QUESTIONS
1 AND 2

1 1 How many people are coming? 2 Who's providing the food? 3 Are you having a disco?

2 1 What time does the boat leave Henley? 2 What time does it get to Sonning? 3 When do they get (back) to Henley?

Practice

- We use the present continuous to talk about things we've already arranged for the future.
- We use the present simple to talk about a programme of future events or a timetable.

1 Look at Anna's diary for next week.

Monday	Cinema 7 pm
Tuesday	Andy's party 8 pm
Wednesday	Meet mum 7.30 pm bus station
Thursday	Spanish lesson 8 pm
Friday	Tennis with Jack at 7.30 pm
Saturday	Free evening

Paul wants to go out with Anna one evening next week. It is not easy because Anna has already made a lot of arrangements. Complete the conversation.

'Are you free on Monday evening?'

'No, (1) .... to the cinema.'

'What are you doing on Tuesday?'

'(2) ....,'

'Are you doing anything on Wednesday?'

'Yes, (3) .... mum at the bus-station.'

'What about Thursday evening?'

'(4) .... Spanish lesson.'

'Friday?' '(5) ....,'

'What are you doing on Saturday?'

'(6) .... anything. What about you?'

2 Look at this timetable for a British Airways flight to Grenada in the West Indies.

London Heathrow Check-in time: 8.00
Departure: 10.15
Stop-over in Antigua: 1 hour
Flight time to Grenada: 9½ hours
Arrival time: 15.45 local time

You are travelling on the flight. Complete the sentences with details of the flight.
Example: *I check in at 8 o'clock.*

1   The plane .... at 10.15.

2   We .... for an hour.

3   The flight .... 9½ hours.

4   We .... at quarter to four, local time.

3 Complete the text, using the present continuous or the present simple.

I (1 go) .... London next Thursday. 'Burning Spear', my favourite reggae band, (2 give) .... a concert at Wembley. I (3 go) .... with Beth. We (4 not go) .... by train; it's much cheaper by coach. The coach (5 leave) .... Plymouth at 12.30 p.m. It (6 stop) .... at Exeter and Taunton to pick up more passengers and (7 arrive) .... in London at 5.30 p.m. We don't want to spend any money on food, so we (8 take) .... some sandwiches to eat on the coach. The concert (9 start) .... at 7.30 p.m. Our coach back to Plymouth (10 leave) .... London at 11.30 p.m. and we (11 get back) .... to Plymouth at about four o'clock on Friday morning!

5 The past simple: *He was/he arrived*

Ruben Kleinsteuber (62) from Cleveland, Ohio, was on a Mediterranean cruise. His wife wasn't with him. She was back home in the States. His children weren't with him either. They were too old to go on holiday with their father and they weren't interested in Mediterranean cruises.

Step 1 | Past simple of the verb *be*

- We use the past simple of the verb *to be* to talk about a past situation.
  *Ruben **was** on a Mediterranean cruise.*
  *His children **weren't** with him.*

- We form the affirmative with *was* or *were*.

  I was   we were
  you were   you were
  he/she/it was   they were
  *His wife **was** back home in the States.*
  *His two children **were** too old to go on holiday with him.*

- We form the negative with *wasn't* (was not) or *weren't* (were not).
  *His wife **wasn't** with him.*
  *His children **weren't** interested in Mediterranean cruises.*

- We form questions and short answers like this:
  ***Was he** on his own? Yes, **he was**.*
  ***Were his children** with him? No, **they weren't**.*

CHECK QUESTIONS 1   **Complete these questions and answers, using *was/wasn't*, *were/weren't*.**
1 ... Ruben on a Caribbean cruise? No, ...
2 Where ... he from? He ... from Cleveland, Ohio.
3 ... his two children with him? No, ...

Step 2 | Past simple of regular and irregular verbs

Last Monday Mr Kleinsteuber's ship arrived in Mallorca. He decided to visit the town of Palma. But he didn't want to go sight-seeing with the other passengers. They always visited churches and museums. He didn't like looking at old churches. So he stopped at a bar and then went to a restaurant. There he ate a large paella and drank several glasses of wine. When he looked at his watch, he saw that it was already 3.55 p.m. He didn't have much time. He only had five minutes! He ran back to the port and got there at 4.02 p.m. His ship was already three metres from the quay. He tried to jump aboard, but he didn't reach the ship. He fell into the water below. 'Why did you do that?' a man on the quay said. 'That wasn't your ship. *Your* ship's over there!'
That evening the other passengers asked him, 'Why didn't you come with us to the cathedral this afternoon? Where did you go?' Mr Kleinsteuber replied, 'Oh, I just went for a swim.'

- We use the past simple of regular and irregular verbs to talk about something that happened and finished in the past, a completed action. We usually say or know when the action happened. The moment in the past is clearly defined.
  > **Last Monday** Ruben's ship **arrived** in Mallorca.
  > He **got** there at **4.02 p.m.**

- Often we don't need to say when something happened. It is understood.
  > He **went** to a restaurant instead.
  > (We know that this happened in the past when he was in Palma.)

- We also use the past simple to describe:
  something that happened regularly or continually in the past.
  > They **always visited** churches and museums.

  a situation that existed in the past over a period of time, not just at one fixed moment.
  > He **didn't like** looking at old churches.

CHECK QUESTIONS 2 **Which sentences refer to the past?**
1 Ruben goes on a cruise every year.
2 Last year he went on a Caribbean cruise.
3 He enjoyed it.
4 His wife doesn't like cruises.

Step 3 | Forms of the past simple

- We form the past simple of most regular verbs by adding -ed to the infinitive. It is the same for all persons.
  look   He look**ed**
  visit   They visit**ed**

- Note the spelling changes:
  like   lik**ed**
  try   tr**ied**
  stop   sto**pp**ed   (See also Appendix 3.)

- The -ed ending can be pronounced in three different ways:
  [id] after the sounds [d] and [t]
  decided   *visited*
  [t] after unvoiced sounds (except [t])
  looked   *asked*
  [d] after voiced sounds (except [d])
  arrived   *tried*

- Many common verbs are irregular. We don't form the past simple with -ed. (A full table of irregular verbs is on page 317.)
  > He **went** to a restaurant. (irregular verb *go*)
  > There he **ate** a large paella. (irregular verb *eat*)
  > He **drank** a lot of wine. (irregular verb *drink*)

CHECK QUESTIONS 3 **What is the past simple of these verbs, and how do you pronounce the final -ed?**
1 wait 2 stop 3 move 4 want 5 watch 6 reply

What is the past simple form of these verbs?
7 get 8 come 9 have 10 say

Step 4 | The past simple: negative

- We form the negative of the past simple with *didn't* (did not) + the infinitive without *to*.

Affirmative	**Negative**
He liked	*He **didn't like** old churches.* (NOT didn't liked)
He reached	*He **didn't reach** the ship.* (NOT didn't reached)
He had	*He **didn't have** much time.* (NOT didn't had)
He went	*He **didn't go** with the others.* (NOT didn't went)

CHECK QUESTIONS 4 **Make these sentences negative.**
1 Ruben's family came on the cruise with him.
2 Ruben liked sight-seeing.
3 The other passengers went to the restaurant.
4 Ruben missed his boat.

Step 5 | The past simple: questions and short answers

- We form questions in the past simple with *did* or *didn't* + the infinitive without *to*. We form short answers with *did* or *didn't*.
  ***Did** Ruben **go** to the cathedral? No, he didn't.*
  (NOT Did Ruben went to the cathedral?)
  ***Did** he **fall** into the water? Yes, he did.*
  *Where **did** you **go**? Why **did** you **do** that? Why **didn't** you **come** with us?*

CHECK QUESTIONS 5 **What questions give these answers?**
1 What ... ? He ate a large paella.
2 How much ... ? He drank several glasses of wine.
3 When ... ? He left the restaurant at 3.55 p.m.
4 What time ... ? He got to the port at 4.02 p.m.

ANSWERS TO
CHECK QUESTIONS
1, 2, 3, 4 AND 5

1 1 Was No, he wasn't. 2 was was 3 Were No, they weren't.
2 2, 3
3 1 waited [id] 2 stopped [t] 3 moved [d] 4 wanted [id] 5 watched [t] 6 replied [d] 7 got 8 came 9 had 10 said

4 1 Ruben's family didn't come on the cruise with him. 2 Ruben didn't like sight-seeing. 3 The other passengers didn't go to the restaurant. 4 Ruben didn't miss his boat.
5 1 What did he eat? 2 How much did he drink? 3 When did he leave the restaurant? 4 What time did he get to the port?

Practice

Past simple	Affirmative	Negative	Question
be	he was	he wasn't	was he
Regular verbs	he visited	he didn't visit	did he visit
Irregular verbs	he went	he didn't go	did he go

1 Complete the conversation between a boy and his girlfriend, using *was/wasn't, were/weren't*.

Rob: Where (1) .... you last night?

Hannah: I (2) .... at home.

Rob: No, you (3) .... I phoned you and you (4) .... there. Who (5) .... you with?

Hannah: I (6) .... with anybody. I (7) .... on my own.

Rob: No, you (8) .... You (9) .... with Jason.

Hannah: No, I (10) .... !

2 You are asking a friend about his holiday. Complete the questions.

'Did (1) .... ?'

'Yes, we liked the food a lot.'

'When (2) .... ?'

'We arrived back yesterday.'

'Where (3) .... ?'

'We stayed on an island called Naxos.'

'How often (4) .... ?'

'It didn't rain at all.'

'Did (5) .... ?

'Yes, we hired a Fiat.'

'How much Greek (6) .... ?

'We learned a few words.'

3 Complete this interview with a girl who has just done a parachute jump.

'Did it cost much?'

'Yes, it (1) .... £120!'

'Did you pay for it yourself?'

'No, I (2) .... My parents (3) .... for it.

'What did you wear?'

'I (4) .... a special suit and a helmet.'

'Did you go with anybody?'

'Yes, I (5) .... with two friends.'

'How high were you when you jumped?'

'We (6) .... at about 1000 metres.'

'How did you feel?'

'I (7) .... very scared.'

'Where did you come down?'

'I (8) .... down in a tree.'

'Did you break anything?'

'Yes, I (9) .... my ankle.'

4 Complete this story using verbs in the past simple. Use each of the following verbs only once: *read, run, put, go, hide, get, say, give, have, be, not have.*

A bank robber (1) ..hide.... into a bank in Sacramento, California. He (2) ..gave.. the cashier a note on the back of an envelope. The note (3) .... 'This is a hold-up. Give me $100,000.' The cashier (4) ..read.... the note. The bank (5) ......put...... $100,000, so she (6) ...?........ $10,000 in a bag. The robber then (7) ..get........ the bag under his coat and (8) ..ran..... out of the bank. When he (9) ..go........ home two hours later, there (10) .... two policemen in a car outside his home. Brilliant detective work? No, not really. The envelope (11) ...have... his name and address on the other side!

6 The past continuous: *He was working*

A detective is interviewing Mrs Jane Garfield about a bank robbery.

Detective: What were you doing at 10.30, at the time of the robbery?

Mrs Garfield: I was walking along King Street.

Detective: Were you going to the bank?

Mrs Garfield: No, I wasn't. I was going to the post office. There were a lot of other people in the street. They were just doing their shopping, quite normally.

Detective: What were the robbers wearing?

Mrs Garfield: They were both wearing jeans and dark sweaters.

Step 1 | Use of the past continuous

- We use the past continuous to talk about something that started before a certain time in the past and was still in progress at that time.
  At 10.30 I was walking along King Street. I was going to the post office.

- We often use the past continuous to describe a situation, to give the background to a scene that happened in the past.
  What were they wearing? They were wearing jeans.
  People were just doing their shopping, quite normally.

- We don't use the past continuous with verbs not normally used in the continuous form. (*know, want,* etc. See Unit 3, Step 3.)

- We don't normally use the past continuous to talk about a repeated action in the past. (See *used to,* Unit 34.)

CHECK QUESTIONS 1 **Which two actions were in progress near the bank at 10.30?**

Step 2 | Forms of the past continuous

- We form the past continuous with *was/were* + the -ing form of the verb.

Affirmative		Negative		Questions
I	was working	I	wasn't working	Was I working?
You	were working	You	weren't working	Were you working?
He	was working	He	wasn't working	Was he working?
She	was working	She	wasn't working	Was she working?
It	was working	It	wasn't working	Was it working?
We	were working	We	weren't working	Were we working?
You	were working	You	weren't working	Were you working?
They	were working	They	weren't working	Were they working?

- Note the short answers.
Were you working? Yes, I was./No, I wasn't.
Were they working? Yes, they were./No, they weren't.

CHECK QUESTIONS 2 **Complete these sentences.**
1 At 10.30 Mrs Garfield/not go/to the bank.
2 Where/she/go? 3 She/go/to the post office.

> Detective: What were you doing when you saw them?
> Mrs Garfield: I was standing outside the post office. I was looking in my bag for my letters when I heard a shout. Then I saw them run out of the bank.
> Detective: And what did you do when you saw them?
> Mrs Garfield: I just stopped. I didn't try to do anything, because one of them was carrying a gun. They ran past me and jumped into a car that was waiting near the bus-stop. People were shouting and screaming. The manager rushed out of the bank and ran towards the car, but it was too late. He couldn't stop them.

- The past continuous and the past simple don't mean the same. We use the past continuous to talk about an action or a situation that was in progress. We use the past simple to talk about a completed action.

   People *were shouting* and *screaming*. (past continuous)
   (That was the situation before and after the robbers ran past Mrs Garfield.)
   They *ran past me and jumped into a car.* (past simple)
   (Two completed actions that started and finished while she was watching.)

- We often use the past continuous and the past simple in the same sentence. The action in the past simple is short and usually unexpected. It interrupts the 'longer' action in the past continuous.

   What *were* you *doing* when you *saw* them?
   I *was standing* outside the post office when I *saw* them.
   I *was looking* in my bag for my letters when I *heard* a shout.
   They *jumped* into a car that *was waiting* near the bus-stop.

- Note the difference:
a) Past continuous + past simple
   What *were* you *doing* when you *saw* them?
   I *was standing* outside the post office when I *saw* them.
b) Past simple + past simple
   What *did* you *do* when you *saw* them? When I *saw* them I *stopped*.
In a) she saw them when she was 'in the middle of' standing outside the post office. (One action 'inside' another.)
In b) she saw them and then, after that, she stopped. (Two separate actions.)

CHECK QUESTIONS 3 | **Complete the sentences with the past continuous or the past simple.**
1 I (walk) past the bank when the door suddenly (open).
2 While I (watch) they (throw) a bag of money into the car.
3 As they (drive) away, the manager (run) out of the bank.

ANSWERS TO
CHECK QUESTIONS
1, 2 AND 3

1 1 Mrs Garfield was walking along King Street.
2 People were doing their shopping.
2 1 At 10.30 Mrs Garfield wasn't going to the

bank. 2 Where was she going? 3 She was going to the post office.
3 1 was walking opened 2 was watching threw 3 were driving ran

23

Practice

> I was walking along King Street. (*past continuous*)
>
> I heard
> a shout.
> (*past simple*)

1 Look at these details of Andrew Hill's journey to Paris.

9.10	He rang for a taxi.
9.20	The taxi arrived.
9.45	He arrived at London Airport.
10.00	He went to the Departure lounge.
10.50	The flight was announced.
11.00	He arrived at Gate 36.
11.10	He got on the plane.
11.20	The plane took off.
12.45	He arrived in Paris.

Write what Andrew was doing at these times.
Example: 9.15 (wait) *At 9.15 he was waiting for the taxi.*

1 9.25 (go)

....

2 10.15 (sit)

....

3 10.55 (walk)

....

4 11.15 (wait)

....

5 12.00 (fly)

....

2 It was Saturday morning. Zoe decided to ring her friend Katy. Put the verbs in brackets into the past continuous or the past simple.

1 Zoe (finish) .... her breakfast

and (ring) .... her friend Katy.

2 Katy (listen) .... to the radio

when Zoe (phone) .... her.

3 She (turn) .... down the radio

when the phone (ring) ....

4 They (try) ....to decide what

to do when Katy (suggest) ....

a game of tennis.

5 Zoe (come) .... round in her

car and they (drive) .... to the

tennis courts.

6 Two other people (use) ....

their court when they (arrive) ....

7 They (buy) .... ice-creams

while they (wait) .... to play.

8 They (play) .... when it

(start) .... to rain.

9 They (stop) .... when the rain

(start) ....

10 When the rain (stop) .... they

(go on) .... with their game.

3 Put the verbs in brackets into the past continuous or the past simple.

Police yesterday (1 stop) .... and

(2 arrest) .... a 105-kilo rugby

player, Jason Carter. Mr Carter (3 stand)

.... by the side of a motorway

outside Bristol. Police Officer Sharon Willis

(4 tell) .... the court that she

(5 drive) .... north along the M32

when she first (6 see) .... Carter. At

the time Carter (7 wear) .... a long

blond wig, a mini-skirt and a pair of high-heeled

shoes. Carter, a student at Bristol University,

(8 say) .... in court: 'I (9 not do)

.... anything wrong. I (10 try) only

.... to get a lift as quickly as

possible.'

7 The present perfect: *I've lost my job*

> Mick: You look miserable. What's the matter? Have you lost your job?
> Dave: No, I haven't.
> Mick: Well, what's happened?
> Dave: I've cut my finger.
> Mick: You've cut your finger! Is that all?
> Dave: It's serious. I can't play the guitar. Our band's playing at a big concert tomorrow night. And they've asked Rick to play instead of me.

Step 1 | The present perfect: the past and the present connected

- The present perfect connects the past and the present. It refers to a past action, but we're more interested in the present effects or results of the action.
  I've cut my finger. (Dave cut his finger in the past, but it hurts now.)

- We often use the present perfect to give people some new information or (in the question form) to ask for information.
  What's the matter? Have you lost your job?
  (Mick's first question shows that he's interested in the situation now. In his second question he asks for information that will explain the present situation.)
  They've asked Rick to play instead of me.
  (It doesn't matter when the band asked Rick. Dave is only interested in the present result – he can't play with the band.)

CHECK QUESTIONS 1

Answer the questions.
1 Is Dave miserable because of his job? No, he hasn't ... job.
2 What's the problem with his finger? He ... it.
3 Can he play at the concert? No, they ... Rick instead.

Step 2 | The forms of the present perfect

- We form the present perfect with *have/has* + the past participle.

Affirmative	Negative	Question
I've (have) started	I haven't started	Have I started?
You've started	You haven't started	Have you started?
He/she's (has) started	He/she hasn't started	Has he/she started?
We've started	We haven't started	Have we started?
They've started	They haven't started	Have they started?

- Note the short answers: Have you started? Yes, I have./No, I haven't.
  Has the film started? Yes, it has./No, it hasn't.

CHECK QUESTIONS 2

Which sentences have a verb in the present perfect?
1 Dave's miserable. 2 Has he lost his job?
3 He's cut his finger. 4 His band's playing tomorrow.

ANSWERS TO
CHECK QUESTIONS
1 AND 2

1 1 No, he hasn't lost his job. 2 He's cut it.
3 No, they've asked Rick to play instead.

2 2, 3

25

Practice

- The present perfect connects the past and the present. We use the present perfect when we talk about the present results or effects of a past action.
- We form the present perfect with forms of the verb *have* + a past participle.
  *The clock **has stopped**.*
  Contracted form: *The clock's stopped.*

1 Caroline has come home after work. Someone has broken into her flat. She is looking round the flat now. Complete her sentences, using the present perfect.
Example: Oh, no. Someone (break into) my flat!
Someone's (has) broken into my flat!

1 They (take) ......taken...... my television
   and my video.

2 And my CD player (go) .... too.

3 They (make) ....made.... a terrible mess.

4 They (throw) .... all my clothes
   all over the floor.

5 I (not phone) .... the police. I
   must do that now.

2 A couple are going on holiday. They are going to drive to the airport. They are checking things. Put the verbs into the present perfect and complete the short answers.
Example: You (fill up)................... ....
the car with petrol? Yes, ... *Have you filled up the car with petrol? – Yes, I have.*

1 You (find) ...have found... the
   passports? – Yes, I ...have...

2 Where you (put) .... the tickets
   and the travellers' cheques?
   – I (put) .... them in my bag.

3 You (leave) .... the key with
   the neighbours? – Yes, I ....

4 You (give) .... the
   neighbours our holiday address?
   – No, I ....

5 You (pack) .... our snorkels
   and masks? – Yes, I ....

3 You have met an old friend in the street. She is asking you about your family. Complete the sentences, using the present perfect.

'How's your brother?'
'He's fine. He (1 not change) .... He
(2 leave) .... college now. He's in
London.'
'How are your mother and father.'
'They're OK. They don't live in the village now.
They (3 move) .... to a
house on the coast.'
'How's your sister?'
'She isn't very happy. She (4 have) ....
a lot of problems.'
'And what about you?'
'I'm fine. I (5 finish) .... my
exams now and I (6 apply) ....
for a few jobs. But I (7 not have) ....
any replies.'

4 You are listening to the main points of the news on the radio. Complete the sentences, using the present perfect. Use these verbs: *vote, damage, be, climb, fly, not find.*

1 There .... fire at Buckingham Palace.

2 The US President .... to
   Moscow for talks with the Russians.

3 The European Parliament ....
   against the legalisation of marijuana.

4 Two British women .... Everest.

5 Rescuers .... any survivors
   from the boat that sank in the Channel.

6 Strong winds .... the roof of
   Canterbury Cathedral.

The present perfect with *just, yet, ever,* etc.

Lucy wants a job. She started looking for work two months ago. She's looked in the newspaper every day. She's visited the job centre in town every week. But she hasn't found anything so far.

Step 1 | The present perfect: past time up to now

- The present perfect connects the past and the present. We use it to talk about what has happened (or hasn't happened) in the period up to the present.
  She's (has) looked in the newspaper every day.
  (Lucy has done this during the last two months and today too.)
  But she hasn't found anything so far.(so far = up to now)
  (She hasn't found a job in the two months up to today.)

CHECK QUESTIONS 1 ▷ 1 Ask Lucy: What/you/do/so far? 2, 3 Give her answers.

Step 2 | The present perfect with *already, yet* and *just*

Dee, a friend, has just met Lucy in town.
Dee: Hi, Lucy. How are you? Have you found a job yet?
Lucy: No, not yet. I've written to four companies so far, but I haven't had any replies yet.
Dee: I've just seen an advert in the newsagent's. They're looking for a shop assistant.
Lucy: I know. I've already phoned them. They've already found someone.

- We use *already* with the present perfect to emphasise that the action has happened before the moment of speaking.
  We normally use it only in affirmative sentences and questions.
  We usually put it between *have, has*, etc. and the main verb.
  *I've **already** phoned them.*
  (Lucy emphasises that she's phoned them before now.)

- We use *yet* with the present perfect to say that something has not happened up to now, but we expect it to happen some time in the future. We use it only in questions and negative sentences. We put it at the end of the sentence.
  *Have you found a job **yet**? I haven't had any replies **yet**.*
  (Lucy expects to have some replies in the future.)

- We often use *just* (= a very short time ago) with the present perfect.
  We put it between *have, has*, etc. and the main verb.
  *Dee has **just** met Lucy in town.* (= a few moments ago)
  *I've **just** seen an advert in the newsagent's.*
  Note: American English. Americans often use *just, already, yet* with the simple past: Dee just met Lucy in town. I already phoned them. Did you find a job yet? (See Appendix 1.)

Answer the questions.

1 Has Lucy found a job? No, she ... one ...
2 Why doesn't Lucy contact the newsagent's? She's ... them.
3 How does Dee know about the job at the newsagent's? She ...

Step 3 | The present perfect with *ever, never, before*

The manager of the local newspaper is interviewing Lucy for a job.
Manager: Have you always lived in Billingham?
Lucy: Yes, I've lived here all my life. I know the town very well.
Manager: Where have I seen you before? I'm sure I've seen you before somewhere.
Lucy: Probably in the Red Lion in King Street. I've often worked behind the bar there.
Manager: Ah, yes. I remember now. Er ... Have you ever worked on a newspaper?
Lucy: No. I've done a few part-time jobs so far, but I've never worked on a newspaper.
Manager: Have you ever worked in an office?
Lucy: No. I've had jobs in shops and restaurants, but I've never worked in an office before.
Manager: Have you travelled much? Have you ever lived abroad?
Lucy: Well, I've been abroad on holiday, but I've never lived abroad.

- We often use *ever* with the present perfect to ask if something has happened at any time up to the present. We normally use it only in questions.
    *Have you **ever** worked on a newspaper?*

- We use *never* with the present perfect to say that something hasn't happened at any time up to the present.
  We put *ever and* never between *have, has*, etc. and the main verb.
    *I've **never** lived abroad.*

- We often use *before* (= before now) with the present perfect. We usually put it at the end of the sentence.
    *I've seen you **before**.   Where have I seen you **before**?*
  Note: We sometimes use *never* and *before* in the same sentence.
    *I've **never** worked in an office **before**.*

Has Lucy worked in an office?

1 Add *ever* to this question.
2 Add *before* to the same question.
3 Answer the question using *never*. No, she ...

1 1 What have you done so far? 2 I've looked in the newspaper every day. 3 I've visited the job centre every week.

2 1 No, she hasn't found one yet. 2 She's already phoned them. 3 She's just seen the advert.

3 1 Has Lucy ever worked in an office? 2 Has Lucy worked in an office before? 3 No, she's (has) never worked in an office.

Practice

We use the present perfect to talk about what has or hasn't happened in the period of time up to now.

.................*already/yet/ever/never*..........................

PAST————————————————|——————|

just NOW (PRESENT)

Questions: *yet, ever*   Affirmative verb: *already, never*

---

1 **You have just come back after 15 years to the village where you were born. Things are different there now. Make sentences using the present perfect.**
Example: The village/change a lot *The village has changed a lot.*

1 They/build/a lot more houses.

....

2 The population/increase/to 5,000

....

3 The railway station/close

....

4 They/cut down/the trees in the square

....

5 But the people/not change. They're still friendly.

....

2 **You are redecorating your flat and a friend has come to see you. Make sentences with the words in brackets, using *just* or *yet*.**
Example: Don't touch that door! (paint) *I've just painted it.*

1 Take your shoes off. (clean the carpets)

....

2 Don't sit on that chair! (not mend)

....

3 Don't use the toilet. (not turn the water on)

....

4 Would you like some tea? (make some)

....

5 We'll sit here. (not finish the living-room)

....

3 **Jack Knight has had a lot of problems recently. His mother is angry with him. Make sentences, using the present perfect with *already* or *yet*.**
Example: You must get up earlier. You/miss the bus/three times/this week. *You've already missed the bus three times this week.*

1 I'm not giving you any more money. I/give you/£70 this month

....

2 I asked you to tidy your room two days ago. You/not do

....

3 I bought you a jacket last week. You/lose it

....

4 I told you to phone your grandfather. You/not ring

....

4 **Alison Brymon (18) has won a competition. The prize is a luxury week in London. Make sentences with *never ... before.***
Example: Try these oysters. Mmm! I/eat oysters *Mmm! I've never eaten oysters before.*

1 Do you like the car? – Yes, I/be in a Rolls Royce

....

2 Try this watch on. – Wow! I/have a gold watch

....

3 Do you like the hotel? – Yes, I/stay at the Ritz

....

4 Champagne? – Yes, please. I/drink real champagne

....

5 Smile at the camera! – Oh no! I/be on television

....

9 The present perfect: other uses

Sally Hardwick's an American anthropologist from Los Angeles. She's been all over the world. She's been to Africa, she's been to South America and she's been to India. Now she's gone to Australia. She's gone to live with a group of Australian aboriginal people.

Step 1 | *She's gone to* OR *She's been to?*

- *Gone to* and *been to* don't mean the same.
  A *She's **gone to** Australia.*   **B** *She's **been to** Africa.*
  (A Sally isn't in LA now. She's in, or on the way to, Australia.)
  (B She isn't in Africa now, but she went there in the past.)

CHECK QUESTIONS 1 **Which questions (Where's Sally gone? Where's Sally been?) give these answers?**
1 To South America and India.   2 To Australia.

Step 2 | Words and phrases often used with the present perfect

Sally's boyfriend has only seen her for two months this year. She's written to him once this month. She's tried to phone him four times this week, but he hasn't answered. She's tried to phone him twice today.

- We often use the present perfect with: *today, this morning, this evening, this week, this year,* etc. when these periods aren't completed at the moment of speaking.
  He's only **seen** *her for two months **this year**.* (The year isn't finished.)
  *She's **tried** to phone him twice **today**.* (Today isn't finished.)

CHECK QUESTIONS 2 **Complete these questions.**
1 How many times (she/write) to him this month?
2 How many times (she/phone) him today?

Step 3 | *It's the first time .../the best ...* + the present perfect

Sally's now in Western Australia. It's the first time she's lived in a desert. It hasn't rained in this region for five years. It's the longest drought they've ever had. Sally's eating with some aboriginals. It's the first time she's eaten kangaroo meat. It's the best meat she's ever tasted.

- We use the present perfect (NOT the simple present) after *It's/This is the first (second, third,* etc.*) time ...* and often after superlatives.
  *It's the first time she's **lived** in a desert.* (NOT *she lives*)
  *the longest drought they've **ever had***

CHECK QUESTIONS 3 **Answer the questions.**
1 Has she eaten kangaroo before? No, it's ... it.   2 Does she like it? Yes, it's ...

ANSWERS TO CHECK QUESTIONS 1, 2 AND 3
1 1 Where's Sally been? 2 Where's Sally gone?
2 1 has she written 2 has she phoned

3 1 the first time she's eaten it. 2 the best meat she's ever tasted.

Practice

> He's gone to X. = He's there now.   ——————▶ X
>
> He's been to X. = He isn't there now.   ⇄▶ X
>
> - We often use the present perfect with *today, this morning, this week, this year*, etc.
> - We use the present perfect after *It's the first time* ... and often after superlatives.

1 **Zoe's boss is angry because she is often away from work. Complete the sentences.**
Example: Zoe (not come to work/today) *Zoe hasn't come to work today.*

1 I (not see her/this morning).

....

2 She (only come twice/this week).

....

3 She (have ten days off/this month).

....

4 She (miss two months' work/this year).

....

5 She (phone/this morning)?

....

2 **A lot of things are happening in the Grey family! Marion Grey wants to know what her family are doing. She asks: "Where ... been?" and "Where ... gone?" Write her questions.**

1 I can't find Henry. .... he

.... ?

2 Megan and John have just come home.

.... they .... ?

3 Jack's just left on his motorbike.

.... he .... ?

4 Ah, Henry, here you are at last!

.... you .... ?

3 **Complete this text with *gone* or *been*.**

Dean isn't at home. He's (1) .... to

America. His wife Joanne has (2) .... to

America with him several times, but she hasn't

(3) .... with him this time. The children

aren't with Joanne. They've (4) .... to

stay with their grandparents.

4 **George is on a plane going to Mallorca. He is talking to the person next to him. They are having lunch. Complete the dialogue.**

A: That's the third glass of whisky (1 you/have)

.... Are you nervous?

B: Yes, very. It's the first time (2 I/fly)

....

A: Ah, I see. So (3 you/not be) ....

to Mallorca before.

B: No, this is the first time.

A: (4 you/be) .... abroad

before?

B: No, this the first foreign holiday (5 I/have)

....

A: Really. So this the first time (6 you/eat)

.... plastic ham and salad?

B: Yes, it is. (7 I/not eat) ....

airline food before.

5 **Complete the answers in this dialogue.**
Example: Did you enjoy the concert last night?
– Yes, it was (good concert/I/be) for a long time.
It was the best concert I've been to for a long time.

1 Have you read 'The Fixer' by John Rix? – Yes,
it's (interesting book/I/read) for a long time.

....

2 Have you seen Spielberg's new film? – Yes, I
think it's (bad film/he/make).

....

3 Did you watch the Liverpool-Inter Milan
match? – Yes, it was (exciting game/I/watch)
this season.

....

The past simple: *He came*
OR the present perfect: *He's come*

Jenny Price is 16. She lives with her mother in Sidmouth.
It's 6 p.m. on Thursday evening and everyone's asking: 'Where's Jenny?'
She left school at 4 o'clock, but she hasn't come home. She hasn't phoned her mother. She hasn't left a note. None of her friends have seen her since 4 o'clock. She's disappeared.
What happened before 4 o'clock this afternoon? Jenny was at school all day. She didn't go straight home after school. At five past four she bought some sweets at the corner shop. Then she said goodbye to her friends.

Step 1 | The difference between the past simple and the present perfect

• We use the past simple to talk about an event or a situation that happened at a particular time in the past, which is now finished.
  *She **left** school at 4 o'clock.*
  (This is a finished action that happened at a particular time.)
  *Jenny **was** at school all day.* (She isn't there now because school is finished.)

• We use the present perfect when we're more interested in the present results or effects of a past action. The action is unfinished at the time of speaking.
  *She **hasn't come** home.* (She isn't at home now.)
  *She**'s disappeared**.* (That's the present situation.)

CHECK QUESTIONS 1

Look at these two sentences.
Present perfect: A *Jenny has had the same boyfriend for six months.*
Past simple: B *Jenny had the same boyfriend for six months.*
1 Does A mean she has the same boyfriend now?
2 Does A mean she doesn't go out with him now?
3 Does B mean she has the same boyfriend now?
4 Does B mean she doesn't go out with him now?

Step 2 | Time words often used with the past simple

Jenny's parents came to live in Sidmouth 18 years ago. Jenny was born two years later. Her father left home when Jenny was twelve. He went to live with another woman. For the next two years Jenny's mother was very poor. Then Jenny's grandfather died and left them a lot of money. They bought a new house. It was Jenny's 16th birthday last Tuesday. Her GCSE exams started yesterday.

- In sentences with the past simple there is often a word, phrase or clause that tells us when the action happened or when a situation existed.

> Jenny's parents came to Sidmouth **18 years ago**.
> Her father left home **when Jenny was twelve**.
> **For the next two years** Jenny's mother was very poor.
> Her GCSE exams started **yesterday**.

We use the past simple (not the present perfect) after the question word *When?*.

> When **did** Jenny's father **leave** home? (past simple)
> NOT When has Jenny's father left home? (present perfect)

- When the time that the action happened is understood, we can use the past simple without time words and phrases.

> He **went** to live with another woman.
> (We understand that this happened immediately after he left home.)
> They **bought** a new house.
> (We understand that this was soon after the grandfather died.)

CHECK QUESTIONS 2 **Which words, phrases or clauses answer the question *When?* in these sentences.**
1 Jenny's parents moved to Sidmouth when they got married.
2 They were happy at first.
3 Her father lost his job in 1990.
4 Jenny met her first boyfriend last year.

Step 3 | Time words often used with the present perfect

> It's now 24 hours after Jenny's disappearance. Detective Inspector Green has come to Sidmouth to investigate. There's been no news of Jenny today. Her mother hasn't seen her since yesterday morning. Inspector Green has already spoken to her mother. He's just checked all the local hospitals. But he hasn't spoken to Jenny's teachers yet. They've known Jenny for five years. The Inspector still hasn't discovered why Jenny has disappeared.

- In sentences with the present perfect there's often a word or a phrase which shows that the action or situation is a present one, or which connects the present situation with the past. These are the most common:

> today this morning, week, etc. just still yet already recently since
> There's been no news of Jenny **today**.
> Her mother hasn't seen her **since** yesterday morning.
> Inspector Green has **already** spoken to her mother.

CHECK QUESTIONS 3 **What is the word in these sentences that often goes with the present perfect?**
1 He's just checked all the local hospitals.
2 He hasn't spoken to Jenny's teachers yet.
3 He still hasn't discovered why Jenny has disappeared.

Step 4 | Time words used with the past simple or the present perfect

Inspector Green went to Jenny's home. He was there for an hour. Now he's at her school. He's been there for two hours. Jenny's headteacher introduced him: 'The police have come to school this morning to ask you about Jenny Price.'
After school, one of the students told his parents: 'The police came to school this morning. They think Jenny Price has been kidnapped.'

- We can use time words and phrases (*for two hours, this morning*, etc.) with the past simple and the present perfect.
  Past simple: *He **was** at Jenny's home **for an hour**.*
    (His visit, which lasted an hour, is now finished.)
  Present perfect: *He's **been** at the school **for two hours**.*
    (His visit to the school is not finished. After two hours he's still there.)
  Present perfect: *'The police **have come** to school **this morning** to ask you about Jenny Price.'* (The morning isn't finished.)
  Past simple: *'The police **came** to school **this morning**.'*
    (The morning is finished. It's now evening.)
- We can also use these words and phrases with either the present perfect or the past simple:
    all morning   all afternoon   all evening   all year   all his life
    this afternoon   this evening   this year
    today   tonight
    for two hours, for three weeks, for ten years, etc.

CHECK QUESTIONS 4 **Answer the questions.**
1 Jenny's mother didn't sleep all night; she was so worried. Is the night finished now?
2 She slept for an hour this morning. Is it the morning now?
3 She has waited by the telephone all day. Is it still today?
4 'I haven't seen the newspaper this evening. Is there any news of Jenny?' Is it the evening now?

Practice

- We use the **present perfect** to talk about the present results or effects of a past action or situation. The action or situation isn't finished at the time of speaking.
  What's the problem? I've lost my passport.
- We use the **past simple** if the action or situation took place at a finished time in the past.
  I lost my passport when I was on holiday last year.

1 Match each item in the first column with one in the second to make a full sentence. Write 1a or 1d, etc.

1 John's gone to bed	a all week.		......
2 He went to bed	b in his life.		......
3 He had a stomach ache at work	c early, at about nine o'clock.		......
4 He's felt ill	d yet.		......
5 He's never been ill	e so he can't speak to you now.		......
6 I haven't phoned the doctor	f so he came home early.		......

2 Complete the dialogue, using either the past simple or the present perfect.

A: What are those people looking at? What .... (1 happen)?

B: There .... (2 be) an accident.

A: An accident! What .... (3 happen) exactly?

B: A cat .... (4 run) out into the road in front of a car. The driver .... (5 swerve) and .... (6 hit) a tree.

A: When .... it .... (7 happen)?

B: About five minutes ago.

A: .... anyone .... (8 call) for an ambulance?

B: No, not yet. But the police .... (9 arrive). They .... probably .... (10 call) for one.

A: This is the second accident we .... (11 have) near here this month.

B: Yes, but the other accident .... (12 not be) as bad as this one.

3 Complete this conversation with the correct form of the verb, present perfect or past simple.

1	I (leave) school in 1994.	A I left	B I've left	......
2	What (you do) after that?	A did you do	B have you done	......
3	I (travel) round the world for a year.	A I've travelled	B I travelled	......
4	When (you come) home?	A have you come	B did you come	......
5	I (come) home six months ago.	A I came	B I've come	......
6	What (you do) since then?	A did you do	B have you done	......
7	I (do) lots of different jobs.	A I've done	B I did	......
8	But I (not have) a job for a month now.	A haven't had	B didn't have	......
9	(you see) the TV news last night?	A Did you see	B Have you seen	......
10	No, I (-n't) Why?	A I haven't	B I didn't	......
11	They (say) they were looking for people to go and work in Berlin.	A They said	B They've said	......
12	Really? I (never work) in Germany.	A I've never worked	B I never worked	......

11 The present perfect continuous: *He's been waiting for hours*

> The rock band Avalon are giving a concert in London. People are queueing to get tickets. A reporter's talking to a man in the queue:
> 'How long have you been standing here?'
> 'I've been waiting for two hours. Some people have been queueing all day. That girl over there has been waiting since 6 o'clock this morning!'

Step 1 | Actions that continue into the present

● We use the present perfect continuous to talk about an action that started in the past, that has continued over a period of time and is still continuing now.

PAST   NOW

|..|...................➤

*I've been waiting **for two hours**.*
(He arrived two hours ago and he's still waiting now.)

● We often use the present perfect continuous with *for* and *since* to say how long an action has been happening.
Note: We don't use the present continuous here.
    *I've been waiting **for two hours**.* (NOT I'm waiting for two hours.)
    *She's been waiting **since 6 a.m.*** (NOT She's waiting since 6 a.m.)
(For the uses of *for, since* see Unit 85.)

CHECK QUESTIONS 1 ▷ **Complete the sentences.**
1 Some people came early this morning, so they/wait/all day.
2 One girl said: 'I/queue/6 o'clock this morning.'

Step 2 | The forms of the present perfect continuous

Affirmative	Negative	Questions
I've been working	I haven't been working	Have I been working?
You've been working	You haven't been working	Have you been working?
He's been working	He hasn't been working	Has he been working?
She's been working	She hasn't been working	Has she been working?
It's been working	It hasn't been working	Has it been working?
We've been working	We haven't been working	Have we been working?
You've been working	You haven't been working	Have you been working?
They've been working	They haven't been working	Have they been working?

● We form the present perfect continuous with *have/has* + *been* + *-ing*.

● *Been* is usually pronounced /bin/.

CHECK QUESTIONS 2 ▷ **Put the sentences a) into the negative b) into the question form.**
1 They've been queueing.
2 He's been waiting.

Step 3 | Actions repeated over a period of time

> The reporter's talking to a young woman in the queue:
> 'Have you ever seen Avalon in concert?'
> 'No, I haven't. I've been trying to get into one of their concerts for years. I've been buying their albums for a long time. In fact, I've been listening to their music since I was 15.'

- We use the present perfect continuous to talk about repeated actions which have continued over a period of time up to now.

PAST   1991   1993   1994   1995   NOW
................|..............|.............|..............|....................|

*I've **been buying** their albums for a long time.*
*I've **been trying** to get into one of their concerts for years.*

Complete the answers.
1 Has she often tried to see them in concert? Yes ... for years.
2 Has she often bought their albums? Yes, ... for a long time.
3 Has she often listened to their music? Yes, ... since she was 15.

Step 4 | Actions that have just stopped

> The reporter has arrived back at the office. His editor's talking to him.
> 'What have you been doing?'
> 'I've been standing in the rain for the last hour. I've been talking to some of the people in the queue for the Avalon concert.'

- We also use the present perfect continuous to talk about an action which started in the past, which continued over a period, and which has just stopped.

1 hour ago   NOW
|..|....|

    *I've **been standing** in the rain for the last hour.*
    (He isn't standing in the rain now. He's just come back to the office.)

Note: We don't use the present perfect continuous with verbs that aren't normally used in the continuous form. (See Unit 2.)
(For the difference between the present perfect continuous and the present perfect simple, see Unit 12.)

1 Was the reporter standing in the rain a short time ago?
2 Is he talking to the people in the queue now?

ANSWERS TO
CHECK QUESTIONS
1, 2, 3 AND 4

1 1 ... so they've been waiting all day. 2 I've been queueing since 6 o'clock this morning. **2** 1a) They haven't been queueing. b) Have they been queueing? 2a) He hasn't been waiting. b) Has he been waiting?

3 1 Yes, she's been trying to see them for years. 2 Yes, she's been buying their albums for a long time. 3 Yes, she's been listening to their music since she was 15. **4** 1 Yes. 2 No.

Practice

> PAST   NOW
> *I've been sitting on the floor for ages.*
> 1 YEAR AGO   January   March   June   NOW
>   *I've been writing to him for a year.*
> PAST   NOW
> *She's been doing some exercises. She's having a rest now.*

1 Complete the text, using the present perfect continuous.

James and Megan (1 go out) ....

.... together for two

years. They (2 plan) ....

to get married. They (3 look for) ....

.... a flat, and they

(4 save up) .... to buy

some furniture. James (5 do) ....

.... his ordinary job

during the day and, to earn some extra money,

he (6 work) .... at a

restaurant three evenings a week. Megan lost

her job three months ago, but since then she

(7 make) .... paper

flowers and selling them at the local market.

Unfortunately she (8 not feel) ....

.... well for the last few

weeks. She (9 go) .... to

the doctor's twice a week. James (10 worry)

.... a lot about her, and

he (11 not sleep) ....

very well. But today, they (12 feel) ....

.... a lot happier. Megan

has just got a new job.

2 The end of a perfect day for the Bloom family! Make sentences with the present perfect continuous.

1 Mrs Bloom's very tired. (work hard)

....

2 Mr Bloom looks pale. (not feel well/all day)

....

3 Tom's got to clean his boots. (play football)

....

4 Alice has got no money left. (buy clothes)

....

5 Andrew's got a headache. (watch TV/all evening)

....

6 They're all depressed. (rain/all day)

....

3 Yesterday you sat next to a professional tennis player on the plane. You talked to her and discovered these facts.

1 She's been playing tennis since she was 6.
2 She's been playing in professional tournaments since she was 13.
3 (She now lives in Monaco.) She's been living there for two years.
4 (She does a lot of yoga.) She's been doing it for five years.
5 (She's coming back from a tournament in Australia. She's tired.) She's been travelling for 28 hours.

What was your question each time? Use *How long ... ?*
Example:
1 *How long have you been playing tennis?*

2 ....

3 ....

4 ....

5 ....

12 The present perfect: continuous or simple?

> Mandy Batista has been cleaning her apartment this morning. So far she's cleaned the kitchen and she's done the bathroom. She hasn't done the bedroom or the living room yet.

Step 1 | Actions over a period of time OR completed actions?

- We use the present perfect continuous to talk about an activity over a period of time. It doesn't matter if it's finished or not. (See Unit 11.)
  *Mandy **has been cleaning** her apartment this morning.*

- We normally use the present perfect simple to talk about a completed action. We're interested in the present result of the action. (See Unit 7.)
  *She**'s cleaned** the kitchen.*
  (The kitchen is finished. It's clean now.)
  *She **hasn't done** the bedroom.*
  (The bedroom isn't done. It's still dirty.)

CHECK QUESTIONS 1
  1 What has Mandy been doing?
  2 What has she done so far?

Step 2 | Actions over a long period OR actions over a shorter period?

> Mandy works at NASA, the American Space Agency in Houston, Texas. She's always worked in the space industry, but this is a new job and she's only been working at NASA for six weeks. She's been trying to get a job there for years. She's lived in Houston all her life, but a few days ago she moved into a new apartment. She's only been living there for four days.

- We can use both the present perfect continuous and the present perfect simple (with verbs like *work* and *live*) to talk about actions that started in the past and still continue now.

- But we normally use the present perfect simple for actions or situations that continue over a long period.
  *She**'s always worked** in the space industry.*

- We normally use the present perfect continuous for actions or situations that continue over a shorter period.
  *She**'s been working** at NASA **for six weeks**.*

- Note that we can use the present perfect continuous for actions that continue over a long period when we're talking about repeated actions.
  *She**'s been trying** to get a job there **for years**.*

CHECK QUESTIONS 2
  1 Has she lived in Houston for long? Yes, she ... all her life.
  2 Has she lived in the apartment for very long? No, she ... only ... four days.

Step 3 | How long OR How many?

> For hundreds of years people have asked the question, 'Are we alone in the universe?' For the last few weeks NASA has been receiving reports from the American public about strange objects in the sky. They've received several letters from a man in Arizona and Mandy has talked to him twice on the phone. He says that a spacecraft has landed three times near his home, and that he's met a 'man' from outer space!

- We can use both the present perfect simple and the present perfect continuous to say how long something has been happening. (See Step 2.)
  *For hundreds of years people **have asked** the question.*
  *For the last few weeks NASA **has been receiving** reports.*
- But we must use the present perfect simple to say how many things we've done or how many times something has happened.
  *They**'ve received several letters** from a man in Arizona.*
  *A spacecraft **has landed three times** near his home.*

CHECK QUESTIONS 3 **Complete these questions.**
1 How many times/a spacecraft/land/near the man's home?
2 How long/NASA/receive/reports about objects in the sky?

Step 4 | Verbs not used in the present perfect continuous

> Mandy has been divorced for three years, and she hasn't had any contact with her ex-husband for the last year. For the last month she's been going out with a pilot. She's known him since she started work at NASA.

- Some verbs like *be, have* (= possess), *know*, etc. (when they describe a state, not an action) aren't used in the present perfect continuous.
  *Mandy **has been divorced** for three years.* (NOT Mandy has been being divorced)
  *She **hasn't had** any contact with her husband for the last year.*
  (NOT She hasn't been having any contact)
  *She**'s known** him since she started work at NASA.* (NOT She's been knowing him)
  (For verbs which aren't normally used in the continuous form, see Unit 3, Step 3.)

CHECK QUESTIONS 4 **Complete the sentences.**
1 Mandy (be) at NASA for six weeks.
2 She (have) a new boyfriend for a month.
3 The pilot (know) her since she started work at NASA.

ANSWERS TO
CHECK QUESTIONS
1, 2, 3 AND 4

1 1 She's been cleaning her apartment. 2 She's cleaned the kitchen and she's done the bathroom.
2 1 Yes, she's lived there all her life. 2 No, she's only been living there for four days.
3 1 How many times has a spacecraft landed near the man's home? 2 How long has NASA been receiving reports about objects in the sky?
4 1 Mandy has been at NASA for six weeks.
2 She's had a new boyfriend for a month.
3 The pilot has known her since she started work at NASA.

Practice

The present perfect continuous: (*I've been trying*)	• for actions happening over a period of time. • for actions happening over a short period. • when talking about 'how long'
The present perfect simple: (*I've tried*)	• for completed actions • for actions happening over a longer period • when talking about 'how many'

1 It is the first day of Kerry's holiday in Spain. Choose the correct tense to complete the sentences.

1 She (has been sunbathing/has sunbathed) .... on the beach since breakfast.

2 The sun (has shone/has been shining) .... all day.

3 She (hasn't had/hasn't been having) .... a swim yet. The sea's a bit cold.

4 She (has read/has been reading) .... a book, but she hasn't finished it yet.

5 She (has only read/has only been reading) .... a few pages.

6 For the last hour she (has been watching/has watched) .... a good-looking Spanish boy who (has surfed/has been surfing) .... just fifty metres away from her.

7 He's a very good surfer and he (has only fallen off/has only been falling off) .... his board a couple of times.

8 He (has been looking/has looked) .... at her several times and each time he (has been smiling/has smiled) .... at her.

9 All the time she (has hoped/has been hoping) .... that he'll come and say hello, but he (hasn't been coming/hasn't come) .... yet.

10 Kerry (has always been wanting/has always wanted) .... to learn a bit of Spanish!

2 Fabian is Colombian. He has recently come to work in England. You are asking him questions. Use the present perfect continuous or the present perfect simple.
Example:
This isn't his first time in England. *How many times have you been to England?*

1 He's living in England now.
How long .... in England?

2 He's a circus acrobat.
How long .... a circus acrobat?

3 He sometimes falls off the trapeze.
How many .... the trapeze?

4 He writes books about the circus.
How many .... ?

5 He's learning English.
How long .... English?

6 He's married to Tessa, an English girl.
How long .... to Tessa ?

13 The past perfect: *He had come*

In 1994 Enzo Manzoni was living in the Italian quarter of Los Angeles. He was an Italian immigrant from Naples. He had come to the USA in 1992. He'd been in America for two years, but he hadn't learnt to speak much English. During those two years he'd worked hard, and by 1994 he'd saved up enough money to go back to Naples for a holiday. On July 16th his plane left Los Angeles airport at 20.30. After Enzo had eaten a large dinner and had drunk some wine, he fell asleep.

Step 1 | Uses of the past perfect

- If we're already talking about the past, we use the past perfect when we want to talk about an earlier past.

  Enzo **had come** to the USA in 1992.

  (We're talking about the past – 1994. So we use the past perfect to talk about what happened in an earlier past – 1992.)

- When something happened in the past before another thing, we use the past perfect for the first action and usually the past simple for the second action.

      (1st action)   (2nd action)

  *After he'**d eaten** a large dinner, he **fell** asleep.*

CHECK QUESTIONS 1 ▸ **Which thing happened first? Which thing happened after that? Write (1st) and (2nd).**

1 He'd emigrated to Los Angeles. ... He worked hard. ...
2 He decided to go to Naples. ... He'd saved up enough money. ...
3 He fell asleep. ... He'd had a big meal. ...

Step 2 | The forms of the past perfect

- We form the past perfect with *had* + a past participle.

Affirmative	Negative	Questions
I'd (had) started	I hadn't (had not) started	Had I started?
You'd started	You hadn't started	Had you started?
He'd started	He hadn't started	Had he started?
She'd started	She hadn't started	Had she started?
It'd started	It hadn't started	Had it started?
We'd started	We hadn't started	Had we started?
You'd started	You hadn't started	Had you started?
They'd started	They hadn't started	Had they started?

- Note the short answers.

  Had Enzo come from Naples ? Yes, he had.

  Had he learnt English ? No, he hadn't.

CHECK QUESTIONS 2 ▸ **Put the verbs into the past perfect.**

1 How long (live) Enzo in America?
2 He (not make) many friends in Los Angeles.
3 He (want) to go back to Naples for a long time.

Step 3 | The past perfect or the past simple?

> Enzo woke up when his plane landed. When he looked at his watch, he was surprised. The flight hadn't taken very long. When he'd been through customs, he came out of the terminal. He was surprised no-one had come to meet him. After he'd waited for a bit, he took a bus into the city. He was amazed when he saw how much Naples had changed.

- When one action is an immediate reaction to another, or when the two actions are almost simultaneous, we use the past simple for both actions.

Past simple	+	**Past simple**
When *he looked at his watch,*		*he was surprised.*

- But when it is clear that the first action was completed before the second started, we often use the past perfect.

Past perfect	+	**Past simple**
After *he'd waited for a bit,*		*he took a bus.*

- Note the difference: *Enzo woke up when his plane **landed**.*
  (Enzo woke up at the same time that the plane landed.)
  *Enzo woke up when the plane **had landed**.*
  (The plane landed, and after that Enzo woke up.)

CHECK QUESTIONS 3 **In which sentence was one action completed before another started?**
1 He went back to Naples as soon as he'd saved enough money.
2 By the time the bus arrived in the city, he was very confused.
3 He was amazed when he saw how different Naples was.

Step 4 | The past perfect continuous

> Enzo sat down on a bench. After he'd been sitting there for a few minutes, he asked a policeman where he was. 'New York, of course!' He hurried back to the airport. When he arrived, the airline had been calling his name for the last 20 minutes. They'd been looking for him everywhere. But they hadn't found him, so the plane had left for Naples. It had only stopped in New York to pick up more passengers!

- We use the past perfect continuous if we want to emphasise that something had been in progress continuously up to a certain time in the past.
  *The airline **had been calling** his name for the last 20 minutes.*
  (This had continued during the 20 minutes before he arrived.)
- We form the past perfect continuous with *had/hadn't been* + an *-ing* form.
Affirmative: He'd (He had) been waiting
Negative: He hadn't been waiting **Questions:** Had he been waiting?

CHECK QUESTIONS 4 **Complete the sentences with the past perfect continuous or the simple past.**
1 Enzo (live) in Los Angeles for two years when he (decide) to go back to Naples.
2 On the plane Enzo (eat) for an hour when he (fall) asleep.
3 Enzo (not sit) on the bench for long, when he (see) a policeman.

ANSWERS TO CHECK QUESTIONS 1, 2, 3 AND 4

1 1 1st 2nd 2 2nd 1st 3 2nd 1st
2 1 had Enzo lived 2 He hadn't made 3 He'd wanted
3 Sentence 1
4 1 had been living decided 2 had been eating fell 3 hadn't been sitting saw

Practice

> - We use the past perfect to say that something happened before a certain time in the past: *I was nervous because I had never driven before.*
> - We use the past perfect continuous to say that something had been in progress up to a certain time in the past: *When I met him, he had been living in Paris for five years.*

1 **Last summer a group of students came to Britain for the first time. These are the things they had not done before they came. Put the verbs in brackets into the past perfect.**

1 Carmen (not speak) .... much English.

2 Maria (not sit) .... on the top of a double-decker bus.

3 Claudio (not drink) .... tea with milk in it.

4 Steffi (not eat) .... fish and chips.

5 Martin (not drive) .... on the left.

2 **Make single sentences, with one verb in the past simple, the other in the past perfect.**

1 We parked our car. We went to the check-in desk. When ....
....

2 They gave us our boarding passes. They weighed our suitcases. Once ....
....

3 We showed our passports at immigration. We went to the café in the departure lounge.
After ....
....

4 We got on the plane. We handed in our boarding passes. ....
after ....

5 We sat down and fastened our seat-belts. We found our seats. As soon as ....
....

6 The plane took off. We didn't unfasten our seat-belts. ....
until ....

3 **Make single sentences. Use either past perfect + past simple or past simple + past simple.**

1 (The alarm clock rang. I woke up.)
As soon as ....
....

2 (I got dressed. I went downstairs.)
When ....
....

3 (I had breakfast. I cleaned my teeth.)
After ....
....

4 (I looked at my watch. I realised I was late.)
When ....
....

5 (I arrived at the bus stop. I remembered it was Sunday.) When ....
....

4 **The Kelly family all came home later than usual yesterday. Why? Complete the sentences using the past perfect continuous.**

1 Daniel and Sarah came home late, because they (jog) ....

2 Gemma came home late, because she (play) .... tennis.

3 Damien came home late, because he (drink) .... with some friends.

4 Jane came home late, because she (study) .... in the library.

44

14 The future: *will/won't, shall/shan't*

Jan and Mike want to go to Eurodisney. They're trying to decide when to go.

Mike: I think it'll be better in October. The hotels will be cheaper then. There won't be as many people. In July we'll probably have to queue for hours to go on the rides. We shan't have time to see everything.

Jan: Yes, but the weather won't be as good in October. It'll probably rain all the time, and it'll be cold. We'll have to take winter clothes.

Step 1 | *Will, won't, shall, shan't* for simple predictions

- We use *will* or *won't* when we make simple predictions about future actions or situations.

    The hotels **will** be cheaper in October.
    But the weather **won't** be as good.

- After *I* and *we*, we can use *will* or *shall* in affirmative sentences. But we normally use the short forms (*I'll, we'll*).

    We**'ll** have to take winter clothes.
    (= We shall have to/We will have to)

In negative sentences, after *I* and *we*, we can use *won't* or *shan't*. *Won't* is more common.

    We **won't** have time to see everything.
    = We **shan't** have time to see everything.

- We often use *I (don't) think, I (don't) expect, I'm sure, I'm afraid* and *probably, definitely, perhaps*, etc. with *will* and *won't*.

    I think it'll be better.   We'll **probably** have to queue for hours.

CHECK QUESTIONS 1 ▶ **Complete the sentences.**

1 Jan prefers July, because she thinks the weather ... be better.
2 Mike prefers October, because they ... have to pay as much for a hotel.
3 Jan says: 'July will be better, because we ... need to take winter clothes.'

Step 2 | *Shall I?/Shall we?* for offers and suggestions

Mike: So, what shall we do? Shall we go in October?
Jan: No, let's go in July. I know it'll be more crowded then, but I'm sure the weather will be better.
Mike: OK. Shall I book the tickets?

- In questions, we use *Shall I/Shall we* (and not *will*) when we make suggestions or offers:

    Shall we go in October?   **Shall** I book the tickets?

- and when we ask for suggestions.

    What **shall** we do?

Complete the questions.
1 Jan asks Mike to suggest a date for their trip. 'When .... go?'
2 Mike offers to go to the travel agent's. '.... to the travel agent's?'

Step 3 | *Will* for intentions (sudden decisions and requests)

> Jan and Mike are now at Eurodisney. Jan's trying to persuade Mike to
> go on the Big Thunder Mountain ride, but Mike won't go. He's sure the
> ride will make him sick.
> Jan: Come on! You'll be all right. I'll sit next to you. I'll hold your hand,
>   I promise!
> Mike: No, I've told you. I won't come. I'll just sit here and watch.
> Jan: Oh, OK. Will you hold my camera ? Will you take a photo of me?
> Mike: Yes, sure.
> Jan: And afterwards we'll have a drink at the Last Chance Café, and I'll
>   tell you all about it.

- We can use *will/won't* when we talk about something we decide to do or not to do
  at the moment of speaking.
    I'll sit next to you.
    We'll have a drink at the Last Chance Café.

- We use *will* to make a request.
    ***Will** you hold my camera?* ***Will** you take a photo of me?*

- We use *won't* when we refuse to do something.
    *I **won't** come.*
    *Mike **won't** go on the Big Thunder Mountain ride.*

**Jan and Mike are in the Last Chance Café after Jan's ride. Complete their
conversation.**
1 What will you have to drink, Jan? I ... anything, thanks. I feel a bit sick.
2 What about you, Mike? I think ... a coffee.
3 Jan, are you all right? No. I think ... to the toilet.

---

1 1 will be 2 won't 3 won't/shan't
2 1 shall we 2 Shall I go
3 1 won't have 2 I'll have 3 I'll go

Practice

> - We use *will* (*'ll*), *won't* (and *shan't* after *I, we*) to talk about a simple prediction of a future event or situation.
> - We use *Shall I ... ? Shall we ... ?* to make a suggestion or an offer.
> - We can use *will/won't when* we decide to do something, or not to do something, at the moment of speaking.
>   *I think I'll go by train. I won't go by car.*
> - *Won't* can also express a refusal.
>   *I won't speak to him again!*

1 Look at these predictions about the future. Match a sentence in the first column with the correct reaction in the second column.

A	Computers won't replace teachers.	1	No, we won't. That's impossible.
B	The world's climate will change.	2	Do you think there will?
C	We'll travel faster than the speed of light.	3	I hope there won't.
D	There won't be a third world war.	4	Yes, we definitely will.
E	There'll be cities on the Moon.	5	I'm sure it will.
F	We'll live longer.	6	I agree. I don't think they will.
G	I'm sure they'll find a cure for AIDS.	7	Yes, I expect they will.

A ......   B ......   C ......   D ......   E ......   F ......   G ......

2 Complete the conversation, using *'ll, will, won't* (or *shan't*).

'(1) .... you phone me tonight?'

'Yes, of course I (2) ....'

'You (3) .... forget, will you?'

'No, I promise I (4) ....'

'(5) .... I see you tomorrow?'

'Yes, I (6) .... see you at the club.'

'(7) .... you meet me outside?'

'Yes, sure.'

'What time?'

'Oh, I (8) .... probably be there at about 9.'

'OK, I (9) .... meet you at 9. You're sure you

(10) .... be late?'

'I promise I (11) .... be late.'

3 You have got an au-pair job with an English family. You have got a lot to do. Complete the sentences.
Example: Will someone do the washing up?
Yes, I'll do it.

'Will someone make the beds?'

'Yes, (1) .... them.'

'We need some eggs for the children's lunch.'

'(2) .... and buy some.'

'The children are getting bored.'

'(3) .... them a story.'

'Will someone take the dog for a walk?'

'Yes, (4) .... him.'

'I can't look after the children this afternoon.'

'(5) .... them.'

4 You are in a car on the motorway. The driver is feeling sleepy. You are making suggestions and offers. Use *Shall I?* or *Shall we?*
Example: (Perhaps you should stop for a few minutes.) *Shall we stop for a few minutes?*

1 (It's very hot in the car. The windows are closed.)

.... ?

2 (The radio isn't on.)

.... ?

3 (You both need a drink. Where can you stop?)

.... the next service area?

4 (The driver's falling asleep. Perhaps you should drive.)

.... ?

15 | *Going to* OR *will?*

> Joe: Hi! What are you going to do today?
> Daniel: I'm going to go for a bike ride.
> Joe: Where are you going to go?
> Daniel: Princetown. I was going to ride to Bovey, but it's too far.
> Joe: I'll come with you, if you like, and I'll bring some sandwiches.

Step 1 | Decisions about the future

- We use *be going to* + infinitive (and not *will*) to talk about future actions we've already decided on.
  I'm going to go for a bike ride. (A decision he made before the phone call.)
  What *are you going to do?* (= What are your plans?)

- We use *was/were going to* + infinitive to talk about intentions or plans we had in the past (but we've now changed our plans).
  I was going to ride to Bovey, but ... (That was his intention, but it isn't now.)

- In contrast, we generally use *will* (NOT *going to*) when we decide to do something at the moment of speaking. (See Unit 14.)
  I'll come with you, if you like. (This wasn't Joe's intention before he phoned.)

CHECK QUESTIONS 1 **Use *going to/will* in your answers.**
1 What does Daniel intend to do today? 2 Where has he decided to go?
3 But what was his first intention?
4 They decide to take some food. What does Joe say?

Step 2 | Predicting future events: *will* or *going to*?

> Daniel's looking at the weather forecast in the newspaper.
> 'It will be fine at first, but rain will spread from the west to all areas by late morning. The westerly wind will become fresh to strong. The temperature will fall to 8° this afternoon.' Now he's phoning Joe.
> Daniel: The weather forecast's awful. It's going to rain and it's going to be very windy. It won't be much fun on the road.
> Joe: Well, what shall we do?
> Daniel: Eat our sandwiches in the kitchen, I suppose!

- We normally use *will/won't* for simple predictions. (See Unit 14.)
  Rain *will spread* from the west. It *won't be* much fun.

- But we use *going to* (NOT *will*) for predictions about the future when there's present evidence of a future event.
  It's going to rain. It's going to be very windy.
  (The weather forecast he's looking at tells him this.)

CHECK QUESTIONS 2 **What does the forecast tell Daniel about this afternoon's temperature?**

ANSWERS TO CHECK QUESTIONS 1 AND 2
1 1 He's going to go for a bike ride. 2 He's going to go to Princetown. 3 He was going to ride to Bovey. 4 "I'll bring some sandwiches."

2 1 It (The temperature) is going to fall (to 8°).

Practice

> - We use *going to* for intentions where we've already decided to do something.
> *I'm going to post this letter. Have you got any letters to post?*
> - We use *will* for intentions where we decide at the moment of speaking.
> *The phone's ringing.   It's OK. I'll answer it.*
> - We use *going to* to predict a future event which seems certain because of present evidence.
> *Look at those black clouds. It's going to rain.*

1 **Complete the dialogue with *will ('ll), won't* or *be going to*.**

'(1) .... you come to the cinema with me at the weekend?'

'No, I can't. I (2) .... be here. I

(3) .... be in London.'

'What (4) .... you .... do in London?'

'I (5) .... see my uncle.'

'When (6) .... be back?'

'I (7) .... be back about four on Sunday afternoon.'

'And what (8) .... you .... do on Sunday evening?'

'I'm not sure. I haven't got any plans. I

(9) .... phone you.'

'OK. Bye! I (10) .... see you on Sunday perhaps.'

2 **Complete this dialogue with *will ('ll)* or *be going to*.**

'I (1) .... take you into town tomorrow, if you like.'

'Great! I want to go to the shops. I (2) ....

be ready at about half past eight. (3) ....

that be all right?'

'Yes. Fine. I (4) .... pick you up at half past eight. What (5) .... you ....

buy?'

'I (6) .... buy a guitar. I

(7) .... get a Gibson.'

'That (8) .... be expensive.'

'Oh, I (9) .... not .... buy a new one.'

'Well, even a second-hand one (10) ....

be expensive.'

'I know, but it's OK because I (11) ....

borrow the money.'

'Good. Well, I (12) .... see you at half past eight tomorrow.'

3 **Look at these pictures and make sentences about the immediate future. Use the verbs: *jump, break, play, sink, drop*.**

1 ....

2 ....

3 ....

4 ....

5 ....

16

The future continuous: *I'll be waiting* and the future perfect: *He'll have left*

It's Saturday morning. Andy's phoning Anna to ask if she's free this evening.
Andy: I could come round at about 7.30.
Anna: No, sorry. I'll be playing volleyball at 7.30. My match starts at 7.15.
Andy: How about 9 o'clock?
Anna: No, I'll be having a swim then, after the match.
Andy: Ah, OK, I understand. Will you be seeing Alison today?
Anna: Yes, I'll be seeing her at lunchtime. She always eats at the same pub as me on Saturdays. Why?
Andy: Can you ask her if she's free this evening?
Anna: She won't be going out this evening. She'll be watching the football on television.

Step 1 | Form and uses of the future continuous

	Subject + *will/won't*	+	*be*	+	*-ing* form of the verb
Affirmative:	*I'll*		*be*		*playing volleyball.*
Negative:	*She won't*		*be*		*going out.*
Question:	*Will you*		*be*		*going out?*

* We use the future continuous (*will be/won't be* + -ing) to say that something will be in progress at a certain time in the future.
  I'll be playing volleyball at 7.30.
  (She'll be in the middle of her game.)
  I'll be having a swim at 9 o'clock.
  (Anna will already be in the swimming pool at 9 o'clock.)

* We also use the future continuous to talk about things that will happen
  a) because they're part of the normal routine:
  I'll be seeing her at lunchtime. She always eats at the same pub as me on Saturdays.
  (Anna always sees Alison at lunchtime on Saturdays.)
  or b) because they've been planned.
  She'll be watching the football on television.
  (Alison decided to watch this football match some time ago.)
  Note: We could also use the present continuous in b). (See Unit 4.)
  She's watching the football on television this evening.
  Note: We can also use the future continuous in questions to ask about somebody's plans because we want them to do something.
  Will you be seeing Alison today?
  (Andy asks this because he wants Anna to give Alison a message.)

CHECK QUESTIONS 1 **Answer the questions.**
1 What will Anna be doing at 7.45?
2 Will Alison be going out tonight?
3 What will she be doing?

Step 2 | Form and uses of the future perfect

> Andy's now phoning Fiona to ask if she's free this evening.
> Fiona: I'm sorry, Andy. I've got a lot of college work to do.
> Andy: What time will you have finished?
> Fiona: I'll have finished my work by 9, but my uncle will have arrived by
> then. He's just come over from Australia. He won't have eaten
> when he arrives, so we'll be having a late dinner. Sorry.

	Subject + *will/won't*	**+**	***have***	**+**	**past participle of the verb**
Affirmative:	*I'll*		*have*		*finished.*
Negative:	*He won't*		*have*		*eaten.*
Question:	*Will you*		*have*		*finished?*

- We use the future perfect (*will have/won't have* + past participle) to talk about something that hasn't happened yet, but that will be or won't be completed before a certain time in the future.
   I'll have finished *my work by 9.*
   (by 9 = not later than 9 o'clock)
   He won't have eaten *when he arrives.*

CHECK QUESTIONS 2 **What will have happened at Fiona's by 9 o'clock? (Two things.)**

Step 3 | Another use of the future continuous and the future perfect

> Andy's still trying to arrange something for this evening.
> Andy: I think I'll phone Lucy.
> Friend: Don't phone her now, Andy.
> Andy: Why not? She won't be in bed. She'll have got up by now.
> Friend: I know, but it's Saturday morning. She'll be doing the shopping
> now. She won't have got home yet.

- We can also use the future continuous and the future perfect (and the simple future) to talk about the present. We use them when we think that something is probably happening at the moment or has probably happened by now.
   *She***'ll be doing** *the shopping now.* (future continuous)
   *She***'ll have got up** *by now.* (future perfect)
   She **won't** *be in bed.* (simple future)

CHECK QUESTIONS 3
1 Is Lucy in bed now? What does Andy think?
2 What's Lucy doing now? What does Andy's friend think?

ANSWERS TO
CHECK QUESTIONS
1, 2 AND 3
1 1 She'll be playing volleyball. 2 No, she won't.
3 She'll be watching the football on television.
2 1 She'll have finished her work. 2 Her uncle
will have arrived.

3 1 She won't be in bed./She'll have got up by
now. 2 She'll be doing the shopping.

Practice

> **We use the future continuous (*will be/won't be* + *-ing*):**
> - to say that something will be or won't be in progress at a certain time in the future because a) it's part of a normal routine, or b) it's been planned.
> - when we say what is probably happening (or not happening) at this moment.
>
> **We use the future perfect (*will have/won't have* + past participle):**
> - to talk about something that hasn't happened yet, but that will be or won't be completed before a certain time in the future.
> - when we say what has probably happened (or not happened) by now.

1 It is Monday. Next Saturday Jenny is going on holiday to Spain. She is thinking about it. Make complete sentences using the future continuous.

Example: This time next week/I/sit/a beach by the Mediterranean *This time next week I'll be sitting on a beach by the Mediterranean.*

1 listen to/flamenco music

....

2 the sun/shine

....

3 it/not rain

....

4 I/not work

....

5 I/not sit/in this boring office

....

2 Joe is 17. He is thinking about what will have happened and what will be happening by the time he is 23. Use the future perfect or the future continuous.

Example: leave college *I'll have left college.*

1 finish my exams

....

2 leave home

....

3 live/in my own flat

....

4 get a job

....

5 earn/a lot of money

....

6 go out/every night

....

3 Ben is going to walk from one end of Britain to the other. He is going to start from Land's End in Cornwall. What will (or won't) have happened by the time he reaches John O'Groats on the north coast of Scotland? Complete the story, using these verbs: *see, walk, eat, pass, use, drink.*

When he reaches John O'Groats he (1) ....
.... eight hundred and seventy-
six miles. He (2) .... through
three countries (England, Wales and Scotland).
He (3) .... at least a
hundred bananas. He (4) .... at
least forty bottles of milk. He (5) ....
......................at least three pairs of shoes. He
(6) .... his family for over five
weeks.

4 You are phoning a friend. You know she is at home, but there is no reply. What do you suppose she is doing? What do you suppose has happened? Make sentences using the future continuous and the future perfect.

1 work/in the garden

....

2 And/forget to put the answering machine on.

....

3 Or/watch TV.

....

4 And/not hear the telephone.

....

5 Or/have a bath.

....

17

The passive (1): *He was sacked*
Forms and main uses

DJ Mark Walsh was sacked yesterday by Radio London. Mark had been given the job of DJ a month ago. Yesterday morning he had an argument with a woman caller, Mrs Dora Hind. The argument was heard by the director of the radio station, Mr Brian Hopkins. The programme was immediately stopped, Mr Walsh was told to leave and old Beatles records were played for the rest of the show.

The morning show on Radio London is listened to by over 1 million people. Mr Hopkins commented: 'Our listeners must be treated with respect. Mrs Hind shouldn't have been insulted. Mr Walsh hasn't been offered his job back. If he'd apologised, he wouldn't have been sacked. A new DJ will be chosen soon and a letter of apology is being sent to Mrs Hind.'

Mr Walsh later agreed to be interviewed by the Daily Express. He told the reporter: 'I hope to be offered a job by another radio station. I was sacked for no good reason. I was being insulted by a silly woman. I was called a lot of rude names. So I insulted her back. What's wrong with that?'

Step 1 | Forms of the passive

- *Radio London sacked Mark Walsh* is an active sentence.
Mark Walsh was sacked by Radio London is a passive sentence.
The object of the active sentence becomes the subject of the passive sentence.

	Subject +	**verb** +	**object**
Active:	*Radio London*	*sacked*	*Mark Walsh.*
Passive:	*Mark Walsh*	*was sacked by*	*Radio London.*

- We form the passive with the verb *be* (*is, was, has been*, etc.) + a past participle (*heard, stopped*, etc.)

	Subject +	**verb** +	**past participle**
	The argument	*was*	*heard by the director.*

- The tense of the verb *be* changes to form the different tenses in the passive.

Present simple:	*The show **is listened to** by 1 million people.*
Present continuous:	*A letter **is being sent** to Mrs Hind.*
Past simple:	*The argument **was heard** by the director.*
Present perfect:	*Mr Walsh **has not been offered** his job back.*
Past continuous:	*I **was being insulted** by a silly woman.*
Past perfect:	*He **had been given** the job a month ago.*
Future:	*A new DJ **will be chosen** soon.*

CHECK QUESTIONS 1 **Make the sentences passive.**

1. A lot of people listen to Mark Walsh's show.
2. Radio London have received a lot of complaints.
3. They won't allow Mark Walsh to work for them again.
4. A lot of people in Liverpool remember the Beatles.

Step 2 | Passive infinitives

- Some verbs are followed by an infinitive, for example modal verbs (*can, must, should, will, would*, etc.). When these verbs are used in a passive construction, we use a passive infinitive (*be* + past participle).
  Active: We must treat our listeners with respect.
  Passive: *Our listeners must **be treated** with respect.*
  Note the past form of the passive infinitive (*have been* + past participle).
  Active: He shouldn't have insulted Mrs Hind.
  Passive: *Mrs Hind shouldn't **have been insulted**.*

- We also use a passive infinitive construction after verbs like *want to, expect to, agree to, hope to*, etc.
  *Mr Walsh agreed to **be interviewed** by the Daily Express.*
  *I hope to **be offered** a job by another radio station.*

CHECK QUESTIONS 2 **Make passive sentences.**
1 DJs mustn't insult their listeners.
2 I don't think they should have sacked Mark Walsh.
3 Mark doesn't expect that they'll give him his job back.

Step 3 | Main uses of the passive

- We use the passive when the person or thing doing the action isn't important or isn't known or is understood.
  *The programme **was** immediately **stopped**.*
  (It isn't necessary to say who stopped the programme.)
  *Mr Walsh **was told** to leave the studio.*
  (We understand that the director told him to leave.)
  *Old Beatles records **were played** for the rest of the show.*
  (We don't know who played them, but it isn't important.)

- A passive sentence is usually more formal than an active one. Compare:
  We'll choose a new DJ soon. (Active. Informal comment)
  *A new DJ **will be chosen** soon.* (Passive. Formal statement)

- The passive is very common in English, especially in news reports, signs and notices, scientific and technical descriptions. In these contexts we're more interested in the things that happen rather than what/who makes them happen.

- In a passive construction we can mention the person or thing that does the action (the agent) after the word *by*.
  *He was sacked **by** Radio London.   He was being insulted **by** a silly woman.*

CHECK QUESTIONS 3 **A or B: Which is better?**
1 A: They opened Radio London in 1994.
   B: Radio London was opened in 1994.
2 A: They told Mr Walsh to apologise to Mrs Hind.
   B: Mr Walsh was told to apologise to Mrs Hind.
3 A: Mr Walsh will be paid until the end of the month.
   B: They'll pay Mr Walsh until the end of the month.

ANSWERS TO
CHECK QUESTIONS
1, 2 AND 3

1 1 Mark Walsh's show is listened to by a lot of people. 2 A lot of complaints have been received by Radio London. 3 Mark Walsh won't be allowed to work for them again. 4 The Beatles are remembered by a lot of people in Liverpool.

2 1 Listeners mustn't be insulted by DJs. 2 I don't think Mark Walsh should have been sacked. 3 Mark doesn't expect to be given his job back.

3 1 B 2 B 3 A

Practice

	Active	Passive
Present simple:	It breaks	It's broken
Present continuous:	It's breaking	It's being broken
Past simple:	It broke	It was broken
Past continuous:	It was breaking	It was being broken
Present perfect:	It's (has) broken	It's (has) been broken
Past perfect:	It had broken	It had been broken
Future *will*:	It'll break	It'll be broken
Future *going to*:	It's going to break	It's going to be broken
Modal (present):	It may break	It may be broken
Modal (past):	It might have broken	It might have been broken

1
The town of Ivybridge has changed a lot in the last five years. Rewrite these sentences, using a passive construction.

1 They've built a new hospital.

....

2 They're building a new shopping centre.

....

3 They'll finish it next October.

....

4 They knocked down the town hall last week.

....

5 They're going to build a new one soon.

....

2
The origin of the word 'jacuzzi'. Put the verbs into the passive.

Candido Jacuzzi (1 be born) ....

in Italy in 1903. In 1913 he (2 take) ....

to the USA by his parents. There he and one of

his brothers (3 kill) .... nearly ....

when their home-made plane crashed. The boys

(4 forbid) .... by their mother to

fly again. Instead they invented a bath with a

water pump which (5 use) .... to

treat their father's arthritis. Candido Jacuzzi's

great grandson (6 lend) ....

$100,000 by the bank to manufacture the bath as

a luxury item which (7 instal) .... now

.... in every new American home.

3
Complete the text, using passive forms.

Sean Kitcher (1 send) .... just ....

to prison. Yesterday he (2 give) ....

a 6-month sentence for stealing a car. The

conditions in the prison are terrible. Sean

(3 shock) .... by them. His cell

(4 not paint) .... for years.

The walls (5 cover) .... in

graffiti. He (6 wake up) ....

every morning at 6.30. He (7 allow) ....

.... to leave his cell for only two

hours a day. If he behaves himself, Sean (8 let

out) .... of prison after

four months. But if he breaks any prison rules,

he (9 keep in) .... for over

six months.

4
Sally Dexter is 16. She thinks young people are treated badly by adults. Rewrite the sentences, using passive infinitive constructions.
Example: I don't want people to treat me like a child. *I don't want to be treated like a child.*

1 I don't want people to tell me what to do.

....

2 I'd like people to listen to me.

....

3 My parents and teachers should have given me more freedom.

....

4 They ought to have allowed me to be more independent.

....

18

The passive (2): other constructions

> Bill Marsh is too old to look after himself. He's in an old people's home called Merrifield. A nurse has to feed him. He hates being fed. She tells him he's very difficult. He doesn't like being criticised, so he gets angry. She tells him to stop shouting, but he's tired of being told what to do. He remembers being treated like this when he was a child.

Step 1 | The passive -*ing* form

- We can use the -*ing* form of a verb in the passive. We use *being* + past participle.
  *He hates **being** fed.*
  (Active: He hates people feeding him.)
  *He's tired of **being told** what to do.*
  (Active: He's tired of people telling him what to do.)
  *He remembers **being treated** like this when he was a child.*
  (Active: He remembers people treating him like this.)

CHECK QUESTIONS 1 > **Make passive sentences.**
1 The nurses call him 'Billy'. He doesn't like ... 'Billy'.
2 They tell him he's difficult. He's tired of ... he's difficult.
3 A doctor examines him every month. He hates ...

Step 2 | Passive verb + infinitive with *to*

> Bill is said to be difficult, but he had a difficult childhood. His parents are thought to have died when he was 14. He went to work on a farm. He was expected to get up at 5.30 a.m. and to work for twelve hours. He was considered to be a good worker. But when he was 16, he was found to have poliomyelitis, and he's believed to have spent two years in hospital.

- We often use an infinitive (*to have*) or a perfect infinitive (*to have had*) in passive constructions with these verbs:
  believe consider expect fear feel find
  intend know report say think understand
  Passive: *Bill's said **to be** difficult.*
  (Active: People say Bill is difficult.)
  Passive: *He was considered **to be** a good worker.*
  (Active: They considered he was a good worker.)
  Passive: *He's believed **to have spent** two years in hospital.*
  (Active: They believe he spent two years in hospital.)
  Passive: *His parents are thought **to have died** when he was 14.*
  (Active: They think his parents died when he was 14.)

- Note the difference between the infinitive and the perfect infinitive. Compare:
  When he was 16, he was found **to have** *poliomyelitis.*
  (= At the age of 16 he had poliomyelitis.)
  When he was 16, he was found **to have had** *poliomyelitis.*
  (At the age of 16 he didn't have poliomyelitis. He had it before he was 16.)

CHECK QUESTIONS 2 **Make passive sentences.**
1 People know that Bill is very independent.
2 People say that Bill has no brothers or sisters.
3 People think that Bill had a difficult childhood.

Step 3 | *It's said …/It's known …/It's reported … etc.*

> It's thought that there are over 1 million old people in Britain who can't look after themselves. It was reported that more than 200 old people died of cold last winter. It's feared that most of them died because they had nobody to look after them. It's often said that this is one of society's biggest problems. It's expected that more old people's homes will be built in the future.

- We can use *it* + a passive verb + a *that* clause to talk about what people in general say or think or feel about a situation. It can be used with these verbs: *agree, announce, decide, expect, fear, feel, find, hope, intend, know, mention, regret, report, say, suggest, think, understand.*
  It's thought *(that) there are over 1 million old people.*
  (= There are thought to be over 1 million old people.)
  It's *often* ***said*** *(that) this is one of society's biggest problems.*
  (= This is often said to be one of society's biggest problems.)
  It was reported *(that) more than 200 old people died of cold last winter.*
  (= More than 200 old people were reported to have died.)

CHECK QUESTIONS 3 **Rewrite the sentences, using *It* + a passive verb.**
1 People think that many old people die because no-one looks after them.
2 The authorities have announced that more old people's homes will be built.
3 People hope that the situation will improve.

Step 4 | *Be supposed to*

> Merrifield is supposed to be a very good old people's home. The nurses are supposed to be well-trained and kind. But Bill doesn't like them. If he gets out of bed at the wrong time, he's told: 'Billy, you're supposed to be in bed.' When he watches a late night film, they say: 'Billy, you aren't supposed to watch television after 10.30.' Bill often gets very angry. 'This is supposed to be a home, not a prison!'

- *Be supposed to* has two different meanings. It can mean that something is the general opinion of most people.
  Merrifield ***is supposed to*** *be a good old people's home.*
  (= People say that Merrifield is a good old people's home.)

- It can also mean that something should happen because it's the rule or because it's been planned.
  *You're **supposed to** be in bed.*
  (You should be in bed because that's the rule.)
  *This **is supposed to** be a home, not a prison.*
  (Merrifield was intended to be a home, not a prison.)

- We use the negative form to say that something isn't allowed.
  *You **aren't supposed to** watch television after 10.30.*
  (This isn't permitted.)

CHECK QUESTIONS 4 **Rewrite the sentences, using *be supposed to.***
1 Bill has to get up at 6.30 a.m. - that's the rule.
2 Bill sometimes smokes, but smoking isn't permitted.
3 People say the nurses at Merrifield are nice.

Step 5 | *He was given .../He's been offered ... , etc.*

Last Thursday Bill was given a boiled egg for his breakfast. 'I've been given a boiled egg three times this week. You know I don't like boiled eggs!' He got very angry. He was promised some toast and marmalade if he was quiet. He just got angrier, so he was given an injection to calm him down. The nurses refused to look after him any more, so he's been offered a room at another home. He was shown his new room this morning but he refuses to move.

- When a verb has two objects (indirect and direct: see Unit 37) it's possible to have two passive sentences.
  (Active: They gave Bill a boiled egg.)
  1 ***Bill** was given **a boiled egg**.*
  2 ***A boiled egg** was given **to Bill**.*
  But we normally make the person the subject, as in sentence 1.
  *He was promised **some toast and marmalade**.*
  *He's been offered **a room** at another home.*

- We can use this construction with these verbs: *allow, give, hand, lend, offer, owe, pay, promise, sell, send, show, teach, tell.*

CHECK QUESTIONS 5 **Make passive sentences.**
1 The authorities have sent Bill a letter saying he must leave.
2 They've offered Bill a better room at the new home.
3 They say they'll give him the kind of food he likes.

ANSWERS TO CHECK QUESTIONS 1, 2 ,3, 4 AND 5

1 1 He doesn't like being called 'Billy'. 2 He's tired of being told he's difficult. 3 He hates being examined.
2 1 Bill is known to be very independent. 2 Bill is said to have no brothers or sisters. 3 Bill is thought to have had a difficult childhood.
3 1 It's thought that many old people die because no-one looks after them. 2 It's been announced that more old people's homes will be built. 3 It's hoped that the situation will improve.
4 1 Bill's supposed to get up at 6.30 a.m. 2 but he isn't supposed to (smoke). 3 The nurses at Merrifield are supposed to be nice.
5 1 Bill's (has) been sent a letter saying he must leave. 2 Bill's been offered a better room at the new home. 3 They say he'll be given the kind of food he likes.

Practice

> The passive -ing form: *I don't like **being photographed**.*
> Passive verb + infinitive with *to*: *George **is said to keep** snakes in his bathroom.*
> Passive verb + perfect infinitive: *The police **are thought to have caught** the thieves.*
> *It* + a passive verb: ***It's said** to be difficult to learn Chinese.*
>   ***It was announced** that the Queen was ill.*
> Two meanings of *be supposed to*: *That restaurant **is supposed to** be good.* (general opinion)
>   *You're **supposed to** work hard.* (the rule or the plan)
> Verbs with two objects: ***A letter** was sent **to him**. He was sent **a letter**.*
>   (The second construction is more common.)

1 **Mireille Lavoisier was a famous French film star in the 1930s. These were her likes and dislikes. Make passive sentences.**
Example: She liked people giving her flowers.
She liked being given flowers.

1 She enjoyed people taking her to the cinema to see her films.

....

....

2 She didn't like people asking how old she was.

....

....

3 She hated people seeing her when she wasn't wearing any make-up.

....

....

4 She was afraid of people forgetting her when she was dead.

....

....

2 **Rewrite these sentences without changing the meaning.**
Example: It's reported that an earthquake has hit the coast of Sumatra. *An earthquake is reported to have hit the coast of Sumatra.*

1 At first it was said that no-one had been killed.

....

....

2 But now it's thought that 250 people have died in the earthquake.

....

....

3 It's expected that the death toll will rise.

....

....

4 It's reported that three coastal villages have disappeared completely.

....

....

3 **Rewrite the sentences, using *be supposed to*.**

1 They say British people are careful drivers.

....

....

2 When you drive in Britain, you have to wear a seat belt.

....

....

3 It's not advisable to drink and drive.

....

....

4 You aren't allowed to park on the pavement.

....

....

4 **Make these sentences passive.**
1 We don't pay nurses much money.

....

2 The government's offering them a 1% pay rise.

....

3 The Minister has promised them a further rise next year.

....

4 She might give them a 2% rise then.

....

5 The nurses have sent the Minister a letter.

....

19

Have/get something done

> When Steve and Louise bought their flat, it was in a terrible state. They couldn't do all the jobs themselves. So they had central heating installed. They also got the windows replaced and they had the flat painted. But they haven't had the carpets cleaned yet. And now they need to have a new lock fitted to the front door because yesterday Louise had her car broken into and her handbag stolen. The front door key was in her bag!

Step 1 | Use of *have/get something done*

- We can say *we have something done* if we don't do the job ourselves. We decide to employ another person to do the job for us. Compare:
  A *Steve and Louise **had** their flat **painted**.* (Someone painted their flat for them.)
  B *Steve and Louise painted their flat.* (They painted their flat themselves.)

- We can use the verb *get* instead of *have*. *Get* is more informal.
  *They **got** (OR had) the windows **replaced**.*

- We can also use *have something done* when we talk about something, often unpleasant, that happened to someone.
  *Louise **had** her car **broken into**. She **had** her bag **stolen**.*
  Note: We don't normally use *get* instead of *have* here.

CHECK QUESTIONS 1 **Which jobs did they do themselves?**
1 They had some new curtains made. 2 They put up some shelves.
3 They had a telephone installed. 4 They decorated the bedrooms.

Step 2 | The forms of *have something done*

Subject	+	*have*	+	object	+	past participle
They		are having		the electricity		checked.
They		have had		central heating		installed.
They		had		a telephone		installed.
They		are going to have		the carpets		cleaned.
Have they		had		the bedrooms		decorated?
Did they		have		the roof		repaired?

- Note that the tense of the verb *have* can change.

- We don't use the contracted forms of *have* (*'ve, 's* and *'d*) with this construction.
  *They **had** the flat painted.* (NOT They'd the flat painted.)

CHECK QUESTIONS 2 **Put in the correct form of *have*.**
1 Last week they ... the roof repaired.
2 At the moment they .... the bedrooms decorated.
3 Next week they ... their new kitchen fitted.

ANSWERS TO
CHECK QUESTIONS
1 AND 2

1 2, 4
2 1 they had 2 they're having 3 they're going
    to have

Practice

Subject	+	*have*	+	object	+	past participle
We		had		a telephone		installed
I		had		my car		broken into
Did you		have		your hair		done?

1 Before we went on holiday, we had to do a lot of things. Rewrite the sentences.

Example: A mechanic serviced our car. *We had our car serviced.*

1 A watchmaker repaired my watch.

I ....

2 A hairdresser cut my hair.

I ....

3 A shoemaker mended my shoes.

I ....

4 A dentist checked my teeth.

I ....

5 An electrician installed a burglar alarm.

We ....

6 A builder fitted stronger locks to the doors.

We ....

7 The passport office renewed my passport.

I ....

8 A garage fitted two new tyres to our car.

We ....

2 Complete this text, using the structure *have something happen*. Use each of these verbs once: *take, search, test, knock out, steal, cut, break*.

When Carl Briggs first arrived in prison, he

.... his pockets (1) .... He ....

his hair (2) .... He .... his blood (3)

.... He .... his photo (4) ....

He also .... his cigarettes (5) ....

Then he .... his nose (6) .... and he

.... one of his teeth (7) .... in a

fight!

3 Answer these questions as in the example.

Example: Did you decorate the room yourself?
No, I ... *No, I had it decorated.*

1 Are you doing most of the work yourself?

No, I ....

2 Did you paint the doors and windows yourself?

No, I ....

3 Are you going to repair that broken window?

No, I ....

4 Did you fit the kitchen yourself?

No, I ....

5 Are you going to build the garage yourself?

No, I ....

4 Camilla Cunningham has got lots of money and she enjoys spending it. Choose a verb from the list and complete the sentences as in the example: *dry clean, massage, do, bring, make, change, clean, redecorate*.

Example: *She has her clothes dry cleaned after she's worn them only once.*

1 She .... her hair .... once a

week at the hairdresser's.

2 She .... her apartment ....

every day.

3 She also .... her apartment ....

every year.

4 She .... all her clothes specially

.... for her.

5 She .... her body and her face

.... once a week.

6 She .... the sheets on her bed

.... every day.

7 She .... breakfast .... to her in

bed every morning.

20

Questions

Libby Johns wants to join an international expedition to the Himalayas. She's answering some of the questions on the application form.

Are you over 18 and under 60? .... *Yes.* ....

Were you 18 before March 30th this year? .... *Yes.* ....

Are you taking any medication at the moment? .... *No.* ....

The expedition will be climbing to altitudes of over 6,000m.

Do you have any problems with your breathing? .... *No.* ....

If so, does your doctor know about the problem? .... *—* ....

Did you have any serious illnesses when you were a child? ..... *No.* ......

Have you been to the Himalayas before? .... *No.* ....

Can you attend a meeting in London on June 6th? .... *Yes.* ....

Step 1 | Basic questions

- To make a question we put the auxiliary verb (*be, have, do* or a modal verb: *can, will, would*, etc.) before the subject.

Auxiliary verb	Subject	Main verb
Are	*you*	*taking any medication?*
Has	*Libby*	*been to the Himalayas before?*
Can	*she*	*attend the London meeting?*

When *be* is the main verb, it comes before the subject.
   Are you *over 18?* ***Were you*** *18 before March 30th?*

- In the present simple we use *do/does* to make questions. (See also Unit 1 Step 3.)

Auxiliary	Subject	Main verb
Do	*you*	*have any problems with your breathing?*
Does	*your doctor*	*know about the problem?*

In the past simple we use *did*. (See also Unit 5.)

Did	*you*	*have any serious illnesses?*

- Note that the main verb is always in the infinitive form.
   *Does your doctor **know**?* (NOT Does your doctor knows?)
   *Did you **have** any serious illnesses?* (NOT Did you had?)

CHECK QUESTIONS 1 ▷ **Make the sentences into questions.**
1 Libby wants to go to the Himalayas.
2 She's hoping to join the expedition.
3 She's over 18.
4 She's filled in the form.

Step 2 | Questions introduced by question words

> Libby's leaving next Sunday. Her friends are asking her questions:
> What time are you leaving on Sunday? – At six in the morning.
> Where do you fly to? – Kathmandu.
> How long does the expedition last? – Two months.
> How many people are there in the group? – Twenty.
> Where do they come from? – From all over the world.
> Who's leading the group? – A man called Richard Lane.
> What does 'Himalaya' mean? – It means 'home of the snows'.

- We often begin questions with the following question words: *What? When? Where? Which? Who? Whose? Why? How?*
  What does 'Himalaya' mean? (NOT What means 'Himalaya'?)
- Or with phrases like: *What time/colour? What kind (of)? How long? How much?* etc.
  What time are you leaving? (NOT What time you are leaving?)
- Note the position of prepositions (*to, from*, etc.) in *Wh-* questions.
  *Where do you fly **to**? Where do they come **from**?*

CHECK QUESTIONS 2 **Put the words in the right order.**
1 is/when/leaving/Libby? 2 is/the expedition/leading/who?
3 to/the/does/expedition/where/fly? 4 does/how long/take/get/it/to/there?

Step 3 | Negative questions

> Libby's packing. A friend has come to say goodbye.
> 'Hi, Libby. Haven't you packed yet? Can I help?'
> 'No, it's all right. But I'd like a drink. Why don't you make a cup of tea?'
> 'OK. ... You haven't packed your camera. Aren't you taking it?'
> 'Yes, but I need some films for it.'
> 'Why didn't you tell me? I'll go to the chemist's. Don't they sell films?'
> 'Yes, but don't worry, I'll get some at the airport tomorrow.'
> 'The Himalayas! Doesn't it sound exciting! Aren't you lucky!'

- We use negative questions: a) to show surprise: ***Haven't you packed*** *yet?*
b) when something seems very probable:
  Don't they sell *films?* (It's probable the chemist sells them.)
c) often with *Why?* to show surprise or frustration, or to make a suggestion:
  Why didn't you tell *me?* ***Why don't you make*** *a cup of tea?*
d) in exclamations (we usually use an exclamation mark, not a question mark):
  Doesn't it sound *exciting!* ***Aren't you*** *lucky!*

CHECK QUESTIONS 3 **Make negative questions.**
1 Libby wants to take photographs. (she/not taking/a camera?)
2 She needs sun cream. (Why/she/not go/to the chemist's?)
3 Look at this photo of Mount Everest. (it/look/great!)

ANSWERS TO
CHECK QUESTIONS
1, 2 AND 3

1 1 Does Libby want to go to the Himalayas?
2 Is she hoping to join the expedition? 3 Is she over 18? 4 Has she filled in the form?
2 1 When is Libby leaving? 2 Who is leading the expedition? 3 Where does the expedition fly to? 4 How long does it take to get to Kathmandu?
3 1 Isn't she taking a camera? 2 Why doesn't she go to the chemist's? 3 Doesn't it look great!

63

Practice

	Auxiliary/main verb	**Subject**	**Main verb**	
Affirmative:	Are	you	studying	English?
Present simple:	Does	your brother	live	in London?
Past simple:	Did	it	rain	yesterday?
Question words:				
Who	is	Jane	talking to?	
What kind of music	do	you	like?	
Negative:	Aren't	you	tired?	
Why	can't	you	come?	
	Didn't	they	play	well!

1 Make the questions to complete the dialogue.

Do you believe in ghosts?   Yes, I do.

1 (you/ever see/a ghost)?

....

Yes, I have. I saw one on the stairs in my house.

2 (you/be/afraid)?

....

Yes, I was. I was very frightened.

3 (you/can/describe/it)?

....

Yes, I can. It was a woman with long grey hair.

4 (you/know/her)?

....

No, I didn't.

5 (the ghost/speak/to you)?

....

No, it didn't. It just looked at me.

6 (you see/it again)?

....

No, I haven't. I only saw it once.

7 (you/would like/to see it again)?

....

No, I wouldn't.

2 Make the questions to complete the dialogue.

1 Where ....?
   I come from Tokyo.

2 Why .... to England?
   I've come to learn English.

3 When .... ?
   I arrived last week.

4 What .... do in Tokyo?
   I'm an engineering student.

5 How long .... in England?
   I'm staying for three months.

6 Who .... in England?
   I don't know anyone.

3 Make negative questions to show your surprise.

1 I didn't enjoy my holiday in the USA!
   (the weather/not be/very good?)

   ....

2 No. The weather was fine, but I didn't have enough money.
   (you/not take/your credit card?)

   ....

3 Yes, I did, but it was stolen on the first day.
   (you/not get/a new one?)

   ....

   Yes, but it arrived too late.

21 Question tags: *You're English, aren't you?*

Two young people are at Melbourne airport waiting for their plane back to London.
A: You're English, aren't you?
B: Yes, I am.
A: Our plane's late, isn't it?
B: Yes, I'm afraid so.
A: The flight back takes 24 hours, doesn't it?
B: No, I think it's 26 actually.

Step 1 | Use of question tags

- A question tag is an expression like *aren't you?/isn't it?* or *doesn't it?* at the end of a sentence. We use question tags in conversation to ask if what we said is true or not, or if the other person agrees or not.

- If we use a rising intonation (if our voice goes up) with a question tag, we're asking a real question. We're not sure if the answer is yes or no.
  *You're English, **aren't you?*** ↗
  *The flight back takes 24 hours, **doesn't it?*** ↗
(In each question his voice rises at the end because he isn't sure if it's true or not.)

- If we use a falling intonation (if our voice goes down), we're expecting the other person to agree with what we've just said.
  *Our plane's late, **isn't it?*** ↘
  (He means 'I'm sure you agree.')

- Question tags are much less common in American English.
Americans often use tag words like *Right?* or *OK?* instead.
You're English, right? (instead of *You're English, aren't you?*)

CHECK QUESTIONS 1 **Are these 'real' questions or not?**
1 You're not Australian, are you? ↘
2 It's hot, isn't it? ↘
3 They take English money on the plane, don't they? ↗

Step 2 | Positive or negative question tag?

A: It's been hot, hasn't it?
B: Yes, very hot. And dry! It hasn't rained for weeks, has it?
A: No, it hasn't.

- If we say something positive, the question tag is usually negative.
  Positive   Negative
  It's been hot,   hasn't it?

- If we say something negative, the question tag is positive.
  Negative   Positive
  It hasn't rained for weeks,   has it?

Choose the correct question tag.

1 Australia's a big country, isn't it?/is it?
2 Things here aren't expensive, aren't they?/are they?
3 Food's cheap, isn't it?/is it?

Step 3 | Forms of question tags

A: You're pretty brown.
B: Yes, I am, aren't I? I spent most of the time on the beach.
A: But Australians don't get brown, do they?
B: No, they all wear hats and T-shirts, don't they?
A: Yes. Everybody's worried about skin cancer, aren't they?
B: Yes, it seems so. You didn't see any sharks, did you?
A: No, no sharks. But I saw plenty of snakes.
B: There are quite a lot of snakes, aren't there?
A: Yes. They've got poisonous spiders too, haven't they?
B: Yes, but I didn't see any. Australian wine's quite good, isn't it?
A: Yes, very good. And the beer. You've tried Australian beer, haven't you?
B: Oh yes. I've drunk some of that.
A: Our plane should be leaving soon, shouldn't it?
B: Yes, let's ask what time it's going, shall we?
A: You go. I'll stay here.
B: Look after my bag, will you?
A: Yes, of course.

- Question tags always have two words: an auxiliary verb (*are, can, have, will*, etc.) + a pronoun (*it, he, they*, etc.). The pronoun refers to the subject of the sentence. *Australians don't get brown, **do they**?* (they = Australians)

- Note the verbs which we use in question tags.
  Present simple: *do/does, don't/doesn't*
  *They all wear hats and T-shirts, **don't they**?*
  Past simple: *did/didn't*
  *You didn't see any sharks, **did you**?*
  Present perfect: *have/has, haven't/hasn't*
  *You've tried Australian beer, **haven't you**?*
  Have got: *have/has, hasn't/haven't*
  *They've got poisonous spiders, **haven't they**?*

- Note the form of the negative question tag after *I am*.
  *You're pretty brown. Yes, I am, **aren't I**?* (NOT *am't I?*)

- If a statement has a modal auxiliary verb (*will, should, would, might, can*, etc.), we use the same auxiliary verb in the question tag.
  *Our plane should be leaving soon, **shouldn't it**?*

- After *There is/There are* the question tags are *is there?/isn't there?* and *are there?/aren't there?*
  *There are quite a lot of snakes, **aren't there**?*

- The question tag after *Let's* is *shall we?*
  Let's ask what time our plane's leaving, **shall we**?

- After an imperative we can use the following question tags: *can you/can't you?*
  will you/won't you? would you? could you?
  Look after my bag, **will you**?

- After *everybody/somebody/nobody*, etc. we use the pronoun *they* in the question tag. (See also Unit 66 Step 1.)
  Everybody's worried about skin cancer, **aren't they**?

CHECK QUESTIONS 3 **Add question tags.**
1 Australians drink a lot of beer, ...
2 Everybody's friendly, ...
3 I suppose you met a lot of nice people, ...
4 Let's have a drink, ...

Step 4 | Other uses of question tags

A: Are you feeling OK?
B: No, not really. I went out to dinner last night.
A: And you had too much to eat, did you?
B: Yes, I did.
A: And now you've got indigestion, have you?
B: Yes, I have. You couldn't lend me a dollar, could you? I need some coffee and I haven't got any Australian money left.
A: Yes, here you are.
B: You don't know where the nearest toilet is, do you?
A: Yes, there's one over there.

- We can use a positive question tag (with a rising intonation) after a positive statement to express interest, sympathy, surprise or sarcasm.

Positive statement	Positive question tag
You had too much to eat,	*did you?* ↗
Now you've got a indigestion,	*have you?* ↗

- We sometimes use a negative statement followed by a positive question tag (with a rising intonation) when we make a request or ask for information.
  You couldn't lend me a dollar, **could you**? ↗
  You don't know where the nearest toilet is, **do you**? ↗

CHECK QUESTIONS 4 **Complete the sentences.**
1 Someone has lost their plane ticket. Show your concern. You've lost ...
2 Ask somebody to help you with your luggage. You couldn't ...
3 Ask somebody if they know when the plane gets to London. You don't know when ...

ANSWERS TO | **1** 1 No. 2 No. 3 Yes. | **4** 1 You've lost your plane ticket, have you?
CHECK QUESTIONS | **2** 1 isn't it? 2 are they ? 3 isn't it? | 2 You couldn't help me with my luggage, could
1, 2, 3 AND 4 | **3** 1 don't they? 2 aren't they? 3 didn't you? | you? 3 You don't know when the plane gets
| 4 shall we? | to London, do you?

Practice

1 Add the correct question tag to the following statements.

1 It's cold, ... ?

2 But it isn't as cold as yesterday, ... ?

3 It was very cold yesterday, ... ?

4 It hasn't been so cold for a long time, ... ?

5 It's snowing in the north, ... ?

6 It often snows there, ... ?

7 There was over 10 centimetres of snow last week, ... ?

8 They haven't had that much snow for a long time, ... ?

9 They didn't have much snow last winter, ... ?

10 But it'll be spring soon, ... ?

2 Zoe's parents do not like her boyfriend. Match her statements with the question tags.

1 You don't like him,   a aren't you?
2 You've never liked him,   b can you?
3 You didn't want me to
   go out with him,   c do you?
4 You think he's lazy,   d did you?
5 You won't let him come
   in the house,   e have you?
6 You're hoping I'll get
   tired of him,   f will you?
7 But you can't stop me
   seeing him,   g don't you?

1 ....   2 ....   3 ....   4 ....   5 ....   6 ....   7 ....

3 Fill in the missing question tags.

Passenger: Take me to Paddington station, (1) .... ?

Taxi driver: Yes, OK.

Passenger: There's a lot of traffic, (2) .... ?

Taxi driver: Yes, it's terrible, (3) .... ?

Passenger: It gets worse every year, (4) .... ?

Taxi driver: Yes, it seems to.

Passenger: It'll be quicker to walk soon, (5) .... ?

Taxi Driver: You're right. You said your train leaves at 10 (6) .... ?

Passenger: Yes, that's right. We haven't got long, (7) .... ?

Taxi driver: Less than 10 minutes.

Passenger: You couldn't drive a bit faster, (8) .... ?

Taxi driver: No, I can't. You can see how bad the traffic is, (9) .... ?

Passenger: I'm going to miss my train, (10) ....

Taxi driver: Probably.

Passenger: Let's try another route, (11) .... ?

22

Who, What, Which?
Do you know who/what/if, etc?

> What did Alfred Nobel invent? – Dynamite.
> What started in April 1861 in the USA? – The American Civil War.
> Who did Lee Harvey Oswald kill in Dallas in 1963? – President Kennedy.
> Who killed Lee Harvey Oswald? – Jack Ruby.
> Which travels faster – light or sound? – Light.
> Which does a herbivore prefer – meat or grass? – Grass.

Step 1 | *What, who, which* as subject or object

● Object	+	Auxiliary verb	+	Subject	+	Main verb
Who		*did*		*Oswald*		*kill?*
				Who		*killed Oswald?*
Which		*does*		*a herbivore*		*prefer?*
				Which		*travels faster?*
What		*did*		*Alfred Nobel*		*invent?*
				What		*started in April 1861?*

● When the question words *who, which, what* are the subject of a sentence, we don't use *do, does, did* with the verb.
(Here we don't say: Who did kill Julius Caesar? Which does travel faster?)
Note: *Who **did** Lee Harvey Oswald **kill**?* (= Who was his victim?)
*Who **killed** Lee Harvey Oswald?* (= Who was his killer?)

CHECK QUESTIONS 1 **Complete these questions.**
1 Who/discover/oxygen? 2 What/Joseph Priestley/discover/in 1774?
3 Which/be/worth more – a US dollar or a British pound?

Step 2 | *What* or *which* + a noun?

> What instrument did Louis Armstrong play? – The trumpet.
> What sea separates England from France? – The English Channel.
> Which way does the Mississippi flow? – South.
> Which president of the USA resigned in 1974? – President Nixon.

● We can often use *what* or *which* + a noun without changing the meaning.
    What (OR ***Which***) *sea separates England from France?*
But *which* is more common with people. And we normally use *which* when there's a limited choice of possibilities, and *what* when there's a large or unlimited choice.
    Which US president *resigned in 1974?* (which + a person)
    Which way *does the Mississippi flow?* (The choice is: north, south, east or west.)
Compare: ***What instrument*** *did Louis Armstrong play?*
    (There are a lot of alternatives, but they aren't given.)
    Which instrument *did he play – the trumpet or the clarinet?*
    (Here we use *which* because the alternatives are given.)

Put in *What* or *Which*.

1 ... languages do they speak in Belgium?   2 ... man gave his name to America?
3 ... language do they speak in Brazil – Spanish or Portuguese?

Step 3 | *Which* for people/things   *Which one(s)*   *Which of ...*

> Which country joined the European Union in 1973?   Britain.
> Which / What German composer was also a famous organist?   Bach.
> Which of the Beatles was killed in New York in 1980?   John Lennon.
> London's clocks. Which one is the most famous?   Big Ben.

● *Who* can only be used for people. *What* on its own is used for things, but with a noun it can be used for people (*What German composer?*). *Which* can be used for people (*Which German composer?*) and things (*Which country?*).

● We can use *which* + *one/ones* and + *of*.
Which one is the most famous?   **Which of** the Beatles was killed?
We can't use *what* and *who* with *of*. We can't say: Who of the Beatles was killed?

Put in *Which* or *What*.

1 Sardinia and Corsica are islands. ... one is French?
2 ... country do the Maoris live in - New Zealand or Australia?
3 ... of the American states is an island?   4 ... is Esperanto?

Step 4 | *Do you know/Could you tell me*, etc. + a question word

> Is English the most widely-used language in the world?
> *Do you know if English is the most widely-used language?*   No.
> Does the River Thames flow east or west?
> *Could you tell me whether the Thames flows east or west?*   East.
> What does 'goodbye' mean?
> *Do you know what 'goodbye' means?*   Yes. 'God be with you'.

● We often begin indirect questions with *Do you know/Could you tell me*.
Simple question: Is English the most widely used language?
Indirect question: *Do you know if English is the most widely used language?*
Simple question: What does 'goodbye' mean?
Indirect question: *Do you know what 'goodbye* **means**?

● Where there is no question word, we use *if* or *whether*.
Simple question: Does the River Thames flow east or west?
Indirect question: *Could you tell me **if/whether** the Thames flows east or west?*

Start the questions with *Do you know*.

1 What did Bell invent?   2 Was Columbus Spanish?
3 Who was Montezuma?   4 What does a speleologist do?

ANSWERS TO
CHECK QUESTIONS
1, 2, 3 AND 4

1 1 Who discovered oxygen? 2 What did Priestley discover in 1774? 3 Which is worth more
2 1 What   2 Which   3 Which
3 1 Which   2 Which   3 Which   4 What

4 1 Do you know what Bell invented?   2 Do you know if/whether Columbus was Spanish?
3 Do you know who Montezuma was?
4 Do you know what a speleologist does?

Practice

Question word used as the subject:	*Who **saw** John this morning?*
Question word used as the object:	*Who **did John see** this morning?*
Which for limited choice:	***Which** trousers shall I wear?*
	***Which** shirt do you want – the red one or the blue one?*
	***Which** of these books do you want?*
	***Which one** are you going to read?*
What for wide choice:	***What's** your telephone number?*
	***What** books have you read this year?*
Word order in indirect questions:	***Is John coming?** Do you know if **John's coming**?*
	*When **did it happen**? Could you tell me when **it happened**?*

1 **Gemma had a party last night. Jack is asking her about it. Complete the questions, using the correct form of the verb.**

'Who (1 you/invite) ....

to the party?'

'I invited James, Rick, Andy, Rosanna and Amy.'

'Sam was there, wasn't he? Who (2 invite/him)

.... ?'

'I don't know. I didn't invite him.'

'Well, who (3 bring/him) .... ?'

'I don't know. He didn't come with anybody.'

'Who (4 Rick/bring) .... ?'

'He brought that tall girl, the one with blond

hair, Beth.'

'And what (5 happen) .... ?'

'Well, Sam started talking to Beth, and Rick got

angry. He threw something at Sam.'

'What (6 he/throw) .... ?'

'A pizza, I think.'

'And what (7 Sam/do) .... ?'

'He left.'

2 **Sally and her husband are going to visit friends in London. Complete the dialogue, using *what* or *which*.**

'We'd better go soon. (1) .... time is it?'

'Nearly nine. (2) .... car shall we take,

mine or yours?'

'Let's take mine. It doesn't use as much petrol.

(3) .... way shall we go?'

'Let's go on the motorway. It's quicker.'

'(4) .... food shall we take?'

'Oh, just a few sandwiches.'

'Well, I've got some cheese or some ham.

(5) .... do you prefer?'

'Cheese, I think.'

'And (6) .... do you want to drink?'

'Orange juice will be fine. We must show them

our holiday photos. (7) .... ones shall we

take?'

'Oh, let's take all of them. Now, (8) .... of

these magazines shall I take to read in the car?'

'Come on. We're going to be late!'

3 **Complete the dialogue, putting the words in brackets in the right order.**

'Do you know where (1 can/find/I/a chemist's)

.... ?'

'In King Street.'

'I don't know where King Street is. Could you

tell me how (2 there/I/get) .... ?'

'Do you know where (3 is/the town hall)

.... ? Well, that's in King

Street.'

'Have you any idea (4 what time/close/they)

.... ? Do you know

(5 they/are/open/if/now)

.... ?'

'Yes, they are. They don't close till six.'

23

Two people are on a flight from London to Barcelona.
'It's a bit bumpy, isn't it? Is it always like this over the Pyrenees?'
'Yes, I'm afraid so, but we'll be there soon.'
'I hope so. Spanish time isn't the same as British time, is it?'
'No, I don't think so. I think they're an hour ahead.'
'That means it's half past seven in Barcelona now.'
'Yes, I think so.'
'The weather's usually good there, isn't it?'
'I believe so.'
'It'll be nice and warm.'
'Yes, I expect so. I don't think it'll rain much.'
'I hope not. Have you got a street map of Barcelona?'
'No, I'm afraid not.'
'Do you think I'll be able to get one at the airport?'
'I imagine so.'
'Do the airport shops close in the evening?'
'I don't suppose so.'
'The problem is though, they won't accept English money, will they?'
'No, I suppose not.'

Step 1 | *I think so/don't think so   I hope so/I hope not*

● In short answers when we want to agree with what someone has said, we use *so* after the following verbs: *believe, expect, guess, hope, imagine, presume, reckon, seem, suppose, suspect, think, be afraid.*
> *We'll be there soon. – I* **hope so**.
> *It's half past seven in Barcelona now. – Yes, I* **think so**.

We don't say: I hope or I hope it or I hope that.

● With all of these verbs except *guess, hope, presume, suspect, be afraid* we often use negative forms with *so*.
> *Spanish time isn't the same as British time, is it? – No, I* **don't think so**.
> *Do the airport shops close in the evening? – I* **don't suppose so**.

But we must use *not* after *guess, hope, presume, suspect, be afraid.*
> *I don't think it'll rain much. – I* **hope not**. (NOT I don't hope so.)
> *Have you got a street map of Barcelona?*
> *No, I'm* **afraid not**. (NOT I'm not afraid so.)

● We can use both forms with *believe, expect* and *suppose.*
> *Do the airport shops close in the evening? – I* **don't suppose so**.
> *They won't accept English money, will they? – No, I* **suppose not**.

CHECK QUESTIONS 1

Give short answers.
1 We'll be able to get a taxi at the airport, won't we? I ... (hope)
2 It won't take long to get to the hotel, will it? I ... (hope)
3 We won't get to the hotel before 9 o'clock, will we? I ... (expect)

Step 2 | *So do I, Neither do I/Nor do I*

> 'We're going to Sitges. It's a place on the coast, not far from Barcelona.'
> 'That's funny! So are we. We haven't been to Sitges before.'
> 'Neither have we.'
> 'The trouble is they eat a lot of fish in Spain, and I don't like fish.'
> 'Nor does my husband. I hope there are other things to eat at the hotel.'
> 'Yes, so do I.' *(Later)* 'I've been learning a bit of Spanish.'
> 'So have I. I bought a little phrase book.'
> 'So did I. I can say a few words in Spanish now.'
> 'Yes, so can I. But I don't like speaking foreign languages.'
> 'Neither do I. You feel so stupid, don't you.'
> 'Oops! It's a bumpy flight. I'll be glad when we get there.'
> 'So will I!'

- When we want to say that we do the same or feel the same as someone else, we can use the short answer *So* + auxiliary verb + subject after positive statements.
  *We're going to Sitges. – **So are we.*** (= We're going to Sitges too.)

- After negative statements we use *Neither* or *Nor* + auxiliary verb + subject.
  I don't like speaking foreign languages.
  *– **Neither do I.*** OR ***Nor do I.*** (= I feel like you. I don't like it.)
  *I don't like fish. – **Nor/Neither does my husband**.*
  (= My husband's the same as you. He doesn't like fish.)

- The auxiliary verb in the short answer will be a form of the verbs *be* or *have*, or a modal verb (*can, could, will*, etc.)
  *We're going to Sitges. – So **are** we.*
  *I've been learning a bit of Spanish. – So **have** I.*
  *I'll be glad when we get there. – So **will** I.*

- When the present simple or the past simple is used in the first statement, we use *do, does* or *did*.
  *I **don't** like speaking foreign languages. – Neither **do** I*
  *I **bought** a little phrase book. – So **did** I.*

- Note the word order.

So/Neither/Nor +	auxiliary verb +	subject
So	*can*	*I.*
Neither	*does*	*my husband.*

- We can replace the *So* construction with *too* and the *Neither/Nor* construction with a negative auxiliary + *either*.
  We're going to Sitges. – So are we. OR ***We are too**.*
  I don't like speaking foreign languages. – Neither do I. OR ***I don't either**.*

CHECK QUESTIONS 2 **Respond with *So ... I* or *Neither/Nor ... I*.**
1 I usually go to Spain for my holiday.   2 I went there last year.
3 But I've never been to Sitges before.   4 I don't like flying.

ANSWERS TO CHECK QUESTIONS 1 AND 2 **1** 1 I hope so. 2 I hope not. 3 I don't expect so./I expect not.

2 1 So do I. 2 So did I. 3 Neither/Nor have I. 4 Neither/Nor do I.

Practice

I	think hope expect am afraid etc.	so.	I don't	think expect believe imagine reckon suppose	so.	I	hope guess believe expect am afraid suppose suspect	not.

I like Spain. – So do I.　　　　*I don't like Greek food. – Neither do I/Nor do I.*
I'd like a drink. – So would I.　　*He can't swim. – Neither can I/Nor can I.*

1 **Two people are waiting at a bus-stop. Complete the dialogue, using *I think so/I hope not*, etc.**

A: Does the number 89 stop here?

B: (1 think) ....

A: Does it go to the town centre?

B: (2 believe) ....

A: It won't be full, will it?

B: No, (3 expect) ....

A: Are the buses normally on time?

B: No, (4 be afraid) ....

　My bus is already ten minutes late. If you're

　in a hurry, you could take a taxi.

A: Yes, (5 suppose) ....

　How much would a taxi cost? £15, £20?

B: No, (6 think) ....

　It won't be as much as that.

A: But it won't be less than £10, will it?

B: No, (7 suppose) ....

A: Well, we'll just have to wait for the bus then.

B: (8 be afraid) ....

2 **Jo and Hannah are on their first date. Complete Jo's replies, using *So ... I* or *Neither/Nor ... I*.**

Hannah: I enjoyed the film.

Jo: (1) ....

Hannah: But I didn't really like the ending.

Jo: (2) ....

Hannah: I don't have to go home yet.

Jo: (3) ....

Hannah: I'm hungry.

Jo: (4) ....

Hannah: I don't really fancy a pizza.

Jo: (5) ....

Hannah: I'd prefer an Indian.

Jo: (6) ....

Hannah: I love hot curries.

Jo: (7) ....

Hannah: There's a new Indian restaurant on the

next corner, but I've never tried it.

Jo: (8) ....

Hannah: Jo, I can't stand people who always

agree with me!

Jo: (9) ....

24

Auxiliary verbs used alone:
Will you come? – I might

Amy Masters works for a market research organisation. She's interviewing people in the street.
A: Excuse me, sir. I'm doing a survey of people's reading habits. Could you answer a few questions, please?
B: I could, if it doesn't take too long. What are the questions?
A: Do you read much?
B: No. I should, I suppose, but I never have time. I would if I had more time.
A: So you aren't reading a book at the moment?
B: I'm not, no. But my wife is. She reads a lot.
(*Later*)
A: Excuse me, madam. Have you got time to answer a few questions?
C: No, I haven't. I'm in a hurry, I'm afraid, so I can't. But my friend here isn't. You could ask her. I'm not really interested in books, but she is.

Step 1 | Single auxiliary verbs used alone

- We often use an auxiliary verb (*be, have, might, would, can*, etc.) alone, without the main verb. We do this when we don't want to repeat the main verb.
  Could you answer a few questions, please?
  *– I **could**, if it doesn't take too long.* (= I could answer)
  So you aren't reading a book at the moment?
  *– I'm **not**, no. But my wife **is**.*
  (= I'm not reading. My wife is reading.)

- The verb *be* can also be used alone when it's a main verb.
  Have you got time to answer some questions?
  *– I'm in a hurry, I'm afraid, but my friend here **isn't**.*
  (= My friend isn't in a hurry.)
  *I'm not really interested in books, but she **is**.*
  (= She's interested in books.)

- The auxiliary verb is used alone in *yes/no* short answers.
  *Have you got time to answer some questions? – No, I **haven't**.*
  *Do you read much? – No, I **don't**.* (For *do* see Step 3.)
  *Is your wife reading a book at the moment? – Yes, she **is**.*

- We use the full form of auxiliaries when they're affirmative.
  *I'm not, but my wife **is**.* (NOT *my wife's*)
  *I **would** if I had more time.* (NOT *I'd*)

- The auxiliary verb(s) in the answer can be different from the one(s) in the question.
  *Do you read much? – No. I **should**, I suppose.* (= I should read, but ...)
  *I **would** if I had more time.* (= I would read.)

CHECK QUESTIONS 1 **Rewrite the sentences, avoiding repetition.**
1 The first person can answer her questions, but the second one can't answer her questions.
2 Could you answer a few questions? I might answer. It depends.
3 Her friend isn't in a hurry, but she's in a hurry.

Step 2 | Two auxiliary verbs

> A: Where did you get the book you're reading at the moment?
> D: I borrowed it from the library.
> A: Would you have bought it, if it hadn't been in the library?
> D: I would if it hadn't been so expensive.
> A: How many books have you read this year? Twenty?
> D: I might have. I can't remember.

- When there are two auxiliary verbs, we usually repeat only the first.
  Would you have bought it, if it hadn't been in the library?
  – I would if it hadn't been so expensive. (NOT I would have)
- But if the verb form changes (for example: *have* changes to *might have*), we use two auxiliaries in the answer.
  How many books have you read this year? Twenty?
  – I might have. (NOT I might.) = I might have read twenty.

CHECK QUESTIONS 2 **Rewrite the sentences, avoiding repetition.**
1 Would you have bought the book if it had been cheaper? – Yes, I would have bought the book.
2 He bought the book, but if it had been in the library, he wouldn't have bought it.

Step 3 | The use of the verb *do*

> Amy Masters is interviewing a middle-aged woman and her husband.
> A: What kind of books do you and your husband read?
> E: Well, I like thrillers. My husband doesn't. He reads historical novels. He reads a lot more than I do.
> A: When did you last go to a bookshop?
> E: About three days ago. Well, I did. My husband didn't. He stayed outside because I was looking for a surprise birthday present for him.

- When the main verb is in the present simple or the past simple, we use the verb *do* to avoid repeating the main verb.
  I like thrillers. My husband doesn't. (= He doesn't like thrillers.)
  He reads a lot more than I do. (= more than I read)
  Did you go into the bookshop? – I did. My husband didn't.
  (= I went into the bookshop. My husband didn't go into the bookshop.)

CHECK QUESTIONS 3 **Rewrite the sentences, avoiding repetition.**
1 Her husband doesn't like thrillers, but she likes thrillers.
2 He reads historical novels, but she doesn't read historical novels.
3 She talked a lot, but her husband didn't talk a lot.

Amy's now talking to a strange old man.
F: I don't really like books.
A: Don't you?
F: No. But I read a good book once.
A: Did you? What was it?
F: It was a book about bees.
A: Was it? That sounds interesting.
F: Yes, it was. You see, these bees could kill.
A: Could they?
F: Yes. But I didn't finish the book.
A: Didn't you?
F: No. And I haven't read a book since then.
A: Haven't you? Why not?
F: Too many pages. I can't read more than 20 pages.
A: Can't you? Why not?
F: I always fall asleep after 20 pages.
A: Do you?
F: And then I forget what I've read, so I have to start the book again.

- We often reply to what someone says by using a short question with an auxiliary verb. We use it to show polite interest or surprise. It means *Really?* or *Is that true?*
  They could kill. – ***Could they?*** (OR *Really?*)

- We use *do/don't/does/doesn't* in reply questions after a statement in the present simple.
  *I always **fall** asleep after 20 pages.* – ***Do** you?*
  *I **don't** really **like** books.* – ***Don't** you?*

- We use *did/didn't* after a statement in the past simple.
  *I **read** a good book once.* – ***Did** you?*
  *I **didn't finish** the book.* – ***Didn't** you?*
  If the statement has an auxiliary verb, we repeat the verb in the reply question.
  *I **haven't** read a book since then.* – ***Haven't** you?*
  If the statement has the verb *be*, used as a main verb, we repeat it in the reply question.
  *It **was** about bees.* – ***Was** it?*

- We use a positive reply question after a positive statement.
  *I **read** a good book once.* – ***Did** you?*

- We use a negative reply question after a negative statement.
  *I **can't** read more than 20 pages.* – ***Can't** you?*
  (For question tags *You're tired, **aren't you**?* see Unit 21.)

CHECK QUESTIONS 4 **Add a reply question.**
1 Amy has worked for the company for ten years. ... ?
2 She's very interested in her work. ... ?
3 Yesterday she interviewed over fifty people. ... ?
4 Several people wouldn't answer her questions. ... ?

ANSWERS TO
CHECK QUESTIONS
1, 2, 3 AND 4

1 1 but the second one can't. 2 I might. It depends. 3 but she is.

2 1 Yes, I would. 2 he wouldn't have.

3 1 but she does. 2 but she doesn't. 3 but her husband didn't.

4 1 Has she? 2 Is she? 3 Did she? 4 Wouldn't they?

Practice

> - We use an auxiliary on its own to avoid repeating a main verb.
> *I'm learning English, but my sister **isn't**.*
> - We use forms of *do* if the main verb is in the present simple or past simple.
> *I **speak** French, but my sister **doesn't**.*
> - If the main verb has two auxiliaries, we normally repeat only the first.
> *I **wouldn't** have paid £50. – Oh, I **would**.*
> - But we use two auxiliaries if we change the verb form.
> *I **didn't buy** the dress. – Oh, I **would have**, if I'd had enough money.*
> - We use an auxiliary on its own in reply questions. *I've just seen a ghost. – **Have** you?*

1 Darren likes to be different. Complete the text, using the correct auxiliary verb.

All his friends can drive a car, but Darren (1) .... They're all members of the local Leisure Club, but Darren (2) .... Everyone in his English class likes the book they're studying, but Darren (3) .... They're all working hard for their exams, but Darren (4) .... They'll all be at Alice's birthday party tomorrow. Darren (5) .... Everyone's going to give Alice a present. Darren (6) .... He isn't sure. None of his friends wears a tie, but Darren (7) .... All his friends have stopped smoking. Darren (8) .... At lunch today in the college canteen hardly anyone ate the fish. It was bad. But Darren (9) .... Everyone went swimming this afternoon, but Darren (10) .... He had stomach-ache.

2 Jack Robertson crashed his car last week. His car hit a tree while he was driving home late at night. A friend has come to see him in hospital. Complete the dialogue, using the following auxiliaries: *must have, might, might have, will, haven't, would have*.

'Did you fall asleep while you were driving?'
'I (1) .... It's possible.'
'Who phoned the police?'
'I don't know, but somebody (2) .... , because the police arrived very quickly.'

'You nearly died, you know.'
'I know. I (3) .... if the ambulance hadn't come so quickly. That's certain.'
'Are you going to get a new car?'
'I (4) .... I haven't decided yet.'
'Have you contacted your insurance company?'
'I (5) .... yet, but I (6) .... as soon as I feel better.'

3 In the following conversation, replace *Really?* with the correct reply question.
Example: I'm afraid I can't play tennis tomorrow evening. Really? ... *Can't you?*

'No. I'm going out for a meal with the family.'
'Really? (1) .... ?'
'Yes. My aunt has just come back from Australia.'
'Really? (2) .... ?'
'We haven't seen her for twenty-five years.'
'Really? (3) .... ?'
'No. This is the first time she's been back.'
'Really? (4) .... ?'
'Yes. She left England when she was eighteen. She married an Australian farmer.'
'Really? (5) .... ?'
'They want me to go and visit them.'
'Really? (6) .... ? That's great!'
'I'll probably go next winter.'
'Really? (7) .... ? That sounds really good. I'd love to go to Australia.'

25

Can, could, be able to

> Hannah Willis is studying languages in London. She's having an interview for a job as a tourist guide.
> 'Miss Willis, how many languages can you speak?'
> 'I can speak Spanish, Italian and German. I'd like to be able to speak a bit of Japanese, but they don't teach it at my college.'
> 'That's a pity, because we get a lot of Japanese visitors in London. We need people who can speak Japanese, but we haven't been able to find any. But this summer there'll be a lot of German and Spanish visitors too, so you'll be able to use your Spanish and German. Can you start work in May?'
> 'No, I'm afraid I can't. I can't miss college. I won't be able to start until the end of term in June.'

Step 1 | Can and *be able to*

- We use *can/can't* (= *cannot*) + an infinitive without *to* to talk about someone's ability or inability to do something.
   *I **can speak** Spanish.* (= I know how to speak Spanish.)
   *I **can't speak** Japanese.* (= I don't have the ability to speak Japanese.)

- We also use *can/can't* (= *cannot*) + an infinitive without *to* when we talk about what is possible or impossible.
   ***Can** you **start** work in May?* (= Is it possible for you to start in May?)
   *I **can't miss** college.* (= It isn't possible for me to miss college.)

- *Can* and *can't* have the same form for all persons. (*I can, he can, we can*, etc.)

- In the present it's often possible to use *be able to* or *can*, but *be able to* is more formal and a lot less common.
   *How many languages **can** you speak?*
   (*How many languages are you able to speak?* is very formal.)

- But because *can* has no infinitive form or present perfect form, we have to use forms of *be able to* here.
   *I'd like **to be able to** speak a bit of Japanese.* (infinitive)
   *We **haven't been able to** find any.* (present perfect)

- When we talk about the future we can normally use *can* or *will/won't be able to*. But if it's important to emphasise the future time, we use *will/won't be able to*.
   ***Can you** start work in May?* (OR Will you be able to start work in May?)
   *I **won't be able to** start until June.* (OR I can't start until June.)
   *You**'ll be able to** use your Spanish and German.*

CHECK QUESTIONS 1

Write the sentences using a different verb.
1 Is Hannah able to speak Japanese? ... Hannah speak Japanese?
2 She isn't able to start work immediately. She ... immediately.
3 She can't start work in May. She ...
4 She can start work at the end of term. She ...

Step 2 | *Could* or *was/were able to?*

Hannah finished college on June 13th and she was able to start work the next day. She took a group of Germans round London. Most of them could speak English. At London Zoo one woman dropped her camera into the lions' enclosure. She could see the camera, but she couldn't reach it. Fortunately a keeper was able to reach it with a fishing net. Later, Hannah's group was in St Paul's Cathedral. One man started to play the organ. He could play very well. Hannah told him that visitors couldn't play the organ, but she couldn't persuade him to stop. Later, in a big department store in Oxford Street, two members of Hannah's group got stuck in the lift. They couldn't get out because they weren't able to open the doors. After about 30 minutes workmen managed to open them and the two Germans were able to get out.

- When we talk about the past we can use *could* or *was/were able to*.
- To talk about a general ability, we use *could* more often than *was/were able to*.
  Most of them **could speak** *English*.
  (More common than *were able to speak English*.)
- But, in affirmative sentences, when we talk about a particular action or situation in the past, we use *was/were able to* and not *could*.
  Hannah finished college on June 13th and she **was able to** *start work the next day*.
  (NOT *could start*)
  The two Germans **were able to** *get out*. (NOT *could get out*)
  (They got out of the lift. This was a particular action.)
- In negative sentences we can use either *couldn't* or *wasn't/weren't able to*, although *couldn't* is more common.
  She **couldn't stop** *the man from playing the organ*.
  (OR She wasn't able to stop the man.)
- Note that *couldn't* can sometimes mean *wasn't/weren't allowed to*.
  She explained to him that visitors **couldn't play** *the organ*.
  (= Visitors weren't allowed to play the organ.)
- Before verbs of perception (*see, hear, feel*, etc.) and verbs like *understand, remember* we normally use *could* rather than *was/were able to*.
  She **could see** *the camera, but she couldn't reach it*.

CHECK QUESTIONS 2 **Put in *could/couldn't* or *was/wasn't/were able to*.**
1 One of Hannah's group ... play the organ very well.
2 The woman who dropped the camera ... reach it herself.
3 But the keeper ... reach it with a fishing net.
4 At last, after 30 minutes, the workmen ... open the lift doors.

ANSWERS TO CHECK QUESTIONS 1 AND 2

1 1 Can Hannah speak Japanese? 2 She can't start work immediately. 3 She won't be able to start work in May.   4 She'll be able to start work at the end of term.

2 1 could 2 couldn't/wasn't able to 3 was able to 4 were able to

Practice

We use *can/be able to*: for ability (*I can ski.   He'll be able to swim soon*)
for possibility (*I can come to the party.   I'll be able to leave early*)

Present	**Future**	**Present perfect**
Can/can't	*will/won't be able to*	*I've been able to/She's been able to*, etc.

Past
Could/couldn't (for general ability)
Was/were able to, wasn't/weren't able to, couldn't (for a particular action in the past)

1 **Complete the sentences with *can/can't* or the correct form of *be able to*.**

I've got a friend who (1) .... play the flute really well. He's studying music at college and when he finishes he (2) .... get a job in an orchestra. I'd like to be a professional musician too. I'd like to (3) .... play a musical instrument well, but I (4) .... I've got a guitar, but I (5) .... play it very well. You need to practise for hours every day, but for the last six months I (6) .... practise much because I've had too much work to do. I dream that one day in the future I (7) .... play like Eric Clapton, but it's only a dream and I'm sure I (8) .... play like him.

2 **Jack Brice is 80. There are a lot of things he cannot do now. He is talking about the things he used to be able to do. Complete the sentences with *could* or *couldn't*.**

My eyes aren't very good now. Five years ago I (1) .... read the newspaper without wearing glasses. A few years ago I (2) .... walk to the shops and back in half an hour, but I prefer to get the bus now. When I was a child we (3) .... watch television or a video in the evening. They didn't exist. My mother used to tell us stories. She (4) .... keep us amused for hours. When I was younger, I (5) .... play tennis very well. No-one

(6) .... beat me. I tried to play tennis again the other day. I (7) .... see my opponent, but I (8) .... see the ball! My memory's not brilliant either. I (9) .... remember my telephone number this morning!

3 **Rob hurt his leg while he was playing football. A friend has come to see him. Complete the sentences with *could/couldn't* or *was/wasn't, were/weren't able to*.**

'How do you feel?'

'I feel terrible.'

'(1) .... go to the doctor's this morning?'

'No, he (2) .... see me this morning. I (3) .... speak to him on the phone. He just told me to stay in bed.'

'(4) .... get any sleep last night?'

'No, not really. I (5) .... feel the pain in my leg all the time.'

'How did it happen?'

'I was playing football yesterday and somebody kicked me. I (6) .... walk home, and it was Sunday so I (7) .... get a bus. None of my friends had a car, so they (8) .... bring me home. But eventually they (9) .... find a taxi for me.'

'Have you eaten anything today?'

'No, I haven't got any food in the flat and I (10) .... get to the shops this morning. I (11) .... make myself a cup of tea, that's all. I'm really hungry!'

> Robert: Can we have a table for two, please? And could we sit over there by the window?
> Waiter: Yes, of course.
> Robert: May we have the menu? And would you take my coat?
> Waiter: Certainly, sir.
> Selina: Can you give us the wine list?
> Waiter: Yes, here it is. ... Can I take your order now?
> Robert: We're not quite ready yet. Could you give us a bit longer?

Step 1 | *Can, could, may, would* in requests

- We use *can, could* and *may* to ask for things or permission.
  Can *we have a table for two?* **May** *we have the menu, please?*
  Could *we sit over there by the window?*
Could is a little more polite than *can*.
May is more polite and formal than *could* and is less common.

- We also use these verbs to ask someone to do something.
  Can *you give us the wine list?* **Could** *you give us a bit longer?*
  Would *you take my coat, please?*
Could I/you? is a little more polite than *Can I/you?*
Would you is more polite and formal than *Could you* and *Can you* and is less common.
Note: In requests we never use *I* or *we* after *would*.
(We can't say: 'Would we have the menu?')
We must say *Can we/Could we/May we have the menu?*

CHECK QUESTIONS 1

Complete these requests with *can/could* or *would*.
1 I'm hungry. (we/have) something to eat?
2 I don't understand some of the things on the menu. (you/tell me) what they are?
3 I haven't got any money. (you/lend me) some?

Step 2 | *Can, could, may* to ask for and to give permission

> Selina: Can I smoke?
> Waiter: No, I'm afraid you can't. This is a non-smoking section.
> Robert: Can I pay by credit card?
> Waiter: Yes, you can. We take Visa, but not American Express.
> Robert: Ah, could I pay by cheque?
> Waiter: Yes, you can, sir. Have you got a cheque card?
> Robert: Yes, I have. May I use your pen, please?
> Waiter: Certainly, sir.
> Selina: May we use the phone to call a taxi?
> Waiter: Yes, of course you can.

- We use *can, could* or *may* to ask for permission.
  Can *I smoke?* **Could** *I pay by cheque?* **May** *we use the phone?*
Could is slightly more polite than *can*. *May* is more polite than *could*.

- To give permission we normally use *can*. We can use *may*, but it's very formal and not common. We don't use *could*.

  *Can I pay by credit card? – Yes, you **can**. Could I pay by cheque? – Yes, you **can** , sir.*
  To refuse permission we use *can't*.
  *Can I smoke? – No, I'm afraid you **can't***.

CHECK QUESTIONS 2 **Complete the sentences.**
1 ... we sit at another table? Yes, you ...
2 ... have an ashtray? No, ... , I'm afraid. Smoking's not allowed.
3 ... speak to the manager? Yes, ...

Step 3 | *Can* and *may* for offers

> Selina: Robert, can I pay half the bill?
> Robert: No, it's all right.
> Waiter: May I help you with your coat?
> Selina: Oh, thank you.

- We use *Can I/May I?* when we offer to do something.
  ***Can** I pay half the bill? – **May** I help you with your coat?*
  Can I is less formal than *May I* and much more common.

CHECK QUESTIONS 3 **Selina does not want Robert to pay for everything. Complete her offers.**
1 ... pay for the tip? 2 ... pay for the taxi home?
3 ... buy you a drink before we go home?

Step 4 | *Would like* in offers and invitations

> Robert: The taxi isn't here yet. I rang ten minutes ago.
> Waiter: Would you like me to ring again, sir?
> Robert: Yes, please.
> Waiter: Would you like to wait at the bar? And would you like more coffee?
> Selina: Yes, that would be nice. Thank you.

- We use *would like* to offer something or to offer to do something.
  ***Would you like** more coffee? **Would you like** me to ring again?*
- We also use *would like* to invite someone to do something.
  ***Would you like** to sit at the bar while you're waiting?*
  (For *would like* see also Unit 43 and Unit 50.)

CHECK QUESTIONS 4 **Complete the offers and invitations.**
1 ... another coffee, Selina? 2 ... me to phone you tomorrow?
3 ... come to a party with me on Saturday?

ANSWERS TO CHECK QUESTIONS 1, 2 AND 3

1 1 Can we/Could we have 2 Can you/Could you/Would you tell me 3 Can you/Could you/Would you lend me
2 1 Can we Yes, you can. 2 May we/Can we No, you can't 3 Could I/Can I/May I Yes, you can.
3 1 Can I/May I 2 Can I/May I 3 Can I/May I)
4 1 Would you like 2 Would you like 3 Would you like to

Practice

Requests: *Can I ...? Could I ...? May I ...? Would you ...?*
Offers: *Can I ...? May I ....?*
Asking for permission: *Can I ...? Could I ...? May I ...?*
Giving permission: *You can ... You may ...* (very formal)
Offers/Invitations: *Would you like a/an/some ...? Would you like (me) to ...?*

1 **Complete the following short dialogues in a Maths class, Use *Can I?/Would you?*, etc.**

Student A: (1) .... I open the

window, please? It's very hot in here.

Teacher: Yes, (2) ....

(*Later*)

Student B: (3) .... give you my

homework next week? I haven't quite

finished it.

Teacher: No, you (4) .... I want it

before then.

Student B: (5) .... give it to you

tomorrow?

Teacher: Yes, (6) ....

(*Later*)

Student C: (7) .... go outside for a

moment ? I'm not feeling very well.

Teacher: Yes, (8) ....

(*Later*)

Teacher: You still don't understand, do you?

(9) .... me to explain it

again?

Student D: Yes, (10) ....

(*Later*)

Student E: (11) .... borrow your

calculator?

Student F: No, I'm sorry, (12) ....

I'm using it myself.

Student G: (13) .... borrow mine?

Student E: Yes, thanks.

2 **A customs officer is talking to a passenger at London airport. Complete the dialogue, using *Can I/Would you?* etc.**

Customs Officer: (1) .... come over

here, please sir? (2) .... tell me

where you've just come from?

Passenger: From Amsterdam.

Customs Officer: I see. (3) .... see

your passport, please?

Passenger: Yes, here you are.

Customs Officer: (4) .... open this

suitcase for me, please? Thank you.

(*Later*)

Passenger: (5) .... go now?

Customs Officer: No, sir, I'm afraid (6)

.... (7) .... open this

second suitcase for me? Is it difficult to

open? (8) .... help you?

Passenger: No, it's all right. I can open it.

Customs Officer: Now, let me just have a quick

look. Ah, (9) .... tell me what this

is, sir? No? Well, (10) .... come

with me? I'd like to ask you a few more

questions - in my office.

Passenger: (11) .... phone my

solicitor?

Customs Officer: Yes, (12) ....

You're going to need a lot of legal advice!

27 *Must/mustn't*
Have to/don't have to

Driving in Britain. Advice for American drivers.
When you come to Britain, remember:
You must drive on the left.
Drivers and passengers have to wear seat-belts at all times.
You must have an international driving licence.
You have to have valid insurance.
You mustn't overtake on the left on motorways.
You mustn't drive with more than 0.45 mg of alcohol in your blood.

Step 1 | Forms of *must* and *have to*

Present and future

Affirmative	**Negative**	**Questions**
I must go	I mustn't (must not) go	Must I go?
You must go	You mustn't go	Must you go?
He/she/it must go	He/she/it mustn't go	Must he/she/it go?
We must go	We mustn't go	Must we go?
You must go	You mustn't go	Must you go?
They must go	They mustn't go	Must they go?

- *Must* is followed by the infinitive without *to*.
(NOT I must to go)

- There's no final *-s* in the 3rd person singular.
(NOT He musts go.   NOT He must goes)

- Questions and negatives are formed without *do*.
(*Must you go?*   NOT Do you must go?)

- For the past tense of *must*, we use *had to*. (See below.)

- (For *must have* + past participle, see Unit 28.)

Present

I have to go	I don't have to go	Do I have to go?
You have to go	You don't have to go	Do you have to go?
He/she/it has to go	He doesn't have to go	Does he have to go?
We have to go	We don't have to go	Do we have to go?
You have to go	You don't have to go	Do you have to go?
They have to go	They don't have to go	Do they have to go?

Past

I had to go	I didn't have to go	Did I have to go?

Future

I'll have to go	I won't have to go	Will I have to go?

CHECK QUESTIONS 1 **Put in the correct form of the verb.**
1 You (have to) drive on the right or the left in Britain?
2 An American driver in Britain (must) have valid insurance.
3 He also (have to) have an international driving licence.
4 A driver (must) drink and drive.

Step 2 | Uses of *must* and *have to*

• We use *must* and *have to* to say that something is necessary or obligatory. Sometimes, it doesn't matter which we use. In the text in Step 1 both *must* and *have to* could be used in all the four affirmative sentences.
   *Drivers and passengers **have to wear** seat-belts.*
   OR *Drivers and passengers **must wear** seat-belts.*

• For questions asking if something is necessary or obligatory, we normally use *Do I, you, etc. have to?* The question form *Must I, you, etc.?* is far less common.
   ***Do you have to** have an international driving licence?*

• For the negative forms, see Step 5.

CHECK QUESTIONS 2 **Answer these questions.**
1 Do you have to drive on the left or the right in Britain? You ...
2 When must you wear seat-belts? You ...

Step 3 | Differences between *must* and *have to*

> Irvine Wallace, an American, is in Britain and has hired a car. He has to wear glasses when he drives, and he's just broken them.
> 'I must get some new glasses. I must go to the optician's.'
> He's made an appointment for tomorrow morning. He's telling his wife:
> 'We can't go to Oxford tomorrow. I have to go to the optician's at 11.30.'

• There's sometimes a clear difference between *must* and *have to*. We use *must* to talk about an obligation that we impose on other people or on ourselves. It's our personal opinion. It's subjective.
   ***I must go** to the optician's.* (Irvine thinks this is necessary.)

• In contrast, we normally use *have to* when the obligation comes from outside the speaker. It's objective, it's outside the speaker's control.
   *I **have to go** to the optician's at 11.30.*
   (The time of Irvine's appointment has been decided by an outsider, the optician.)

• Note that the obligation or necessity is often habitual.
   *Irvine **has to wear** glasses when he drives.*   (This is an habitual necessity.)

CHECK QUESTIONS 3 **Put in *must* or *have to/has to*.**
1 Irvine can't go to Oxford tomorrow. He's thinking: 'I ... phone the hotel to say we aren't coming.'
2 He's phoning the hotel: 'I'm afraid we can't come tomorrow. I ... go to the optician's here in London.'
3 Irvine's eyesight isn't very good. He ....have an eye-test once a year.

Step 4 | *Have got to*

> Irvine's got to take a taxi to the optician's because he can't drive his car. He's talking to the taxi driver:
> 'First, I've got to stop at a bank to change some travellers' cheques. Then we'll have to hurry, because I've got to get to the optician's by 11.30.'

- *Have got to* usually means the same as *have to*.
  It's more informal and colloquial than *have to*, but it's used a lot in spoken English.
    I've got to get to the optician's by 11.30.
  OR *I have to get to the optician's by 11.30.*
- We often use *have got to* in preference to *have to* when we're talking about a specific, not habitual, situation.
    First, I've got to stop at a bank.   (Rather than *I have to stop at a bank.*)

CHECK QUESTIONS 4 **Put in forms of *have got to*.**
1 What time ...you ... be at the optician's?
2 I ... be there at 11.30.
3 The taxi driver doesn't know the way to the optician's. He ... to stop to look at a map.

Step 5 | *Mustn't* or *don't have to/haven't got to*?

> Usually in the USA you mustn't drive at more than 55 m.p.h. It's the law. Irvine drives at this speed on the motorway in Britain. But he doesn't have to drive so slowly, because the speed limit in Britain is 70 m.p.h.

- The negative forms *mustn't* and *don't have to/haven't got to* don't mean the same. We use *mustn't* to tell people not to do something, that something is wrong or against the law.
    *Usually in the USA you **mustn't** drive at more than 55 m.p.h.*
- But we use *don't have to* or *haven't got to* to say that there's no obligation to do something.
    *He **doesn't have to** drive so slowly.* (It isn't necessary.)
  Mustn't = You have no choice. You can't choose.
  Don't have to/haven't got to = You have a choice. You can choose.

CHECK QUESTIONS 5 **Put in *mustn't* or *don't have to*.**
1 You ... drive at more than 30 m.p.h. in towns in Britain.
2 On American highways you ... overtake on the left; you can overtake on the right if you want to.

ANSWERS TO CHECK QUESTIONS 1, 2, 3, 4 AND 5

1 1 Do you have to drive 2 must have 3 has to have 4 mustn't
2 1 You have to/must drive on the left. 2 You have to/must wear them at all times.
3 1 I must 2 I have to 3 He has to
4 1 have you got to be 2 I've got to be 3 He's got to stop
5 1 mustn't 2 don't have to

Practice

- *Must* and *have to* sometimes mean the same.
  You **must** be fit if you want to go scuba-diving.
  OR You **have to** be fit if you want to go scuba-diving.
  But there is sometimes a difference.
  Must: obligation coming from the speaker. *This is important. You **must** listen to me!*
  Have to: obligation coming from outside. *He **has to** wear a suit at work.*
- *Mustn't*: You have no choice. *You **mustn't** smoke in here.*
  Don't have to: You have a choice. *You **don't have to** come. Stay here if you want.*

---

1 Match a sentence on the left with a sentence on the right.

1 I've got terrible toothache.
2 My teeth aren't very good.
3 I must phone my boss.
4 I've got to go to work this afternoon.

a I'm seeing an important client at three o'clock.
b I must tell her I'm not coming to work this morning.
c I have to go to the dentist's quite often.
d I must make an appointment at the dentist's.

1 ...... 2 ...... 3 ...... 4 ......

2 What do these signs and notices mean? Write sentences with *must, mustn't* or *don't have to*.

1 ....
2 ....
3 ....
4 ....
5 ....
6 ....

1 NO SMOKING
2 STOP
3 Hairdressers
NO APPOINTMENT NECESSARY
4 SILENCE
5 FREE EYE TESTS
6 FASTEN YOUR SEAT BELTS

3 Travelling by plane. Put each of the following into the correct column.

A watch the film
B sit in the seat marked on your boarding card
C try to open a door
D take a gun on board the plane
E show your boarding card to get on the plane
F look out of the window
G smoke in the non-smoking section
H speak to the person next to you
I sit in your seat during take-off and landing

You must/ you have to	You mustn't	You don't have to
....	....	....
....	....	....
....	....	....

4 How to play tennis. Complete these sentences with *must, mustn't* or *don't have to*.

1 You .... wear white clothes.

2 You .... hit the ball over the net.

3 You .... hold your racket in your right hand.

4 You .... let the ball bounce twice.

5 You .... serve from behind the base-line.

6 You .... hit the ball before it bounces.

28

Must, can't
Must have done, can't have done

There's an area in the Atlantic called the Bermuda Triangle. A lot of boats and planes have mysteriously disappeared there. It must be a strange place. People must feel worried when they cross it. It can't be easy for them. A friend of mine is on a yacht in the Triangle at the moment. He must be feeling nervous. He can't be enjoying the trip. So, is he crazy? He must be. I wouldn't go there. Does he know the risks? He must do.

Step 1 | Deductions about the present: *must/can't* + infinitive

- We can use *must* + infinitive without *to* when we make a logical deduction from the information or evidence we have. We use *can't* + infinitive without *to* (not *mustn't*) when we talk about a logical impossibility.

  People **must feel worried**. (Because of the disappearances.)
  It **can't be** easy for them. (Because they're worried.)

- Note the continuous forms *must be/can't be* + *-ing*.
  He **must be** feeling nervous.
  (You're sure he's feeling nervous.)
  He **can't be** enjoying the trip.
  (You're sure he isn't enjoying the trip.)

- Note the short answers: *Is he crazy?* – **He must be**.
  Does he know the risks? – **He must do**.

(For other uses of *must* see Unit 27.)

CHECK QUESTIONS 1 **Put in *must* or *can't*.**
1 People who cross the Triangle ... be very happy about it.
2 They ... know about the strange disappearances.
3 The writer's friend ... be feeling worried at the moment.

Step 2 | Deductions about the past: *must have, can't have*

Last July Art Fidler left Miami in his private jet to fly to Bermuda. He never arrived. He had plenty of fuel when he left, so he can't have run out of fuel. His radio can't have been working, because there was no radio contact with him. There must have been something wrong with his plane. And it must have crashed into the sea and sunk immediately, because nothing was found. Did he make a stupid mistake? He can't have done. He was an experienced pilot. Was he killed? He must have been.

- We use *must have* + past participle to say we're almost certain something happened in the past, because of the information we have. We use *can't have* (NOT *mustn't have*) + past participle to say we think something was impossible.
  *It **must have sunk** immediately.*
  (Nothing was found.)
  *He **can't have run out** of fuel.*
  (Impossible. He had plenty.)
- Note the continuous forms *must/can't have been* + *-ing*.
  *His radio **can't have been** working.*
- Note the short answers.
  *Did he make a mistake? – **He can't have done**.*
  *Was he killed? – **He must have been**.*

CHECK QUESTIONS 2 **Put in *must have* or *can't have*.**
1 Nothing was found, so the plane ... exploded in the air.
2 Fidler ... felt scared.
3 He ... been expecting a normal flight.

ANSWERS TO
CHECK QUESTIONS
1 AND 2
1 1 can't 2 must 3 must
2 1 can't have 2 must have 3 must have

Practice

> Must + infinitive or must be + -ing when we feel sure something is true.
> Can't + infinitive or can't be + -ing when we think something is impossible.
> Must have + past participle or must have been + -ing when we feel certain something was true.
> Can't have + past participle or can't have been + -ing when we think something was impossible.

1 **Rewrite the marked sentences using *must/can't* + infinitive or *must be/can't be* + -ing.**
Example:
Jane Ross has three expensive holidays a year. She's obviously got plenty of money. *She must have plenty of money.*

1 She's got lots of friends. She's obviously very popular.

....

2 She owns three dogs and two cats. She obviously likes animals.

....

3 She plays tennis in national tournaments. She's obviously a very good player.

....

4 She never watches the news on TV. She's obviously not very interested in current affairs.

....

5 She's got to go into hospital for an operation on her arm. She obviously isn't looking forward to it.

....

6 She won't be able to play tennis for two months. She's obviously feeling depressed.

....

2 **Complete the dialogue using *must/can't* + infinitive, *must have* or *can't/couldn't have* + a past participle and the verbs in brackets.**

'I had a £20 note this morning, and I can't find it.'

'You (1 spend) .... it.'

'I (2 spend) .... it. I didn't buy anything today.'

'It (3 fall) .... out of your pocket.'

'It (4 fall) .... out of my pocket because I left it here in my room.'

'Well, it (5 be) .... still .... in your room, then.'

'It isn't. I've looked everywhere. Gillian (6 take) .... it.'

'It (7 be) .... Gillian. She'd never take your money without asking.'

'Well, where is it? Money (8 disappear) .... just .... like that. Somebody (9 take) .... it.'

3 **Harriet has been trying to contact her boyfriend Martin. She is talking to her flatmate. Complete the sentences, using *must have* or *can't have* + a past participle, or *must have been/can't have been* + -ing.**

'Harriet? Has Martin phoned yet?'

'No. He (1 get) .... my message. I rang him this morning, but he wasn't there. He (2 go) .... to work early. I left a message on his answer-phone. Wait a minute. He (3 go) .... to work. It's Saturday. I forgot. He (4 go) .... away for the weekend. He often goes away at the weekend.'

'No, I saw him last night at the Indian take-away.'

'He (5 buy) .... his dinner.'

'Well, he was with a girl I didn't know.'

'Oh, that (6 be) .... his sister.'

'It (7 be) .... his sister. They were holding hands.'

'You (8 make) .... a mistake. You (9 wear) .... your glasses. It (10 be) .... Martin.'

'I'm sorry, Harriet, but I'm sure it was.'

29 May (have), might (have), could (have)

John Speight keeps snakes at home. Monty, his favourite python, has escaped. His wife's terrified.

'John, that snake may be dangerous. It may attack someone. It might eat the cat. It could be under the bed and I might not see it when I get into bed. Ugh! It could be anywhere. It might be in the garden.'

'No, it couldn't be in the garden because all the doors and windows are closed. Don't worry. I'll find it. It may be under the floorboards. I didn't feed it this morning. It may be feeling hungry. It could be looking for food.'

'And you may not find it. We need some help. We could phone the police.'

Step 1 | *May, might, could* for present and future possibility

- We can use *may, might* or *could* + an infinitive without *to* when we want to say that something is possible (in the present or the future). There is no significant difference between them.

  It **may attack** someone. (= It's possible it'll attack someone.)
  It **might eat** the cat. (= It's possible it'll eat the cat.)
  It **could be** under the bed. (= It's possible it's under the bed.)

- But we use *could*, not *may* or *might*, to make suggestions.

  We **could** phone the police. (= Shall we phone the police?)

- We use the negative forms *may not* or *might not* (or *mightn't*) to talk about possibility, but not *couldn't*.

  I **might** not see it when I get into bed. (= It's possible I won't see it.)

  Couldn't means that something is totally impossible.

  It **couldn't** be in the garden. (= That's not possible.)

- We often use the continuous form: *may be, might be, could be* + *-ing* to talk about a present possibility.

  It **may be feeling** hungry. (= It's possible it's feeling hungry.)
  It **could be looking** for food. (= It's possible it's looking for food.)

- *May, might, could* have the same form for all persons.

  I *may/might/could come. He may/might/could come*, etc.

(For *could*, see also Unit 25.)

CHECK QUESTIONS 1

Rewrite these sentences.
1 Perhaps the snake will attack someone. The snake ...
2 Perhaps it's under the floorboards. It ...
3 It's possible John won't find it. He ...
4 Perhaps the snake's hiding in a cupboard. The snake ...
5 It isn't possible that it's in this cupboard. It ...

May have, might have, could have for past possibility
May as well/might as well

A police officer has come to talk to John about his snake.

'Have you any idea where the snake may have gone?'

'It might have gone under the floorboards. It may have fallen asleep somewhere in the house. It could have gone down the toilet.'

'Could someone have stolen it?'

'No. A thief couldn't have got into the house. I was here all the time.'

'How did it escape?'

'I found the cover of its tank on the floor. I might not have put it on. I might have forgotten. I can't remember. The snake may have moved it itself. It may have been feeling hungry. It might have been looking for food. I could have given it some this morning, but it didn't seem hungry.'

'Are you sure you've looked under all the beds?'

'Yes, I think so.'

'Well, we may as well look again, just in case.'

'I suppose you're right. We might as well.'

'Wait a minute. That plant over there ... It's moving.'

- We can use either *may have, might have* or *could have* + a past participle to say that something was possible in the past.
  It **may have fallen** asleep. (= It's possible it's fallen asleep.)
  It **might have gone** under the floorboards. (= That's possible.)
  It **could have gone** down the toilet. (= That's possible.)

- *Could have* can also mean that something was possible, but didn't happen.
  I **could have given** it some food this morning. (He didn't give it any food.)

- Note the negative forms: *may not have/might not(n't) have*.
  I **might not have** put the cover on. (= It's possible I didn't.)

- *Couldn't have* means that something was totally impossible.
  A thief **couldn't have** got into the house. (= It wasn't possible.)

- We often use the continuous form: *may have been, might have been, could have been* + *-ing* to talk about a past possibility.
  It **may have been feeling** hungry. (= It's possible it was feeling hungry.)

- Note the expressions *may as well* and *might as well* which mean the same. We use them when we suggest doing something because it seems the only sensible thing to do, but we aren't very enthusiastic.
  We **may as well** look again. (= There's nothing better to do.)

CHECK QUESTIONS 2

Rewrite the sentences.

1 Perhaps the snake went under the floorboards. The snake ...
2 Perhaps the snake was feeling hungry. The snake ...
3 It was possible for John to feed it, but he didn't. John ...
4 Perhaps it hasn't gone very far. It ...

ANSWERS TO
CHECK QUESTIONS
1 AND 2

1 1 The snake may/might/could attack someone. 2 It may/might/could be under the floorboards. 3 John may not/might not find it. 4 The snake may/might/could be hiding in a cupboard. 5 It couldn't be in this cupboard.

2 1 The snake may have/might have/could have gone under the floorboards. 2 The snake may have/might have/could have been feeling hungry. 3 John could have fed it, but he didn't. 4 It may not have/might not have/mightn't have gone very far.

Practice

Present and future possibility:	may, might, could	She may phone.
	may not, might not	She might not come.
Impossibility:	couldn't	She couldn't be in her office now. It's 8 p.m.
Past possibility:	may/might/could have	She might have gone home.
Impossibility:	couldn't have	She couldn't have been at work this morning. She was ill.

1 Sophie seems very depressed. Her friends are not sure what the problem is. Write sentences using *may (not), might (not)* or *could*.
Example: Perhaps she's worried about something. *She might be worried about something.*

1 Perhaps she isn't feeling well.

....

2 Perhaps she's worrying about her exams.

....

3 Perhaps she needs help.

....

4 But perhaps she doesn't want to talk to anybody.

....

2 Helen told Jack she would be at home at 8, so he rang her then. But there was no reply. Jack is thinking of possible reasons. Make sentences using *may (not) have, might (not) have* or *could have*.
Example: (Had she gone out?) *She might have gone out.*

1 (Had she stayed late at work?)

....

2 (Or did she hear the phone?)

....

3 (Was she having a bath?)

....

4 (Did she want to talk to him?)

....

5 (Had she forgotten about the arrangement?)

....

3 Mr Benson has lost his hat. He is telling his wife. Use *might have, might not have* or *could have, couldn't have* to complete the dialogue.

'I don't know where I (1) .... lost it.'

'You (2) .... left it in the cinema. '

'I (3) .... left it in the cinema. I saw it this morning on the hall table.'

'Somebody at work (4) .... taken it by mistake. They (5) ....

realised it was yours.'

'Only Alison and Claire were in the office today. They (6) .... taken it because they don't wear men's hats!'

'Are you sure you took it to work? You (7)

.... taken it. You (8) ....

left it here.'

'I (9) .... left it here. I always wear it when I go to work.'

'Well, you (10) .... worn it today, because it's here, on the hall table!'

4 You are going shopping with a friend. Make sentences with *may/might as well*.

1 You've missed the bus. The next one's in half an hour. It only takes ten minutes to walk.

    We ....

2 It's starting to rain. You're outside a café. You don't really want to have a drink, but it seems the sensible thing to do.

    We ....

3 You're buying a sweater. You like the green one more than the red one, but it costs more.

    Your friend says: You ....

    ....because it's silly to buy something you don't like.

4 It's half past five. The shops are closing. You don't really want to buy anything else.

    We .... go home.

30 *Should/ought to, had better*
Should have/ought to have

> There's too much traffic on British roads. People have different opinions.
> – We ought to make petrol more expensive.
> – We shouldn't make so many cars.
> – People should pay to use the roads.
> – We oughtn't to allow cars in city centres.

Step 1 | The main use of *should/ought to*

- We use *should* + infinitive without *to* or *ought to* + infinitive when we think something is the right thing to do.

   People **should pay** to use the roads = People **ought to pay**.

- We use *shouldn't* (should not) or *oughtn't to* (ought not to) when we think something isn't a good idea.

   We **shouldn't make** so many cars = We **oughtn't to make**.

CHECK QUESTIONS 1

Put in *should(n't)* or *ought(n't) to*.
1 We ... build more roads. That will only make the problem worse.
2 We .... build more railways. I think that's the best answer.

Step 2 | *Should* and *ought to* + *be* + *-ing*

> Sam Travis is in his car. The police have stopped him.
> 'Excuse me, sir. You should be wearing your seat-belt. And your back lights aren't working. You oughtn't to be driving this car.'

- We use *should(n't)/ought(n't) to* + *be* + *-ing* to talk about something that should(n't) be in progress now.

   You **should be wearing** your seat-belt.   You **oughtn't to be driving** this car.

CHECK QUESTIONS 2

Put in *should(n't)* or *ought(n't) to*.
1 Is Sam wearing his seat-belt?   No, but he ...it.
2 Are his back lights working?   No, so he ... his car.

Step 3 | Other uses of *should/ought to*

> Sam's going to a football match at 7.30. He's telling his wife about it.
> 'England should win tonight. Scotland aren't very good this year.'
> 'Are you going to the match by train?'
> 'Yes. If I get a train at 6 p.m., I shouldn't be late. I ought to be there by 7.
> Or do you think I should catch an earlier train?'
> 'Yes, I think you should.'

- We use *should* and *ought to* when we talk about how probable something is, or what we expect to happen in the future.
  *England **should** win.*
  (Sam expects this, because Scotland aren't very good.)
  *I **shouldn't** be late. I **ought to** be there by 7 p.m.*
  (This is probable if he catches a train at 6 p.m.)
- Note the use of *should/ought to* without a main verb.
  *Do you think I **should** catch an earlier train?*
  *Yes, I think you **should**. (OR Yes, I think you **ought to**.)*

CHECK QUESTIONS 3 **Put in *should(n't)/ought(n't) to*.**
1 If the train's on time, Sam .... be late.
2 His wife thinks he .... catch an earlier train.

Step 4 | *Had better* + infinitive without *to*

> 'Sam! You're going to miss your train. You'd better hurry. It's ten to six!'
> 'What! I'll never catch that train now. I'd better go by car.'
> 'Yes, you'd better. But wait a minute. The lights don't work. Perhaps you'd better not take the car.'

- We use *had better* (*'d better*) + infinitive without *to* to say that something is the right thing to do. We use it with *I* and *we* to talk about an immediate intention.
  *I**'d better** go by car.*
  We use it with *you* or *he, she, it, they* when we're giving advice or a warning about the present or the immediate future.
  *You**'d better** hurry.*
- Note the negative form *had* (*'d*) *better not*.
  *You**'d better not** take the car.*
- Note the use of *had better (not)* without a main verb.
  *I'd better go by car.   Yes, you**'d better**.*

CHECK QUESTIONS 4 **Put in *had better (not)*.**
1 Your car lights don't work, Sam. ... fix them.
2 You ... drive without lights.

96

Step 5 | *Should have/ought to have* + past participle

> Sam decided to take the car. On his way home he was eating a hamburger. He hit the car in front. He's telling his wife what happened. 'There was too much traffic! I shouldn't have taken the car. I ought to have gone by train.'
> 'Well, it's your fault. You ought to have listened to me. You should have left home earlier. And you oughtn't to have been eating a hamburger in the car. You should have been watching the road.'

- We use *should have* or *ought to have* + a past participle to say that something in the past was a mistake.
  *I **shouldn't have** taken the car.* (But he took it. It was a mistake.)
  *I **ought to have gone** by train.* (But he didn't go by train.)

- We use *should(n't) have* or *ought(n't) to have* + *been* + *-ing* when we talk about something that should(n't) have been in progress at a particular moment in the past.
  *You **should have been watching** the road.*
  (But he wasn't watching the road.)
  *You **oughtn't to have been eating** a hamburger.*
  (But he was eating a hamburger.)

CHECK QUESTIONS 5

Put in *should(n't) have* or *ought(n't) to have*.
1 Sam took the car. That was a mistake. He .... it.
2 He didn't listen to his wife. That was a mistake. He ... to her.
3 He wasn't watching the road. That was a mistake. He .... the road.

ANSWERS TO
CHECK QUESTIONS
1, 2, 3, 4 AND 5

1 1 shouldn't/oughtn't to 2 should/ought to
2 1 should be/ought to be wearing 2 shouldn't be/oughtn't to be driving
3 1 shouldn't/oughtn't to 2 should/ought to

4 1 You'd better 2 You'd better not
5 1 shouldn't have/oughtn't to have taken 2 should have/ought to have listened 3 should have been/ought to have been watching

Practice

> We use:
> - *should/shouldn't* or *ought to/oughtn't to* + infinitive without *to* to say something is or isn't the right thing to do: *You should go to the doctor. You shouldn't smoke.*
> - *should/shouldn't* etc. + *be* + *-ing* to say something should be in progress now: *You should be working now.*
> - *had ('d) better* to say what we should do immediately: *We'd better phone the police.*
> - *should have/ought to have* (and their negative forms) + past participle to say that something in the past was a mistake: *I shouldn't have said that.*

1 **Your grandfather cannot sleep at night. You're giving him some advice. Answer *Yes* or *No* to the questions.**

1 You shouldn't drink so much coffee. Does he drink a lot of coffee? ......
2 You oughtn't to have eaten that cheese. Did he eat the cheese? ......
3 You should take sleeping tablets. Does he take sleeping tablets? ......
4 You ought to go and see a doctor. Has he been to the doctor's? ......
5 And you shouldn't be watching this late-night film. Is he watching the film? ......

2 **Mark Boulder has got an important exam tomorrow. Complete these sentences, using *should(n't)* or *ought(n't) to* + infinitive or + *be* + *-ing*.**

1 He isn't very interested in his work. He (be)

.... more interested.

2 He goes out every evening. He (go out)

.... so often.

3 He's watching a film at the moment. He

(watch) .... TV.

4 He (study) .... , but he

isn't.

3 **Gerry Martin has got financial problems. Describe the mistakes he has made, using *should(n't) have* or *ought(n't) to have* + a past participle.**

1 He bought a luxury flat in London. He

.... flat like that.

2 He's had three expensive holidays this year.

He .... so many

holidays.

3 He hasn't paid any tax for three years. He

.... at least a bit

of tax!

4 He hasn't spent much time with his family.

He .... more time

with them.

5 He's been very irresponsible. He ....

.... more responsible.

4 **You have arrived at the scene of a car accident. A man is lying on the road. He is badly hurt. What is the best thing to do? You are telling the people who are there. Use *had ('d) better (not)* and the following verbs to complete the sentences: *move, put, stop, phone***

1 You .... him.
2 We .... the police.
3 We .... a coat over him.
4 We .... the traffic.

31

Have got/have

> Marie Thomas hasn't got many friends so she put an advertisement in the Personal column of a local newspaper. She received this reply.
>
> Dear Marie,
>
> First the good news. I've got blue eyes and I've got brown hair. I've got a flat and I've got a job. But I haven't got a girlfriend!
>
> Now for the bad news. I've got big ears and I haven't got much hair left. I've got asthma too. I used to have a good job, but I lost it. The job I've had for the last year is badly paid. I had a car a month ago, but I haven't got one now. I didn't have enough money, so I sold it. My flat's very small - it's only got one bedroom, and it hasn't got a very big kitchen ...

Step 1 | Uses of *have got*

● *Have got* and *have* mean the same. But in informal English we normally use *have got* rather than *have* when we talk about:

Possessions: *I've got a flat. It's only got one bedroom.*

Relatives: *I haven't got a girlfriend.*

Illnesses: *I've got asthma.* (*I've got a headache, a cold, a bad back, etc.*)

Personal characteristics: *I've got blue eyes and brown hair.*

● We could use *have* in all the above examples. But *have got* is far more common.
I have a flat. It only has one bedroom. I don't have a girlfriend.

● In American English we use the affirmative forms of *have got*, but we rarely use the negative or question forms.

British English: *Have you got a car? I haven't got a car.*

American English: *Do you have a car? I don't have a car.*

● The forms of *have got* **Present simple:**

Affirmative	Negative	Question
I've got	I haven't got	Have I got?
He's got	He hasn't got	Has he got?
They've got	They haven't got	Have they got? etc.

Contracted forms: 's got = has got   hasn't got = has not got

                 've got = have got   haven't got = have not got

● Note the short answers: *Yes, I have/Yes, he has/No, they haven't*, etc.
(NOT Yes, I've got/Yes, he's got/No, they haven't got)
Has he got a girlfriend? **No, he hasn't.** (NOT No, he hasn't got)

● In the past simple we can use either *had/didn't have* or *had got/hadn't got* but *had/didn't have* is more common.
I had a car a month ago. (NOT I'd got a car a month ago.)

● In other tenses (present perfect, past perfect, future, etc.) and forms (the infinitive) only *have* (NOT have got) is possible.
The job I've had for the last year. (NOT The job I've had got.)
I used to have a good job. (NOT I used to have got.)

CHECK QUESTIONS 1 **Put in forms of *have got*.**

1 ... Marie ... many friends? No ...

2 She ... a boyfriend last year, but she ... not ... one now.

3 Her girlfriends ... all ... husbands and children.

Step 2 | *Have* for actions

... I haven't got any bad habits although, I must admit, I usually have dinner in front of the television and I sometimes have a cigarette afterwards. And I don't have a bath every day!

At weekends I often have a long walk in the country. Then I have a meal in a country pub. Once a year I have a holiday on the south coast. But I'm not having one this year because I haven't got enough money.

I'd really like to meet you. Perhaps we can have dinner together soon.

Best wishes,

Raymond

PS I could meet you any evening next week except for Thursday. That evening I'm having a game of badminton with a friend. And then we're having a drink together afterwards.

- We use *have* (NOT have got) to talk about actions/activities.
  I have dinner in front of the television.   (NOT I've got dinner)
  I have a holiday on the south coast.   (NOT I've got a holiday)

- When we use *have* like this, we can use continuous forms because we're describing actions.
  I'm not having a holiday this year.
  We're having a drink together afterwards.

- Note the negative and question forms in the present simple.
  I don't have a bath every day.
  Does he have a holiday every year?

- We don't use contractions with *have* when it's describing an action.
  I have a cigarette afterwards. (NOT I've a cigarette)

- Look at this list of further examples of *have* used for actions.
  have breakfast, dinner, a drink, a sandwich, etc.
  have a bath, a shower, a wash, a shave, a sauna, etc.
  have a rest, a sleep, a dream, etc.
  have a holiday, a nice time, a day off, etc.
  have a swim, a game, a walk, a ride, etc.
  have an argument, a talk, a discussion, a meeting, etc.
  have a go, a try, etc.
  have a baby   have a look   have a lesson

CHECK QUESTIONS 2 **Put in forms of *have*.**
1 Raymond (not have) a shower in the morning. He usually (have) a bath.
2 He (have) his breakfast at the moment.
3 he (have) a holiday in July? Yes normally, but he (not have) a holiday this year.

ANSWERS TO
CHECK QUESTIONS
1 AND 2
1 1 Has Marie got many friends? No, she hasn't.
2 She had a boyfriend last year, but she hasn't got one now. 3 Her girlfriends have all got husbands and children.

2 1 Raymond doesn't have a shower in the morning. He usually has a bath. 2 He's having his breakfast at the moment. 3 Does he have a holiday in July? ... he isn't/he's not having a holiday this year.

Practice

We use *have got* for possessions, relatives, personal characteristics, illnesses:
They've got a new car.   I haven't got a sister.   Sarah's got dark hair.   Have you got a headache?
Have for actions or activities:
They're having a meeting.   They don't always have sandwiches for lunch.   Does the dog have a walk every morning?

1 **Michael Wells is at the dentist's. Complete this dialogue, using forms of *have got*.**

Michael: Good morning. My name's Wells. I

(1) .... an appointment with Mr

Rees at 10.30.

Receptionist: Yes, that's right. Mr Rees

(2) .... a patient in with him at the

moment. Could you take a seat please?

(Later)

Dentist: What's the problem?

Michael: I (3) .... bad toothache.

Dentist: How long (4) .... you .... it?

Michael: I (5) .... it for over a week.

(Later)

Dentist: Well, you (6) .... good teeth

but this tooth here at the back (7) ....

a big hole in it.

Michael: (8) .... you ....

time to fill it now?

Dentist: No, I (9) .... , I'm afraid. But I

think I might (10) .... some free

time at the end of the week.

2 **Are forms of *have got* possible in these sentences? Answer *Yes* or *No*.**

We (1 have) a house in the middle of London and we (2 have) full-time jobs. During the week we (3 have) very little free time. I come home from work, (4 have) a quick shower and then (5 have) something to eat. Then we usually go out together, because we (6 have) so many friends in London. But weekends are different. We (7 have) a small cottage in the country. When we're there in the summer we (8 have) long country walks. I sometimes (9 have) a

swim in the river. My wife (10 have) riding lessons. We (11 have) meals in the garden and in the evenings we often (12 have) a drink in the local pub. We don't watch television when we're there because we (13 not have) a TV. We sit in front of the fire and (14 have) long discussions or sometimes we (15 have) a game of cards. In fact we (16 have) a complete rest and we (17 have) a really good time.

1 ......   2 ......   3 ......   4 ......   5 ......   6 ......   7 ......

8 ......   9 ......   10 ......   11 ......   12 ......   13 ......

14 ......   15 ......   16 ......   17 ......

3 **Complete this paragraph with forms of *have* or *have got*. Use forms of *have got* where possible.**

My brother and I are completely different. We

look different for a start. I (1) .... long

hair but he (2) .... very short hair. He

(3) .... glasses but I (4) ....

I (5) .... very good eyesight. He

(6) .... lots of money because he

(7) .... a well-paid job. I (8) ....

a job at all at the moment. He and his family

(9) .... holidays in the Caribbean.

The last holiday I (10) .... was a week

in Spain three years ago.

We (11) .... lunch together today. We

usually (12) .... a meal together

about once a month. He's very excited at the

moment, because his wife (13) .... a

baby.

32

Phrasal verbs: *He took off his coat*

> Monday, February 3rd
> A bad day! I woke up with a headache. I got up late. I turned on the radio. The news was bad, so I turned off the radio and had a shower. The water was cold. Then I went out for a walk. It was raining.

Step 1 | What are phrasal verbs?

- Phrasal verbs are usually two-word verbs (a verb + an adverbial particle): *wake up, go out, turn on*, etc.
- We can use different particles with the same verb. The particle changes the meaning of the verb.
  *I turned **on** the radio.   I turned **off** the radio.*
- Phrasal verbs are very common, especially in informal English.
  We could say *I awoke with a headache*, but this is very formal. We normally say: *I **woke up** with a headache.*

CHECK QUESTIONS 1 **What are the five phrasal verbs?**
I sat down, had breakfast, washed up and set off for work. When I went out, it was still raining. It went on raining all day.

Step 2 | Different types of phrasal verb

> Tuesday, February 4th
> The car broke down. I rang up a garage. The mechanic found out why I'd stopped – I'd run out of petrol!
> I don't get on with the people at work, so today I filled in an application form for a new job. I put it down somewhere in the office. Now I can't find it!
> At home I switched on the TV. Cigarette prices are going up. I must give up smoking. And the government's planning to put up taxes. I'm not looking forward to that. They've already put them up twice this year. I've just worked out that I'll soon have no money. I can't go on like this.

- Some phrasal verbs never take an object.
  *The car **broke down**.   I can't **go on** like this.   Prices are **going up**.*

- Most phrasal verbs can take an object. The object can usually go before or after the particle.

verb	+	particle	+	object		verb	+	object	+	particle
I rang		*up*		*a garage.*	OR	*I rang*		*a garage*		*up.*
I switched		*on*		*the TV.*	OR	*I switched*		*the TV*		*on.*

- But if the object is long, it usually goes after the particle.
  *I filled in **an application form**.* (NOT I filled an application form in.)

- If the object is a pronoun the construction is always:

verb	+	pronoun	+	particle	
I put		*it*		*down*	(NOT I put down it.)
They've put		*them*		*up*	(NOT They've put up them.)

- Some phrasal verbs are three-word verbs with a particle + a preposition. The object can only come after the preposition.
  *I don't get **on with** the people at work.*
  *I'd run **out of** petrol.   I'm not looking **forward to** that.*

- (For a list of phrasal verbs see Appendix 4.)

CHECK QUESTIONS 2

Are these right or wrong?
1 They're going to put taxes up.
2 They're going to put up taxes.
3 They shouldn't put up them.
4 I'm not looking it forward to.

ANSWERS TO
CHECK QUESTIONS
1 AND 2
1 1 sat down 2 washed up 3 set off
4 went out 5 went on
2 1 Right. 2 Right. 3 Wrong. `4 Wrong.

Practice

> **Look** the word **up** in the dictionary. OR **Look up** the word in the dictionary.
> But: **Look it** up in the dictionary. (NOT Look up it in the dictionary.)
> **Look up** the words you don't know. (NOT Look the words you don't know up.)
> She's going out **with him**. (NOT She's going him out with.)

1 Replace the verbs in brackets with phrasal verbs. Use each of the following verbs once: *turn down, carry on, get back, ring up, go on, work out, put off, pay back, hold on, find out, call in.*

I'd just (1 returned) .... from work when my bank manager (2 telephoned) .... me .... He wanted me to (3 visit) .... to see him as soon as possible because he'd just (4 discovered) .... that I hadn't (5 repaid) .... the money I owed the bank. He said the situation couldn't (6 continue) .... like this. I asked him to (7 wait) .... to the end of the month. But he said I couldn't (8 delay) .... it .... any longer. He (9 continued) .... like this for several minutes. I'm now trying to (10 calculate) .... where I can get the money from. I've tried two other banks but they've both (11 rejected) .... me ....

2 Complete the following paragraph with phrasal verbs. Use each of the following verbs once: *come round, get on with, get up, go away, go on, look forward to, put up with, switch on, throw away, turn down, wake up.*

I share my flat with another girl but we don't (1) .... each other. When I (2) .... the television .... she always tells me to (3) .... it .... And if friends (4) .... late at night she tells them to (5) .... If I leave something on the floor, she (6) .... it .... ! I really (7) .... Sunday mornings when I don't have to (8) .... early. But on Sunday mornings she (9) .... at six and listens to the radio in bed. We can't (10) .... like this. I can't (11) .... it for much longer.

3 Which alternative is correct and which is wrong, a or b? (Sometimes both alternatives are correct.)

I'll never forget my French teacher at school. I never (1a got on with her 1b got her on with.) If there was a word I didn't understand she always said '(2a Look up it 2b Look it up) in the dictionary.' If I couldn't understand the meaning of a sentence she always told me to (3a work it out 3b work out it) but she never helped me. I never dared to (4a put up my hand 4b put my hand up) because I was afraid she'd (5a tell me off 5b tell off me.) And if I (6a handed in my homework 6b handed my homework in) a day late she was furious. I always (7a looked forward the end of the lesson to 7b looked forward to the end of the lesson). I'm not surprised I (8a gave up French 8b gave French up) as soon as I could.

1 .... 2 .... 3 .... 4 .... 5 .... 6 .... 7 .... 8 ....

33

Look, feel, etc.
+ adjective or like/as if

> Justin Cox works at an advertising agency. He's writing a TV commercial for a new product called Vitamax.
> 'You seem depressed. What's the problem?'
> 'I just feel tired all the time. When I see my face in the mirror, I look terrible. Food doesn't taste good any more. I've got no appetite.'
> 'Try Vitamax, the drink with five essential vitamins. It will change your life.'
> 'That sounds interesting. I'll try it. Mmm! It smells good. And it tastes good too!'
> (3 days later. She's walking around singing.)
> 'Well, you sound happy!'
> 'I feel happy! And all my friends say I look great. Thanks to Vitamax!'

Step 1 | look, feel, sound, taste, smell, seem + adjective

- We use these verbs to talk about our impression of things. We use an adjective after them, not an adverb.
  *I **look terrible**.* (NOT terribly) *Food doesn't **taste good**.* (NOT well)
  We use *look* to talk about visual appearance.
  *I **look terrible**.* (= When she sees her face in the mirror, that's her impression.)
  We use *sound* to talk about things that we hear.
  *That **sounds interesting**.* (= What you said seems interesting.)
- *Seem* is never used in the continuous form.

CHECK QUESTIONS 1 **Answer the questions.**
1 Before she takes Vitamax how does she feel all the time?
2 But 3 days later, how does she sound?   3 And how does she look?

Step 2 | look, feel, sound, taste, smell, seem + like

> Justin Cox is writing an advertisement for a new non-alcoholic beer called Old Gold.
> 'It looks like beer. It smells like beer. It tastes like beer. And when you drink it, it feels like liquid gold in your mouth. Why not have a glass of Old Gold?'
> 'That seems like a great idea. Cheers!'

- We use *like* + a noun after these verbs to describe what someone or something is similar to.
  *It **smells like** beer.   It **feels like** liquid gold.*
  When we use these verbs to describe what something is like, we usually use the present simple (not the present continuous).
  *It **looks** good.   It **looks** like beer.* (NOT It's looking)

Note: We use *like* to make a comparison, but we use *taste, smell* + *of* when there is a particular smell or taste on something.
> *This glass **tastes of** lipstick. My shirt **smells of** beer.*

CHECK QUESTIONS 2 **Answer the questions.**
1 What does Old Gold look like? 2 What does it feel like in your mouth?

Step 3 | Look, feel, sound, seem + as if/as though

> Justin's writing a TV commercial for British Telecom's new Helpline.
> ● 'The washing machine isn't working. Who can I phone on a Sunday?' It doesn't sound as if she can repair it herself. She sounds as though she needs help. She needs Helpline on 0800 56 56 56.
> ● Here's Mr Thorpe. He's missed his last bus home. He can't find a taxi. It looks as though he'll have to walk home. Wait a minute. He can use the telephone. But now he looks as if he's got another problem. He hasn't got any change! Don't panic, Mr Thorpe. You can call Helpline free.
> ● 'Oh, I feel terrible. It feels as though the whole room's going round and round. I feel as if I'm going to faint. The doctor. I must phone the doctor. Oh no, I've forgotten his number.'
> When it seems as if there's no one who can help you, call Helpline, a number you won't forget.

● We can use *as if/as though* + a subject and a verb after these verbs to describe our impressions. *As if* and *as though* mean the same.
> *She sounds **as though** she needs help.* (= She sounds **as if** she needs help.)

● We often use the impersonal *it* with these verbs, with the meaning 'it seems'.
> ***It looks** as though he'll have to walk home.* (= It seems as though …)
> ***It feels** as though the room is going round and round.*
> ***It doesn't sound** as if she can repair it herself.*

Note: In informal English we often use *like* instead of *as if/as though*. In American English *like* is frequently used.
> *It doesn't sound **like** she can repair it herself.*
> (= It doesn't sound **as if** she can repair it herself.)
> *It looks **like** he'll have to walk home.*
> (= It looks **as though** he'll have to walk home.)
> *It feels **like** the room's going round and round.*
> (= It feels **as though** the room's going round and round.)
> *When it seems **like** there's no one who can help you …*
> (= When it seems **as if** there's no one who can help you …)

(For *like* and *as* and other uses of *as if/as though* see Unit 89.)

CHECK QUESTIONS 3 **Rewrite these sentences, using *as if/as though*.**
1 She sounds in need of help. She ...
2 He'll probably have to walk home. It ...
3 I think I'm going to faint.

ANSWERS TO CHECK QUESTIONS 1, 2 AND 3

1 1 She feels tired. 2 She sounds happy. 3 She looks great.

2 1 It looks like beer. 2 It feels like liquid gold.

3 1 She sounds as if/as though she needs help (OR she's in need of help). 2 It looks as if/as though he'll have to walk home. 3 I feel as if/as though I'm going to faint.

Practice

> *Look, feel, sound, taste, smell, seem*
>
> **+ adjective**   **+ *like* + a noun**   **+ *as if* / *as though* + a subject + a verb**
> *He looks happy.*   *He looks like a film star.*   *He looks as if he's won the lottery.*

---

1 **A group of friends have all got an important exam this morning. Complete this description of how they seem, how they look or how they sound. Use these adjectives: *happy, well, tired, nervous, angry*.**
Example: Nick's got a big smile on his face. (look) *Nick looks happy.*

1 Martha's biting her fingernails. (seem)

   ....

2 Adam's yawning and rubbing his eyes. (look)

   ....

3 Joanne's shouting at everyone. (sound)

   ....

4 Simon's face is pale. (not look)

   ....

2 **Two people are looking through some old things in a cupboard. Complete the dialogue, using *look, feel, sound, smell* + *like*.**

'What's in this old bottle?'

'It (1) .... perfume.'

'What's this little box?'

'It (2) .... a jewellery box.'

'Hey! Who's this in the photo?'

'It (3) .... me when I was a baby.'

'Let's play this old cassette. Who's singing on it?'

'It (4) .... Elvis Presley.'

'Look at this old doll. It's got beautiful hair. Is it real?'

'Yes, I think so. It (5) .... real hair.'

3 **Complete the dialogue with *like* or *of*.**

'You smell (1) .... paint. What have you been doing?'

'I've been painting my bike. Come and have a look.'

'Wow ! It looks (2) .... a new one.'

'I've got some home-made beer. Would you like a glass?'

'Yes, thanks. Ugh! This glass tastes (3) .... paint.'

'Oh, sorry. I'll get you another one. Well, what do you think of my beer? What does it taste (4) ....?'

'It tastes very good. In fact, it tastes (5) .... real beer.'

4 **Complete the text with *like* or *as if/as though* or no word at all.**

That girl over there looks (1) .... she's got a problem. That man standing next to her looks (2) .... suspicious. He doesn't look (3) .... someone she knows. He sounds (4) .... angry too. He looks (5) .... he's asking her for something. She looks (6) .... frightened. She keeps looking over her shoulder. It seems (7) .... she's looking for help. Perhaps I should go and find out. But I feel (8) .... so embarrassed in situations like that. Wait a minute. It looks (9) .... they've finished their conversation. It seems (10) .... he's pushing her into his car. Oh no, this looks (11) .... a kidnapping. I'd better call the police.

34 Used to

Harry Titmus (68) used to collect golf balls. He used to walk with his dog every day on the local golf course, and his dog used to find a lot of balls. Harry took them home and put them in boxes, then in drawers, then in cupboards. 'I didn't use to play with them,' Mr Titmus commented, 'although I used to be quite a good player, when I was younger. I simply used to enjoy counting them. But when I'd collected 15,389 there were no more drawers and no more cupboards left, so I used to put them in the bath. My wife didn't use to like that.'

Step 1 | The forms of *used to*

Affirmative: *used to* + infinitive
Negative: *didn't use to* + infinitive
Questions: *did* + subject + *use to* + infinitive

Affirmative	Negative	Question
I used to go	I didn't use to go	Did I use to go?
You used to go	You didn't use to go	Did you use to go?
He used to go	He didn't use to go	Did he use to go?
She used to go	She didn't use to go	Did she use to go?
It used to go	It didn't use to go	Did it use to go?
We used to go	We didn't use to go	Did we use to go?
You used to go	You didn't use to go	Did you use to go?
They used to go	They didn't use to go	Did they use to go?

- Note the final *-d* in the affirmative (*used to*).
  *Harry **used** to collect golf balls.* (NOT Harry use to collect)
But note that there's no final *–d* in the negative and question forms (*didn't use to/did he use to?*).
  *I didn't **use** to play with them.*
  (NOT I didn't used to play with them.)
  *Where did he **use** to put them?*
  (NOT Where did he used to?)

- Note the short answers.
  *Do you collect golf balls, Harry? No, but **I used to**.*
  *Do you wear glasses now, Harry? Yes, but **I didn't use to**.*

- Note that the *-s-* in *used to* is pronounced [s], *to* in *used to* is pronounced [tə] before a consonant and [tu:] before a vowel sound.
  I used to [tə] be … I used to [tu:] enjoy …

- We use the negative form … *never used to* for emphasis:
*I **never used to** play with them* is a stronger version of *I didn't use to play with them.*

CHECK QUESTIONS 1 **Write three sentences with *use(d) to*.**
1 (affirmative) His wife/find golf balls in the bath
2 (negative) She/play golf
3 (question) Why/Harry/collect golf balls?

Step 2 | *Used to* to describe regular actions in the past

- We use *used to* to talk about a habit or regular activity in the past that doesn't happen now. *Used to* emphasises that the activity was repeated many times.

    He **used to** collect golf balls.

    His dog **used to** find a lot of balls.

  If we use the past simple here, the idea that the action happened many times isn't emphasised.

    He collected golf balls.   His dog found a lot of balls.

  Note: If we describe a number of regular activities in the past, it isn't necessary to repeat *used to* each time. We can use the past simple instead.

    Harry **took** them home and **put** them in boxes.

    (= Harry used to take them home and he used to put them in boxes.)

- We can also use *would* + infinitive without *to* to talk about past habits. When we use *would*, we usually say when or how often the action happened.

    He **used to walk** with his dog on the local golf course.

  OR He **would walk** with his dog **every day** on the local golf course.

  Note: *Would* is generally more formal and less common.

CHECK QUESTIONS 2 **Answer these questions with either *Yes* or *No*.**

1 Does Harry collect golf balls now?
2 Did he regularly look for golf balls in the past?
3 Does he still put golf balls in the bath?
4 Did his dog often find balls for him?

Step 3 | *Used to* to describe situations in the past

- We also use *used to* to talk about situations in the past which don't exist now.

    Harry **used to** be quite a good player.

    All the drawers in the house **used to** be full of golf balls.

  Note: We don't use *would* when we talk about a past situation. We can't say: 'Harry would be quite a good player.'

CHECK QUESTIONS 3 **Answer these questions with *Yes* or *No*.**

1 Is Harry a good player now?
2 Was he quite a good player when he was younger?
3 Are the drawers full of golf balls now?
4 Were the drawers full of golf balls at one time in the past?

ANSWERS TO
CHECK QUESTIONS
1, 2 AND 3

1 1 His wife used to find golf balls in the bath.
2 She didn't use to play golf. 3 Why did Harry use to collect golf balls?

2 1 No. 2 Yes. 3 No. 4 Yes.
3 1 No. 2 Yes. 3 No. 4 Yes.

Practice

> *I used to smoke* = I smoked regularly in the past, but I don't smoke now.
> *My brother didn't use to smoke.* = Smoking wasn't his habit in the past. He might smoke now.
> We don't know.
> *Did you use to smoke?* = Was smoking one of your habits in the past?

1 **An old man remembers the time when he was young. Complete these sentences.**
Example: His hair/be/black. Now/grey. *His hair used to be black. Now it's grey.*

1 He/play/football. Now/watch/on television.

....

....

2 He/stay up till 12.00. Now/go to bed/at 9.30.

....

....

3 He/ride/a motorbike. Now/drive/a car.

....

....

4 He/not wear glasses. Now/wear glasses all the time.

....

....

2 **Gemma and Paul used to go out together. But then Gemma got tired of Paul. Describe how things have changed.**
Example: see each other every day/never *They used to see each other every day, but now they never see each other.*

1 Gemma/go out with Paul/go out with Ben.

....

....

2 Paul/go out a lot/stay in in the evening

....

....

3 Gemma/be in love with Paul/feel nothing for him

....

....

4 Paul/not think about her much/miss her a lot

....

....

3 **Andy Hart used to be a professional football player, but then he broke his leg and could not play again. Complete the journalist's questions and Andy's answers where necessary, using *used to*.**

1 Which team/you play for? – Leeds United.

....

....

2 How much/you/earn? – About £1,500 a week.

....

....

3 Be/good player? – I/the best.

....

....

4 Where/live? – I/big house.

....

....

5 What kind of car/have? – A Mercedes.

....

....

6 How many friends/have? – I/hundreds.

....

....

35 *Get used to   Be used to*

Dimitri Poulos, a Greek student, has come to London to learn more English. At first things were very strange. English money was a problem at first, but now he's got used to it. English food is different from Greek food, but he's getting used to it, slowly! He's also getting used to speaking English all the time. But he hasn't got used to the traffic in England. He hasn't got used to looking right before he crosses the road. That's still a problem.

Step 1 | *to get used to* + a noun/pronoun OR + - *ing*

- We use *get used to something* or *get used to doing something* when we talk about the process of becoming accustomed to something. Something that was strange and unfamiliar, at first, becomes more familiar and normal.

  He's getting used to English food. (+ a noun)
  (At first English food was strange, but it's becoming less strange.)
  He's getting used to it. (+ a pronoun. *it* = English food)
  He's getting used to speaking English. (+ the *-ing* form)
  (When he speaks English, he now finds it easier than before.)
  He's (has) got used to English money.
  (The process of understanding English money has finished. Now it isn't strange.)

- Note the forms of *get used to*.

Affirmative	Negative	Question
Present continuous		
I'm getting used to	I'm not getting used to	Am I getting used to?
He's getting used to	He isn't getting used to	Is he getting used to?
Present perfect		
He's got used to	He hasn't got used to	Has he got used to?
Past simple		
He got used to	He didn't get used to	Did he get used to?
Future		
He'll get used to	He won't get used to	Will he get used to?

- We don't use an infinitive after *get used to*. *To* here is a preposition, so it is followed by the *-ing* form of the verb.

  *He's getting used to **speaking** English all the time.*
  (NOT *He's getting used to speak English all the time.*)

- *Used* is pronounced /ju:st/.

CHECK QUESTIONS 1 **Put in forms of *get used to*.**
1 Dimitri hasn't ... English food yet.
2 English money was a problem, but after a few days he ... it.
3 Slowly he ... (live) in London.

Step 2 | *be used to* + a noun/pronoun OR + *-ing*

Dimitri has been in England for six weeks now, and he's used to a lot of things that were strange at first. He's used to speaking English all the time. He's used to the English weather. Traffic in England doesn't worry him any more – now he's used to looking right before he crosses the road. But there are some things he still isn't used to. He isn't used to having milk in his tea and coffee and he's not used to drinking instant coffee. And he isn't used to swimming in a cold sea.

- We use *be used to* + a noun or a pronoun or + the *-ing* form of a verb when we say that something isn't strange any more.
  *He's **used to** the English weather.*
  (The English weather doesn't surprise him any more.)
  *He's **used to** speaking English all the time.*
  (This was a problem, but it isn't now.)
  *He's **not used to** drinking instant coffee.*
  (In Greece he drinks 'real' coffee. So instant coffee is strange to him.)

- Note the forms of *be used to*.

Affirmative	Negative	Question
Present		
I'm used to	I'm not used to	Am I used to?
He's used to	He isn't used to	Is he used to?
Past simple		
He was used to	He wasn't used to	Was he used to?
Future		
He'll be used to	He won't be used to	Will he be used to?

- Note that we don't use an infinitive after *be used to*. *To* here is a preposition, so it is followed by the *-ing* form of the verb.
  *He's used to **speaking** English all the time.*
  (NOT He's used to speak English all the time.)

- Compare:
  A Dimitri **is used to eating** English food.
  B Dimitri **used to eat** English food.
  Note: These two sentences have completely different meanings.
  A means 'Eating English food isn't strange to him any more and he often eats it now.'
  B means 'Eating English food was his habit in the past, but he doesn't eat it now.'
  (For the verb *used to* see Unit 34.)

CHECK QUESTIONS 2 **Put in forms of *(not) be used to*.**
1 Dimitri's ... (hear) English now.
2 He still ... (drink) tea with milk in it.
3 The sea's warm in Greece. So he ... (swim) in a cold sea.

ANSWERS TO
CHECK QUESTIONS
1 AND 2
1 1 Diimitri hasn't got used to English food yet.
2 English money was a problem, but after a few days he got used to it. 3 Slowly he's getting used to living in London.

2 1 Dimitri's used to hearing English now. 2 He still isn't used to drinking tea with milk in it. 3 he's not (he isn't) used to swimming in a cold sea.

112

Practice

be	used to	something	*I'm not used to English weather.*
get		do**ing** something	*I'm not used to carrying an umbrella.*
			I'm getting used to living here.
			I'm getting used to the traffic.

1 Three months ago Matthew was a university student. Now he has just started his first job and he is finding it difficult. Why is it difficult?
Example: get up/6.45 *He isn't used to getting up at 6.45.*

1 travel/to work

....

2 start work/8.30

....

3 wear/a suit and tie

....

4 sit/at a desk all day

....

5 work/nine hours a day

....

6 have/money to spend

....

2 Peter and Liz Harvey emigrated to Australia a year ago. Kerry Merton, a journalist on a local newspaper, interviewed them. Complete the interview, using forms of *get used to* or *be used to* + noun or *-ing*.

Kerry: Was it difficult when you first arrived in Australia?

Peter: Yes, some things were difficult to (1) .... Other things were easy. We soon (2) .... the Australian accent, for example. That wasn't a problem. And of course we (3 drive) .... already .... on the left. But we had to (4) .... the road signs and distances in kilometres, not miles.

Kerry: How did you find the climate when you first arrived?

Liz: We (5 not be) .... the heat. When we were in England, we (6 be) .... short, warm summers. But now here in Australia we're trying to (7) .... long, hot summers.

Kerry: Is there anything else you find strange?

Liz: Yes, we still (8 not be) .... the feeling of space.

Peter: And I (9 not see) .... dead kangaroos by the side of the road!

Liz: And we will never (10 have) .... Christmas dinner on the beach, in the middle of summer!

3 Bob Summers is 78. His wife died last year and now he is living on his own. He is not finding it easy. Complete the text, using *get/be used to* + noun, pronoun or *-ing*.

We were married fifty years ago, so I (1 share) .... everything. I (2 do) .... everything together with her. Now it's very different. I (3 not be) .... (live) on my own. I'm trying to (4) .... it, but it isn't easy. I can't (5 have) .... nobody to talk to. I (6 be) .... (cook) for myself, that isn't a problem. But the biggest problem is in the mornings. I (7 not be) .... still .... (wake up) and finding nobody in bed beside me. I (8) .... never .... that.

113

36 The verb *need*

Nick wants to go to New York. He's in a travel agent's.
'Do I need a visa?'
'If you're British, you don't need a visa. You just need to take a
passport.'
'I need to hire a car while I'm over there. Do I need an international
driving licence?'
'Yes, you do, and you'll also need a credit card.'
'What about the violence and crime in New York?'
'You don't need to worry too much. You just need to be careful where
you go, especially at night.'
'So I needn't buy a gun then?'
'No, you needn't.'
'If I go in September, what sort of clothes do I need to take?'
'It's warm in New York in September, so you needn't take winter
clothes.'

Step 1 | Uses of *need*

- We use *need* + noun/pronoun when we talk about the things it's necessary to have.
  > You'll **need** *a credit card.* (= It'll be necessary to have one.)
  > *Do I* **need** *a visa?* (= Is it necessary to have a visa?)

Note: *Need* has two negative forms: *don't need/doesn't need* and *needn't*. When we're talking about something that isn't necessary we use *don't need/doesn't need* + noun, not *needn't*.
  > You **don't need** *a visa.* (NOT You needn't a visa.)

- We use *need* + infinitive with *to* when we talk about an obligation or necessity in the present or the future.
  > *I* **need to drive** *while I'm over there.* (= That's necessary.)
  > *You* **need to be** *careful.* (= It's necessary to be careful.)

- We use *don't/doesn't need to* or *needn't* when we mean it isn't necessary to do something.
  > *I* **needn't buy** *a gun then?* OR *I* **don't need to** *buy a gun.*

- Note that *You don't need to/You needn't* mean the same as *You don't have to.* (See Unit 27.)
  > You **don't need to** *worry too much.*
  > OR *You* **needn't** *worry too much.*
  > (= You don't have to worry too much.)

- *Needn't* isn't used much in American English.

CHECK QUESTIONS 1 **Rewrite the sentences, using *need*.**
1 It's necessary for Nick to hire a car when he's in the States.
2 Is it necessary for him to have an international licence?
3 It isn't necessary for him to buy a gun.

Step 2 | Forms of the verb *need*

Affirmative
I need to go
He needs to go
They need to go

Negative
I don't need to go
He doesn't need to go
They don't need to go

OR I needn't go
He needn't go
They needn't go

Questions
Do I need to go?
Does he need to go?
Do they need to go?

● The verb *need* has no continuous form. You can't say, for example: 'You're needing a passport.'

CHECK QUESTIONS 2 **Put in forms of the verb *need*.**
1 Nick ... a visa.
2 But he ... a passport.
3 ... take winter clothes? No, he doesn't.

Step 3 | *Needn't have* + past participle or *didn't need to* + infinitive?

Six weeks later Nick goes back to the travel agent's.
'New York was great! I needn't have worried about the crime and violence. I didn't see any.'
'So you didn't need to take a gun?'
'No, I didn't. And I needn't have had travel insurance. I was never ill and nothing was stolen. And you were right. I didn't need to take winter clothes. The temperature never went below 30°!'

● We use *needn't have* + past participle when someone did something that wasn't necessary. It was a waste of time or effort. But at the time they didn't know this.
 *I **needn't have worried** about it.* (But he worried about it.)
 *I **needn't have taken** insurance.* (But he took insurance.)

● We use *didn't need to* + infinitive when it wasn't necessary to do something. But it isn't always clear if it was done or not.
 *I **didn't need to take** winter clothes.*
(It wasn't necessary, but it isn't clear if he took winter clothes or not.)

● Compare *I **needn't have taken** winter clothes.*
(= He took winter clothes, but it wasn't necessary.)
 *I **didn't need to take** winter clothes.*
(= Perhaps he took them, perhaps not, but it wasn't necessary.)

CHECK QUESTIONS 3 **Add a sentence with *didn't need to* or *needn't have*.**
1 He took £1,000. He didn't spend it all. He ...
2 He took two credit cards, but he only used one. He ...
3 He didn't have a visa. The agent said it wasn't necessary.

ANSWERS TO CHECK QUESTIONS 1, 2 AND 3 **1** 1 Nick needs to hire a car when he's in the States. 2 Does he need an international licence? 3 He doesn't need to buy a gun. OR He needn't buy a gun.

2 1 doesn't need 2 needs 3 Does he need to
3 1 He needn't have taken £1,000 (OR so much money). 2 He needn't have taken two credit cards. 3 He didn't need to have a visa.

Practice

1 **A journalist is talking to the manager of Bristol City, an English football team. The team is not playing well at the moment. Complete the dialogue, using parts of the verb *need*.**

Journalist: What (1) .... you .... to make the team more successful?

Manager: We (2) .... a bit of luck and we (3) .... win a few matches.

Journalist: But can you do that with the present team?

Manager: No, I (4) .... buy one or two new players.

Journalist: How much money (5) .... ?

Manager: I (6) .... much, only about a million pounds.

Journalist: Wouldn't it be cheaper just to get a new manager?

Manager: No, we (7) .... a new manager and I (8) .... advice from people like you who know nothing about the game!

2 **Suzy has come home late. Her mother is waiting for her. Complete the sentences, using *needn't have* + past participle.**

Suzy: Hi, mum. Why aren't you in bed? You (1 wait up) .... for me.

Mum: I was worried about you.

Suzy: But you (2 worry) .... I was OK.

Mum: I didn't know where you were so I rang Rachel's mother.

Suzy: But you (3 ring) ....

I was perfectly OK.

Mum: I even phoned the police.

Suzy: Oh no. You (4 phone) .... the police. I was only an hour or two late.

Mum: How did you get home? I gave you money for a taxi.

Suzy: You (5 give) .... me the money. A boy called Chris gave me a lift.

3 **Simon took a history exam yesterday. Complete the sentences, using *didn't need to* or *needn't have*.**

1 The exam didn't start till 10.30 so he knew he (get up) .... early.

2 He (get) .... there till 10.15 but he got there at 10.00 so he (worry) .... about being late.

3 He took three pens with him. He (take) .... so many because he only used one!

4 He knew there wouldn't be any questions about the American Civil War so he (read) .... the chapter about it in his history book.

5 Just before the exam he read all his notes on the American War of Independence. He (look at) .... them because there weren't any questions about it.

6 When he left the examination hall he knew he (worry) .... about the result because he was certain he'd pass.

On July 17th, 1965 Micky Nash of Finchley, north London wrote a letter to his brother, Frank. He gave it to his wife and asked her to post it for him when she went to the shops. Micky wrote his brother a letter because he needed money. He explained the problem to him. He'd just lost his job, and he wanted to buy a pram for his new baby. He wrote: 'Can you lend me £20? I'll give you the money back when I get a new job.'

On July 13th, 1995 Micky received the reply. 'I got your letter yesterday, asking for £20. I can lend it to you, but nowadays I think a pram will cost you a bit more than that! And do you really need a pram for your 30-year-old son?!' Frank then went to the post office and showed them the letter. They promised him an official apology.

Step 1 | Verb + indirect object + direct object

- Some verbs can have two objects, an indirect object and a direct object. Normally the indirect object refers to a person, and comes first.

verb +	indirect object +	direct object
Micky wrote	*his brother*	*a letter.*

(*His brother* is the person who Micky wrote to – the indirect object. *A letter* is what Micky wrote – the direct object.)

He showed	*them*	*Micky's letter.*
Can you lend	*me*	*£20?*
I'll give	*you*	*the money.*

CHECK QUESTIONS 1 **Write the correct word order.**

1 Micky/his brother/wanted/him/to lend/some money.
2 He/a letter/him/sent.

Step 2 | Verb + direct object + *to* + indirect object

- We sometimes use *to* with the indirect object, which then comes after the direct object.

verb +	direct object +	indirect object
Micky wrote	*a letter*	*to his brother.*
He gave	*it*	*to his wife.*

- We use *to* + the indirect object when we want to emphasise the indirect object. Compare these two sentences from the text:

    A *Micky wrote a letter to his brother.*
    B *Micky wrote his brother a letter because he needed money.*

In sentence A we want to say who Micky sent the letter to, so we emphasise *his brother* by saying *to his brother*.

In sentence B, we already know he's written to his brother. Now we want to say why he wrote, so we don't need to emphasise *his brother*.

- We also use *to* with the indirect object:
when both objects are pronouns (*it, him, you, them*, etc.).
> *I can lend **it to you**.*
(In informal English we can say: *I can lend you it.* OR *I can lend it you.*)
or when the direct object is a pronoun (*it, them*).
> *He gave **it to his wife**.*

- We must use *to* with the verbs *describe, explain, mention, report, suggest*.
> *He explained the problem **to him**.*
(NOT He explained him the problem.)

CHECK QUESTIONS 2 **Complete the sentences, using *to*.**
1 Micky wrote the letter and (sent/his brother/it)
2 (He/the letter/his wife/showed) when he'd finished it.
3 (He/her/it/read)

Step 3 | *To or for?*

- We often use an indirect object or *to* + an indirect object with the following verbs:
bring, give, hand, lend, offer, pass, owe, pay, read, recommend, sell, send, show, teach, tell, throw, write.
> *Micky Nash **wrote** a letter **to his brother**.*
We use *to* + the indirect object when we're talking about something which passes from one person to another.

- But we use *for* + the indirect object when we're talking about doing something that will be of value to another person, or when one person does something instead of another person.
> *He wanted to buy a pram **for** his new baby.*
(OR *He wanted to buy his new baby a pram.*)
> *Do you really need to get a pram **for** your son?!*
(OR *Do you really need to get your son a pram?!*)
> *He asked her to post the letter **for** him when she went to the shops.*

- We often use *for* + an indirect object with the following verbs: *book, bring, build, buy, choose, cook, cut, do, fetch, find, get, keep, leave, make, order, play, prepare, reserve, save, sing, take*.

- With some verbs (*allow, cause, charge, cost, fine, promise, refuse, wish*) we must use the indirect object on its own. We don't use *to* or *for*.
> *A pram will cost **you** a bit more than that!*
> *They promised **him** an official apology.*

CHECK QUESTIONS 3 **Write complete sentences, adding either *to* or *for*.**
1 Micky didn't post the letter himself. (his wife/him/it/posted)
2 Micky and his wife went to the shops (the baby/a new pram/to buy)
3 Frank/the letter/the post office/took
4 They couldn't/him/explain/why the letter had arrived so late

---

ANSWERS TO CHECK QUESTIONS 1, 2 AND 3

1 1 Micky wanted his brother to lend him some money. 2 He sent him a letter.

2 1 Micky wrote the letter and sent it to his brother. 2 He showed the letter to his wife 3 He read it to her.

3 1 His wife posted it for him. 2 to buy a new pram for the baby. 3 Frank took the letter to the post office. 4 They couldn't explain to him why the letter had arrived so late.

Practice

- An indirect object on its own goes before the direct object:.
  *She gave **the man** some money.*   *She made **him** some sandwiches.*
- Order: we put the object that gives more important information second.
- We use *to* or *for* when we want to emphasise the indirect object.
- An indirect object with *to* or *for* goes after the direct object.
  The man gave the money to his friends.   *And he bought some food for his dog.*
- If the direct object is a pronoun, we normally use *to* or *for* with the indirect object.
  Give it to me.   *Show them to your son.*

---

1 Last week Mrs Julia Carter won £50,000 in a competition. Complete the sentences in the dialogue, using a direct and an indirect object after the verb. Decide which object is more important and put it in the best position. Use *to* or *for* where necessary.

A: What did Mrs Carter get for her family?
B: (1 She/her husband/gave/a new car.)

....

(2 And/some new clothes/her daughter/ bought/ she)

....

A: And what about her parents?
(3 Did she/them/ give/anything?)

....

B: Yes, (4 she/a holiday in Thailand/them/ booked)

....

A: Who else did she buy things for?
B: (5 She/her brother/bought/a new computer.)

....

(6 And she/all her neighbours/some flowers/got)

....

A: What did she do with the rest of the money?
B: She put some of it in the bank, (7 and/she/the rest/gave/charity)

....

A: Which charities did she send it to?
B: (8 She/£3,000/Save the Children/sent)

....

(9 And she/gave/£2,000/the Red Cross)

....

A: You seem to know her very well. What did she give you?
B: (10 She/me/didn't give/anything)

....

(11 She just showed/the £50,000 cheque/me)

.... !

2 It is Gemma's birthday. Paul has got a present for her. Complete the sentences, using *to* or *for*.

'I bought something (1) .... you in town this

morning.'

'What is it? Show it (2) .... me. I like the

wrapping paper!'

'Yes, it's nice, isn't it? Save it (3) .... me, then I

can use it again.'

'OK. I'll open it carefully. I need some scissors.'

'Can you fetch them (4) .... me?'

'Here you are. Well, what do you think?'

'It's a blue envelope.'

'Well, blue's your favourite colour. That's why I

chose it (5) .... you! Go on, open it.'

'It's a hotel reservation! 3 nights in Venice.

That's absolutely brilliant!'

'I haven't got the plane tickets yet. The travel

agent's going to send them (6) .... me. And

I've booked a table (7) .... us at the

Vietnamese restaurant this evening. They're

going to cook something special (8) .... you

because it's your birthday.'

'That sounds brilliant! Thanks, Paul. Why don't

you sit down and have a cup of tea. I'll make

one (9) .... you now.'

38

If sentences:
1st and 2nd conditional

> Cal and Lee are football fans. Their team, Leeds United, are playing tonight. Cal's talking about the game.
> 'They'll win the championship if they beat Arsenal tonight. And if they win the championship, they'll play in the European Cup next season.'

Step 1 | 1st conditional: *If* + present simple + *will*

- We use *if* + a verb in the present simple to talk about a possible future action or situation. The *if* clause is often followed by another clause with *will* or *won't*.
  *If they **win** the championship, they'**ll play** in the European Cup.*
  (Leeds may win the championship or they may not. Winning is a factual possibility.)

- *If* + present simple (*if* clause) + future *will* (main clause)
  *If they **win** the championship, they'**ll play** in the European Cup.*
  This sentence is about the future, but we don't use a verb in the future in the *if* clause. We don't say 'If they will win the championship.' We use a present tense, often the present simple.

- We can put the *if* clause at the beginning or at the end.
  *They'll win the championship **if they beat Arsenal tonight**.*
  OR ***If they beat Arsenal tonight**, they'll win the championship.*
  Note: Don't confuse *if* and *when*.
  ***If** they beat Arsenal tonight, they'll win the championship.*
  (*If* = a condition. We're talking about a possibility.)
  ***When** they beat Arsenal tonight, they'll win the championship.*
  (*When* = a point in time. It's certain they'll beat Arsenal.)

CHECK QUESTIONS 1 ▷ **Complete the questions.**
1 What (happen) if ...? They'll win the championship.
2 What (happen) if ...? They'll play in the European Cup.

Step 2 | *If* + a present tense + *can, should, may, might*, etc.

> Cal's still talking about Leeds United.
> 'And if they play in the European Cup, they might make a lot of money. If they make a lot of money, they can buy some new players. And if they buy new players, they should win the championship again next year ...'

- In addition to the future *will*, we can also use *can, could, should, ought to, may, might, must* in the main clause.
  *If they play in the Cup, they **might** make a lot of money.*
  (= Perhaps they'll make a lot of money.)
  *If they make a lot of money, they **can** buy new players.*
  (= They'll be able to buy new players.)
  *If they buy new players, they **should** win the championship again.*
  (= They'll probably win the championship again.)

Write these sentences in a different way. Use *should, can, might*.
1 If Leeds play badly, perhaps Arsenal will win tonight. If Leeds play badly, ...
2 If Leeds play well, they'll probably beat Arsenal. If Leeds play well, ...
3 If they buy new players, they'll be able to improve the team. If they buy ...

Step 3 | *If* + a present tense + the present simple or the imperative

'Listen, Cal, if we don't leave now, we'll miss the bus. So, if you've finished talking, can we go? Come on! If you're coming to the match, hurry up! And if you want to get in, don't forget your ticket! They don't let people in if they don't have a ticket.'
'OK, OK! I'm looking for my scarf. Leeds always win if I wear my scarf.'

- We can use the construction *If* + present simple + present simple when we're talking about something that's always true.

Present simple (main clause)   **If + present simple (*if* clause)**
*Leeds always **win***   *if I **wear** my scarf.*
(= Every time I wear my scarf, Leeds win.)
*They **don't let** people in*   *if they **don't have** a ticket.*
(= They never let people in without a ticket.)

- We can use an imperative (a command) in the main clause.

If + present (*if* clause)   +   **imperative (main clause)**
If you're coming to the match,   ***hurry up**!*
If you want to get in,   ***don't forget** your ticket!*
Note also:
If + present perfect
*If you**'ve finished** talking, can we go?* (= If you've finished now.)
If + present continuous
*If you**'re coming**, hurry up!* (= If you intend to come.)

Put the verb in the correct tense.
1 If you (want) to get into the ground, (not forget) your ticket!
2 If you (go) to an 'all-ticket' match, you (need) a ticket to get in.
3 If Cal (wear) his scarf, Leeds always (win).
4 Come on, Cal! If you (come) to the match, hurry up!

Step 4 | 2nd conditional: *If* + a past tense + *would*

Lee and Cal have missed the bus! The next bus is in 35 minutes. An old man on a bike is giving them some advice.
Old man: If I were you, I wouldn't wait for the next bus, I'd walk.
Lee: We haven't got time. If we walked, it would take us an hour to get there, and we'd miss the first 20 minutes of the game.
Cal: There wouldn't be a problem if there were more buses.
Lee: If we had a car, we'd be all right.
Cal: No, we wouldn't. If we went by car, we might not find a place to park.
Lee: If we had £30, we could get a taxi.
Old man: Well, If I was going to a big match, I'd leave home much earlier. I wouldn't risk missing the bus, like you two. It's your own fault.
Lee: Cal, if we asked him nicely, we could borrow this old man's bike!

- We use *if* + a verb in the past simple to talk about an action or situation in the present or the future which is improbable, hypothetical or imaginary. The *if* clause is often followed by the conditional *would* or *wouldn't*.

  If + past simple   +   would
  If we **had** a car,   we**'d be** all right.
  (Imaginary: They haven't got a car.)

- Note the difference between the 1st and 2nd conditional:

  *If we **walk**, it **will take** us an hour to get there.* (1st)

  (This is a factual possibility. It's an open choice. They can walk or not. See Step 1.)

  But Lee says: *If we **walked**, it **would take** us an hour to get there.* (2nd)

  (This is an unreal hypothesis, because Lee doesn't want to walk. He doesn't want to miss the beginning of the game.)

- To emphasise the improbability or the impossibility we often use *were* instead of *was*, but *was* can also be used here.

  *If I **were** you, I wouldn't wait.* (OR If I was you)

- We can use *could* or *might* in the second clause.

  *If we had a car, we **might not** find anywhere to park.*
  (= Perhaps we wouldn't find anywhere to park.)
  *If we had £30, we **could** get a taxi.*
  (= It would be possible to get a taxi.)

- If necessary, we can use the past continuous in the *if* clause.

  *If I **was going** to a big match, I'd leave home much earlier.*

- We form the conditional with *would* + an infinitive without *to*.

Affirmative	**Negative**	**Question**
I'd (would) be late	I wouldn't be late	Would I be late?
He'd be late	He wouldn't be late	Would he be late? Etc.

CHECK QUESTIONS 4 **Complete the sentences.**
1 Why don't they walk? Because if ...
2 There aren't many buses. If ... , ... a problem.
3 Could they get a taxi? They could, if ...

ANSWERS TO
CHECK QUESTIONS
1, 2, 3 AND 4

1 1 What will happen if they beat Arsenal?
2 What will happen if they win the championship?

2 1 If Leeds play badly, Arsenal might win tonight.   2 If Leeds play well, they should beat Arsenal.   3 If they buy new players, they can improve the team.

3 1 want don't forget! 2 go need 3 wears win 4 you're coming

4 1 Because if they walked, it would take them an hour to get there.   2 If there were more buses, there wouldn't be a problem.   3 if they had £30.

Practice

> - For a possible action or situation: *If* + the simple present + *will/won't*
>   *If* Leeds United **win** 1-0, the fans **will** be happy.
> - For an improbable or hypothetical action or situation: *If* + the simple past + *would/wouldn't*
>   *If* Leeds United **won** 7-0, the fans **would** be very happy.

1 The Wright family are talking about a possible holiday in the south of Spain. Complete the text using the correct tense of the verbs (present simple or future).

Mark: If we (1 go) .... in the

summer, there (2 be) .... more

tourists and it (3 be) .... very

hot. If we (4 go) .... at Christmas,

there (5 not be) .... as many

tourists and the weather (6 be) ....

cooler.

Carol: If we (7 take) .... the car, it

(8 take) .... much longer to get

there, but we (9 be able to) ....

take more luggage with us.

Anna: If we go by plane it (10 be) ....

quicker, but it (11 cost) ....

more too, and we (12 not see) ....

anything of France.

2 Oliver is depressed at the moment. He is talking about things he has not got and things he cannot do. Complete the sentences with the correct tense of the verb (past simple or conditional).

1 If I (have) .... more money, I

(be able to) .... get a flat.

2 I (find) .... a better job if there

(be) .... more jobs available.

3 I (be) .... happier if I

(have) .... more friends.

4 If I (be) .... more adventurous, I

(go) .... abroad.

5 My parents (not be) .... so critical

if they (understand) .... me better.

3 Complete the dialogue, putting the verbs into the correct tense.

'If you (1 want) .... to learn Spanish, you

must go to Spain. If I (2 be) .... you, I

(3 spend) .... a month in Spain.'

'No, I couldn't afford it. If I (4 go) .... to

Spain, I (5 have to) .... pay for

my lessons and my accommodation.'

'Well, (6 you go) .... if you

(7 not have to) .... pay for your

accommodation? You see, I've got some

Spanish friends in Cordoba. You (8 be able to)

.... stay with them. I (9 write) ....

to them if you (10 like) ....'

'But if I (11 stay) .... with your friends, I

(12 have to) .... pay them.'

'No, it (13 not be) .... necessary.

They want to learn English, so if you (14 give)

.... them English lessons, you

(15 be able to) .... stay there

free.'

39

If in past situations: 3rd conditional

On Tuesday evening, November 16th last year, David Lynch flew back to England from Tunis. In England the weather was terrible. If the weather had been good, David would have arrived home on Tuesday evening, quite normally, and his life wouldn't have changed. If it hadn't been foggy, they would have landed at London Airport. But they didn't land in London.

Step 1 | *If* + past perfect + *would have*

- We use the past perfect in the *if* clause to talk about something that didn't happen or a situation that didn't exist in the past.
  *If the weather **had been** good, they **would have landed** in London.*
  (The weather wasn't good. It was terrible.)
- We use the past conditional in the main clause.

Past perfect	Past conditional
*If the weather **had been** good,*	*they **would have landed** in London.*

Note: We don't use the past conditional in the *if* clause. We don't say 'If the weather would have been good, ...'

CHECK QUESTIONS 1 **If it hadn't been foggy, they would have landed at London Airport, and David's life wouldn't have changed.**
1 Was it foggy?
2 Did they land at London Airport?
3 Did David's life change?

Step 2 | Forms of the past conditional

- The past conditional = *would have* + a past participle.

Affirmative	Negative	Questions
I'd (would) have won	I wouldn't have won	Would I have won?
He'd have won	He wouldn't have won	Would he have won?
We'd have won	We wouldn't have won	Would we have won?
Etc.		

- There are two possible contracted forms:
  I'd have won OR I would've won, etc.
- Note the pronunciation: I'd have /aidəv/ won. I would've /wʊdəv/ won. I wouldn't have /wʊdntəv/ won.

Note: *had* and *would* both have the contracted form *'d*.
  If he'd (= had) landed in London, he'd (= would) have got home on time.

CHECK QUESTIONS 2 **Complete the sentences.**
1 If I'd been on the plane, I (be) worried.
2 I (not take) the plane if it had been foggy.
3 If the plane had landed in London, he (get) home on time?

Step 3 | *If* + past perfect + *could have* or *might have*

> If the weather had been better, there wouldn't have been a problem. They could have landed in London quite easily, and it wouldn't have been necessary to fly to Scotland. If David had needed to get home that night, he could have gone back to London by train. But he decided to stay in a hotel. At the reception desk a woman dropped her pen. He picked it up for her. If he hadn't been standing there, he wouldn't have seen her. If she hadn't dropped her pen, he might not have noticed her. If he hadn't been there, someone else might have picked it up.

- We can also use *could have* and *might have* in the main clause.
  *If the weather had been better, they **could have landed** in London.*
  (= They would have been able to land. It would have been possible to land.)
  *If he hadn't been there, someone else **might have picked it up**.*
  (= Perhaps someone else would have picked the pen up.)
  (For *could have* and *might have* see also Unit 29.)
- We sometimes use the past perfect continuous (see Unit 13) in the *if* clause.
  *If he **hadn't been standing** there, he wouldn't have seen her.*

CHECK QUESTIONS 3 **Answer the questions.**
1 If he'd needed to get home that night, what could he have done?
2 What might have happened if the woman hadn't dropped her pen?

Step 4 | *If* + past perfect + *would* or *would be* + *-ing*

> David and Hannah, the woman he met in the hotel, are now married and living in Scotland. They often talk about their first meeting.
> 'If I hadn't dropped my pen, I wouldn't know you now and I wouldn't be wearing this ring.'
> 'Yes, it's funny. If I hadn't met you, I'd still be living in London. And if someone else had picked your pen up, I wouldn't be here with you now.'

- We sometimes link the past with the present by using *would* or *would be* + - *ing*.
  If + past perfect (past action) + **would (present situation)**
  *If I **hadn't dropped** my pen,*   *I **wouldn't know** you now.*
  If + past perfect (past action) + **would be + -ing (present situation)**
  *If I **hadn't met** you,*   *I'd still **be living** in London now.*

CHECK QUESTIONS 4 **Make sentences with *if*.**
1 He met her. He isn't living in London now.
2 She dropped her pen. He knows her now.
3 He picked her pen up. He's here with her now.

ANSWERS TO CHECK QUESTIONS 1, 2, 3, AND 4

1 1 Yes, it was.   2 No, they didn't.   3 Yes, it did.
2 1 I'd have been worried.   2 I wouldn't have taken   3 would he have got home on time?
3 1 He could have gone back to London on the airline bus.   2 He might not have noticed her.

4 1 If he hadn't met her, he'd still be living in London now.   2 If she hadn't dropped her pen, he wouldn't know her now.   3 If he hadn't picked her pen up, he wouldn't be here with her now.

Practice

If + past perfect   +   **would have, could have, might have**
If the train had been late,   Jenny and I would have missed the plane.
= The train wasn't late. We didn't miss the plane.
If + past perfect   +   **would or would be + -ing**
If the train had been late,   we'd be very angry now.
= The train wasn't late. We aren't angry now.

1 Sally's boyfriend, Rory, has just arrived home from Sweden. She did not know he was coming. Complete the dialogue using the past perfect and *would have*.

'If I (1 know) .... you were

coming, I (2 make) .... you a

meal.'

'I (3 phone) .... you if I (4 have)

.... time, but I've been travelling

all day. And if I (5 phone) ....

you, it (6 not be) .... a surprise!'

'Yes, but what (7 you do) ....

if I (8 not be) .... here?'

'I (9 go) .... to a hotel, I suppose.'

'But you said you were going to be in Sweden

for a month.'

'I know, but if I (10 stay) .... there

any longer, I (11 go) .... crazy. I

was missing you so much.'

2 Rosie March does not usually go on the motorway to work. But this morning she did and she was involved in an accident with a lorry carrying dangerous chemicals. Complete the sentences with these clauses:

he would have seen Rosie's car.
if the fire brigade hadn't arrived and put out the fire.
she might have been killed.
the driver could have stopped in time.
if she'd taken her normal route to work.

1 If she hadn't been wearing her seat-belt,

....

2 If the lorry's brakes had been working.

....

3 Rosie wouldn't be in hospital now

....

4 If the lorry driver hadn't been looking at his map

....

5 The lorry might have exploded

....

....

3 Jerry Stamp had a very lucky day yesterday. Look at these situations and write sentences using *if* + the past perfect (simple or continuous) + the past conditional.
Example: That morning there was a big traffic jam because a lorry had crashed. *If the lorry hadn't crashed, there wouldn't have been a big traffic jam.*

1 Fortunately Jerry didn't take his car, so he got to work on time.

....

....

2 At the office there was a big mistake in the sales figures. Jerry found the mistake because he checked the figures.

....

....

3 At lunch he didn't choose the chicken. The people who chose the chicken had food poisoning.

....

....

4 It was raining when Jerry went home, but he didn't get wet because had his umbrella.

....

....

5 He bought a paper at the newsagent's. The newsagent persuaded him to buy a lottery ticket. Jerry won £500.

....

....

40 Unless, provided (that) As long as, in case

Rosanna Fisher works at an outdoor activities centre on the west coast of Scotland. She teaches mountain climbing, scuba diving and hang-gliding. She's talking to some young people who've just arrived at the centre.
'You can't do any of the activities unless you're with an instructor. We won't let you start an activity unless you have the correct equipment. You can't go scuba diving unless you've done the training course. And remember, you can't leave the centre unless you say where you're going.'

Step 1 | Unless

- *Unless* = *if ... not*.

	unless +	affirmative verb
You can't leave the centre	*unless you*	*say where you're going.*
OR	**if** +	**negative verb**
You can't leave the centre	*if you*	*don't say where you're going.*

- *Unless* is followed by the same tenses as *if* in the 1st and 2nd conditional (see Unit 38). It can't be followed by *will* or *would*.
  *We won't let you start an activity **unless you have** the correct equipment.*
  (NOT unless you will have the correct equipment)

CHECK QUESTIONS 1 **Rewrite these sentences using *unless*.**
1 You can't go hang-gliding if you aren't 16 or over.
2 If you haven't got a medical certificate, you can't go scuba diving.

Step 2 | As long as, provided (that)/providing (that)

Two young people are asking Rosanna if they can do certain things.
'Can I go into town this evening, Rosanna?'
'Yes, provided that you go with a friend, and as long as you get back by 10.30 p.m.'
'Will it be safe to go windsurfing this afternoon?'
'Yes. You'll be OK providing there's an instructor with you and as long as you don't go too far out to sea.'

- We use *provided/providing (that)* or *as long as* to talk about a condition. They're stronger than *if* and mean *only if*.
 As long as and *provided/providing (that)* all mean the same and they're followed by the same tenses as *if* (in the 1st and 2nd conditional).
   *You can go into town, **provided that** you go with a friend.*
   (= You can go, *only if* you go with a friend.)

*You'll be OK, **as long as** you don't go too far out to sea.*
(= You'll be OK, *only if* you don't go too far out to sea.)

- We often leave out *that* after *provided* and *providing*.
*You'll be OK, **providing** there's an instructor with you.*
(= *You'll be OK, **providing that** there's an instructor with you.*)

CHECK QUESTIONS 2 **Complete these sentences with *as long as* or *provided/providing (that)*.**
1 Mark can go windsurfing ... there (be) enough wind.
2 Emily can go into town ... (get back) late.

Step 3 | In case

> Rosanna's taking a group of young people into the mountains tomorrow.
> 'Bring a waterproof jacket with you in case it rains and an extra sweater in case it gets cold. We'll take survival bags with us in case we have to spend the night on the mountain. Last month I took a group out and we took survival bags and extra sweaters in case the weather changed. Well, it suddenly got very foggy and we were on the mountain for 48 hours. So, don't forget your survival bags in case we can't get home tonight.'

- We use *in case* to talk about the precautions we take before we do something. We use a present tense after *in case* when we talk about the future. We don't use *will*.
*You'll each need a jacket **in case** it **rains**.* (NOT it will rain)
(= Take a jacket as a precaution because it might rain.)
*Take your survival bags **in case** we **can't get home** tonight.*
(= Take them as a precaution because we might not get home.)

- *In case* doesn't mean the same as *if*. Compare:
      A   B
Bring a waterproof jacket   *in case it starts to rain.*
(= Bring a waterproof jacket when we leave, because it might start to rain later.)
      B   A
Bring a waterproof jacket   *if it starts to rain.*
(= Bring a waterproof jacket after the rain has started.)
In both sentences A happens first.

- We can also use *in case* to talk about precautions we took in the past.
*We **took** survival bags and extra sweaters **in case** the weather **changed**.*
(= We took survival bags and extra sweaters because it was possible the weather would change.)

CHECK QUESTIONS 3 **Put in *if* or *in case*.**
1 We should get back for dinner ... we leave now.
2 We'll take plenty of food with us ... we don't get back for dinner.
3 We'll also take some matches ... we need to light a fire.

ANSWERS TO
CHECK QUESTIONS
1, 2 AND 3

1 1 You can't go hang-gliding unless you're 16 or over. 2 Unless you've got a medical certificate, you can't go scuba diving.

2 1 Mark can go windsurfing provided/providing (that) there's enough wind. (OR as long as)
2 Emily can go into town as long as she doesn't get back late. OR provided/providing

3 1 if 2 in case 3 in case

Practice

> - *They won't play the match tomorrow unless the weather changes.*
> (= They won't play the match tomorrow if the weather doesn't change.)
> *Unless* + an affirmative verb = *if* + a negative verb.
> - *As long as, provided/providing (that)* have the meaning of *only if.*
> - We use *in case* to talk about precautions we take.
> - In future sentences we don't use *will* after *unless, as long as, provided/providing (that)* and *in case.* We use a present tense.

1 **Simon Spellar is making a speech for the Alternative Party. Rewrite the sentences, using *unless*.**

1 If we don't stop polluting the sea, we'll kill everything that lives in it.

   ....
   ....

2 We must forget about economic growth, or we'll use up all the earth's natural resources.

   ....
   ....

3 We must act now, or there won't be a future for our grandchildren.

   ....
   ....

4 But we can't change the world if we don't change ourselves.

   ....
   ....

5 If people don't cooperate with each other, we'll destroy ourselves.

   ....
   ....

2 **Gemma is phoning Martha to see if she wants to go camping with her. Use *unless* or *as long as/provided/providing* to complete the dialogue.**

'Hi, Martha. I'm going camping this weekend
(1) .... the weather's fine. Can you come?'

'Jerry's invited me to a party on Saturday night, so I can't come (2) .... I say no to Jerry. Where are you going?'

'To Fistral Beach. I'm taking the surfboards, so
(3) .... there's some good surf, we should have a great time. I can pick you up at

about 8.30 on Saturday morning, (4) ...., of course, you don't want to come.'

'I'd love to come! (5)........................ you don't drive too fast. I'm not coming (6) .... you promise to drive slowly.'

'I promise. But what about Jerry? You said you couldn't come (7) .... you said no to him.'

'I know. But I think it'll be OK (8) .... I can think of a good excuse.'

'Tell him your mother's ill and that you're going to see her on Saturday (9) .... she gets better before then. Anyway, I'll pick you up at 8.30 (10) .... the weather's good.'

3 **Mr and Mrs Crimp are going on holiday abroad. They are preparing their trip. Rewrite the sentences, using *in case*.**

1 We'd better reserve our seats on the train. It might be full.

   ....
   ....

2 I'm going to insure the video camera. It might get stolen.

   ....
   ....

3 I gave the travel agent our telephone number this morning. They said it was possible they would need to contact us.

   ....
   ....

4 I phoned the bank yesterday. I thought they might have forgotten to get our travellers' cheques.

   ....
   ....

41

I wish .../If only ...

Louise, Melissa and Brad all share a flat just outside London. The two girls don't like some of Brad's habits.
'I wish Brad would stop smoking. The whole flat smells of cigarette smoke.'
'And I wish he wouldn't leave his clothes everywhere. He's so untidy.'
'And he never does any housework. If only he'd do the washing-up sometimes.'
'I sometimes wish we could persuade him to leave. If only he'd go and find another flat!'
'I wish I could just say to him 'Brad, we'd like you to leave'. But it's difficult.'

Step 1 | *Wish/If only + would*

- We use *wish* or *If only + would* when we want something or someone to change or when we want someone to do something.
    I wish Brad *would* stop smoking.   (Brad smokes; they want him to stop.)
    I wish he *wouldn't* leave his clothes everywhere.
    (Brad leaves his clothes everywhere. They want him to be more tidy.)

- We don't use *would* after *I wish I ...* and *I wish we ...* . We often use *could* after *I* and *we* to talk about a regret about a present or future inability.
    I wish I could just say to him "Brad, we'd like you to leave."
    (NOT: I wish I would just say to him ...)
    I wish we could persuade him to leave.
    (NOT: I wish we would persuade him to leave.)

- *I wish ...* and *If only ...* mean the same, but *If only ...* can express the wish more strongly.
    If only he'd go and find another flat!

CHECK QUESTIONS 1 **Complete the sentences.**
1 Melissa wishes that Brad ... the washing-up occasionally.
2 Louise: 'Brad, I wish you ... leave your clothes everywhere.'
3 Melissa: 'If only we ... persuade Brad to find another flat.'

Step 2 | *Wish/If only + the past simple/the past continuous*

Brad works in central London. He's talking to Louise and Melissa.
'I wish the flat was nearer the office. It's a long way to travel every day.'
'Yes, I bet you wish you had a nice flat in Chelsea.'
'Too expensive. I wish I was earning a lot more money.'
'Well, why don't you give up smoking, then you'd save some money?'
'I wish I didn't smoke, but I can't stop.'
'Yes, you could, if you tried.'
'You're criticising me again! If only you two were more tolerant. Sometimes I wish I lived on my own, then I could do what I want!'

- We use *wish* (or *If only*) + the past simple or the past continuous when we talk about a regret about a present situation.

    I wish I **didn't smoke**. (He smokes, but he regrets it.)

    I wish the flat **was** nearer the office. (It isn't near the office.)

    I wish I **was earning** a lot more money. (He isn't earning a lot more.)

    Note: We don't use *would* here. We don't say: 'I wish the flat would be nearer the office.'

- Note that with this construction we can use either *was* or *were* after *I, he, the flat*, etc. (1st and 3rd person singular):

    I wish the flat **was** (OR **were**) nearer the office.

    I wish I **was** (OR **were**) *earning a lot more money.*

CHECK QUESTIONS 2
Complete the sentences.
1 Brad wishes he (live) in his own flat.
2 He wishes he (have) a lot of money.
3 He wishes he (not smoke).

Step 3 | Wish/If only + the past perfect

It's a month later. Brad has left the flat. The two girls are talking about him.

'It seems strange without Brad, doesn't it?'

'Yes, I sometimes wish we hadn't asked him to leave. He was a very nice guy really. He had a great sense of humour. I wish we'd tried to discuss things with him.'

'I know. I wish I hadn't criticised him so much.'

'If only he hadn't been so untidy.'

'If only he hadn't smoked in the flat.'

'If only, if only! If only things had been different! Why are we talking like this? We can't change the past.'

- We use *wish* and *if only* + the past perfect when we talk about a regret we have about something that happened or didn't happen in the past.

    I wish we **hadn't asked** him to leave.

    (But they asked him to leave.)

    If only he **hadn't smoked** in the flat.

    (But he smoked in the flat.)

- We don't use *would have* after *wish/if only*.

    I wish we **'d tried (had tried)** *to talk to each other more.*

    (NOT I wish we would have tried.)

CHECK QUESTIONS 3
Complete the sentences.
1 They asked Brad to leave. Now they wish they ... him to leave.
2 Brad was untidy. Now Louise says: 'I wish he ... so untidy.'
3 Brad smoked a lot. They wish he ... in the flat.

ANSWERS TO
CHECK QUESTIONS
1, 2 AND 3

1 1 would do 2 wouldn't leave 3 could persuade

2 1 lived 2 had 3 didn't smoke

3 1 hadn't asked 2 hadn't been 3 hadn't smoked

Practice

Wish or *If only*
- We use *would* when we want something or someone to change or when we want someone to do something. We can't say "I wish I would, I wish we would".   *I wish it would stop rainng.*
- We use the past simple or the past continuous when we talk about a regret we have about a present situation.   *I wish the sun was shining.*
- We use the past perfect when we talk about a regret we have about something that happened or didn't happen in the past.   *I wish we hadn't come.*

---

1 **Steve plays the electric guitar. His father does not like it. They are having an argument. Write sentences using *I wish* or *If only*. Use *would ('d)/wouldn't* (or *could* where necessary).**
Example: Play something tuneful! I wish ...
I wish you'd play something tuneful.

1 Steve! Turn the volume down!

   I wish you ....
2 Don't make so much noise!

   I wish you ....
3 I want to break that guitar!

   I wish I ....
4 Dad, I've got to practise. Try to understand!

   If only you ....
5 Well, practise somewhere else!

   If only you ....
6 Dad, don't be so intolerant!

   I wish parents ....
7 I want to get my own flat.

   I really wish I ....

2 **Sophie always watches the advertisements on television. She wants a lot of the things she sees. Make sentences using *I wish/If only* + the past simple or continuous.**
Example: She hasn't got a video camera.
I wish ...   *I wish I had a video camera.*

1 Her computer doesn't have a CD ROM. I

   wish my computer ....
2 Her dad hasn't got a Mercedes.

   If only ....
3 She isn't going to the Caribbean this winter.

   I wish ....

   ....
4 There isn't a swimming pool in her garden.

   If only ....

   ....

5 She doesn't look like a fashion model.

   I wish ....
6 She's got ordinary light brown hair.

   I wish .... ordinary light brown hair.
7 She lives in England.

   I wish .... in England.
8 She doesn't live in New York.

   If only ....

3 **Linda is having a party on Saturday. Gary is asking her about it. Complete the dialogue with the correct form of the verb after *I wish*.**

'How many people are coming to the party?'

'Only about ten. I wish there (1 be) ....

more people coming. I wish I (2 invite)

.... more.'

'Who's coming?'

'Er, James, Rick, Maggy, Rachel, er ...'

'Oh, I wish Rick (3 not come) ....

I wish you (4 not invite) ....

him. You know I don't like him.'

'I wish you (5 not talk)................................. like

that. Rick's a good friend of mine.'

'Sorry. I wish I (6 not say) .... it

now. Please don't tell Rick what I said.'

'Well, I wish you (7 not be) ....

so rude. I like Rick a lot. I wish I (8 not tell)

.... you he was coming. If you

don't want to come, just say so.'

'Listen, I wish you (9 stop) ....

talking about it. And I wish you (10 try) ....

.................to understand why I don't like him.'

'You're jealous, that's all!'

42

The infinitive of purpose
In order to   So that, so

> Sarah Judd's a student. She's saving up to pay for a trip to India. She's going to sell her motorbike and her CD player to make some money. In order to sell them she put an advert in the local paper last week. She works in a bar two evenings a week in order to earn some extra money. Her parents have given her £500 to help her pay for her trip.

Step 1 | Talking about the purpose of an action

- To talk about the purpose of an action we can use the infinitive of purpose (*to* + infinitive).

  *She's saving up **to pay** for a holiday.*
  *She works in a bar **to earn** some extra money.*

- We can also use *in order to* + infinitive. It is more formal.

  ***In order to** sell them she's put an advert in the local paper.*
  *She works in a bar **in order to** earn some extra money.*

We can use these two structures only if each part of the sentence has the same subject.

  Sarah's saving up to pay for a holiday.
  (Sarah's saving up. Sarah wants to pay for a holiday.)

- Note that there's no negative form of the infinitive of purpose.

We can't say: Sarah stays in most evenings not to spend money.
We use *so that* + a verb in the negative or *so as not to* + infinitive. (See Step 3.)

CHECK QUESTIONS 1 **Answer the questions with the infinitive of purpose or *in order to.***
1 Why does Sarah need money?
2 Why has she put an advert in the local paper?
3 Why did she phone the local paper last week?

Step 2 | Talking about the purpose or use of a thing

> Sarah doesn't have time to have breakfast at home. She takes something to eat on the bus and a book to read, usually a travel book about India. In the evening, if there's nothing to watch on television and she hasn't got any work to do, she plans her trip. She'll need a guide book to help her plan her route, and enough money to pay for her food and lodging. She's also going to take a notebook to write her experiences in. She's looking for someone to go with because she doesn't want to go alone.

- We use the infinitive of purpose (not *in order to*) to talk about the purpose or use of something.

  *She doesn't have **time to have** breakfast at home.*
  *She takes **something to eat** on the bus.   She takes **a book to read**.*

- Note that the preposition is still included when we use a verb as an infinitive of purpose. When the verb has an object, the preposition comes after the object.
  (She wants **to go with** someone.)
  *She's looking for someone **to go with**.*
  (She'll **write** her experiences **in** a notebook.)
  *She's going to take a notebook **to write** her experiences **in**.*

CHECK QUESTIONS 2 **Answer the questions, using the infinitive of purpose.**
1 Why does she take a book with her in the mornings?
2 Why will she need a guide book?
3 Why will she need money on the trip?

Step 3 | So that/so

> Every week Sarah puts her money in the bank so that she won't spend it! A travel agent has given her a lot of information so that she can choose the cheapest return flight to India. Sarah has found a friend to go with. His name's Sanjit. He's an Indian student at the same college. Yesterday Sarah invited Sanjit to her house so that they could discuss their plans. She told him to bring all his maps of India so they could both look at them.

We use *so that* (and not the infinitive of purpose) to talk about the purpose of an action:

- when there is a different subject in each part of the sentence.
  *A **travel agent** has given her a lot of information **so that she** can choose the cheapest return flight to India.*
- when the purpose is negative.
  *Every week Sarah puts her money in the bank **so that** she **won't spend** it!*
- Note that we can also use *so as not to* + infinitive. The meaning stays the same.
  *Every week Sarah puts her money in the bank **so as not to spend** it!*
- *So that* is often followed by *will, won't, would, wouldn't, can, can't, could, couldn't.*
  *Sarah puts her money in the bank **so that** she **won't** spend it!*
  *She invited Sanjit **so that** they **could** discuss their plans.*
- Note that *so that* is often shortened to *so.*
  *She told him to bring all his maps **so** they could look at them together.*
  *She told him to bring all his maps **so that** they could look at them together.*
  These two sentences mean the same.

CHECK QUESTIONS 3 **Answer the questions with *so that* (or *so*).**
1 Why does Sarah put her money in the bank?
2 Why has the travel agent given Sarah a lot of information?
3 Why did Sarah invite Sanjit to her house?

ANSWERS TO
CHECK QUESTIONS
1, 2 AND 3

1 1 To pay for/In order to pay for her trip to India. 2 To sell/In order to sell her motorbike and her CD player. 3 To put/In order to put an advert in (the paper).

2 1 To read on the bus. 2 To help her plan her route. 3 To pay for her food and lodging.

3 1 So (that) she won't spend it. 2 So (that) she can choose the cheapest return flight. 3 So (that) they could discuss their plans.

Practice

- We use *to* + infinitive and *in order to* + infinitive to talk about the purpose of an action, where the subject of each part of the sentence is the same.
- We use the infinitive of purpose, and not *in order to*, to talk about the purpose or use of a thing.
- If the purpose of an action is negative, or if there is a different subject in each part of the sentence, we use *so that* or *so*, usually followed by the verbs *can, can't, will, won't*, etc.

---

1 **Look at Sarah's diary. What is she going to do next week? Use the infinitive of purpose.**

Monday	Indian Embassy - get a visa
Tuesday	Doctor's - have vaccinations
Wednesday	Bookshop - buy Hindi dictionary
Thursday	Camping shop - choose a tent
Friday	Travel agent's - book ticket
Saturday	

1 On Monday she's going to the Indian

Embassy ....

2 On Tuesday she's going to ....

....

3 On Wednesday she's going to ....

....

4 On Thursday ....

....

5 On Friday ....

....

2 **You are going walking for a day in the mountains. What things do you need?**
Example: You wear a waterproof jacket if it rains. *I need a waterproof jacket to wear if it rains.*

1 You plan your route using a map. I need

....

2 A compass will help you find your way. I'll

take ....

3 Your food must last for two days. I need

enough ....

4 You may need to light a fire/some matches.

I'll take ....

3 **Matthew starts work very early. He leaves the house at 5.30 a.m. Make sentences using *so that* or *so as not to*.**

1 He sets his alarm clock for 5 a.m. He doesn't want to be late.

....

....

2 He puts the alarm clock near his bed. He wants to hear it.

....

....

3 He makes his sandwiches the night before. He wants to have more time in the morning.

....

....

4 He listens to the weather forecast. He wants to know what to wear.

....

....

5 He doesn't make too much noise. He doesn't want to wake the family.

....

....

6 He shuts the front door carefully. He doesn't want to disturb the neighbours.

....

....

43

Verb + infinitive with *to*:
I want to go

In June 1921 a Scotsman, Arthur Ferguson, met an American tourist in Trafalgar Square, London. Ferguson managed to convince him that Nelson's Column, the famous statue in the square, was for sale. He offered to sell him the monument for only £6,000. The American agreed to buy it immediately, and he could afford to, because he was very rich. He didn't know how to get it back to his ranch in Texas, but he certainly intended to. Ferguson claimed to work for the Bank of England, so the American decided not to ask for a contract and didn't hesitate to give him a cheque immediately. Ferguson had £6,000 and Nelson's Column is still in Trafalgar Square!

Step 1 | Verbs + infinitive with *to*

- When these verbs are followed by another verb, the second verb is normally the infinitive with *to*: *afford, agree, aim, appear, arrange, ask, attempt, beg, choose, claim, consent, decide, demand, deserve, endeavour, expect, fail, guarantee, happen, help, hesitate, hope, hurry, intend, know (how), learn, long, manage, mean (= intend), neglect, offer, omit, plan, prepare, pretend, promise, prove, refuse, seek, seem, swear, tend, threaten, train, want, wish*.

   He **managed to convince** him that it was for sale.
   He **offered to sell** him the monument for £6,000.
   He **didn't know how to get** the monument back to his ranch.

- Note the negative form of the infinitive:
   The American decided **not to ask** for a contract.
   We don't normally use a negative infinitive after *fail, hesitate, hurry, mean, neglect, omit, prepare, refuse, train, want, wish*.

- With many of these verbs (*afford, expect, intend, mean, seem, want*, etc.) it isn't necessary to repeat the second verb if it's understood from the context. We just use *to* instead.
   The American agreed to buy it, and he could **afford to**, because he was very rich.
   (= He could afford to buy it.)
   He didn't know how to get it back to his ranch in Texas, but he **intended to**.
   (= He intended to get it back.)

CHECK QUESTIONS 1

Complete the sentences.
1 Ferguson (hope/make) a lot of money quickly.
2 He (decide/sell) Nelson's Column.
3 The American (learn/not/believe) everybody he met.

| *Dare, help* + infinitive with and without *to*

> The American soon realised he'd lost his £6,000. At first he didn't dare tell the police because he didn't want to look foolish. But finally he asked them to help him find Ferguson. They said they couldn't help him to get his money back because they had more important crimes to solve.
> Ferguson was planning to sell something else. 'I daren't sell Nelson's Column again,' he thought. 'How about Big Ben? Do I dare sell Big Ben?'
> He sold the famous clock for £10,000 to an Italian millionaire!

- In the present, we can use *dare* as a modal verb or an ordinary verb. The modal verb is more common.
   *I **daren't** sell Nelson's Column again.* (modal)
   OR *I **don't dare (to)** sell Nelson's Column again.* (ordinary)
   In the past we normally use *dare* as an ordinary verb.
   *He **didn't dare** (to) tell the police.* (Rather than: *dared not*)
   In questions *dare* can be used as a modal verb or an ordinary verb (but in past questions the ordinary verb form is more common).
   ***Do I dare (to) sell** Big Ben?* OR ***Dare I sell** Big Ben?*

- When we use *dare* as an ordinary verb it can be followed by an infinitive with or without *to*. The infinitive without *to* is more common in informal spoken English.

- Note that *dare* is normally used only in questions and negative sentences.

- The verb *help* can be followed by an infinitive with or without *to*. The meaning is the same.
   *He asked them to **help** him **find** Ferguson.*
   OR *He asked them to help him **to find** Ferguson.*
   *They couldn't **help** him **to get** his money back.*
   OR *They couldn't help him **get** his money back.*

CHECK QUESTIONS 2 **Complete the sentences.**
1 Ferguson (dare/sell) Nelson's Column again?
2 No, he (dare/try) to sell it a second time.
3 The police (not help the American/find) Ferguson.

| *Come and see/go and work*

> After that Ferguson decided to go and work in the USA. Outside the White House in Washington he stopped and talked to some visitors from Chicago. He rented them ten rooms in the White House for $5,000! He said they could come and see their rooms later!

- After verbs like *go, come, stop, run, stay, hurry up* we often use *and* + infinitive without *to*.
   *He decided to **go and work** in the States.*
   *They could **come and see** their rooms later.*

And we always use *and* in commands like *Come and help me! Go and look!* etc. (NOT Come to help me!)

- Note that *and* can also be followed by a past tense.
*He stopped **and talked** to some visitors from Chicago.*
(= He stopped to talk to some visitors)

CHECK QUESTIONS 3 **Complete the sentences using *and* and the verbs.**

1 After the sale Ferguson (not stay/talk) to the people from Chicago.
2 He (go/catch) a bus the airport.

Step 4 | Verb + question word + infinitive with *to*

Ferguson then considered what to do next. He had to decide where to go. He decided to go to New York. When he arrived he asked someone how to get to Liberty Island. There, he sold the Statue of Liberty to some people from Brazil! But Ferguson didn't know when to stop. And he was finally arrested while he was trying to sell the Empire State Building! He was sent to prison for five years.

- After the following verbs we often use a question word + the infinitive with *to*:
ask, consider, decide, discover, discuss, explain, find out, forget, know, learn, remember, show, teach, tell, understand, wonder.
*Ferguson then **considered what to do** next.*
*He had to **decide where to go**.*
*He didn't **know when to stop**.*

- The question words we use in this construction are:
how   what   who   where   when   (NOT why)
We also use the word *whether* in this construction.
*At first Ferguson couldn't decide **whether** to stay in New York or not.*

- Note that the verb *know* can't be followed directly by an infinitive. We say *I know how to drive a car.* (NOT I know to drive a car.)

CHECK QUESTIONS 4 **Complete the sentences.**

1 Ferguson had discovered (how/become) rich.
2 He knew (what/say) to make people believe him.
3 After the Statue of Liberty, he didn't know (what/sell) next.

ANSWERS TO
CHECK QUESTIONS
1, 2, 3 AND 4

1 1 Ferguson hoped to make a lot of money quickly.   2 He decided to sell Nelson's Column.   3 The American learned not to believe everybody he met.

2 1 Did Ferguson dare (to) sell Nelson's Column again?   2 No, he didn't dare (to) try to sell it a second time.   3 The police didn't help the American (to) find Ferguson.

3 1 Ferguson didn't stay and talk to the people from Chicago.   2 He went and caught a bus to the airport.

4 1 Ferguson had discovered how to become rich.   2 He knew what to say to make people believe him.   3 he didn't know what to sell next.

Practice

1 Complete the dialogue, using these verbs. Use each verb once: *decide, go, work, complete, study, be, do, fill in, not find, become.*

Stephanie hopes (1) .... to university. She was asked (2) .... a lot of forms.

Now she's having an interview.

Interviewer: Why have you chosen (3) .... Maths?

Stephanie: Because Maths happens (4) .... my best subject.

Interviewer: What do you plan (5) .... after university?

Stephanie: I haven't decided yet. I'm sure that three years at university will help me (6) .... Perhaps I'll train (7) .... a teacher.

Interviewer: Most students tend (8) .... the course easy. Maths is a difficult subject.

Stephanie: Well, I intend (9) .... hard, and I'm sure I'll manage (10) .... the course.

2 Complete the text, using these verbs: *take, steal, drive, get, start* (x 2), *leave, go, be* (x 2), *open, contact, wait.*

It was late. Two young men in south London couldn't afford (1) .... a taxi, so they decided (2) .... a car instead. They planned (3) .... the car home and sell it the next day. They managed (4) .... into a red Ford Escort without too much difficulty. They then attempted (5) .... the car. But it wouldn't start They decided (6) .... it and steal another. At that moment a police car happened (7) .... past. The policemen offered to help them (8) ....

the car. The two young men pretended (9) .... the owners of the car and they accepted the offer. But the car still wouldn't start. One of the policemen decided (10) .... the bonnet. He quickly discovered that the car had no battery. The two men didn't dare (11) .... any longer. They ran off. The next day the police managed (12) .... the real owner of the car. She didn't seem (13) .... very surprised. She said someone had stolen the battery of her car the day before.

3 Complete the sentences, using these words: *how/speak, how/write, how/ask, whether/take, what/do* (x 2), *how/spell, how/translate, what/say, how/use.*

When I learned English at school, I learned (1) .... from English to Spanish, and I knew (2) .... essays in English, but I didn't learn (3) .... English. After I'd finished school, I didn't know (4) .... Some American friends of my family offered me a job as an au pair in California. At first I couldn't decide (5) .... the job or not. But finally I decided to go. When I first arrived in the States I had terrible problems. The people I worked for told me (6) .... , but I didn't understand a word! I didn't even know (7) .... my name in English. I didn't know (8) .... for the simplest things like a hot dog or a hamburger. I didn't know (9) .... the phone. When boys asked me for a date I never knew (10) .... I felt so stupid.

44

Verb + object + infinitive:
I want you to listen   You make me laugh

> Carla Finch is 17. She's a rebel.
> 'Society encourages me to be the same as everyone else. But I'm not. At school they don't allow me to be different. They advise me to conform. I ask them to listen to me, but they tell me to be quiet. They teach me to speak French, but they don't teach me how to live my life. My parents expect me to work hard and to get a job. They warn me not to waste time. For them the most important thing is to earn money. Big multi-national companies produce things and then get people to buy them. If you haven't got the money to buy them, you aren't a good citizen.'

Step 1 | Verb + object (noun or pronoun) + infinitive with *to*

- We use the following verbs in the structure **verb + object (noun or pronoun) + infinitive** when we say or do something to influence someone else: *advise, allow, ask, beg, cause, compel, encourage, expect, forbid, force, get, instruct, invite, oblige, order, persuade, recommend, remind, request, teach, tell, warn.*

verb	+	object	+,	infinitive
They don't allow		*me*		*to be different.*
They warn		*me*		*not to waste time.*
They get		*people*		*to buy their products.*

- With these verbs we use the infinitive with *to* (negative *not to*).

- After the verb *teach* we often add *how* before the infinitive.
  *They **teach me to speak** French.* (OR how to speak French.)
  *But they **don't teach me how to live** my life.*

- The verb *get* is often used with the meaning *persuade.*
  *They **get** people to buy them.*
  (=They persuade people to buy them.)

- Many of these verbs are reporting verbs used in reported speech. (See Unit 54.)

CHECK QUESTIONS 1 **Write complete sentences.**
1 Her parents/expect/Carla/get a job.
2 They/warn/her/not be lazy.
3 Society/encourage/people/earn money.

Step 2 | *Make* and *let* + infinitive without *to*

> My parents make me work every evening. They make me feel guilty if I watch television. They don't let me go out during the week. My friends' parents let them do what they like. My parents make me so angry!

- Note the use of this construction with *make* and *let*.

Make/let	+	object	+	infinitive without *to*
They make		*me*		*work.*
They don't let		*me*		*go out.*

- Make has two meanings – *force* and *cause*.
  *They **make** me work.* (=They force me to.)
  *They **make** me feel guilty.* (=They cause me to.)

- *Make* meaning *cause to be* can be followed by an adjective.
  They make me so angry.

- *Make* can be used in a passive construction. It's followed by the infinitive with *to*.
  *Carla is **made to work** every evening.*

Note that *let* can't be used in a passive construction. We use *allow* + infinitive with *to*.
  *Her friends **are allowed to do** what they like.*

CHECK QUESTIONS 2 **Rewrite the sentences, using *make* or *let*.**
1 They don't allow her to watch television.
2 They force her to stay in during the week.
3 They only allow her to go out on Saturday evening.
4 Her friends cause her to be envious.

Step 3 | Want, would like, would love, would prefer, would hate

Carla's grandfather enjoys talking to her. They have endless discussions.
'I want society to change.'
'But what would you like people to do?'
'I'd like them to take control of their own lives. And I want the government to see that people are more important than economic growth.'
'Well, I'd hate you to be very ill if there were no hospitals or doctors. Governments need money to pay for health care and education.'
'I know, but I'd prefer them not to make money by selling arms. If we want wars to stop, we must stop the arms trade now.'
'But you want things to change too quickly. These things take time.'

- We use *want, would like, would love, would prefer, would hate* + object + infinitive with *to* when we talk about our wishes.

verb	+	object	+	infinitive
I want		*society*		*to change.*
What would you like		*people*		*to do?*
I'd prefer		*them*		*not to make money.*

Note: With *want* we use the structure **verb + object + infinitive**.
(NOT I want that society changes. OR If we want that wars stop.)

CHECK QUESTIONS 3 **Write complete sentences.**
1 Carla/want/the government/listen to people.
2 She/would like/the government/stop selling arms.

ANSWERS TO CHECK QUESTIONS 1,2 AND 3

1 1 Her parents expect Carla to get a job.
2 They warn her not to be lazy. 3 Society encourages people to earn money.
2 1 They don't let her watch television. 2 They make her stay in during the week. 3 They only let her go out on Saturday evening. 4 Her friends make her envious.
3 1 Carla wants the government to listen to people. 2 She'd like the government to stop selling arms.

141

Practice

Tell, ask, want, etc.	+	Object (noun/pronoun)	+	Infinitive with *to*
He told		*me*		*to work harder.*
I want		*people*		*to listen to me.*
They ask		*their visitors*		*not to smoke.*

Make/let	+	**object**	+	**infinitive without *to***
They make		*me*		*speak English.*
She lets		*her brother*		*use her car.*

Make	+	**object**	+	**adjective**
He made		*her*		*unhappy.*

1 **I was in France for a few days, visiting friends. Write sentences using verb + object + infinitive.**
Example: A friend in Paris phoned me. She asked me to have dinner with her. A friend invited ...
A friend invited me to have dinner with her.

1 She said: 'Don't leave anything valuable in your car.'
She warned ....
....

2 I forgot, and my passport and some other things were stolen. She said: 'Go to the police station.'
She advised ....
....

3 At the police station I asked the police officer to give me a written report of the theft.
I got ....
....

4 I said: 'Will you sign the report, please?'
I asked ....

5 In case I forgot, he told me again to phone the ferry company to tell them I'd lost my passport.
He reminded ....
....

6 When I arrived back at Dover, the immigration officer said: 'Show me the police report, please.'
He asked ....
....

7 He said: 'You must get a new passport as soon as possible.'
He told ....
....

8 Then he said: 'You can go through now.'
Then he allowed ....

2 **Megan is applying for a hotel job in Spain. She is showing her letter to her friend Mark. Complete the sentences, using *want* or *would like/prefer/hate* + object + infinitive.**

Mark: What (1 you/want/me) ....
.... do?

Megan: I (2 like/you/translate) ....
.... this letter for me. They (3 want/me/write) ....
it in Spanish.

Mark: My Spanish isn't very good. I (4 hate/you/find) ....
that I'd made some terrible mistakes. I (5 prefer/you/ask) ....
someone else.

Megan: I haven't got time to ask someone else. They (6 want/me/reply) ....
by Friday and it's Tuesday today. I (7 like/you/do) .... it.

3 **Rewrite the sentences, using *make* and *let*.**

1 Most schools in Britain force their students to wear a uniform. They ....

2 Most schools don't allow their students to smoke. They ....
....

3 Some schools don't allow their students to leave the school during school hours.
They ....
....

4 This causes some students to feel very angry. This ....
....

A policeman is talking to the driver of a sports car he's just stopped.
'Good evening, sir.'
'Good evening, officer.'
'I suppose it's easy to break the speed limit in a fast car like this. It must be an exciting car to drive.'
'Er, yes, it is.'
'It must be hard not to drive fast.'
'Yes, it isn't easy.'
'And it isn't easy to remember that the speed limit's 70 m.p.h.'
'No, sometimes it isn't.'
'How fast do you think you were going?'
'It's difficult to say.'
'Would you be surprised to know that you were breaking the limit?'

Step 1 | Adjective (+ noun) + infinitive with *to*

	adjective	+	**infinitive with *to***
It's	difficult		to say.
It isn't	easy		to remember that the speed limit's 70 m.p.h.

- We sometimes use a negative infinitive with *not* after the adjective.
  *It must be hard **not to drive** fast.*

- The most common adjectives used with an infinitive are: *cheap, dangerous, difficult, disappointed, easy, exciting, expensive, good, hard, important, impossible, interesting, lucky, nice, pleased, possible, ready, safe, sensible, silly, stupid, surprised, terrible, wonderful.*

- We sometimes use the construction:

	adjective	+	**noun**	+	**infinitive**
It must be an	*exciting*		*car*		*to drive.*

CHECK QUESTIONS 1 | **Complete the sentences using the words in brackets.**
1 It's ... the speed limit. (important/remember)
2 It's ... with the police. (stupid/argue)
3 It's ... too fast. (sensible/drive)

Step 2 | Adjective + *for* + noun/pronoun + infinitive with *to*

'But it's normal for drivers to break the speed limit by a few miles an hour.'
'You aren't the first person to say that, sir. I admit, it isn't unusual for people to do 75 or 80 m.p.h. But you were doing over 100 m.p.h.! Now, I'm afraid it's necessary for me to have your name and address.'

- **adjective** + ***for*** + **noun/pronoun** + **infinitive with *to***

It's normal	*for*	*drivers*	*to break the limit.*
It's necessary	*for*	*me*	*to have your name.*

We use this construction with adjectives like: *common, difficult, easy, essential, important, necessary, normal, rare, unnecessary, unusual, usual.*

- It's also used with *the first, the second,* etc. and *the next, the last.*
  You aren't **the first person to say** that, sir.

CHECK QUESTIONS 2 **Rewrite the sentences.**
1 A lot of people drive too fast. It's common for ...
2 But not many people drive at over 100 m.p.h. It's unusual for ...
3 Drivers shouldn't break the speed limit. It's important for ...

Step 3 | To be+ adjective + of + noun/pronoun + infinitive with to

'All right, officer. It was wrong of me to break the speed limit. It was stupid of me to drive so fast. I'm sorry. Now, can I go?'
'Well, it was good of you to apologise, sir. But you can't go yet, I'm afraid. Your name and address, please.'

- Note this construction:

be +	**adjective** +	***of*** +	**noun/pronoun** +	**infinitive with *to***
It was	*wrong*	*of*	*me*	*to break the limit.*
It was	*good*	*of*	*you*	*to apologise.*

We use this construction with adjectives that describe how someone behaves: *careless, clever, generous, good, kind, mean, nice, polite, silly, stupid, wrong.*

CHECK QUESTIONS 3 **Complete the sentences.**
1 He drove too fast. It was stupid of ... fast.
2 He didn't see the police car behind him. It was careless of ...
3 He thought the police officer would let him go. It was silly of ...

ANSWERS TO
CHECK QUESTIONS
1, 2 AND 3

1 1 It's important to remember the speed limit.
2 It's stupid to argue with the police.
3 It's sensible not to drive too fast. OR It's not sensible to drive too fast.

2 1 It's common for people to drive too fast.
2 It's unusual for people to drive at over 100 m.p.h. 3 It's important for drivers not to break the speed limit.

3 1 It was stupid of him to drive too fast. 2 It was careless of him not to see the police car behind him. 3 It was silly of him to think that the police officer would let him go.

Practice

Adjective + infinitive with *to*	Adjective + *for* + noun/pronoun + infinitive with *to*
It's difficult to say.	It's difficult for me to answer.
It's difficult not to laugh.	Adjective + *of* + noun/pronoun + infinitive with *to*
I'm pleased to meet you	It's nice of you to come.

1 The basic rules of scuba diving. Rewrite these sentences in a different way.

1 You must have the right equipment. (essential)

It's ....

....

2 You mustn't dive on your own. (not safe)

It isn't ....

3 You mustn't take any risks. (important)

It ....

4 You mustn't stay under the water for too long. (dangerous)

It ....

....

2 These people are talking about learning English. Rewrite the sentences in a different way.
Example: English is a useful language to learn.
It's useful to learn English.

1 Many English words are hard to pronounce.

It's ....

....

2 I find some English people are difficult to understand when they talk.

It's difficult for ....

....

3 It's easy to make mistakes when you speak .

It's difficult ....

....

4 I don't think it's important to understand all the grammar.

It ....

....

5 A teacher gave me extra lessons. He was very kind.

It was very kind of ....

....

3 Ethel Taylor has won the national lottery and is being interviewed on a TV show. Complete the sentences.

'Hello, Ethel. It was (1 good/you/come)

....,'

'It was (2 kind/you/ask) ....

me.'

'Now tell me, Ethel. How does it feel to be the

winner of the national lottery?'

'That's (3 difficult question/answer) ....

.... It would be (4 easy/me/say)

.... I felt happy. But it

would be more (5 honest/me/say) ....

.... I felt shocked.'

'You must have been (6 amazed/hear) ....

.... that you'd won £11 million.'

'Yes. I was (7 surprised/hear) ....

.... that I'd won so much.'

'What are your plans, Ethel?'

'It's too (8 early/me/say) ....

.... I think it would be (9 nice/spend)

.... a few days here in

London. Then I'll go home and start my new

life. It would be (10 silly/me/not enjoy) ....

.... spending the money,

but it'll be (11 hard/know) ....

.... what to spend it on.'

'Well, I'd be (12 happy/help) ....

you. Ladies and gentlemen, Ethel Taylor!'

Verb + -ing: I enjoy swimming

It's the weekend. Rowan's asking Emma what she wants to do.
'What do you fancy doing? Shall we go for a walk?'
'No, I can't imagine doing anything more boring!'
'Do you fancy going round to Pete's place?'
'No, I don't want to risk seeing his sister. I owe her £20, so I'm trying to avoid meeting her, if possible.'
'Well, I haven't finished cleaning the windows. Do you mind helping me?'
'No, you know I don't enjoy doing that. That's your job.'

Step 1 | Verbs that are followed by the -ing form (gerund)

- If these verbs are followed by another verb, we use the -ing form (gerund) of the second verb: *admit, avoid, consider, deny, detest, dislike, enjoy, escape, fancy, finish, imagine, keep, mind, miss, practise, recall, regret, risk, suggest.*
  *What do you **fancy doing**?* (NOT fancy to do)
  *I don't want to **risk seeing** her.* (NOT risk to see)
  *Would you **mind helping** me?* (NOT mind to help me)

CHECK QUESTIONS 1 **Complete the sentences using the verbs *go, do, make.***
1 Rowan keeps ... suggestions. 2 He suggests ... for a walk.
3 Emma dislikes ... for walks. 4 She doesn't enjoy ... that.

Step 2 | *Go* and *come* followed by the -ing form

'Well, shall we go swimming? Or we could go windsurfing.'
'I've never been windsurfing and I don't fancy starting now.'
'Do you want to come jogging with me?'
'Jogging! No, thanks!'
'Well, I might go into town. Do you want to come shopping?'
'No. I went shopping yesterday. I don't want to do anything.'

- We use *go* and *come* + -ing when we talk about sports or outside activities.
  *Shall we **go swimming**?* (NOT Shall we go to swim?)
  *I've never **been windsurfing**.*
  *I **went shopping** yesterday. Do you want to **come jogging** with me?*

CHECK QUESTIONS 2 **What do you do with these things? (Example: a bike - *You go cycling.*)**
1 a fishing rod 2 skis 3 a credit card

ANSWERS TO
CHECK QUESTIONS
1 AND 2

1 1 Rowan keeps making suggestions. 2 He suggests going for a walk. 3 Emma dislikes going for walks. 4 She doesn't enjoy doing that.

2 1 You go fishing. 2 You go skiing. 3 You go shopping.

Practice

> - We use the -ing form after certain verbs (enjoy, finish, suggest, etc.)
>   I enjoy listening to music.
> - We use the -ing form after go and come when we talk about sports and outside activities.
>   I went swimming yesterday.

1 Complete the dialogue, using these verbs:
learn, write, do, stop, be, give up, look, work, talk.

'Mr Aubrey-Woods, you're now 90. Have you

finished (1) .... books now?'

'No, I'll keep (2) .... till I die. I can't

imagine (3) .... anything else. I've

never really considered (4) .... '

'Do you mind (5) .... old?'

'No, not at all. I enjoy (6) .... back

over my life. Of course a lot of my friends are

dead, and I miss (7) .... to them.'

'Do you have any regrets?'

'Yes, I regret not (8) .... smoking and

not (9) .... how to use a computer.'

**2 Two detectives are talking about a robbery at
a jeweller's shop. One of them has just
interviewed a suspect. Use these verbs to
complete the dialogue:** *let go, say, ask,
be (x 2), buy, answer, go.*

'Did he admit (1) .... in town that

morning?'

'Yes, but he denied (2) .... in the

jeweller's at the time of the robbery.'

'Did he admit (3) .... a newspaper

at the shop next door?'

'No, he said he didn't recall (4) ....

into the newsagent's. He kept (5) ....

he was innocent. But he avoided

(6) .... most of my questions.'

'Can we risk (7) .... him .... ?'

'No, not yet. I suggest (8) .... him

some more questions might be a good idea.'

**3 Complete the following advertisement, using
these verbs:** *sail, swim, windsurf, sight-see,
explore, ride, dance, fish, shop.*

Hotel Santa Ponsa

The hotel is on the beach, so you can go

(1) .... in the clear, blue waters of

the Mediterranean any time you like. The hotel

also has its own boats and windsurfers so you

can go (2) .... or (3) ....

at any time, or you can go (4) ....

with one of the local fishermen.

If you want adventure, you can go

(5) .... in the mountains behind the

hotel. Why not hire a pony and go

(6) .... through the woods and

along quiet mountain paths?

But if you're not feeling energetic, why not take

a bus and go (7) .... in the

picturesque town of Santa Cruz? And when

you've looked round the old churches and

medieval streets, why not go (8) ....

in the fashionable shops of the Calle Petra?

And then, at the end of the day, why not come

(9) .... in our lively pool-side

disco?

Judy Barnard's being interviewed for a job with a travel company.
'Thank you for coming, Miss Barnard. Before starting, I'd like to say that
I'm not interested in interviewing people who simply like the idea of
travelling round the world. The job is more difficult than that.'
'Don't worry. I'm fed up with doing temporary jobs. I'm keen on doing a
real job for a change.'
'Good. Now, I see you left school without taking any exams.'
'Yes. I was tired of studying. I was more interested in earning some
money. By staying at school, I was just wasting my time.'
'What did you do after leaving school?'
'Well, I wanted to go to Australia, and by working hard for six months, I
saved up enough money to pay for the fare.'

Step 1 | (Adjective) + preposition + -ing

- When a verb follows a preposition (*in, at, on*, etc.), the verb ends in -*ing*. The preposition is sometimes on its own.
  Before start**ing**, I'd like to say that ...   **by** stay**ing** at school
  without tak**ing** any exams.   **after** leav**ing** **school**

- There's sometimes an adjective before the preposition.
  I'm not **interested in** interviewing people.   I'm **keen on** doing a real job.
Here are some other common adjectives + preposition: *afraid **of** do**ing** something, excited **about** do**ing** something, angry **about** do**ing** something, fond **of** do**ing** something, bad **at** do**ing** something, good **at** do**ing** something, clever **at** do**ing** something, proud **of** do**ing** something.*

- There's sometimes a noun before the preposition.
  *people who simply like the **idea of** travelling*
  *I don't like the **thought of** not getting the job.*
  *That's the **advantage of** working for a travel company.*

CHECK QUESTIONS 1 **Add a preposition + an -ing form.**
1 Why do a lot of people want to work for travel companies? Because they like the idea ...
2 Why does she want a real job for a change? Because she's fed up ...
3 How did Judy get enough money to go to Australia? By ...

Step 2 | Verb + preposition + -ing

'What did you do in Australia, Miss Barnard?'
'I travelled a lot. I worked for a bit, and when I felt like moving on, I just
got on a bus. I don't believe in staying in the same place all the time. I
think I succeeded in visiting every Australian state.'
'And did you come home then?'
'Yes. I thought about staying longer, but my visa ran out, and I was
looking forward to coming home and seeing my friends again.'

- Some verbs are followed by a preposition + an -*ing* form.

verb +	preposition +	the -*ing* form of a verb
I thought	*about*	*staying longer.*
I felt	*like*	*moving on.*
I was looking forward	*to*	*seeing my friends.*

- Here are some other common verbs + preposition: *to **apologise for** doing something, to **dream of** doing something, to **approve of** doing something, to **insist on** doing something, to **decide against** doing something, to **talk about** doing something.*

- Note that *to* is normally the infinitive mark (*I wanted to come home*). But *to* is sometimes used as a preposition.

  *I was looking forward **to** com**ing** home.*
  (*To* here is a preposition so you can't say 'I was looking forward to come home.')
  *I wanted **to come** home.*
  (*To* here is the infinitive mark, so you can't say 'I wanted to coming home.')

CHECK QUESTIONS 2 **Answer the questions.**
1 Why did Judy keep moving on? She ... (not believe)
2 How many states did she visit? She ... (succeed)
3 Why did she want to come home? She ... (look forward to)

Step 3 | Verb + object + preposition + -*ing*

'Well, Miss Barnard, I'd like to thank you for coming. And I congratulate you on getting the job!'
'I've got the job? Really? Thanks very much! Um, forgive me for asking, but what will my salary be?'

- Some verbs are followed by an object, usually a person, and a preposition.

verb +	object +	preposition +	verb ending in -*ing*
I'd like to thank	*you*	*for*	*coming.*
I congratulate	*you*	*on*	*getting the job.*
Forgive	*me*	*for*	*asking*

- Here are some other verbs + object + preposition:

to accuse	*someone*	*of*	*doing something*
to blame	*someone*	*for*	*doing something*
to prevent	*someone*	*from*	*doing something*
to stop	*someone*	*from*	*doing something*
to succeed		*in*	*doing something*
to suspect	*someone*	*of*	*doing something*

CHECK QUESTIONS 3 **Answer the questions.**
1 What does he thank Judy for? He thanks ...
2 How does she know she's got the job? He congratulates ... it.

ANSWERS TO CHECK QUESTIONS 1, 2 AND 3

1 1 the idea of travelling round the world.
2 Because she's fed up with doing temporary jobs. 3 By working hard for six months.
2 1 She didn't believe in staying in the same place. 2 She succeeded in visiting every state.

3 She was looking forward to seeing her friends.

3 1 He thanks her for coming.
2 He congratulates her on getting it.

Practice

Adjective	+	Preposition	+	-ing	Verb	(+ object)	+	preposition	+	-ing
(I'm) tired		of		waiting	They left			without		paying
		After		leaving	He thanked	them		for		coming

1 Make one sentence from two sentences.
Example: I usually set my alarm clock. I go to sleep. *Before Before going to sleep, I usually set my alarm clock.*

1 Last night I went to bed. I didn't set my alarm clock. *without*

....

....

2 I slept well for eight hours. I got up. *After*

....

....

3 I left home. I didn't lock the door. *without*

....

....

4 I sat in a traffic jam. I arrived at work an hour late. *After*

....

....

5 I left work. I was told I was going to lose my job. *Before*

....

....

6 I arrived home. I found my TV and video had been stolen. *After*

....

....

....

2 Here is an advertisement in a local newspaper. Choose the correct preposition and put the verb in the -ing form: *with, about, on, to, against, at, in, of.*

Are you tired (1) .... (spend) ....

evenings on your own? Are you interested

(2) .... (meet) .... a young,

attractive girl? I'm keen (3) .... (swim)

.... and (4 cycle) .... and I'm fond

(5) .... (cook) .... But I'm not

(6) .... (spend) .... the evening at

home if there's a good film on television – I'm

just fed up (7) .... (watch) ....

them alone! I'm not afraid (8) .... (show)

.... my feelings. But I don't believe (9)

.... (meet) .... someone one night,

then (10 forget) .... him the next.

I'm bad (11) .... (remember) ....

names, but I'm very good (12) .... (remember)

.... faces, so how (13) ....

(send) .... me your photo? If you think

you're the man I'm looking for, I look forward

(14) .... (hear) .... from you.

3 An angry football manager is talking to his team after they have lost a match 5-0. Put two sentences together, using these prepositions + the verb in the -ing form: *against, of, for, on.*
Example: I blame our goalkeeper. He let in the first goal. *I blame our goalkeeper for letting in the first goal.*

1 I warned you last week. You thought you could win every match.

....

....

2 I'd like to congratulate Wayne. He scored a goal. (But for the other team!)

....

....

3 But I'm not just accusing Wayne. He played badly.

....

....

4 I blame the whole team. You lost the game.

....

....

48

Do you mind + -ing? I don't mind + -ing
It's no use, there's no point, etc. + -ing

'Tom! Do you mind taking these books off my desk? And would you mind not leaving my computer switched on?'
'Sorry, Dad. I was doing my homework.'
'I don't mind helping you with your homework. I don't mind you using my computer, but would you mind asking me before you use it?'

Step 1 | Do/Would you mind? I don't mind/he doesn't mind

- When *mind* is followed by a verb we always use the *-ing* form.
  *Do you **mind taking** your books off my desk?*
  *I don't **mind helping** you with your homework.*
  *Would you **mind asking** me before you use it?*
  Do you mind? and *Would you mind?* are polite ways of asking someone to do something. *Would you mind?* is a little more polite.

- When we say we don't mind what someone else does, we use:
  | **don't mind** | + | **a noun or pronoun** | + | **-ing** |
  | *I* *don't mind* | | *you* | | *using my computer.* |

- Note that we can use a negative *-ing* form after *mind*:
  *Would you mind **not leaving** my computer switched on?*

- Note that we only use the negative and question form of *mind*.

CHECK QUESTIONS 1 **Complete the sentences.**
1 He (not mind/help) Tom with his homework.
2 He (mind) Tom using his computer?

Step 2 | can't stand   can't help

Now Tom's father is talking to Tom's sister, Kate.
'Kate! Turn that music down! I can't stand listening to that terrible noise! And I can't stand you wasting your time. Do some homework!'

(*Later*) 'Mum. What's the matter with Dad? Why's he so angry?'
'He can't help being irritable sometimes. I can't help thinking he's got problems at work. We all get angry, and sometimes we can't help it.'

- We use *can't stand* to show strong dislike. It means *hate* or *detest*. When it's followed by a verb, we always use the *-ing* form.
  *I **can't stand listening** to that terrible noise.*
  (The expression *can't bear* means the same as *can't stand*, so we can say 'I **can't bear listening** to that awful noise.' But *can't bear* can also be followed by the infinitive with *to*: 'I **can't bear to listen** to that awful noise.')

- When we say we can't stand what someone else does, we use:
  | **can't stand** | + | **noun or pronoun** | + | **-ing** |
  | *I* *can't stand* | | *you* | | *wasting your time.* |

151

Or we can say:

can't stand + **it** + **when clause**
I can't stand it when you waste your time.

- *Can't help* means that you can't stop yourself from doing something. It's often followed by *it*. When it's followed by a verb, we always use *-ing*.
  *Sometimes we **can't help it**.* (= We can't stop ourselves.)
  *He **can't help being** irritable.* (= He can't stop himself)

CHECK QUESTIONS 2 **Rewrite the sentences.**
1 He hates Kate to waste her time. He can't ...
2 He can't stop himself from getting angry. He can't ...

Step 3 | *It's no use, there's no point, it's (not) worth + -ing*

Kate's talking to her brother later in the evening.
'Tom, there's a good film on television at 10.15. People at school say it's really worth seeing. Shall we ask Dad if we can watch it?'
'It's no use asking him at the moment. It isn't worth it. He'll say no. There's no point asking him.'
'He might say yes. It's worth trying.'
(*Later*)
'I tried, but it was no good. He said no.'
'You see, it wasn't worth asking him. I told you.'

- *It's no use/There's no point/It's (isn't) worth* are followed by the *-ing* form of the verb, not the infinitive with *to*.
  *It's no use **asking** Dad.* (NOT It's no use to ask Dad.)
  *There's no point **asking** him. It's worth **trying**.*
  It's no use, There's no point and *It isn't worth* mean more or less the same (= there's no sense in doing something).

- We can also use *worth* + *-ing* to (or not to) recommend something.
  *The film's really **worth seeing**. Dad isn't **worth talking to** at the moment.*

- We can say *It's no good* instead of *It's no use*.
  It's no good asking Dad. (= It's no use asking Dad.)
  We sometimes say *There's no point **in** doing something*, but *in* is often omitted.
  There's no point (in) asking him.

- Sometimes we don't need to repeat the following verb.
  *I tried, but **it was no use**.* (= It was no use trying.)
  *There's no point asking him. **It isn't worth it**.*
  *It's no use asking him. **There's no point**.*

CHECK QUESTIONS 3 **Rewrite the sentences.**
1 There was no point asking their father. It was ...
2 It wasn't worth trying. There ...

ANSWERS TO
CHECK QUESTIONS
1, 2 AND 3

1 1 He doesn't mind helping Tom with his homework. 2 Does he mind Tom using his computer?

2 1 He can't stand Kate wasting her time.
2 He can't help getting angry.

3 1 It was no use/no good asking their father. OR It wasn't worth asking their father. 2 There was no point trying. OR It was no use/no good trying.

Practice

> I don't mind (+ noun or pronoun) + -ing: *I don't mind staying at home.* *I don't mind you coming.*
> I can't stand (+ noun or pronoun) + -ing: *I can't stand watching football.* *I can't stand people shouting.*
> I can't help + -ing: *I can't help feeling tired.*
> It's no use/It's (not) worth/There's no point + -ing: *It's no use waiting.*

1 **Sally Gregg is a flight attendant. She is on a plane which is waiting to take off. She is asking some passengers to do various things. She is asking them 'Would you mind (not) ...?'**
Example: Someone hasn't put their seat in the upright position. *Would you mind putting your seat in the upright position?*

1 Someone's smoking.

....

2 Someone isn't sitting down.

....

3 Someone hasn't put their seat-belt on.

....

4 Someone's using their mobile phone.

....

2 **Complete the dialogue, using *Do you mind?* *don't/doesn't mind* and the future form *won't mind* with the verbs in brackets.**
'We need some more eggs. Can someone go to the shop and get some?'

'I (1 go) .... I'll

take Sarah's bike.'

'You'll have to ask her first.'

'No, I'm sure she (2 me/take) ....

it. It's only an old bike, and she (3 people/use)

.... it.'

'You (4 get) ....

some butter too?'

3 **Five people were asked what they hated most. Use *can't stand* + -ing or *can't stand it when* to complete their answers.**

1 I (drink/cold coffee)

....

2 I (parents/hit/their children)

....

3 I (be stopped/by a customs officer)

....

4 I (people/smoke in a restaurant)

....

4 **Rewrite the sentences, using *can't help* or its past form *couldn't help*.**

Our English teacher is rather boring, but (1) *I can't stop myself from liking her.*

.... Our
class is a bit noisy, so (2) *it isn't her fault if she gets angry sometimes.*

....

Yesterday I dropped all my books on to the floor. (3) *I couldn't stop myself,*

....

because someone pushed me. She got very angry and knocked a pile of books off her desk. (4) *I couldn't stop myself from laughing.*

....

5 **Some people are stuck in a lift in a big department store. The store has just closed. Make sentences with *It's no use (good)*, *There's no point* or *It's (isn't) worth*.**

1 There's a phone in the lift, but it's out of order. (try to phone)

....

....

2 No one will hear them. (shout)

....

....

3 They're getting angry. But (get angry)

....

....

4 They might be able to force the doors open. (try)

-ing clauses: *He sat listening*

> Salesman Barry Tate of Solihull, Birmingham sat in his car listening to the radio and thinking about his next customer. Suddenly a car went past. Mr Tate couldn't believe it – two legs were hanging out of the back! He decided to follow the car. He nearly had an accident trying to phone the police on his mobile phone. He couldn't contact them. Taking a pen out of his pocket, he then wrote down the car's registration number. Having written down the number, he tried to call the police again.

Step 1 | The *-ing* form for one of two actions

- If two actions happen at the same time, we can use a verb in the *-ing* form for one of the actions.

  *He **sat** in his car **listening** to the radio.*
  (= He sat and listened at the same time.)
  *He **sat thinking** about his next customer.*
  (= He sat and thought about his next customer.)

We often use this construction after the verbs *be, lie, sit, stand.*

- If one action happens while another action is going on, we can use a verb in the *-ing* form for the longer action.

  *He nearly **had** an accident **trying** to phone the police on his mobile phone.*
  (= He nearly had an accident while he was trying to phone the police.)

- If one action immediately follows another action, we can use a verb in the *-ing* form for the first action.

  ***Taking** a pen out of his pocket, he **wrote down** the car's registration number.*
  (= He took his pen out, then immediately wrote down the number.)

- If we need to emphasise that one action was completed before another action started, we use *having* + a past participle.

  ***Having written down** the number, he **tried** to call the police again.*

CHECK QUESTIONS 1 **Rewrite the two sentences as one.**

1 He was sitting. He was watching the car in front.
2 He used his mobile phone. He tried to call the police.
3 He failed to contact the police the first time. He tried to phone them again.

Step 2 | The -ing form to say why something happened

Thinking that the legs must belong to a murder victim, Mr Tate was very excited. Imagining that he'd be a hero the next day, he tried to stop the car by flashing his lights. Not understanding what Mr Tate's signals meant, the driver kept going. But when Mr Tate flashed his lights again, he stopped. A man got out of the boot of the car and explained everything. They were mechanics. There was a strange noise at the back of the car. Having tried without success to find the reason for the noise at the garage, they'd decided to take the car out on the road. Wanting to listen more carefully, he'd climbed into the boot. It was his legs that were hanging out of the back!

- We can use a clause with a verb in the -ing form to explain why something happened.
  Thinking *that the legs must belong to a murder victim, Mr Tate was very excited.*
  (Mr Tate was excited because he thought the legs belonged to a murder victim.)
  Imagining *that he'd be a hero the next day, he tried to stop the car.*
  (He tried to stop the car because he imagined he'd be a hero.)
- We can use a negative form.
  Not understanding *what Mr Tate's signals meant, the driver kept going.*
  (The driver kept going because he didn't understand.)
- If we need to emphasise that the action giving the reason was completed before another action started, we use *having* + a past participle.
  Having tried *without success to find the reason for the noise, they'd decided to take the car out on the road.*

CHECK QUESTIONS 2 | **Rewrite the two sentences as one.**
1 The driver thought there must be something wrong. He stopped.
2 He was in the boot of the car. It was easier for him to hear the noise.
3 Mr Tate stopped the car in front. He got out to speak to the driver.
4 Mr Tate felt stupid. He asked them not to tell anyone what had happened.

ANSWERS TO
CHECK QUESTIONS
1 AND 2

1 1 He was sitting watching the car in front. 2 Using his mobile phone, he tried to call the police. 3 Having failed to contact the police the first time, he tried to phone them again.
2 1 Thinking there must be something wrong, the driver stopped. 2 Being in the boot of the car, it was easier for him to hear the noise.

3 Having stopped the car in front, Mr Tate got out to speak to the driver. OR Mr Tate, having stopped the car in front, got out ... 4 Feeling stupid, Mr Tate asked them not to tell anyone what had happened.

Practice

> We sat **talking**. = We sat and talked at the same time.
> He broke his leg **playing** football. = He broke his leg while he was playing football.
> **Locking** the door behind him, he left. = He locked the door and then immediately left.
> **Having left** school, he got a job. = He left school and then got a job.
> **Feeling** hungry, I bought a hamburger. = I felt hungry, so I bought a hamburger.
> **Not having** any money, I couldn't buy it. = I couldn't buy it because I didn't have any money.
> **Having seen** the film once, he didn't want to see it again. = He didn't want to see the film because he'd already seen it once.

1 **Zoe had a party last night. Her parents came home early. Rewrite the two sentences as one, using a verb in the -ing form.**
Example: One boy was lying on their bed. He was snoring. *One boy was lying on their bed snoring.*

1 Two boys were standing on the stairs. They were arguing.

   ....

2 A girl was sitting in the hall. She was crying.

   ....

3 A boy was in the toilet. He was feeling sick.

   ....

4 Three people were in the kitchen. They were making themselves something to eat.

   ....

   ....

2 **There are some people in a hospital waiting room. Rewrite the two sentences as one sentence.**
Example: One man had broken his nose. He'd been playing squash. *One man had broken his nose playing squash.*

1 An old woman had been knocked over. She'd been crossing the road.

   ....

2 A woman had burnt her hands. She'd been trying to light a barbecue.

   ....

3 A man had cut himself. He'd been sawing wood.

   ....

   ....

3 **Rewrite the sentences, using *having* + past participle.**

1 We went to the cinema and then we decided to go to a restaurant.

   ....

   ....

2 We decided to have a Chinese meal. We went to the Mandarin restaurant.

   ....

   ....

3 We looked at the menu. We ordered our food.

   ....

   ....

4 We waited for half an hour for our food. We decided to leave.

   ....

   ....

4 **Camilla is taking a History exam. Rewrite the sentences, using a verb in the -ing form.**

1 Because she's feeling very nervous, she's arrived at the examination half an hour early.

   ....

   ....

2 Because she's chosen to do History at university, she wants to do well in this exam.

   ....

   ....

3 But because she stayed up late last night, she's feeling very tired ....

   ....

4 But because she's a very clever girl, she'll probably pass the exam. ....

   ....

50 | *Like, love, hate* + infinitive with *to* or + *-ing*

During a Health and Leisure programme on TV, people were asked,
'What do you like doing in your spare time?' These were some of their
answers:
'I like doing active things. I like swimming and going for walks. I hate
sitting around and doing nothing.'
'I love to go to the coffee shop and meet friends. I hate playing sport,
but I enjoy watching it on TV. I don't like people telling me I'm lazy.'
'I don't like to go out much. I enjoy relaxing at home. I like watching
television and listening to music. And I like friends coming round to see
me.'

Step 1 | *Like, love, hate* + infinitive with *to* and *-ing*, *enjoy* + *-ing*

- The verbs *like, love* and *hate* can be followed by *-ing* or by the infinitive with *to*.
The meaning is the same. The construction with *-ing* is more common.

verb + *-ing*		**verb + infinitive with *to***
I like doing active things.	OR	*I like to do active things.*
I hate playing sport.	OR	*I hate to play sport.*
I love going to the coffee shop.	OR	*I love to go to the coffee shop.*

- The verb *enjoy* can only be followed by *-ing*.
  *I **enjoy watching** sport.* (NOT I enjoy to watch sport.)
(For the verb *prefer* + infinitive with *to* or *-ing* see Unit 51.)

- When we say we like or don't like what someone else does, we normally use this
construction:

like/love/hate/enjoy	+	**noun/pronoun**	+	***-ing***
I like		*friends*		*coming round.*
I don't like		*people*		*telling me I'm lazy.*

CHECK QUESTIONS 1 ▶ **Write complete sentences.**
1 A lot of people/enjoy/go to the coffee shop/and/meet friends.
2 Some people/not like/go out much. They/like/read/and/listen to music.
3 Some people/hate/play football/but/enjoy/watch it.

Step 2 | *Like* + infinitive with *to*

> Another question was: 'What do you do to stay healthy?'
> 'I like to eat fruit and fresh vegetables at least once a day. And I like to take at least half an hour's exercise every day. I like to look after myself.'
> 'I like to go to the doctor's twice a year. I like him to check my blood pressure.'

- When we use *like* to say that something is a good idea, *like* is followed by the infinitive with *to*, not *-ing*.
  > *I **like to go** to the doctor's twice a year.*
  > (= I go because it's a good thing, not because I enjoy it.)
  Note: 'I **like going** to the doctor's' = 'I enjoy going to the doctor's.'

- When we say what someone else does is a good idea, we use this construction:

like, etc.	+	noun/pronoun	+	infinitive with *to*
I like		*him*		*to check my blood pressure.*

CHECK QUESTIONS 2 **Complete the sentences.**
1 I like chocolate, but I don't like (eat) it every day.
2 I like (go) swimming. I really enjoy it.
3 I like (go) to the dentist's regularly.

Step 3 | *Would like/would love/would hate* + infinitive with *to*

> The presenter then asked: 'Would you like to make any changes in your life?'
> 'I'd like to take more exercise because I'd like to lose weight.'
> He asked the smokers in the audience: 'Would you like to give up smoking?' Most of them said: 'I'd love to, but I can't.'
> He then asked a beer-drinker if he'd like to give up drinking beer. He replied: 'I'd hate to give up my only pleasure in life!'

- *Would like, would love, would hate* are followed by the infinitive with *to*, not the *-ing* form.
  > *I'd **like to lose** weight.* (NOT I'd like losing weight.)
  > *I'd **hate to give up** my only pleasure.* (NOT I'd hate giving up)

- Note that sometimes after *would like/love/hate* it isn't necessary to repeat the complete infinitive. We just use *to*.
  > *I'd **love to**, but I can't.* (= I'd love to give up smoking.)

- (For *I'd like/hate/prefer* + object + infinitive with *to*, see Unit 44.)

CHECK QUESTIONS 3 **Put in *would like/would hate* + verb.**
1 I'm too heavy. I ... weight. (lose)
2 I ... smoking. It isn't good for me. (stop)
3 I love going to the pub. I ... drinking beer. (give up)

The presenter then asked people if they had any regrets. 'What would you like to have done?' These were some of their answers:
'I'd like to have played more sport when I was younger.'
'I've always worked in an office. I'd like to have had a more active job.'
'I'm lucky. I've never been ill. I'd hate to have had problems with my health.'

● *would like*, etc. +	*to have* +	**past participle**
I'd like	*to have*	*played more sport.*
I'd hate	*to have*	*had problems.*

We use this construction to talk about the present regrets we have about a past situation.

I'd like to have had a more active job.

(= I didn't have an active job in the past. I regret it now.)

CHECK QUESTIONS 4 **Put in *would like/would hate to have.***
1 I didn't eat well when I was young. I ... less junk food. (eat)
2 I gave up smoking last year. I (give it up) ... ten years ago.
3 In the 1950s London was polluted. I (live) ... in London then.

ANSWERS TO
CHECK QUESTIONS
1, 2, 3 AND 4

1 1 A lot of people enjoy going to the pub and meeting friends. 2 Some people don't like going out (to go out) much. They like reading (to read) and listening (to listen) to music. 3 Some people hate playing (to play) football, but enjoy watching it.

2 1 eating 2 going (less common: to go) 3 to go
3 1 I'd like to lose weight. 2 I'd like to stop smoking. 3 I'd hate to give up drinking beer.
4 1 I'd like to have eaten 2 I'd like to have given it up 3 I'd hate to have lived

Practice

> - The verbs *like, love, hate* are usually followed by the *-ing* form, but can be followed by the infinitive with *to*: *I like going for walks.* OR *I like to go for walks.*
>   Note: *enjoy* must be followed by *-ing*, not the infinitive with *to*.
> - When we think something is a good idea, we use *like* + the infinitive with *to*: *I like to tidy my room at least once a week.*
> - We must use the infinitive with *to* after *would like/love/hate*: *I'd love to be fit.*
> - For present regrets about the past, we use *would like/love/hate* + *to have* + past participle: *I'm a teacher. I'd like to have been an actor.*

1 Joshua Gillingham lives in a flat near Hyde Park in London. Complete these sentences about him, using the verb in brackets and one of these verbs: *wash up, live, stay, go* (x 2), *write, eat, cook, do.*
Example: Joshua lives near Hyde Park. He (like) *likes living* in the middle of a city.

1 Joshua doesn't live with anyone. He

   (like) .... on his own.
2 His flat's always in a mess. He

   (hate) .... housework.
3 His kitchen is always full of dirty dishes. He

   (not enjoy) ....
4 He always goes out to eat. He (not like)

   .... his own meals.
5 He usually has a hamburger and chips. He

   (not like) .... healthy food.
6 He never gets up before 11 a.m. He

   (enjoy) .... in bed.
7 He drinks a lot. He (love) ....
   to the pub.
8 But he's a very successful song-writer. He

   (love) .... songs.
9 He spends all his money on expensive

   holidays. He (love) .... to
   Hawaii.

2 Helen Black is very different from Joshua Gillingham. Complete these sentences about her, using the verb *like* and the verb in brackets.
Example: She always wants to look smart, so she (go) *likes to go* to the hairdresser's once a week.

1 She takes great care of her car. She (clean)

   .... it every weekend.
2 For her, arriving late is terrible. She always

   (get to) .... work on time.

3 She takes plenty of exercise. She (keep)

   .... fit.
4 The company she works for wants to keep its

   employees happy. It (give) ....
   them a bonus every year.
5 Helen doesn't spend all her money at once.

   She (spend) .... it carefully.

3 Natasha has just finished school and she is looking for a job. She is talking to her friend David. Complete the dialogue with *would like/would hate* + **infinitive** or *would like/would hate to have* + **past participle**, using the verbs in brackets.

David: What sort of job (1 you get) ....

.... ? What (2 you be)

.... ?

Natasha: I (3 work) ....

abroad, if possible. I (4 spend) ....

.... all my life in England.

David: Well, you could be an English teacher,

like my friend Anna. She's spent ten years

abroad.

Natasha: I (5 meet) ....

her.

David: She's just gone back to Tokyo, I'm

afraid.

Natasha: That's a pity! I (6 talk) ....

.... to her. I (7 ask) ....

.... her about her job.

David: Why don't you write to her?

Natasha: Yes, I (8 like) ....

David: Have you got your exam results yet?

Natasha: Yes, I did quite well. I (9 do)

.... badly.

51

I prefer to do/I prefer doing
I'd prefer to/I'd rather

Justin and Rachel have only been married for six months, but they've already discovered that they prefer doing different things. Rachel doesn't like staying at home in the evening. She prefers going out and meeting people. Justin prefers staying in to going out. He prefers to sit in front of the television.

Rachel: Shall we go to Jake's party?

Justin: I don't want to go out this evening. I'd prefer to stay at home. OK?

Rachel: No, it's not OK! You always prefer doing nothing.

Justin: That's not true. But this evening I'd prefer to watch television rather than go to a party.

Rachel: But you always say: 'I'd prefer not to go out this evening.' You're so boring!

Step 1 | *Prefer to do/prefer doing* or *would prefer*

- When we talk about what someone generally prefers, we can use either *prefer* + *-ing* or *prefer* + infinitive with *to*. The meaning is the same.

  They each prefer doing different things.
  (= They each **prefer to do** different things.)
  *He **prefers to sit** in front of the television.*
  (= He **prefers sitting** in front of the television.)

- When we're talking about a particular situation, we normally use *would* (*'d*) *prefer* + infinitive with *to*.

  *I'd **prefer to stay** at home.*

  Note: *Would prefer* is never followed by *-ing*.

- When we talk about two alternatives, we say:

  *Justin prefers **staying in to going out**.*

  OR *Justin prefers **to stay in rather than go out**.*

  When we use *prefer* + *-ing* we join the alternatives with *to*.
  When we use *prefer* + infinitive with *to* we join the alternatives with *rather than* followed by an infinitive without *to*.

- Note that we can use a negative infinitive.

  *I'd prefer **not to go** out this evening.*

- The verb *prefer* is never used in continuous tenses. We can't say: 'I'm preferring to stay at home.'

  (For *would prefer* + object + infinitive, see Unit 44.)

CHECK QUESTIONS 1 **Complete the sentences, using *(would) prefer to do/prefer doing*.**

1 Tonight Justin ... (watch) a video.
2 He usually ... (stay) at home to ... (go out)
3 This evening Rachel ... (go) to a party rather than ... (watch) television.
4 She always prefers ... (go out) with her friends rather than ... (stay) at home.

Step 2 | *Would prefer to/would rather*

> Rachel: Well, if we don't go to the party, I'd rather go to a pub than stay at home. Would you rather stay at home or come with me?
>
> Justin: Oh, all right then, I'll come. But I'd rather not go to a pub. I'd prefer to go to the cinema. Would you like to do that?
>
> Rachel: No, I'd rather not. Listen, why don't we go to Jake's party? You enjoyed the party we went to last week, didn't you?
>
> Justin: No, not really. I'd rather have watched the football on television.
>
> Rachel: Well, I'm going out!
>
> Justin: I'd rather you didn't go. I'd rather you stayed here with me.
>
> Rachel: And I'd rather we went out together. But you don't want to.

- To talk about what we prefer in a particular situation, we say:
  I'd prefer to go to the cinema. OR **I'd rather go** to the cinema.
  These two sentences mean the same.
  Note: After *would prefer* we use the infinitive with *to*.
  After *would rather* we use the infinitive without *to*.

- Note the question forms:
  Would you rather stay at home or come with me?
  OR **Would you prefer to stay** at home or come with me?

- Note the negative short answers:
  Would you like to do that? No, **I'd rather not**. OR No, **I'd prefer not to**.

- When we talk about two alternatives, we say:
  I'd rather go to a pub **than** stay at home.
  OR **I'd prefer** to go to a pub **rather than** stay at home.

- When our preference includes another person, we use a verb in the form of a past tense after *would rather*.
  I'd rather you **didn't go**. (OR I'd prefer you not to go.)
  I'd rather you **stayed** here. (OR I'd prefer you to stay here.)
  I'd rather we **went** out together. (OR I'd prefer us to go out together.)
  Although the verb has a past form, we're talking about the present or future.

- When we talk about regrets we have now about something that happened in the past, we can use these constructions:

	would rather + **have**	+	**past participle**
	I'd rather	*have*	*watched the football.*
OR:	**would prefer** + **to have**	+	**past participle**
	I'd prefer	*to have*	*watched the football.*

  We use *would rather have* more often.
  Note: With these constructions we're talking about actions that didn't happen. In the example Justin didn't watch the football.

CHECK QUESTIONS 2 **Complete these sentences.**
1 What/Rachel/prefer/do? 2 She/rather/go/to a pub.
3 Last night they went to a pub. Justin/rather/stay at home.
4 Rachel often says: I/rather/we/go out more.

ANSWERS TO
CHECK QUESTIONS
1 AND 2

1 1 would prefer to watch 2 prefers staying ... to going out 3 would prefer to go ... rather than watch 4 prefers to go out ... rather than stay

2 1 What would Rachel prefer to do? 2 She'd rather go to a pub. 3 Justin would rather have stayed at home. 4 I'd rather we went out more.

Practice

> I prefer **going** by car. OR I prefer **to go** by car.
> I**'d** prefer (not) **to eat** later. OR I**'d rather** (not) **eat** later.
> I**'d rather** play **than** watch. OR I**'d** prefer to play **rather than** watch.
> I**'d** prefer **you to go**. OR I**'d rather you went**.
> I**'d rather have gone** to Greece. (But I didn't.)

1 **It is the first time Chris and Lucy have been out together. They have just got back to Chris's flat. Complete Lucy's replies.**
Example:
Chris: Do you want to take your coat off?
Lucy: (prefer/keep on) *I'd prefer to keep it on.*

Chris: Would you like some tea?
Lucy: (1 rather/have/coffee)

....

Chris: Why don't you come and sit on the sofa?
Lucy: (2 rather/sit/chair)

....

Chris: Shall I put on some music?
Lucy: (3 prefer/watch/news)

....

Chris: Would you like some more coffee?
Lucy: (4 rather/go/home)

....

Chris: Why don't you stay a bit longer?
Lucy: (5 prefer/go/now)

....

2 **Rewrite these sentences, using the word in brackets.**
Example: I want to go in June, not July. (rather)
I'd rather go in June than July. (prefer) *I'd prefer to go in June rather than July.*

1 I want to go to Canada, not the USA. (prefer)

....

2 I think it would be better to go for two weeks, not just one. (prefer)

....

3 Why don't we stay in an apartment, not a hotel? (rather)

....

....

4 Can't we fly from Manchester instead of London? (rather)

....

....

5 I want to decide now, not later. (prefer)

....

....

3 **Jamie and Lisa are lying on a beach. Jamie is reading a book. Change *would prefer* to *would rather*, and *would rather* to *would prefer*.**

Lisa: Do you want to go for a swim?
Jamie: I'd rather stay here.

(1) ....
Lisa: Why don't we go for a walk together?
Jamie: I'd prefer you to go on your own.

(2) ....
Lisa: Shall I go and get us something to eat?
Jamie: I'd rather you waited a bit.

(3) ....
Lisa: Would you like to go that pizza restaurant again tonight?
Jamie: I'd rather not go to the same place twice.

(4) ....
Lisa: But you liked that pizza we had, didn't you?
Jamie: I'd prefer to have gone to a sea-food restaurant.

(5) ....
Lisa: You're glad we came to the beach, aren't you?
Jamie: I'd prefer to have gone somewhere quieter.

(6) ....
Lisa: You don't mind me talking to you, do you?
Jamie: I'd prefer you to keep quiet so I can finish my book.

(7) ....

52

Verb + infinitive with *to* or + *-ing*
Remember to do or *remember doing*

Gavin Armstrong began writing his first novel while he was on holiday in Italy. When he got back to England he bought himself a second-hand computer and started writing his book again, on screen. He was slow, because he didn't bother to learn to type - he only used two fingers. He continued typing every evening after work. He intended to finish the book before Easter.

Step 1 | Verbs that can be followed by infinitive with *to* or *-ing*

- Some verbs can be followed by the infinitive with *to* or the *-ing* form. The meaning is usually the same. The most common verbs are: *begin, bother, continue, intend, start.*

verb	+	-ing		verb	+	infinitive
He began		*writing*	OR	*He began*		*to write*
He started		*writing*	OR	*He started*		*to write*
He didn't bother		*learning*	OR	*He didn't bother*		*to learn*
He continued		*typing*	OR	*He continued*		*to type*
He intended		*finishing*	OR	*He intended*		*to finish*

- We don't use the *-ing* form after a verb in a continuous tense (where the main verb ends in *-ing*).
  He **was beginning to think** of ideas for his book.
  (NOT He was beginning thinking of ideas)

CHECK QUESTIONS 1 ▶ **Choose from these verbs to complete the sentences: *use, buy, send, write.***
1 He began ... when he was still at school.
2 He didn't bother ... a new computer.
3 He continued ... two fingers to type.
4 He was intending ... his novel to two or three publishers.

Step 2 | *Go on, need, stop* + the infinitive with *to* or *-ing*

Gavin went on writing for seven months. He was sure that if he could finish this first novel, he could go on to become a famous writer. One evening, just before Easter, he sat down and started writing. Now he only needed to write the last chapter. He wrote for six hours. He only stopped writing twice. First, when the cat needed feeding, he stopped to give it something to eat. Then, when he felt tired, he stopped to make a cup of strong black coffee.

- These verbs can also be followed by the infinitive with *to* or the *-ing* form, but the meaning is not the same: *go on, need, stop.*

- *Go on to do* OR *go on doing*?
We use *go on* + infinitive with *to* when a situation or an action comes later.
  *He could **go on to become** a famous writer.*
  (= Then, later, he could become a famous writer.)
We use *go on* + *-ing* when we continue doing the same thing.
  *He **went on writing** for seven months.*
  (= He continued writing for seven months.)

- *Need to do* OR *need doing*?
We use *need* + the infinitive with *to* when we say what it's necessary to do.
  *He **needed to write** the last chapter.*
  (= It was necessary to write the last chapter.)
We use *need* + *-ing* when we say that something is in need of attention.
  *The cat **needed feeding**.* (= The cat was in need of food.)

- *Stop to do* OR *stop doing*?
We use *stop* + the infinitive with *to* when we stop one action in order to do a different one. The infinitive here is the infinitive of purpose. (See Unit 42.)
  *He **stopped to make** a cup of strong black coffee.*
  (He stopped writing in order to make a cup of coffee.)
We use *stop* + *-ing* to say that an action finishes.
  *He only **stopped writing** twice.*
  (He was writing, then he stopped. He didn't stop in order to write.)

CHECK QUESTIONS 2 **Put in the right form of the verb.**
1 He needed ... the book by Easter. (finish)
2 For a long time he didn't stop ... (work)
3 Then he stopped ... something to drink. (have)
4 After that he went on ... for another three hours. (type)

Step 3 | *Forget, remember, regret, try* + infinitive with *to* or *-ing*

Gavin was typing the final page of the last chapter of his book when there was a power cut. Suddenly everything disappeared from the computer screen. Normally he remembered to save his work, but this time he'd forgotten to save what he'd written. When the power came back, he desperately tried to find the work he'd done. He tried pressing every button on the computer. He tried phoning the software company. But his last chapter had simply disappeared.
He'll never forget losing that last chapter! He'll always regret not saving it. He'll always remember seeing the computer screen go blank.

- The verbs *forget, remember, regret, try* can be followed by the infinitive with *to* or the *-ing* form, but the meaning is not the same.

- *Forget to do* OR *forget doing*?
We use *forget* + the infinitive with *to* to say we didn't do something we should have done.
  *He'**d forgotten to save** what he'd written.*
  (= He didn't save what he'd written. He should have done.)

We use *forget* + the *-ing* form (normally in negative sentences) when we talk about memories of things we did in the past.

> *He'll never **forget losing** that last chapter.*
> (= He'll always have the memory of losing the chapter.)

- *Remember to do* OR *remember doing*?

We use *remember* + the infinitive with *to* when we remember that we have to do something.

> *Normally he **remembered to save** his work.*
> (= He remembered he had to save his work.)

We use *remember* + the *-ing* form when we talk about something we did in the past.

> *He'll always **remember seeing** the screen go blank.*
> (= He'll always have the memory of seeing the screen go blank.)

- If the remembering or the forgetting comes:

before the action	*remember/forget* + infinitive with *to*
after the action	*remember/forget* + *-ing*

- *Try to do* OR *try doing*?

We use *try* + the infinitive with *to* when we say we make an effort to do something or see if we can do something.

> *He **tried to find** the work he'd done.*
> (He made an effort to find it.)

We use *try* + the *-ing* form when we talk about a possible solution to a problem.

> *He **tried phoning** the software company.*
> (= He phoned the company to see if they could help him.)
> *He **tried pressing** every button on his computer.*

- *Regret to do* OR *regret doing*?

We use *regret* + the infinitive with *to* to announce bad news.

> *I **regret to say** that I lost the last chapter.*

We use *regret* + the *-ing* form when we wish we had/hadn't done something.

> *He'll always **regret** not **saving** it.*

CHECK QUESTIONS 3

Put in the right form of the verb.
1 Normally he remembered ... what he'd written. (copy)
2 He tried ... his computer, but that didn't work. (hit)
3 He'll never forget ... the empty computer screen. (see)
4 The next day he tried ... what he'd written, but he couldn't. (remember)
5 Now he regrets ... more careful. (not be)

Practice

begin bother continue + intend start	infinitive with *to* or *-ing* The meaning is the same.	go on need stop + forget remember try regret	infinitive with *to* or *-ing* The meaning changes.

1 **Andrea has got a daughter aged three. She is going out for the evening and giving instructions to her baby-sitter. Complete the sentences, using the infinitive with *to* or the *-ing* form with the verbs in brackets.**

If she starts (1 cry) .... , don't

panic! She'll probably stop (2 cry) ....

before long. But if she goes on (3 cry) ....

for a long time, you could try (4 give) ....
her a drink. And if that doesn't work, try

(5 read) .... her a story. And if she
still keeps crying, her nappy might need

(6 change) .... I hope you won't

need (7 do) .... that, but you

never know. Don't bother (8 phone) ....
unless it's urgent. Remember (9 check)

.... she's all right every half hour.

I don't intend (10 stay) .... out

late. Don't forget (11 lock) .... the
front door after I've left.

2 **Complete this newspaper report. Use the infinitive with *to* or the *-ing* form of these verbs: *get, read* (x 2), *see, put* (x 2), *examine, look at, stop, hear, think.***

William Cox left his car on the quay at Poole,

Dorset, while he stopped (1) ....
the boats. Two minutes later he looked round
and saw his new Ford rolling slowly towards

the edge of the quay. 'I tried (2) ....
it, but it was too late,' commented Mr Cox. 'I

remember (3) .... out of the car

and (4) .... that it was a bit near
the edge of the quay. I think I remember

(5) .... the handbrake on, but I

must have forgotten (6) .... it on.'
Brian Bungay, the owner of a luxury yacht,
commented: 'I was on my boat and I remember

(7) .... a shout. I stopped

(8) .... the newspaper, but I
couldn't see anything wrong, so I went on

(9) .... Then I remember

(10) .... a car about to fall on top
of me. I jumped out of the way just in time.'

Insurance experts need (11) ....
the damage to the car and the yacht. The cost
of repairs will probably be more than £100,000.

3 **Daniel is going on a camping holiday for the first time. His father is not worried, but his mother is. Complete the sentences, using the verbs in brackets.**

Mother: Don't forget (1 send) ....
    us a postcard.

Father: I'll never forget (2 go) ....
    on a camping holiday when I was your age. I

    remember (3 do) .... all sorts
    of things I've never told your mother about.

Mother: Remember (4 brush) ....
    your teeth. And your clothes will need

    (5 wash) .... , so remember

    (6 take) .... washing powder.

    And you'll need (7 take) ....
    some shampoo too.

Daniel: Yes, all right, Mum. There's no need to

    go on (8 repeat) ....
    everything. You've already told me that.

Mother: Try (9 phone) .... every
    night, won't you? And if we're not in, try

    (10 leave) .... a message with
    your grandmother. And don't forget, you

    must stop (11 find) .... a camp-
    site before it gets dark.

Daniel: You never stop (12 worry) .... ,
    do you, Mum!

53

Reported speech:
He said it was a good car

> Anna Radford bought a second-hand car from a man who seemed honest.
> 'He said it was a good car. He told me he'd had it for two years. He thought it had a new engine.'

Step 1 | Uses of reported speech

- We often report what another person said but we don't use exactly the same words. This is called reported speech or indirect speech.

Direct speech	Reported speech
'It's a good car.'	*He said it was a good car.*
'I've had it for two years.'	*He told me he'd had it for two years.*

We use ' ... ' (inverted commas/speech marks) to show direct speech. We don't use ' ... ' in reported speech. We don't write: He said 'it was a good car.'

- We often leave out *that* after the reporting verb.
  He said it was a good car.   (Less formal)
  He said that it was a good car.   (More formal)

- We can use both *say* and *tell* as reporting verbs. If we mention who we're talking to, we use *tell* + indirect object (*me, him, the man*, etc.). We don't put *to* before the indirect object.
  *He **told me** it was a good car.*
  (NOT He told to me it was a good car.)
If we don't mention who we're talking to, we use *say*.
  *He **said** it was a good car.*
  (NOT He said me it was a good car.)

CHECK QUESTIONS 1

Change to reported speech.
1 'It isn't expensive.' He said ...
2 'It's got a good radio.' He told ...

Change to direct speech.
3 He said it had new tyres. 'It ... '
4 He told her it was very reliable. 'It ... '

Step 2 | How verb forms change in reported speech

> 'He said he'd never had any problems with the car. He bought it from an old lady. He told me he wasn't selling it because he wanted to. He'd been hoping to keep it but his company had given him a new car. He promised that he would send me all the papers. He said I wasn't going to regret buying the car.'

- If the reporting verb is in the past (*He said … He told me …*), the verb in reported speech usually changes. It 'goes back' one tense into the past.

Direct speech	Reported speech
Present simple	Past simple
'It's a good car.'	*He said it was a good car.*
Present continuous	Past continuous
'I'm not selling it'	*He said he wasn't selling it*
Past simple	Past perfect
'… my company gave me a new car.'	*He said his company had given him a new car.*
Past continuous	Past perfect continuous
'I was hoping to keep it.'	*He said he'd been hoping to keep it.*
Present perfect	Past perfect
'I've never had any trouble with it.'	*He said he'd never had any trouble with it.*
Future: will/shall	Would/should
'I'll send you all the papers.'	*He promised he would send me all the papers.*
Future: going to	Was/were going to
'You're not going to regret buying the car.'	*He said I wasn't going to regret buying the car.*

- Note that a verb in the past simple in direct speech can stay the same in reported speech.
*'I **bought** it from an old lady.'*
*He said he **bought** it from an old lady.* (OR: he **had bought**)

- Note that if we use the past perfect in direct speech, we use the same tense in reported speech.
*'When I bought the car, it **had** only **done** 10,000 miles.'*
*He said the car **had** only **done** 10,000 miles.*

CHECK QUESTIONS 2 **Change to reported speech.**
1 'It always starts first time.'   2 'It doesn't use much petrol.'
3 'I've taken it to France a couple of times.'   4 'I'll take you for a ride in it.'

Step 3 | Modal verbs in reported speech

'He told me the car shouldn't give me any trouble. It ought to last for years. He also said I could ring him if I had any problems, although he might not be at home. He told me I must pay him as soon as possible.'

Direct speech	Reported speech
Can	Could
'You can ring me if you have any trouble.'	*He said I could ring him if I had any trouble.*
May	Might
'I may not be at home.'	*He said he might not be at home.*

- Note that the verbs *would, could, should, might* and *ought do* don't change in reported speech.

*'It **shouldn't** give you any trouble.'*	*He said it **shouldn't** give me any trouble.*
*'It **ought to** last for years.'*	*He said it **ought to** last for years.*

- *Must* either stays the same in reported speech or changes to *had to*. *Must* is more common.
  'You must pay me as soon as possible.'
  *He told me I **must** (OR **had to**) pay him as soon as possible.*

CHECK QUESTIONS 3 **Change to reported speech.**
1 'You can pay me cash or give me a cheque.' He told her ...
2 'You must phone me if there's a problem.'
3 'You should use unleaded petrol.'

Step 4 | Other changes in reported speech

'He said his name was Leach and he wanted £1,250 for the car. I gave him £1,000 and said I would give him the rest the following day. The next day the car wouldn't start so I rang him. The woman who answered said Leach had left the day before. Then the police rang me and said the car didn't belong to him - he'd stolen it the week before. They also said the real owner wanted his car back - that day!'

- The pronouns (*I, we, me*, etc.) and possessive adjectives (*my, our*, etc.) also change in reported speech.

Direct speech	Reported speech
*'**My** name's Leach'*	*He said **his** name was Leach.*

- The following words also change in reported speech:

this	that
*'There's nobody called Leach at **this** address.'*	*She said there was nobody called Leach at **that** address.*
tomorrow	the following day OR the next day
*'I'll give you the rest **tomorrow**.'*	*I said I would give him the rest **the following day**.*
yesterday	the day before OR the previous day
*'He left **yesterday**.'*	*She said he'd left **the day before**.*
last week	the week before OR the previous week
*'He stole it **last week**.'*	*They said he'd stolen it **the week before**.*
today	that day
*'He wants his car back **today**.'*	*He said he wanted his car back **that day**.*

- Note also these changes:

next week/next month, etc.	the following week / month, etc.
now	then
this morning/evening, etc.	that morning/evening, etc.
tonight	that night
three days ago	three days before

CHECK QUESTIONS 4 **Change to reported speech.**
1 'I first met Leach two days ago.' She said she ...
2 'I got the money out of the bank this morning.' She said she ...
3 'You must return the car to the owner next weekend.' The police said she ...

'And now I've spoken to a lawyer and he says he'll see me next week but he doesn't think I'll ever get my money back. But my boyfriend said he'll find Leach and get the money.'

- Note that words and phrases in direct speech don't change in reported speech if it's still the same day or week, etc.

Direct speech	Reported speech
*'I'll see you **next week**.'*	*He says he'll see me **next week**.*

(It's still this week when she reports what the lawyer said.)

- If the reporting verb is in the past but the situation still exists, we can keep the same tense.

'I'll find Leach and get the money.'	*But my boyfriend said he'll find Leach and get the money.*

(Her boyfriend is still looking for Leach when she says this.)

- If the reporting verb is in the present, the future or the present perfect, the tense of the verb in reported speech doesn't change.

Direct speech	Reported speech
'You'll never get your money back.'	*He **says** I'll never get my money back.*

CHECK QUESTIONS 5

Change to reported speech.

1 'I've lost £1000.' (Anna still hasn't got her money back.) She said she ...
2 'I don't think I'll buy another car.' She says she ...

Practice

Direct speech	Reported speech
'I'm English'	*She said she was English.* OR *She told me she was English.*
'I can speak English.'	*She said she could (OR can) speak English.* BUT *She says she can speak English.*
'I'm going to England next week.'	*She said she was going to England the following week.*

1 Change the following jokes into reported speech.

Patient: I've got a problem, doctor. I feel a pain in my right eye every time I drink a cup of tea.

Doctor: I don't think it's serious. I think you should take the spoon out of the cup before you drink the tea.

The patient said she ....

....

....

....

....

....

Patient: Doctor, you must help me.

Doctor: I will if I can, but I haven't got much time today, so it may not be possible.

Patient: I've got a terrible pain in my right leg. It started two days ago.

Doctor: That's interesting. I want you to stand at the window and put your tongue out.

Patient But that won't stop the pain in my right leg!

Doctor: No, but it's going to help me, because I don't like the man who lives opposite.

The patient told the doctor he ....

....

....

....

....

....

....

....

....

....

....

....

2 When Amanda moved into her new flat, several things needed repairing. The landlord telephoned her and said:

'I'm busy now, but I'll come round today or tomorrow. I'll fix the roof this week and I'll redecorate the bathroom next week. I checked the central heating last month, and I had the washing-machine serviced a week ago. The carpets were all cleaned yesterday. If you've got any problems, you can ring me tonight at home.'

A month later the landlord had done none of the things he had promised. Amanda is telling a friend about what he said, using reported speech. Complete the text.

When he first rang me, he said he was busy

(1) .... but he (2) ....

....

But he never came. He said he (3) ....

the roof (4) ...., and he

(5) .... the bathroom

(6) .... But he

never did. He also said he (7) .... the

central heating (8) ....

and he (9) .... the washing-machine

serviced (10) .... But

neither of them has ever worked. He told me

the carpets (11) ....

Then he said if I (12) .... any problems, I

(13).. at home. I

rang him, but he wasn't in.

54

Reported questions, commands, etc.:
She asked me where I was from

Nick, a British tourist, is telling his American girlfriend about the questions he was asked at Kennedy Airport, New York.
'To start with the immigration officer asked me where I was from and why I'd come to the States. That wasn't a problem. But then she wanted to know how much money I had. When I told her, she said $800 wasn't enough for three weeks. She wondered why I hadn't brought more. She then asked me if I intended to work. She wanted to know whether I really planned to go back to the UK after three weeks.'

Step 1 | Changes in reported questions

● In reported questions, the word order is subject + verb. This is not the same as in the direct question.

Direct question	Reported question
verb + subject	**subject + verb**
*'Where **are you** from?'*	*She asked me where **I was** from.*
	(NOT She asked me where was I from.)
*'Why **have you come**?'*	*She asked me why **I had come**.*
	(NOT She asked me why had I come.)

Note: There's no question mark at the end of a reported question.

● Notice how questions in the present simple and the past simple change in reported speech.

Direct question	Reported question
'How much money	*She asked me how much*
***do you have**?'*	*money I had.*
*'Where **did you buy***	*She asked me where*
your ticket?'	*I **bought** my ticket.* (OR *I **had bought***)

● If there's no question word like *why, who, where*, etc. in the direct question, we use *if* or *whether* in the reported question.

Direct question	Reported question
'Do you intend to work?'	*She asked me **if** I intended to work.*
'Do you really plan	*She wanted to know **whether** I*
to go back?'	*really planned to go back.*

● We often use these verbs in reported questions:
  ask want to know wonder (NOT say)

Direct question	Reported question
'How much money	*She **wanted to know** how much*
do you have?'	*money I had.* (OR *She **asked** ...*)
'Why haven't you	*She **wondered** why I hadn't*
brought more?'	*brought more.*

CHECK QUESTIONS 1

Change to reported questions.
1 'What's your name?' She asked me ...
2 'When are you returning to Britain?' She asked me ...
3 'Do you have friends in the USA?' She wanted to know ...

Step 2 | The infinitive with *to* in reported commands, requests, etc.

> 'Then she told me to show her my return ticket. She warned me not to try to get a job. She also asked me to give her my address in the States. I told her I was staying with you in New York. She said New York could be a bit dangerous, and she advised me not to carry a lot of money on me.'

- We normally use this construction in reported commands, warnings, requests and advice.

subject +	verb +	object +	infinitive with *to*
She	*told*	*me*	*to show her my ticket.*

Direct speech

Reported speech

Commands

'Show me your ticket.'	She told me to show her my ticket.
'Don't try	She warned me not to try
to get a job!'	to get a job.

Requests

| 'Can you give me your | She asked me to give her my |
| address in the States?' | address in the States. |

Advice

| 'You shouldn't carry a | She advised me not to carry a lot |
| lot of money on you.' | of money on me. |

- Note that in reported requests with the verb *ask*, we can sometimes use the construction *ask (someone) for something.*

    She asked me to give her my address in the States.

OR *She **asked (me) for** my address in the States.*

CHECK QUESTIONS 2 **Change to reported speech.**
1 'Show me your passport!'
2 'Can you fill in an immigration form?'
3 'You shouldn't go to some parts of Manhattan.'

Step 3 | Other reporting verbs

> 'Then she offered to give me the address of the American Youth Hostel organisation. She explained that there were hundreds of hostels all over the States. She suggested I visited Boston, where she came from. I promised to go there, if I had time. She apologised for asking me so many questions. She reminded me to be careful.'

- We use *agree, invite, offer, promise, refuse, remind, threaten* as reporting verbs with this construction.

subject +	verb	(+ object)	+	infinitive with *to*
She	*offered*			*to give me the address.*

(Direct speech: 'I'll give you the address.')

| *She* | *reminded* | *me* | | *to be careful.* |

(Direct speech: 'Don't forget to be careful.')

| *I* | *promised* | | | *to go there.* |

(Direct speech: 'I'll certainly go there.')

- We can use *add, admit, agree, comment, claim, complain, deny, explain, insist, mention, promise, remind, suggest* as reporting verbs with this construction.

verb +	*that* clause
She suggested	*(that) I visited Boston.*

(Direct speech: 'Why don't you visit Boston?')

| *She explained* | *that there were hundreds of hostels* |

(Direct speech: 'You see, there are hundreds of hostels.')

- We use *apologise for + -ing* as a reporting verb.

She apologised for asking me so many questions.

(Direct speech: 'I'm sorry I asked you so many questions.')

CHECK QUESTIONS 3

Change to reported speech.

1 'I'll show you on a map.' She offered ...
2 'Why don't you go to New England.' She suggested ...
3 'It's the most beautiful part of the States.' She added ...
4 'Remember. Don't try to get a job.' She reminded me ...

Practice

1 A policeman has just stopped a motorcyclist. Change the conversation to reported speech. Use *The policeman (he) asked him ...* and *He said ...*

Policeman: What's your name?
Motorcyclist: Jason Cox.
Policeman: Who does the motorcycle belong to?
Motorcyclist: It belongs to me.
Policeman: Have you got a driving licence?
Motorcyclist: Yes, I have.
Policeman: Can I see it?
Motorcyclist: I haven't got it on me.
Policeman: Can you bring it to Redland Police station tomorrow?
Motorcyclist. Yes, I can.
Policeman: Did you know your back light isn't working?
Motorcyclist: No, I didn't.
Policeman: You must fix it or walk home.

The policeman asked him ....

....

....

....

....

....

....

....

....

....

....

....

2 A doctor is talking to a patient. Change what the doctor says to reported speech.

Doctor: (1) What's the problem?
Mr Welch: I collapsed while I was at work.
Doctor: (2) Do you know why you collapsed?
Mr Welch: I've been working very hard recently.
Doctor: I see. (3) Could you roll up your sleeve please. Well your blood pressure's quite high. (4) I think you should take a complete rest. (5) I suggest you go away on holiday. (6) If you don't take it easy, you may make yourself seriously ill. (7) You're not a young man any more. (8) Take the sleeping pills to help you sleep. (9) You must come and see me again on Thursday.

1 The doctor wanted to know ....

....

2 She asked ....

....

3 She asked ....

....

4 She advised him ....

....

5 She suggested ....

....

6 She warned him ....

....

7 She reminded him ....

....

8 She told him ....

....

9 She insisted ....

....

55 | The definite article: *the* (1)

> We noticed the advertisement in the travel agent's.
> 'Going to the USA? Go with the airline that really looks after you, the
> one that gives you real value for money. The honest airline. Fly USAir!'
> The price was so low we booked the tickets the same day.

Step 1 | The form and pronunciation of *the*

- The definite article has only got one form: *the*. It is used before singular and plural nouns:

    the *tickets*   **the** *same day*

- *The* is pronounced /ðə/
before words beginning with a consonant (*b, d, y,* etc.):

    the *travel agent's*   **the** *price*

before vowels that have a consonant sound:

    the *USA* /ðə ju: es eɪ/   **the** *one* /ðə wʌn/

- *The* is pronounced /ði:/ before words starting with a vowel sound (*a, e, i,* etc.).

    the *advertisement*   **the** *easy way*   **the** *honest airline*

CHECK QUESTIONS 1 **How do you pronounce *the* before these words? Write /ðə/ or /ði:/.**
1 the /   / holiday 2 the airport /   / 3 the /   / United States 4 the /   / Americans

Step 2 | The basic use of *the*

> We phoned for a taxi. The taxi was late. On the way to the airport there
> was a traffic jam on the motorway. Because of the traffic jam we arrived
> at the airport late, at half past twelve. The flight left at quarter past
> one.

- We use *the* when we talk about a particular person or thing. Note the difference between:

    We phoned for **a taxi**. (Any taxi. Not a specific taxi.)

and **The taxi** *was late*. (The particular taxi they phoned for.)

See also: **The flight** *left at quarter past one*.

    (The particular flight they had tickets for.)

- Note also that we use the indefinite article *a, an* when a noun is mentioned for the first time. After that we use the definite article *the* with that noun.

    We phoned for **a taxi**. **The taxi** *was late*.

    There was **a traffic jam** *on the motorway. Because of* **the traffic jam** *we arrived at the airport late.*

CHECK QUESTIONS 2 **Complete the sentences with *a/an* or *the*.**
1 ... taxi they phoned for arrived late at their house, at quarter past twelve.
2 ... taxi-driver didn't say he was sorry.
3 ... traffic jam was caused by ... accident on ... motorway. ... car had collided with ... lorry.

Step 3 | Other uses of *the*

It was the longest flight I'd ever been on (and also the most expensive!). We left London in the afternoon. After an hour we were flying over the south of Ireland and after 7 hours we were flying over the centre of New York - and it was still the afternoon! Out of the window on the right we could see Manhattan, and on the left the Statue of Liberty.

We also use *the*

- with superlatives:
  the *longest flight* ***the*** *most expensive flight*

- with parts of the day to say when something happens:
  *in **the** afternoon in **the** morning*
  *in **the** evening* (BUT *at night*)

- with words which describe geographical position and place:
  the *south of Ireland* ***the*** *centre of New York*
  the *window on the right*

CHECK QUESTIONS 3 **Complete these sentences.**
1 We sat at ... back of the plane.
2 ... best part of the flight was the in-flight movie, ... worst was the coffee!
3 New York is ... ... north-east of the United States.
4 At two o'clock ... ... afternoon in London, it's nine o'clock ... ... morning in New York.

Step 4 | When we don't use *the*

On the plane we had lunch and dinner. When we arrived in New York we just wanted to go to bed. We went by bus to the centre of town. It was Saturday, so the streets of Manhattan weren't too crowded. Most New Yorkers don't go to work on Saturdays; they stay at home in the suburbs. Our hotel was on 42nd Street. We took a taxi. The taxi-driver was Puerto Rican and he spoke mainly Spanish. I didn't learn Spanish at school.

We don't use *the*

- in the phrases *in bed/to bed, at work/to work, at home.*
  *we wanted to go **to bed** they don't go **to work***
  *they stay **at home***

- before days, months and festivals in phrases like:
  *It was Saturday. They don't go to work **on Saturdays**.*
  in June at Christmas before Easter

- before meals in sentences like: *We had **lunch** and **dinner**.*

- before school subjects: *I didn't learn **Spanish** at school.*

- before time expressions like: *last week next month next Monday*

- in the phrases *by bus, by train*, etc.: *We went **by bus**.*

CHECK QUESTIONS 4 **Put in *the* where necessary.**

1 We had ... breakfast at ... home in London before we left.
2 ... bus station was on ... 38th Street.
3 We went to ... hotel by ... taxi.
4 We're flying home ... next Thursday.

Step 5 | Other cases where *the* is or is not used

> The taxi driver took us all over Manhattan. We saw the Hudson River, the Empire State Building, the Metropolitan Opera House and Fifth Avenue, where the rich and the famous do their shopping. On the sidewalks there were people from China, Italy, the West Indies, Africa and Asia. Forty minutes later we arrived at the Wellington Hotel on 42nd Street and the taxi-driver asked for $78! Our room was on the fifth floor. In our room we looked at a map of New York for the first time. The hotel was only 200m from the bus station! That taxi-driver must think the English are stupid!

We use *the*:

- with the names of rivers, oceans, and groups of mountains and islands.
  the *Hudson River* ***the*** *Atlantic* ***the*** *Rocky Mountains* ***the*** *Azores*
  BUT not with the names of lakes and individual mountains and islands.
  Lake Eyrie   Mount Everest   Mallorca

- with the names of buildings like cinemas, hotels, etc.
  the *Wellington Hotel* ***the*** *Empire State Building* ***the*** *Metropolitan Opera House*
  BUT not with the names of churches, castles, palaces, squares, streets, etc.
  St Patrick's Cathedral   Windsor Castle   42nd Street
  Buckingham Palace   Washington Square   Fifth Avenue

- with the names of 'plural' countries like:
  the *United States* ***the*** *West Indies* ***the*** *Netherlands*
  and note also: ***the*** *United Kingdom*.
  BUT not with the names of most countries and continents:
  Puerto Rico   Japan   Spain   Africa   Europe   Asia   America   North America

CHECK QUESTIONS 5a **Put in *the* where necessary.**

1 ... United Nations Headquarters faces ... East River.
2 ...White House is probably ... most famous building in ... United States.
3 ... Rocky Mountains are in ... west of ... America.

We also use *the*

- when we use an adjective (for example: *English*) to refer to the people of a country.
  the *English* ***the*** *French* ***the*** *Dutch* ***the*** *Spanish* ***the*** *Japanese* ***the*** *Chinese*
  BUT when we use a plural noun (*Americans*) to refer to the people of a country or a continent, *the* is normally optional.
  *(**the**) Americans (**the**) Puerto Ricans (**the**) Italians (**the**) Europeans*

- with an adjective to describe groups of people.
  the *rich* ***the*** *famous*

- with ordinal numbers: ***the*** *first* ***the*** *third* ***the*** *fifth* (5th) *floor* etc.
  BUT not with positions in a race, a competition, etc.
  *He came **third** in the race.*

Complete the sentences, using *the* where necessary.
1 ... first American we met said he preferred ... Irish to ... English.
2 ... Americans seem to work harder than ... British.
3 ... Long Island is where many of ... rich and ... famous live.

Step 6 | When we don't use *the* before *school, hospital, church*, etc.

On Sunday we went to church. We went to the church on Broadway. On the way back to the hotel we saw a shooting at the university on 39th Street and two students were taken to hospital.

- We don't use *the* when we're talking about the main purpose or use of these places: *church, hospital, school, university, college, prison, court.*
  *On Sunday we went **to church**.*
  *Two students were taken **to hospital**.*
- We use *the* before these words when we're talking about a particular church, a particular university, etc.
  *We went to **the** church on Broadway.*
  *We saw a shooting at **the** university.*

Complete the sentences, using *the* where necessary.
1 Our hotel manager went to ... school in England, then went to ... university in the States.
2 The New York police arrested a man for the shooting. He was a cleaner at ... university.
3 He'll appear in ... court next week. He'll definitely go to ... prison.

ANSWERS TO
CHECK QUESTIONS
1, 2, 3, 4, 5 AND 6

1 1 /ðə/ 2 /ði:/ 3 /ðə/ 4 /ði:/
2 1 The 2 The 3 The an the A a
3 1 the 2 The the 3 in the 4 in the in the
4 2 The bus station 3 the hotel

5a 1 The the 2 The the the 3 The Rocky
   Mountains the west
5b 1 The the the 2 (The) the 3 the rich and
   (the) famous
6 2 the

180

Practice

1 Complete this conversation using *the* where necessary.

'Do you go to (1) .... church?'

'No, not very often. At (2) .... Christmas and

(3) .... Easter usually. We go to (4) ....
church in Clifton Street.'
'Where do your children go to (5) ....
school?'

'Both our children go to (6)........... local school,

just down (7) .... road.'

'And after (8) .... school ? Will they go to (9)

.... college or to (10) .... university?'

'I doubt it. (11) .... older one, Emma, wants
to be a nurse. You see, she's got a friend who

works in (12) .... hospital in (13) ....
centre of town. Her brother will probably go to

(14) .... prison! He attacked a man and they

had to take him to (15) .... hospital.'

'And is your son still at (16) .... school?'
'No, not really. In fact, he spends most of

(17) .... time in (18) .... bed. I just want

him to leave (19) .... home and go out to

(20) .... work!'

2 Fill in the gaps with *the* where necessary.

I hate (1) .... November! It doesn't get light

till (2) .... 8 o'clock in (3) .... morning.

Then it's dark again as early as (4) ....

4 o'clock in (5) .... afternoon. After

(6) .... Christmas, (7) .... days start to

get a bit longer, but (8) .... weather starts to

get colder. On (9) .... Friday (10) .... last

week, (11) .... temperature was minus 10°.

(12) .... next week (13) .... weather

forecast is (14) .... same.

**3 Complete this telephone conversation, using
the where necessary.**

'Hi! This is Nick. We met at (1) .... party at

(2) .... Sarah's house on (3) .... Saturday.
Remember?'
'Oh, yes. I remember.'
'Are you free this evening? There's a good band

playing at (4) .... Red Lion.'
'Sounds interesting. Yes, OK. But I can't get

there before (5) .... 9 o'clock at (6) ....

earliest. I haven't had (7) .... dinner yet.'
'That's OK. I can pick you up and we can go by

(8) .... car. Where do you live exactly?'

'In (9) .... Granby Road. Do you know it ?'
'I'm afraid not.'

'Take (10) .... first turning on (11) ....

right after (12) .... bridge over (13) ....
River Avon.'

'Is that opposite (14) .... Odeon Cinema?'

'That's right. Then take (15) .... second

turning on (16) .... left after (17) .... St

Luke's Church. That's (18) .... Granby Road.'
'OK. I'll see you later.'

**4 Complete this advertisement, using *the* where
necessary.**

Come to Quebec:

● where (1) .... France meets (2) .... Canada.

● where (3) .... Canadians speak (4) ....

French. (But if you didn't learn (5) .... French

at high school, don't worry. They all speak

(6) .... English.)

● where you can have (7) .... dinner in some

of (8) .... finest French restaurants outside

(9) .... France.
● where you can swim or sail on (10) .... Lake
Batiscan.
● where you can climb to (11) .... top of

(12) .... Mount Apita.
● where you can go by (13) .... boat down

(14) .... St Lawrence River.
● above all, where you can experience a bit of

(15) .... France in (16) .... North America.

Life isn't simple any more. The world is a dangerous place. Water and food are often polluted. Chemicals, additives and pesticides are everywhere. They're in the water we drink and the food we buy. We need clean water and clean air. We need food that is produced without additives and pesticides. Life in the big cities of the world is unhealthy and unsafe. The lakes and the rivers of Europe are dying. Do we care more about nature or profit? We need better public transport, not new roads. The people of Britain need jobs, not unemployment. We need generosity, not selfishness. We need the Alternative Party!

Step 1 | Nouns without *the*

We don't use *the* when we use the following nouns in a general sense:
- plural nouns. **Chemicals, additives** and **pesticides** *are everywhere.*
- uncountable nouns. **Water** *and* **food** *are often polluted.*
- abstract nouns. **Life** *isn't simple any more.*
We need **generosity***, not* **selfishness***.*

CHECK QUESTIONS 1

Which is right, A or B?
1 ... is becoming more difficult. (A Life   B The life)
2 ... are damaging our food. (A The pesticides   B Pesticides)
3 People are worried about ... (A the pollution   B pollution)

Step 2 | When to use *the* before nouns

- We use *the* with plural and uncountable nouns when we mean particular people or things.
   The people *of Britain need jobs.* **the water** *we drink*   **the food** *we buy*
   The lakes *and* **the rivers** *of Europe are dying.*
Here, we don't mean all people, all water, all food, all lakes and rivers. We mean particular water (the water we drink), particular food (the food we buy), etc.
- Note that we sometimes talk about a particular thing, but use it in a general sense. So we don't use *the*.
   Life *in the big cities of the world is unhealthy and unsafe.*
   (Not all life in the world, but all life in the big cities, which is still a general idea.)
   We need **food** *that is produced without additives.*
   (Not all food, but all food that is produced without additives)

CHECK QUESTIONS 2

Complete the sentences, using *the* where necessary.
1 All over the world ... cars cause ... pollution.
2 Is there room on ... roads of Britain for ... cars we're making?
3 Nowadays ... people seem to prefer ... food with ... additives.

ANSWERS TO
CHECK QUESTIONS
1 AND 2

1 1 A 2 B 3 B
2 2 the the

182

Practice

1 Do these sentences refer to the particular or the general? Write 'Particular' or 'General'.

1 Motorbikes can be dangerous.

....

2 Trains in France usually run on time.

....

3 All the trains we went on in France were late.

....

4 Cars with diesel engines are more economical than cars with petrol engines.

....

5 The cars they make in Japan are sold all over the world.

....

6 All the cars I've owned have been Japanese.

....

7 Bikes are very popular in Holland.

....

8 Buses in London are red.

....

2 Complete the sentences with *the* where necessary.

1 They say .... English people drink a lot of tea. But .... English people I know prefer .... coffee.

2 Everybody thinks that .... French people always wear .... smart clothes, but .... French students I met all wore ....T-shirts and .... jeans.

3 A lot of .... Europeans think that .... American people drive .... big cars, but .... people we know in America all have .... small Japanese cars.

4 .... Swedish students we sat next to on the plane both had dark hair. We thought all .... Swedish people had blond hair.

5 They say .... Spanish people have dinner very late in the evening, but .... people I stayed with in Spain were in bed by half past nine!

3 This morning Steven went to the doctor. The doctor told him what he can and cannot eat. Complete the sentences with *the* where necessary.

1 He must be very careful about .... food he eats.

2 He can eat .... meat, but he can't eat .... red meat. He can only eat .... chicken or .... fish.

3 He can have .... potatoes, but .... potatoes mustn't be fried.

4 He must eat .... raw vegetables if possible.

5 He mustn't put .... salt on his food.

6 He can have .... coffee, but .... coffee must be decaffeinated.

4 An old man is complaining about modern Britain. Use these words or phrases, with or without *the*, to complete the sentences: *marriage, young people, music, drugs and sex, respect, crime, money*.

1 .... on the streets of London has increased.

2 .... you hear today is just noise.

3 Spending .... seems to be the most important thing in life.

4 .... has no value for young people.

5 They're only interested in ....

6 .... that children have for their parents has decreased.

7 .... don't know the meaning of hard work.

57 A, an, some

Amy Clarke's a university student. She lives in a house with a dozen other students. She shares a room with a friend. Money is usually a problem, so Amy's got a job. She works two evenings a week. She's a waitress at a pizza restaurant. She earns £5 an hour so she makes about £30 an evening. She has to wear a uniform. 'I have an enormous breakfast, but I don't have lunch. I have a big dinner at work – a huge pizza and an ice cream. It's an interesting job and I meet a lot of people.'

Step 1 | A or an?

- We use a/ə/ before words that begin with a consonant sound.
  a *restaurant* **a** *part-time job* **a** *uniform*
- We use an/ən/ before words which begin with a vowel sound.
  an *ice cream* **an** *interesting job* **an** *hour*

Note: The first sound in *hour* is the vowel sound /aʊə/. We don't pronounce the *h*, so we say **an** *hour*. But note **a** *house* because we pronounce the *h*.

Note also **a** *university student,* **a** *uniform.* The first sound in these words is the consonant sound /j/ not the vowel sound /ʌ/.

CHECK QUESTIONS 1   **Put *a* or *an* before these words:**
1 job 2 union 3 unusual name 4 enormous ice cream 5 holiday 6 honest man

Step 2 | Main use of a/an (the indefinite article)

- We usually use *a/an* with singular countable nouns.
  a **house** *a* **friend** *an* **evening**
- We use *a/an* when we talk about a person or a thing for the first time. We don't identify the person or thing.
  She lives in **a** *house.* (We don't say which house.)
  She shares **a** *room with* **a** *friend.* (We don't say which room or which friend.)

CHECK QUESTIONS 2   **Put in *a/an* where necessary.**
1   She works in restaurant in street near the station.
2   For lunch she only has apple and glass of milk.

Step 3 | Other uses of a/an

- We use *a/an* before occupations, jobs and religions, etc.
  She's **a** *student. She's* **a** *waitress. He's* **a** *Muslim.*
- We use *a/an* when we talk about numbers or quantities.
  a dozen other students *a lot of people* *£100 (**a** hundred pounds)* *a few friends*
- We can use *a/an* with the meaning *per.*
  two evenings **a** *week* *£4* **an** *hour* *£2* **a** *kilo*
- We also use *a/an* in exclamations like:
  What **a** *huge pizza! What* **an** *interesting job!*

CHECK QUESTIONS 3 **Put in *a/an* where necessary.**
Amy's friend works in pub. She's barmaid. She works three evenings week. She earns $4.50 hour.

Step 4 | When not to use *a/an*

We don't use *a/an*:

- before uncountable nouns (see Unit 59).
  ***Money** is usually a problem for students.* (NOT A money)
- before the names of meals (*breakfast, lunch, dinner*, etc.).
  I don't have lunch. (NOT I don't have a lunch.)
  But if we use an adjective before the meal, we must use *a/an*:
  *I have **a big** dinner at work.* (NOT I have big dinner)

CHECK QUESTIONS 4 **Put in *a/an* where necessary.**
Amy likes good food, but food's expensive for student, and she doesn't like spending money. She has big breakfast; she only has apple for lunch, but she has dinner at work.

Step 5 | The plural of *a/an*: *some* + noun, or noun on its own

In the street where Amy lives there are some people who don't like students. They say students have an easy life and don't do any work. Is this true? In fact, students usually have very little money. Some students get jobs to pay for their food and accommodation. Some students borrow money from their parents. A lot of Amy's friends are students. They don't all have rich parents. And they can't all find part-time jobs.

- We often use *some* as the plural of *a/an* when we mean a certain number.
  *There are **some** people who don't like students.*
  (A certain number of people, but not all.)
  ***Some students** borrow money from their parents.*
  (Not all students borrow money from their parents.)

We don't use *some*:

- when we're interested in the things or people themselves, not the number of them.
  *They get **jobs** to pay for their food and accommodation.*
  *They don't all have **rich parents**.*
- when we talk about things or people in general.
  *They say **students** have an easy life.* (= all students)
  ***Students** usually have very little money.*

(For the use of *some* with uncountable nouns see Unit 61.)

CHECK QUESTIONS 5 **Put in *some* where necessary.**
1 There are people who say that students have an easy life.
2 There are very nice students who live in our house.
3 People understand students' problems, and people don't.

ANSWERS TO
CHECK QUESTIONS
1, 2, 3, 4 AND 5

1 1 a job 2 a union 3 an unusual name
4 an enormous ice cream 5 a holiday
6 an honest man
2 1 a restaurant a street 2 an apple a glass

3 a pub a barmaid a week an hour
4 a student a big breakfast an apple
5 1 (some) people 2 some very nice students
3 Some people some people

Practice

1 **Put these words and phrases into two columns:**
empty glass, honest answer, US citizen, Eastern European country, European country, untidy room, one-way street, unusual name, international airport, CD-player, Chinese restaurant, used car.

a	an
....	....
....	....
....	....
....	....
....	....
....	....
....	....

2 **Complete the following texts, using *a* or *an* where necessary.**

He's (1) .... 20. He's (2) .... American citizen, but he's got (3) .... Italian name – Luigi Cabello. He's (4) .... university student. He lives in (5) .... small apartment. He's got (6) .... old American car – (7) .... Chevrolet.

He's (14) .... English, but he's got (15) .... unusual name – Yves. He's (16) .... electrician. He lives in (17) .... house with his parents in (18) .... old English city called (19) .... Exeter. He's got (20) .... Italian motorbike – (21) .... Ducati.

She's (8) .... teacher. She was (9) .... British, but now she's got (10) .... Australian passport. She lives in (11) .... Melbourne which is (12) .... enormous city in (13) .... South East Australia.

She's from (22) .... island in the Caribbean called Antigua. She's (23) .... air hostess with (24) .... West Indian airline. She lives in (25) .... small apartment with her boyfriend who's (26) .... pilot.

3 **Complete the dialogue, using *a* or *some* where necessary.**

'Can I help you?'

'Yes, I want to make (1) .... fruit salad for (2) .... supper this evening, so I need (3) .... apples, please. (4) .... people buy fruit salad in tins, I prefer to make mine.'

'These are (5) ....very nice apples. These green ones. Would you like (6) .... ?'

'Yes, please.'

'Anything else?'

'Yes, I'd like (7) .... bananas, please. Good heavens! They're expensive, aren't they!'

'I'm afraid (8) .... bananas are very expensive at the moment. But (9) .... oranges are cheap. How about (10) .... kilo of (11) .... oranges?'

'Yes, OK.'

'Do you want (12) .... big ones or (13) .... small ones?'

'I'll take half (14) .... kilo of (15) .... small ones, please.'

58

Nouns: singular and plural:
book/books, child/children

<table>
<tr><td>

**ROBBERY IN
STAPLETON ROAD**

● ● ● ● ● ● ● ● ● ● ● ● ●

Thieves stole cameras and
videos from two shops in
Stapleton Road yesterday.
They also took several
boxes of video cassettes
and hundreds of audio
cassettes.

</td><td>

**FIGHT IN CITY CENTRE
CAR PARK**

● ● ● ● ● ● ● ● ● ● ● ● ● ● ● ●

Two police officers were injured in
a fight last night. One policeman
lost four teeth. Three other people
were also injured. The police were
called to the Central car park where
there was a fight involving about
two dozen young men and women.
Dozens of cars and two buses were
damaged.

</td></tr>
</table>

Step 1 | The plural form of nouns

● Most nouns have a plural ending in *-s*.
a camera > two cameras   an officer > two officers
(For the spelling of plural endings, see Appendix 3.)

● This final *-s* is pronounced in two different ways:
/s/ after the consonants *c, p, t, k, f* and *th*: *sho**ps**, casse**ttes***
/z/ after all other consonants and after vowels (*a, o*, etc.):
*thiev**es**   camer**as**   vide**os**   car**s***
When the plural ends in *-es* (after *c, s, x, z, ss, sh, ch*) *-es* is pronounced /ɪz/:
*bo**xes**   bu**ses***

● A few common words have irregular plural forms.

Singular	**Plural**		**Singular**	**Plural**
man	*men*		*foot*	*feet*
woman	*women*		*tooth*	*teeth*
person	*people*		*child*	*children*
(*Persons* is very formal.)			*mouse*	*mice*

● These are sometimes part of other words:
policewoman > policewomen   grandchild > grandchildren
a Frenchman > Frenchmen   (BUT *a German > two Germans*)

● In compound nouns the more important word takes the plural form.
*police officer > police **officers**   credit card > credit **cards**
video cassette > video **cassettes**   car park > car **parks***

● Some nouns (usually numbers) don't change in the plural.
*a dozen > two dozen   a hundred > two hundred
a thousand > two thousand   a million > two million*
BUT when these words are used to talk about an indefinite number, they have the
plural *-s*.
***Dozens** of cars were damaged.   **hundreds** of audio cassettes*

CHECK QUESTIONS 1 **Put in the plural forms.**
1 a policeman, two ...
2 a businesswoman, two ...
3 a young person, two ...
4 a police station, two ...
5 an Englishman, two ...
6 a thousand, ... of people

<table>
<tr>
<td>

United buy Baresco

• • • • • • • • • • • • • • •

Manchester United have paid £8 million for Baresco, the Italian goalkeeper. 'People in Manchester want to see the world's best players,' commented the manager.

</td>
<td>

New shop opens

• • • • • • • • • • • • • • • • •

Clothes are cheaper at Stax. If your family need new clothes, why not try Stax? 'I bought some trousers for £25,' said Benny Sampson. 'Nowadays £25 isn't a lot to pay for a pair of trousers. Jeans are cheap too. And my wife bought some tights for only £2.99!'

</td>
<td>

Government says politics is 'honest'

• • • • • • • • • • • • • •

The government has formed a new committee. The committee have produced a document called 'Politics in Britain is an honest profession'.

</td>
</tr>
</table>

● A few nouns look singular, but are used with a plural verb.
  people   police   Manchester United (or any sports team)
  ***People want** to see the world's best players.* (NOT wants)
  ***Manchester United have** bought* (NOT has)

● Collective or group nouns can be followed by a singular verb (if we're thinking of the group as a single unit), or by a plural verb (if we're thinking of the group as a number of individuals). The most common are: *family, government, team, crowd, army, audience, company, group.*
  *If your family **need** new clothes   My family **isn't** very big.*
  *The government **has** formed a committee.*
  *The government **have** discussed the problem.*

● When we think of a certain quantity of money, distance or time as a single unit, we use a singular verb.
  ***£25 isn't** a lot of money to pay for a pair of trousers.*
  *Stax is two miles from town. **Two miles is** a long way to walk.*

● Some nouns are only plural. The most common are: *belongings, clothes, contents, headquarters, savings, surroundings, thanks.*
  ***Clothes are** cheaper at Stax.*

● There's another group of nouns that are also only plural: *glasses, pants, knickers, pyjamas, jeans, scissors, shorts, tights, trousers.*
  *I bought **some trousers** for £25.* (NOT a trousers)
  *Jeans **are** cheap.   She bought **some tights**.* (NOT a tights)
  Before these words you can also use the phrase *a pair of* + a singular verb.
  ***A pair of** trousers **costs** £25.*

● Some nouns end in *-s*, but are followed by a singular verb: *news, politics, mathematics, physics, economics.*
  ***Politics is** an honest profession.*

CHECK QUESTIONS 2 **Choose the correct form of the verb.**
  1 Clothes (isn't/aren't) cheap nowadays.
  2 People (doesn't/don't) buy clothes that are too expensive.
  3 £60 (is/are) a lot of money for a pair of jeans.
  4 The government (is/are) trying to keep prices low.

ANSWERS TO CHECK QUESTIONS 1 AND 2 **1** 1 policemen 2 businesswomen 3 young people 4 police stations 5 Englishmen 6 thousands   **2** 1 aren't 2 don't 3 is 4 is trying/are trying

Practice

1 Complete the sentences with the plural form of the words in brackets.

A postcard from Africa.

My hotel's a bit primitive. I've seen (1 mouse) .... in my room! And there are (2 fly) .... everywhere during the day and (3 mosquito) .... at night. But the (4 beach) .... are beautiful. There are a lot of old (5 church) .... on the island and I've taken lots of (6 photo) .... of them.

Every day I buy two small (7 loaf) .... of bread and some (8 fruit) .... , usually (9 peach) .... , (10 orange) .... and (11 tomato) .... But the (12 shelf) .... in the shops are almost empty, so yesterday I went fishing and caught two (13 fish) .... for my lunch!

There aren't any (14 bus) .... so I walk everywhere. My (15 foot) .... really hurt. I want to go into the mountains. They say there are (16 wolf) .... there. The (17 person) .... are very friendly. Sometimes (18 family) .... come out to say hello when I walk past. The (19 man) .... have two or three (20 wife) .... and dozens of (21 child) .... I don't think their (22 life) .... have changed for (23 century) .... It's certainly one of the most unspoilt (24 country) .... I've ever been to.

2 Put the words in bold into the plural with the word in brackets.

1 I went to **a party** at the weekend. (two)

....

2 I saw **a person** I knew. (a lot of)

....

3 I spoke to **a woman** I was at school with. (two)

....

4 I talked about my **child**. (three)

....

5 **A man** asked me to dance. (two)

....

6 An Arab sheikh arrived with his **wife**. (three)

....

7 He said he owned **an oil company**. (several)

....

8 I told him about the **Arab country** I'd visited. (many)

....

9 I wasn't very hungry. I only ate **a sandwich**. (a few)

....

10 But I had **a glass** of wine. (two or three)

....

3 Choose the correct verb forms.

His clothes (1 are/is) .... very old. His trousers (2 has got/have got) .... holes in them and his glasses (3 are/is) .... broken. All his belongings (4 is/are) .... in a bag on his back. The police often (5 stops/stop) .... him and (6 asks/ask) .... him questions. People (7 avoid/avoids) .... him in the street. His earnings (8 are/is) .... very small; he gets £40 a week from Social Security. For him £40 (9 is/are) .... a lot of money. 'I'm not interested in possessions,' he says, 'Mathematics (10 are/is) .... my passion.'

59

Countable and uncountable nouns:
cars, traffic, pollution

> Hi! You're listening to GWR Radio. What a terrible morning! There have been several accidents on the roads. A number of people were hurt in an accident on the M32 motorway when two cars crashed near Junction 4. And there are a few problems for rail travellers. Many trains between cities in the west and London are running twenty to thirty minutes late.

Step 1 | Countable nouns: *car, problem*, etc.

- Countable nouns are people or things which we can count. They have both a singular and a plural form.

Singular	Plural
train	*trains*
city	*cities*
problem	*problems*

- We can use *a* or *an* or numbers with a countable noun.
  a car   two cars   a minute   twenty minutes

- We use these words and phrases only with countable nouns:
  many   several   a few   a number of   both   a couple of
  *several accidents   **a number of** people   **a few** problems*

- Note the use of the exclamation *What...!*
  Singular: *What a terrible morning!* (NOT What terrible morning!)
  Plural: *What terrible drivers!*

CHECK QUESTIONS 1 **Which are the eight countable nouns in this news report?**
'Four cows escaped from the market at Winford this morning. It took three police officers and several farmers over an hour to catch them. Two old women were hurt when the cows ran down the main street.'

Step 2 | Uncountable nouns: *air, courage*, etc.

> An explosion has destroyed a chemical factory in Brislington. Thanks to the courage of the firefighters no-one was hurt. The air around the factory is still thick with smoke, and, for their own safety, residents have been told not to drink the water. Residents are worried about their children's health and the damage to the environment caused by the explosion.

- Uncountable nouns are things that we can't count. They have no plural form. *Air*, for example, is an uncountable noun. We can't say *one air, two airs*.
- Most uncountable nouns are:
materials or substances: *air, water, smoke*, etc.
feelings or qualities: *courage, love, anger*, etc.
abstract ideas: *safety, justice, freedom*, etc.

- The exclamation *What …!* (see Step 1) can be followed by an uncountable noun without *a, an*.
  What terrible damage! (NOT What a terrible damage!)

CHECK QUESTIONS 2 **What are the eight uncountable nouns in the news report of the explosion at Brislington?**

Step 3 | Words not used with uncountable nouns

> There's less violence in the St Paul's district of Bristol than there was two years ago. But many young people still have nothing to do in the evenings. Several youth leaders have asked for a new youth club. A number of local councillors have accepted the idea, but the council has very little money and the government hasn't offered financial support. So there isn't much hope that the youth club will be built.

- We can't use *a* or *an* with uncountable nouns, even if there's an adjective before the noun.
  financial support (NOT a financial support)
- We can't use numbers with uncountable nouns. We can't say 'two violences'.
- We can't use these words and phrases with uncountable nouns:
  many several a few a number of both a couple of each every these those
  many *young people* (countable)
  But NOT many violences (uncountable)
- These words and phrases can only be used with uncountable nouns:
  (a) little very little much less
  less *violence* *very **little** money* *there isn't **much** hope*
  (But some people use *less* with countable nouns nowadays.)
- For the use of *some, any, no* with countable and uncountable nouns, see Unit 61.

CHECK QUESTIONS 3 **Choose the correct word.**
1 The council hasn't got (many/much) money.
2 The young people of St Paul's like (a/-) loud music.
3 That's why (a few/a little) local people don't want a youth club.

Step 4 | Countable or uncountable?

> Some interesting research has been done recently in the food industry. One piece of research is particularly interesting. Scientists have looked at spaghetti, which normally takes 15 minutes to cook. They've produced a spaghetti that takes only a minute to cook. They've also worked on beer. There's some good news for beer-drinkers who drive. You can now have several glasses of beer and drive your car safely afterwards. A new beer has been produced which is non-alcoholic, but which tastes like real beer.

- Some words are countable in most languages, but are uncountable in English and are used with a singular verb. The most common are: *accommodation, advice, baggage, behaviour, bread, damage, equipment, evidence, furniture, garbage, homework, information, knowledge, luck, luggage, money, news, nonsense, progress, research, rubbish, spaghetti, traffic, transport, weather.*

  *Some interesting **research has been** done.* (NOT have been done)
  ***spaghetti** which normally **takes** 15 minutes to cook* (NOT take)
  *There's some good **news.*** (NOT there are)

- The following words are normally uncountable, but can also have a plural use: *business, grass, hair, travel, work.*

  ***Business** in St Paul's **is** getting better.* (uncountable)
  *Several new **businesses have** been started.* (countable)
  (*businesses* = 'companies, firms')

- If we want to talk about a certain quantity of these things, we normally use a countable noun + *of* + the uncountable noun.

  *One **piece of** research is particularly interesting.*
  *You can now have several **glasses of** beer.*

  These words are often used in this construction:
  A cup of tea/coffee, etc. *A glass of beer/milk*, etc.
  A bottle of whisky/wine, etc. *A bowl of soup/salad*, etc.
  A packet of sugar/flour/washing-powder, etc.
  A jar of jam/marmalade, etc. *A tin of salmon/soup*, etc.
  A loaf of bread A slice of bread/ham, etc. *A piece of toast/cake*, etc.
  A piece of furniture/information/advice, etc.
  All these phrases can be used in the plural.
  Two cups of tea, a few tins of soup, etc.

- Note that with words like *tea, coffee, beer, whisky* we can say:
  I'd like a glass of beer OR *I'd like a beer.*
  Do you want a cup of coffee? OR *Do you want a coffee?*

- Many words in English for food and drink can be used sometimes as uncountable nouns (when used in a general sense), sometimes as countable nouns (when used to talk about a particular type of something).

  *They've looked at **spaghetti.*** (*spaghetti* in general: uncountable)
  ***a spaghetti** that takes only a minute to cook*
  (*a spaghetti* = a particular type of spaghetti: countable)
  *They've worked on **beer**.* (*beer* in general: uncountable)
  *A new **beer** has been produced.*
  (*A beer* = a particular type of beer: countable)

  Here are some other words that can be countable or uncountable: *cheese, wine, meat, soup, coffee, tea, whisky.*

CHECK QUESTIONS 4 **Choose the correct word.**

1 There (isn't/aren't) any more information about the new beer.
2 Progress (has/have) been made on producing non-alcoholic beer.
3 The English like (cheese/cheeses), but there aren't many different (cheese/cheeses) produced in Britain.

ANSWERS TO CHECK QUESTIONS 1, 2, 3 AND 4

1 cow, market, morning, police officer, farmer, hour, woman, street
2 courage, air, smoke, safety, water, health, damage, environment

3 1 much money 2 loud music 3 a few people
4 1 There isn't much information 2 Progress has been made 3 The English like cheese many different cheeses

Practice

<table>
<tr><td>

Countable nouns
- can be counted
  two cars/many people
- can be singular or plural
  a house/several houses
- can be used with *a* or *an*
  Take an umbrella.

</td><td>

Uncountable nouns
- can't be counted
  water/air/love
- don't have plural forms and are used with a singular verb
  This information is important.
- can't be used with *a* or *an* when used in a general sense
  What awful weather!

</td></tr>
</table>

1 **You need to buy the following things. Look at these words and put them into the correct columns. Write the countable nouns in the plural:** *salt, cooking oil, potato, rice, toilet-paper, washing-powder, fruit, vegetable, milk, toothpaste, meat, banana, egg, mushroom, tomato, marmalade, sausage, coffee, tea, match.*

Countable	Uncountable
potatoes	coffee
....	....
....	....
....	....
....	....
....	....
....	....
....	....
....	....
....	....
....	....

2 **Mark has moved into a new flat. He is looking out of his window. Complete the description with 's (= is) or are, isn't or aren't.**

There (1) .... a main road, but there (2) .... much traffic. There (3) .... many cars. But there (4) .... a lot of people in the street and there (5) .... a lot of noise. On the other side of the road there (6) .... a park. There (7) .... a few trees, but there (8) .... much grass and there (9)................. rubbish everywhere.

3 **Complete this dialogue at a hotel reception desk.**

Guest: It was (1 a luck/a bit of luck) .... you had a room free. (2 An/-) .... accommodation (3 is/are) .... difficult to find in this part of town.

Receptionist: Yes, sir. And it's (4 a/-) .... nice room; the furniture (5 is/are) .... all new.

Guest: Good. Which are the best restaurants round here? Can you give me (6 an/some) .... advice? And I'd like (7 an/some) .... information about buses and taxis.

Receptionist: I'm afraid my knowledge of the town (8 isn't/aren't) .... very good. I'm new here. But I know that transport (9 is/are) .... difficult to find after 11 p.m.

Guest: That isn't (10 a problem/problem) .... I've got (11 work/a work) .... to do tomorrow, so I won't be back late. You see I sell (12 an/-) .... office equipment and it isn't (13 an/-) .... easy job. Oh, my luggage (14 is/are) .... in my car outside and I need (15 a help/help) .... to take it to my room. Is there (16 a/-) .... porter?

Receptionist: Yes, sir. No problem.

60

Much, many, a lot, plenty, (very) little, (very) few A little, a few

British people eat a lot of Italian, Indian and Chinese food, and lots of junk food. Nowadays there aren't many people who have a traditional English breakfast (eggs and bacon). Many people eat cereals like cornflakes instead. They also eat a lot of things with sugar in. Shops sell plenty of biscuits - the British spend £500 million on biscuits every year! There's plenty of food for cats in the supermarkets too. The British don't spend much on their children's shoes, but they spend a lot on cat food - £250 million a year! The British drink a lot of wine nowadays. But because of the climate there aren't many vineyards so they don't make much wine. But they import 500 million litres each year!

Step 1 | A lot, much, many, plenty

- We use *much* with uncountable nouns (*food, wine*, etc.) to talk about a quantity of something. We use it only in questions and in negative sentences.
  *Do they make **much** wine? They **don't** make **much** wine.*

- We use *many* with plural nouns (*people, vineyards*, etc.) to talk about a number of things or people. We use it in questions and in negative sentences. (It's sometimes used in affirmative sentences, particularly at the beginning of a sentence.)
  *Do **many** people eat a traditional English breakfast?*
  *There **aren't many** vineyards in Britain. **Many** people eat breakfast cereals.*

- We use *a lot of/lots of* with countable and uncountable nouns to talk about a number of things or people or a quantity of something. They are used mainly in affirmative sentences, but can also be used in negative sentences and questions. *Lots of* means the same as *a lot of*. It's more informal.
  *They eat **a lot of** Chinese food.* (NOT **much** *Chinese food*)
  *Do they eat **a lot of** Indian food?* (OR **much** *Indian food*)
  *They eat **a lot of** things with sugar in.* (More common than: *many things*)
  *They don't make **a lot of** wine.* (OR **much** *wine*)

- We use *plenty of* with countable and uncountable nouns to talk about a number of things or people or a quantity of something.
  Plenty (of) means 'more than enough', but it's often used with the meaning of 'a lot (of)'.
  *There's **plenty of** food for cats.   Shops sell **plenty of** biscuits.*

- *Much, many, a lot, lots, plenty* can be used alone, without a noun.
  *They don't spend **much** on children's shoes,* (= much money)
  *but they spend **a lot** on cat food.* (= a lot of money)

- Note the question forms:
  How much? (with uncountable nouns) *How many?* (with countable nouns)

CHECK QUESTIONS 1 **Put in *much, many* or *a lot*.**
1 Do the British eat ... Italian food? Yes, they eat ...
2 How ... do they spend on their children's shoes? Not ...
3 Are there ... vineyards in Britain? No, there aren't ...
4 How ... people have a traditional English breakfast? Not ...

Step 2 | Little/very little few/very few a little/a few

Many British people are unfit. They take very little exercise, and do few active sports. They eat very little fruit and very few vegetables. If you want to be healthy, you should eat a little fresh fruit every day and a few fresh vegetables. You should also take a little exercise.

- We use *little/very little* with uncountable nouns to talk about a small quantity. We use *few/very few* with plural nouns to talk about a small number. *Very little* and *very few* have a negative meaning. We use them more often than *little* and *few*.
  They take **very little** exercise/**little** exercise.
  (= not much exercise, not enough exercise)
  They eat **very few** vegetables/**few** vegetables.
  (= not many vegetables, not enough vegetables)
- *A little* and *a few* have a more positive meaning.
  You should take **a little** exercise. (not much, but enough to be healthy)
  You should eat **a few** fresh vegetables. (not many, but enough to be healthy)

CHECK QUESTIONS 2   **Are these positive or negative things to do?**
1 I eat very few vegetables.   2 I take a little exercise every day.
3 I do a few active sports.   4 I eat little fresh fruit.

Step 3 | So much/so many too much/too many

So much food is wasted nowadays because we throw away so much. It's terrible when you think that so many people in the world don't have enough food. Many adults and children in the rich countries are overweight because they eat too much, and because there's too much sugar and fat in their diet. Many children have got bad teeth because they eat too many sweets and too much junk food.

- We use *so much* to emphasise that we're talking about a big quantity, and *so many* to emphasise that we're talking about a large number of people or things.
  So much food is wasted. **So many** people don't have enough food.
- We use *too much* and *too many* to mean 'more than necessary'.
  Too many people eat **too much**. (An excessive number eat more than is necessary.)
- *So much* and *too much* (unlike *much*) can be used in affirmative sentences.
  So much food **is wasted**. **There's too much** sugar.

CHECK QUESTIONS 3   **Answer these questions using *so much/too much/too many*.**
1 How do we waste food? We throw away ...
2 Do British people eat many sweets? Yes, they eat far ...
3 Do they eat much junk food? Yes, far ...

ANSWERS TO
CHECK QUESTIONS
1, 2 AND 3

1 1 much/a lot of a lot 2 much much (a lot)
3 many/a lot of many/a lot 4 many many/a lot

2 1 Negative 2 Positive 3 Positive 4 Negative
3 1 We throw away so much/too much. 2 Yes, they eat far too many. 3 Yes, far too much.

195

Practice

	Affirmative	**Negative**	**Questions**
Countable nouns	*a lot of* cars *plenty of* cars *many* cars *(very) few/a few* cars	*not many* cars *not a lot of* cars	Are there *many* cars? Are there *a lot of* cars?
Uncountable nouns	*a lot of* time *(very) little/a little* time	*not much/not a lot of* time	How *much* time?

- *Very little/little* and *very few/few* have a negative meaning.
  A little and *a few* have a more positive meaning.
- *Too much* and *so much* can be used in affirmative sentences (unlike *much*).

1 Joe Sloper grows his own fruit and vegetables. What has happened this year? Complete the sentences using the given words in the correct place.

1 He's grown .... tomatoes, but he hasn't grown .... peppers. (a lot of/many)

2 He's got .... courgettes. He's going to give .... to his neighbour. (a lot/too many)

3 He hasn't got .... celery and there aren't .... peas this year. (many/much)

4 There's .... fruit. He's given .... to his neighbour. (a lot/so much)

5 He's got .... apples he'll be able to make .... cider this year. (so many/a lot of)

2 Complete this dialogue. Use the given words in the correct place.

'How (1) .... college work do you do each evening?'

'I don't do (2) .... , only about an hour. I spend (3) .... time with my friends (much/a lot of)'

'Have you got (4) .... friends?'

'Yes, I've got (5) .... (lots/many)'

'Do you watch (6) .... television?'

'Yes. there are (7) .... programmes I like. (a lot of/much)'

'How (8) .... times do you go to the cinema?'

'Not very often. There aren't (9) .... cinemas round here, and it's (10) .... trouble to go into London. (many/too much)'

3 Two people are driving into town to see a film. Make sentences using *plenty of*.
Example: We don't need to hurry. *We've got plenty of time.*

1 We don't need to stop at a service station. We've got ....

2 The car park won't be full at this time of the evening. There'll be ....

3 I'll pay for the film and the drinks afterwards. I've got ....

4 We'll easily find somewhere to have a drink. There are ....

4 Charlotte Webb is worried about what she eats. Complete the sentences, using *very little* or *very few* and *a little* or *a few*.

1 I know that a lot of coffee isn't good for you. So I drink .... coffee.

2 I eat .... cooked vegetables. I prefer raw vegetables.

3 For breakfast I have .... orange juice and .... grapes.

4 For lunch I have .... cheese and .... raw vegetables.

5 For dinner, I have .... rice, perhaps some fish, and I drink .... wine.

6 In general I eat .... sugar, ... fat and .... snacks like crisps or biscuits or chocolate.

61 *Some, any, no, none*

Joss and Anna have arrived at a camp site. Joss is going to the shop.
Joss: I'll get some burgers and some fruit. And we need some milk too.
Anna: OK. Have we got any cooking oil?
Joss: Yes, there's some in that bag. Oh no, I didn't bring any matches.
Anna: You'll have to buy some.
Joss: What about bread?
Anna: We haven't got any. Get some bread rolls.

Step 1 Basic uses of *some, any*

- *Some* and *any* can be used with uncountable nouns:
  Get **some fruit**. Have we got **any cooking oil?**
  and plural countable nouns.
  Get **some burgers**. I didn't bring **any matches**.

- We usually use *some* in affirmative sentences and *any* in questions and negative
  sentences. (But see Steps 3 and 4.)
  *We need **some** milk. Have we got **any** cooking oil? I didn't bring **any** matches.*

- *Some* and *any* can be used alone, without a noun.
  *There's **some** in that bag. We haven't got **any**.*

CHECK QUESTIONS 1 **Put in *some* or *any*.**
1 Joss bought ... burgers from the shop.
2 He also bought ... milk, because they didn't have ...
3 Did they bring ... cooking oil with them? No, but they need ...

Step 2 Uses of *no, none*

The camp site isn't very good. There are no showers, and there's no hot
water in the washroom. It's got no public telephone. It's difficult at
night because there are no lights at the entrance and there are none in
the toilets.

- *No* and *none* are used with a verb in the affirmative.
  *There **are no** showers.* (= There aren't any showers.)
  *There **are none**.* (= There aren't any.)
  No/none with an affirmative verb = *any* with a negative verb.

- *No* is used with countable and uncountable nouns.
  *There are **no showers**.* (= There aren't any showers)
  *There's **no hot water**.* (= There isn't any hot water.)

- *None* is used alone, without a noun.
  *There are **none** in the toilets.* (= There aren't any in the toilets.)

- We often use *no/none* with *there is/there are* and *have got*.
  *There's **no** hot water. It's got **no** public telephone.*
  With other verbs we normally use *not + any*.

Put in *no* or *none*.
1 This camp site is awful! There are ... doors on the toilets!
2 There's ... paper in the toilets, and there's ... room in the rubbish bins.
3 We've got ... camping gas left and they've got ... at the shop.

Step 3 | *Some* used in questions

> Joss is talking to the people in the next tent.
> Joss: Have you got any camping gas?
> Man: Yes, we have.
> Joss: Could we have some, please?
> Man: Yes, no problem. Would you like some coffee? We've just made
>   some.

- We use *some* in questions when we expect the answer *Yes*.
  *Could we have **some**, please?*
  (Joss knows that they've got some camping gas, so he expects the answer *Yes*.)
  BUT: *Have you got **any** camping gas?*
  (Here Joss doesn't know if they've got any camping gas or not, so he uses *any*.)
- We also use *some* in offers. *Would you like **some** coffee?*

**Anna and Joss are having supper with the people in the next tent. Complete the
sentences with *some* or *any*.**
1 Would you like ... spaghetti, Joss? – Yes, please.
2 Have you got ... cheese in your tent? We haven't got ... here.
3 Yes, we have. Shall I go and get ...?

Step 4 | *Any* used in affirmative sentences

> A notice in the camp site office said:
> Any campers making a noise after 11 p.m. will be asked to leave the
> camp site. If you need any information, ask at the camp office. If you
> have any problems, consult the manager at any time.

- *Any* can be used in affirmative sentences where it means *it doesn't matter
  which/how much/when*, etc. It's often used after *If...*
  ***Any** campers making a noise after 11 p.m. will be asked to leave.*
  *If you need **any** information, ask at the camp office.*

Complete the sentences with *some* or *any*.
1 If you need extra blankets, there are ... in the camp office.
2 Don't damage ... equipment on the camp site. ... damage must be paid for.
3 Please leave ... money or valuables at the camp office.

1	1 some	2 some	any	3 any	some
2	1 no	2 no	no	3 no	none

3	1 some	2 any	any	3 some
4	1 some	2 any	Any	3 any

Practice

- We usually use:
  some in affirmative sentences.
  any in questions and negative sentences.
- *Some* can be used in certain questions where we expect the answer *Yes*, and in offers.
- *Any* can be used in affirmative sentences, with the meaning *doesn't matter which/how much/ when*, etc.
- *No* and *none* are used with a verb in the affirmative (*no* + noun, *none* without a noun).

---

1 Make a conversation. Put these sentences in the right order. (Write the letters a–f.)

a Well, if there are none in the bathroom, I'll have to go and buy some.

b I've got a bad headache. Have we got any aspirins?

c No, I've looked in the bathroom. There aren't any.

d The chemist's open on Sundays. I'll buy some there.

e I think there are some in the bathroom.

f But there are no shops open. It's Sunday.

....

2 The effects of war on a big city. Complete the sentences with *any* or *no*.

1 There's .... electricity.

2 There isn't .... clean water.

3 There are .... anaesthetics at the hospital.

4 There isn't .... food in the shops.

5 .... food is reaching the city.

3 A man is in a village pub forty miles from London. His car has broken down. It is 10 p.m. Complete his conversation at the pub, using *some, any, no, none.*

'My car's broken down. Are there (1) ....

trains to London?'

'No, there are (2) .... this evening, I'm

afraid.'

'Are there (3) .... buses?'

'I'm afraid not. There are (4) .... buses

after 6 p.m.'

'Can I stay here tonight? Have you got

(5) .... rooms?'

'Yes, no problem. Do you want to eat? We've got

(6) .... sandwiches left.'

'Yes, I'll have (7) .... sandwiches, and

could I have (8) .... change for the

phone?'

4 Complete the sentences with *some* or *any*.

1 Doctor: Take the tablets and if there are

.... problems, come and see me

immediately.

2 Teacher: If there's .... more noise, I'll

give you .... extra homework.

3 Car salesman: You can put .... petrol in

it – super or regular, leaded or unleaded.

4 Hotel receptionist: You can have ....

room you like.

5 Shopkeeper: There are .... oranges

over there. Choose .... you like.

62

> Natasha's a refugee. She's escaped from the war in her own country and has come to live in Eccleston, a village in the south of England. She's feeling very strange.
> Everything is new. Everything is different. But everybody is very kind to her. They give her everything she needs. They do all they can to help her. She thanks everyone for their kindness with a smile, because she can't speak English. All she can say is 'Hello'. She isn't happy because all she wants to do is go home.

Step 1 | *All* or *everything/everybody/everyone*?

- When we mean 'all the things' we usually say *everything*, not *all*. When we mean 'all the people' we use *everybody* or *everyone*, not *all*.
  Everything is new. (NOT All is new.)
  Everybody is kind to her. (NOT All are kind to her.)
  She thanks everyone for their kindness. (NOT She thanks all …)

- *Everything* and *everybody/everyone* are followed by a verb in the singular.
  Everything's (is) different. (NOT Everything are different.)
  Everybody is kind. (NOT Everybody are kind.)

- But we use *they, them, their* after *everybody/everyone*.
  Everybody is very kind to her. They give her everything she needs.
  She thanks everyone for their kindness. (NOT: his kindness)

- Note that we can use *all* followed by a relative clause. It has two meanings: 'everything' or 'the only thing(s)'.
  They do all they can to help her. (= They do everything they can)
  All she wants to do is go home. (= The only thing she wants to do)
  We usually leave out the relative pronoun *that* after *all*.
  All (that) she can say is 'Hello'.
  Note: We say *All she can say* or *All that she can say*, but NOT All what she can say.

CHECK QUESTIONS 1 **Rewrite the sentences, using *all, everything* or *everybody/everyone*.**
1 All the things Natasha sees are new. 2 All the people want to help her.
3 The only thing she can do is wait for the war to stop.

Step 2 | *All, every* or *each*?

> All the families in Eccleston have offered to help Natasha. People have been to every house to collect money for her. All the money goes into a special bank account. There are three pubs in the village. The owner of each pub is collecting money too. They've each collected about £100. The newsagent has also asked each of his customers to give money. Some people are decorating Natasha's flat. They're painting every room. Each room's a different colour. Each colour is part of her national flag.

- *All* and *every* often mean the same.
  All the families in Eccleston = **Every family** in Eccleston
  all the houses in the village = **every house** in the village
  Note: *every* is followed by a singular noun.

- But we use *all* not *every* with uncountable nouns.
  All the money *goes into a special bank account.* (NOT every money)

- We use *every* and *each* + a singular noun when we talk about all the people or all the things in a group. We can often use either.
  Every *family in Eccleston* **has** *offered to help Natasha.*
  OR **Each** *family in Eccleston* **has** *offered to help Natasha.*

- But, if we see the people or the things individually, if we talk about them separately, we normally use *each*.
  They're painting **every room**. (= **all** the rooms)
  They're painting **each room** *a different colour.* (= the rooms one by one)

- We can use *each* (NOT every) on its own or with *of*.
  They've **each** *collected about £100.*
  The newsagent has asked **each of his customers** *to give money.*

CHECK QUESTIONS 2 **Put in *every* or *each*.**
1 Natasha needs ... penny she can get.
2 The council has asked ... shop in the village to give money.
3 They've asked ... shop to give £30.
4 ... of the two farmers in Eccleston has given £50.

Step 3 | Whole

> Natasha's whole life has changed. She had spent the whole of her life in Akabi, a mountain village. But now the whole of Akabi has been destroyed and she's lost her whole family. On the day she arrived in Britain she was very hungry and tired. They gave her bread, fish and milk. She ate a whole loaf of bread and a whole tin of tuna and she drank all the milk.

- We use *whole* mainly with singular countable nouns.
  Natasha's **whole** *life has changed.* (= Her life has changed totally.)
  She's lost her **whole** *family.* (= all her family)
  She ate a **whole** *loaf of bread.* (= She ate a complete loaf of bread.)

- We don't use *whole* with uncountable nouns.
  She drank **all the** *milk.* (NOT the whole milk)

- We can use the phrase *the whole of* + a noun:
  She had spent **the whole of her life** *in Akabi.* (= her whole life)
  We must use this phrase with the names of places.
  The whole of Akabi *has been destroyed.* (NOT the whole Akabi)

CHECK QUESTIONS 3 **Rewrite the sentences, using *whole*.**
1 She drank all the bottle of milk.
2 Natasha's village has been completely destroyed.
3 All Eccleston is trying to help Natasha.

Step 4 | *All* + a preposition

> There are refugees like Natasha all over the world. They know all about war and suffering. Natasha's still so unhappy that she often cries all through the night. She'd like to tell her friends in Eccleston all about her life in Akabi. But she can't speak English yet.

- We can use *all* before prepositions (*about, along, down, over, round, through*).
  *There are refugees **all over** the world.* (= over the whole world)
  *They know **all about** war and suffering.* (= everything about)

CHECK QUESTIONS 4 | **Rewrite the sentences, using *all* + a preposition.**
1 There are refugees living everywhere in Britain.
2 Natasha wants to tell people the whole story of her experiences.

Step 5 | *All/every/the whole* in time expressions

> Natasha dreams about her terrible experiences every night. Sometimes she's awake all night. Her doctor has given her some tablets that she has to take every three hours. And every two weeks she goes to see a psychiatrist. She has an English lesson every day. Her teacher comes to the flat every morning at 10 a.m. and they spend all morning together. Every Wednesday she spends the whole day at college. She has a busy life now, but all day she thinks of her family and friends.

- In time expressions with words like *minute, hour, day, week, month, year, Monday, Tuesday*, etc. we use *every* to say how often something happens.
  ***Every morning** at 10 a.m. her teacher comes to the flat.*
  *She dreams about her terrible experiences **every night**.*
  ***Every two weeks** she goes to see a psychiatrist.*

- We use *all* or *the whole* with *morning, evening, day, week, month, year*, etc. to say how long something lasts.
  *They spend **all morning** together.* (OR the whole morning)
  *She spends **the whole day** at college.* (OR all day)
  *Sometimes she's awake **all night**.* (OR the whole night)

CHECK QUESTIONS 5 | **Put in *all* or *every*.**
1 She goes to college ... Wednesday.
2 She's at college ... day on Wednesdays.
3 Her English teacher comes to see her ... day.
4 Yesterday they spent ... evening listening to music.

ANSWERS TO
CHECK QUESTIONS
1, 2, 3, 4 AND 5

1 1 Everything Natasha sees is new.
2 Everybody (Everyone) wants to help her.
3 All she can do is wait for the war in her country to stop.
2 1 every penny   2 every shop   3 each shop
4 Each
3 1 She drank the whole bottle of milk.

2 Natasha's whole village/The whole of Natasha's village has been destroyed.
3 The whole of Eccleston is trying to help Natasha.
4 1 There are refugees living all over Britain.
2 Natasha wants to tell people all about her experiences.
5 1 every   2 all   3 every   4 all

202

Practice

> *Everything she does is good.* (Everything = all the things)
> *Everybody is happy.* (Everybody/everyone = all the people)
> *All she does is laugh.* (All = the only thing)
> *All the houses are painted white.* (All + a plural noun)
> *Every house is painted white.* (Every + a singular noun = all the houses)
> *Each house has a different front door.* (Each = the houses seen separately)
> *Each of the houses has a different front door.* (NOT Every of the houses)
> *He drank the whole bottle.* (= all the bottle)
> *Every day* (= how often)   *All day* (= how long)

1 Complete the dialogue, using *everything, everybody (everyone)* or *all*.

'Have you been to that new restaurant in Mill

Street? (1) .... says it's very good.'

'Yes, I went last weekend. But (2) ....

was so expensive. (3) .... I had was
a mixed salad and a glass of orange juice. That's

(4) .... I could afford. (5) ....
else on the menu cost a fortune!'
'Were there many people there?'
'Yes, but the atmosphere was very formal.

(6) .... was wearing their best

clothes, and (7) .... was talking
very quietly. It was so boring!'

2 Complete the sentences, using *all, every* or *each*. Sometimes more than one answer is possible.

The government is planning to build a new road
round the village of Melcombe. They're going to

cut down (1) .... the trees in Melcombe

wood. They're going to demolish (2) ....
house on the route. The Department of
Transport has written to the owners of

(3) .... the houses to say that it will give

(4) .... of them a good price for their
house. But the families don't want to sell their

homes and they've (5) .... written to

the Department to protest. (6) .... time
the government plans to build a new road,

people ask: What about (7) .... the

pollution ? Doesn't (8) .... new road just
create more traffic?

3 Eric Worth does not believe in moderation!
Complete the sentences, using *the whole* or *a whole*.
Example: When he has a packet of nuts, *he eats the whole packet.*

1 When he has a bottle of wine, he

....
2 When he buys wine, he doesn't buy just one
   or two bottles. He

.... case.
3 The Saturday sports programme on TV goes
   on for three and a half hours. He

....
4 Eric doesn't like foreign food, so when he

   goes on holiday, he ....
   suitcase full of English food with him.

4 Complete the sentences, using *every* or *all* or *the whole*. Sometimes more than one answer is possible.

Last week I spent (1) .... week studying

for my exams. I got up at 7 a.m. (2) ....

day. I worked (3) .... morning until
about 12.30 and then I had lunch. Then I

worked (4) .... afternoon till six

o'clock. I stopped work (5) .... half an
hour to make a cup of coffee and to stretch my

legs. I also worked (6) .... evening on

Friday. I usually go out (7) .... Friday
evening, but last Friday I decided not to. When
I've finished my exams, I'm going to have a
week's holiday. I'm going to spend

(8) .... day of the week doing what I
want to do. This year I've worked hard

(9) .... year, so after the exams I'm
going to enjoy myself.

203

63

All (of), most (of), some (of), etc.
Both (of), neither (of), either (of)

Most British people watch a lot of television. Most young people watch more than 20 hours a week. Most of the young people interviewed recently in a survey said they watched at least 24 hours a week. And some of them watched up to 28 hours.

Some old people watch 40 hours a week. Some of them aren't really interested in half the programmes. Most of the time they watch because they're bored or lonely.

Many viewers have special interests. Some watch all the wildlife programmes, for example, and some watch all the sport.

Some people say that all violence on TV should be banned. They say that some of it encourages children to be violent. But the TV companies say that all parents should control what their children watch. All of them are responsible.

Most of us see television as a problem. But none of the viewers interviewed recently have thrown their televisions away! None of them has stopped watching!

Step 1 | All, most, some, none, etc. + noun or + of

- We use:
  all, most, some, any, many, a few + plural noun
  all, most, some, any, much + uncountable noun.
  most *people* **some** *old people* **all** *violence* **all** *parents*
  ('Most' = 'nearly all'. 'Some' = 'a part, but not all'.)

- *All, most*, etc. have a general, unlimited meaning.
  All of, most of, etc. have a more specific, limited meaning.
  Compare:
  Most young people *watch 24 hours a week.* (= most young people in general)
  most of the young people *interviewed* (= a specific group of young people)

- But we often leave out *of* after *all* and *half*.
  all (of) the *sport* **half (of) the** *programmes*

- With *all, most, some*, etc. we must use *of* before a pronoun (*it, us, you, them*).
  some **of it** (= some of the violence. NOT some it)
  most **of us** (= most of the people in Britain. NOT most us)
  all **of them** (= all (of) the parents. NOT all them)

- We can use *all, most, some*, etc. as pronouns on their own.
  Some *watch all the wildlife programmes.* (= some viewers)

- We can use a singular or plural verb after *none of*.
  None of the viewers interviewed have *thrown their televisions away!* **None of them has** *stopped watching!* (Here, we could say *has thrown* or *have stopped*.)
  (For *all*, see also Unit 62.)

CHECK QUESTIONS 1 **Put in *of the* or nothing at all.**
1 Some ... people think there's too much violence on television.
2 Many ... people I know don't watch much television.
3 I don't watch any ... programmes my friends like.
4 Not all ... television programmes are of high quality.

Both Mr and Mrs Hope watch television regularly. So do their children. They all enjoy soaps and wildlife programmes. But both parents think that the children watch too much. Both their children watch television for four hours a day. Neither child reads very much. And neither of them has other interests. If Mrs Hope asks either of the children to turn the television off, there's usually an argument. For both of them television is a drug. Neither Mr Hope nor his wife know what to do. They've both talked about the problem a lot, with other parents. It seems they're all experiencing the same problem. They can either force the children to watch less often, or they can get rid of the television.

- We use *both, either, neither* when we talk about two people or things. Note the possible constructions:

both/either/neither +	*(of)* +	*(the*, etc.) +	*noun/pronoun*
Both			*parents*
Both		*the*	*parents*
Both	*of*	*the*	*parents*
Both	*of*		*them* (NOT both them)
Either/Neither			*child*
Either/Neither	*of*	*the*	*children*
Either/Neither	*of*		*them*

- We can say *both X and Y, neither X nor Y, either X or Y.*
  Both *Mr* **and** *Mrs Hope watch television regularly.*
  Neither *Mr Hope* **nor** *his wife know what to do.*
  They can **either** *force them to watch less often,* **or** *they can ...*

- After *Neither of ...* and *Neither ... nor ...* we can use a singular or plural verb.
  Neither of them **has** *other interests.* (OR *have*)
  Neither Mr Hope nor his wife **know** *what to do.* (OR *knows*)
  BUT *Neither* + noun is always followed by a singular verb.
  Neither child **reads** *very much.*

- *All* and *both*, used on their own, usually come in mid-position (before the main verb or between the auxiliary verb and the main verb).
  They **all enjoy** *soaps and wildlife programmes.*
  They've **both talked** *about the problem a lot.*

CHECK QUESTIONS 2

Put in *both, either of* or *neither of*.
1 ... children watch television too often.
2 ... them reads books.
3 There are two possible solutions. Mr Hope doesn't like ... them.

Add the words in brackets to the sentences.
4 They want to solve the television problem. (all)
5 The two children have agreed to watch less television. (both)

ANSWERS TO
CHECK QUESTIONS
1, 2 AND 3

1 1 Some people 2 Many of the people 3 any of the programmes 4 Not all television programmes

2 1 Both children 2 Neither of them 3 either of them 4 They all want to solve the television problem. 5 The two children have both agreed to watch less television.

Practice

1 Complete the text, using *all, some, most, many, any, none, a few* with or without *of*.

(1 most) .... British holidaymakers go abroad for their holiday. (2 many) .... them go to France, Italy, Greece or Spain. But not (3 all) .... them go to Europe. (4 some) .... people go to the USA, the West Indies, Australia or New Zealand. I don't think (5 any) .... the people I know have their holiday in Britain. (6 all) .... them go abroad. I usually go on holiday with (7 a few) .... my friends. We went to Turkey last year. (8 all) .... my friends spent (9 half) .... the time on the beach and (10 half) .... the time in the hotel swimming pool. Unfortunately I was ill, so I spent (11 most) .... the time in bed. The hotel food was delicious, but (12 none) .... the things on the menu tempted me. I couldn't eat (13 any) .... them. (14 some) .... us are going back to Turkey this summer. But this time I'm not going to spend (15 all) .... the time in bed!

2 Complete this dialogue in a clothes shop, using *both, either* or *neither* with or without *of*.

'I really like (1) .... these sweaters. What do you think of them?'

'(2) .... them suits you. I don't like (3) .... them very much. I don't think (4) .... red or green is your colour.'

'Oh, I think I look nice in (5) .... colours. Which one shall I have?'

'(6) .... , I really don't mind. But be quick. (7) .... we leave here in three minutes or we miss the bus. Which sweater is cheaper?'

'Well (8) .... them is very cheap, but the red one's cheaper.'

'Buy the red one then.'

3 Mark the correct position for *all* or *both* in the sentence using *.

My girlfriend Sadie and I like flying (1 both). But our last flight was very unpleasant. We flew through a storm. At the time we were having lunch (2 all). The flight attendants were serving us coffee (3 all). Then the plane started to shake. Sadie looked at me. We stopped eating (4 both). Then we fastened our seat-belts (5 both). The captain told us to keep our seat-belts fastened (6 all). The other passengers were scared. They had stopped talking (7 all). The flight attendants had returned to their seats (8 all). Sadie's face was pale. We held hands (9 both). Then the captain spoke to us again (10 all). We'd flown out of the storm. We cheered (11 all).

64

Demonstratives:
This, that, these, those

> Polly and James are at the beach. James has just had a swim.
> James: Can I borrow that towel?
> Polly: No, this towel's mine. That's your towel over there.
> James: Oh, OK.
> Polly: Do you want one of these chicken sandwiches?
> James: No thanks. But I'd like one of those apples. ... Thanks. Did you
> see? I swam out to those rocks.
> Polly: Which rocks?
> James: Those over there. Where that man is now.
> Polly: Which man?
> James: That man with the mask on.

Step 1 | Main use of demonstratives *this, that, these, those*

- We use *this* + a singular noun for something which is near the speaker.
  This *towel's mine.* (This towel **here**.)
  We use *that* + singular noun for something further away.
  *Can I borrow **that** towel?* (That towel **there**.)

- We use *these* + plural noun for things near the speaker.
  *Do you want one of **these** sandwiches?*
  (These sandwiches **here**.)
  We use *those* + plural noun for things further away.
  *I'd like one of **those** apples.* (Those apples **there**.)

- Note that *this, that, these, those* can be used as adjectives or pronouns.
  This *towel's mine.* (adjective)
  This *is my towel.* (pronoun)

- We use them as pronouns when it's clear what we're talking about.
  *Which rocks? **Those** over there.*
  (He doesn't repeat *rocks* because they've already been mentioned in the
  question.)

- This is only true if we're talking about things, not people.
  That man *with the mask on.* (NOT That with the mask on.)
  BUT we use *this/these* on their own when we introduce people:
  This *is my wife, Polly. And **these** are my children, Mark and Anna.*

CHECK QUESTIONS 1 **Put in *this, that, these* or *those*.**
1 What's in ... sandwich you're eating?
2 Look at ... people over there.
3 I can't use ... towel. It feels wet.
4 Ugh! I can't eat ... sandwiches. They've got sand in them.

Step 2 | Other uses of *this, that, these, those*

> Polly: That sandwich was nice. Are you sure you don't want one?
> James: Quite sure, thanks.
> Polly: This is the life! I know we're very busy these days but we should spend more time like this. Do you remember when we were students? In those days we spent a lot of time just doing nothing.
> James: What's that noise?
> Polly: It's your mobile phone!
> James: Hello? Who's that?
> Simon: This is Simon. Listen, this is important. You must come into the office this afternoon. I've got a problem with this new computer program.
> James: Simon, that's your problem, not mine. This is my day off.

- We use *this* and *these* when we're talking about a present situation or something near in time.
  This is the life. We're very busy *these* days.
  *We should spend more time like **this**.*
  *You must come into the office **this** afternoon.*

- We can also use *this* to refer to a subject we're going to talk about.
  *Listen. **This** is important.*

- We use *that* and *those* when we're talking about something further away in time.
  ***That** sandwich was nice.* (Past: She's finished eating it.)
  Compare: ***This** sandwich is nice.* (Present: She's still eating it.)
  *In **those** days we spent a lot of time doing nothing.* (Past)
  Compare: *We're very busy **these** days.* (Present)

- We can also use *that* to refer back to a subject or an idea that's already been mentioned.
  I've got a problem with this new computer program.
  ***That's** your problem, not mine.*

- Note that when we speak on the telephone in British English we use *this* to introduce ourselves and *that* to ask who the caller is.
  ***This** is Simon. Who's **that**?*
  In American English *this* is used for both.
  ***This** is Simon. Who's **this**?*

CHECK QUESTIONS 2 **Put in *this, these, that* or *those*.**
1 A: Hello. Who's ...? B: ... is Simon. Is ... James?
2 Do you remember ... computer programs you bought last month?
3 Can you help me? I can't solve all ... problems on my own.
4 I can't help you now. I'm very busy ... week.

ANSWERS TO
CHECK QUESTIONS
1 AND 2
1 1 that 2 those 3 this 4 these
2 1 that This that 2 those 3 these 4 this

Practice

1 Complete this dialogue with *this, these, that* or *those*.

Customer: Can I have half a kilo of (1) .... tomatoes on the shelf behind you?

Assistant: (2) .... here, do you mean?

Customer: Yes, that's right. And have you got any of (3) .... oranges you had last week?

Assistant: No, we haven't got any of (4) .... but (5) .... here are just as nice.

Customer: All right, I'll have a kilo of (6) .... please.

Assistant: Anything else?

Customer: Yes, can I have a cabbage please.

Assistant: How about (7) .... one?

Customer: Yes, (8) ....looks fine.

Assistant: Anything else?

Customer: No, (9) ....'s all thanks.

Assistant: (10) ....'s £3.45 altogether.

2 Complete this dialogue with *this, these, that* or *those*. A doctor is talking to one of his patients in hospital.

Doctor: How are you feeling (1) .... morning?

Patient: A bit better, thanks. But I've still got a pain in (2) .... leg.

Doctor: (3) .... isn't surprising. (4) .... accident you had was quite serious. Now, did you take (5) .... pills I gave you yesterday?

Patient: Yes, but I still couldn't sleep. (6) .... man in the bed over there snored all night.

Doctor: I see. Well, if you take (7) .... pills (8) .... evening, at about 10 o'clock, they should help you to sleep.

3 Complete this dialogue with *this, that, these* or *those*.

Jane Ford: Hello.

Matthew: Who's (1) .... ?

Jane Ford: (2) .... is Jane Ford.

Matthew: Oh, I'm sorry. I didn't recognise your voice. Is Sasha there please?

Jane Ford: Is (3) .... Matthew?

Matthew: Yes, it is.

Jane Ford: No, I'm afraid Sasha isn't here. Um, (4) .... is the second time you've phoned (5) .... evening, isn't it?

Matthew: Yes, it is.

Jane Ford: Matthew, I don't know how to tell you (6) .... but I think you should know that Sasha's out with another boy.

Matthew: One of (7) .... boys she works with?

Jane Ford: Yes, (8) .... 's right.

Matthew: Oh, I see. OK, I won't phone her again (9) .... evening. But I'll try again (10) .... weekend. I suppose she'll be at home one of (11) .... days.

65

Reflexive and emphatic pronouns: *myself, himself, themselves,* etc.

> Mrs Betty Withers is 89 and lives alone. Last week she fell and hurt herself badly. But she doesn't want to go into an old people's home. 'I may be 89, but I can still look after myself. The man next door is only 80, but he can't even make a piece of toast without burning himself! I told him the other day: 'Reg Dwyer, you'll kill yourself one day if you aren't more careful.' Men aren't very good at looking after themselves, are they? Women are much better. We know how to look after ourselves, don't we?'

Step 1 | The main use of reflexive pronouns

- We use a reflexive pronoun (*myself, himself,* etc.) when the subject and the object of the verb are the same person. The action is directed back to the person who does it.

subject	verb	object
She	*hurt*	*herself.*

(*She* and *herself* are the same person.)

You	*'ll kill*	*yourself.*

(*You* and *yourself* are the same person.)

- The reflexive pronouns are:

	Singular		**Plural**
I	*myself*	We	*ourselves*
You	*yourself*	You	*yourselves*
He	*himself*	They	*themselves*
She	*herself*		
It	*itself*		

Note that when there is more than one person, the ending of the reflexive pronoun changes from *-self* to *-selves*:

yourself = one person (singular)
yourselves = two or more people (plural)
*I can still look after **myself**.* (singular)
*We know how to look after **ourselves**.* (plural)

CHECK QUESTIONS 1 **Put in reflexive pronouns.**
1 Betty Withers thinks she can look after ...
2 She thinks the man next door might kill ... one day.
3 Most old people prefer to look after ...

'I wake up at about half past six every morning. I get up at seven. I wash and dress and then I make myself a good breakfast. I keep myself busy by doing the housework. Of course, by the evening, I feel tired and I go to bed early. I don't enjoy myself very often - I don't go out much. But I never feel sorry for myself. I never complain. I don't mind living by myself,' said Mrs Withers.

Mrs Withers' social worker blames himself for her accident. He's angry with himself because he didn't insist that she went into an old people's home. 'She's too old to be responsible for herself. I worry that one day she might kill herself if she has another accident.'

- A few verbs in English are often used with a reflexive pronoun. The most common are:

to amuse yourself to behave yourself to blame yourself to burn yourself
to control yourself to cut yourself to dry yourself to enjoy yourself
to help yourself to hurt yourself to kill yourself to look after yourself
to make yourself something   to keep yourself busy, warm, etc.

> I **make myself** a good breakfast.
> I **keep myself** busy by doing the housework.
> I don't **enjoy myself** very often.
> She might **kill herself** if she has another accident.

- Many verbs are reflexive in other languages, but not normally in English:

to change (clothes)   to dress
to wake up   to get up   to go to bed
to shave   to wash
to stand up   to sit down   to lie down
to feel (+ adjective)   *to relax   to rest*
to complain   to concentrate   to remember   to worry

> I **wake up** at half past six. (NOT I wake myself up)
> I **feel** tired. (NOT I feel myself tired)
> I never **complain**. (NOT I never complain myself)
> I **worry** that she might kill herself. (NOT I worry myself)

- We sometimes use a reflexive pronoun after an adjective + preposition:

to be angry with yourself   to be ashamed of yourself   to be pleased with yourself
to be proud of yourself   to be responsible for yourself   to be sorry for yourself

> I'm never **sorry for myself**.
> The social worker's **angry with himself**.

- Note the expression *by myself* which means 'on my own' or 'alone'.

> I don't mind living **by myself**.

We can use it with all the reflexive pronouns: *by herself, by themselves,* etc.

CHECK QUESTIONS 2 **Put in reflexive pronouns if necessary.**
1 Mrs Withers gets ... up early.
2 She doesn't often enjoy ...
3 But people like her prefer to live by ...
4 The social worker blames ... for Mrs Withers' accident.

Step 3 | Emphatic pronouns: *myself, yourself,* etc.

> Mrs Withers doesn't want to go into an old people's home, and the social worker himself admits that she's very independent. 'Why should I go into a home?' asked Mrs Withers. 'The doctor himself said I was still very healthy. I can do most of my housework myself. And look at this cake I've made. Could that social worker make a cake like this himself?'

- We often use these pronouns as emphatic pronouns to emphasise that someone does something without help. We put the pronoun at the end of the sentence.
  *I can do my housework **myself**.* (= No one helps me.)
  *Could that social worker make a cake like this **himself**?* (= without help)
- We sometimes use the emphatic pronoun to emphasise a noun or pronoun. We put it immediately after the noun or pronoun.
  *The doctor **himself** said that I was still very healthy.*
  (She's emphasising that it was the doctor who said this.)
- When we speak, we stress the final syllable (*-self* or *-selves*).

CHECK QUESTIONS 3 **Add emphatic pronouns.**
1 Mrs Withers can't do all her housework.
2 Mrs Withers admits that she finds some things difficult.

Step 4 | *Ourselves, yourselves, themselves* OR *each other?*

> Mrs Withers continued: 'The old people in the village are very independent. They prefer to look after themselves. But they look after each other too. In fact, we often do things for each other. I cook hot meals for Reg Dwyer next door and he does the shopping for me. We all help one another when it's necessary.'

- Compare these two sentences. They don't mean the same.
  A *The old people in the village look after **themselves**.*
  B *They look after **each other** too.*
  A means that they do things independently, on their own.
  B means that one old person helps another old person. It's a two-way action involving different people.
- We can say *each other* or *one another*. (But *one another* usually means we are talking about more than two people. It is also more formal.)
  *We all help **each other**. = We all help **one another**.*

CHECK QUESTIONS 4 **Rewrite these sentences using *each other*.**
1 Reg helps me and I help him. We ...
2 He does things for me and I do things for him. We ...

Practice

- He's looking at himself in the mirror. (*He* and *himself* are the same person.)
- *-self* = singular   *-selves* = plural.
- A ——————▶ A
  myself, yourself, themselves, etc.
  I enjoyed myself.
- A ⇄ B
  each other/one another
  Adam and I love each other.

---

1 Complete the dialogue, using *myself, himself, themselves,* etc.

'Hi! How was your weekend? Did you enjoy

(1) .... ?'

'No, we didn't enjoy (2) .... '

'Why? What happened?'

'Well, I told the children to look after

(3) .... while I went to buy

(4) .... some cigarettes. When I

came back I found that Tim had fallen and hurt

(5) .... quite badly. I blame

(6) .... for leaving them by

(7) .... , but it was only for ten

minutes.'

'Is that all?'

'No, it isn't. Then Sarah tried to make

(8) .... something to eat and

burnt (9) .... on the cooker. And

the dog cut (10) .... on a piece of

glass. But how about you? Did you enjoy

(11) .... ?'

'Yes, thanks. I bought (12) .... a

new computer and I played with that for most

of the weekend. Greg looked after the children.

They really enjoyed (13) .... '

2 A Spanish student is in England, learning English. She is talking to a French friend. Complete the text with reflexive pronouns (*myself, yourself,* etc.) or *each other.*

A funny thing happened to me yesterday. Juan

and I were sitting in a restaurant, speaking

Spanish to (1) .... , of course. I

noticed that the English couple at the next

table were listening. After a few minutes they

introduced (2) .... and we started

talking to (3) .... The English

couple said they were trying to teach

(4) .... Spanish. They were finding

it difficult because they could only speak to

(5) .... and they knew they were

making a lot of mistakes. So, we arranged to

give (6) .... language lessons. I

would teach them Spanish and they would

teach me English! It's very difficult to teach

(7) .... a language, because you

don't get a chance to speak it, unless you talk to

(8) .... of course!

3 Complete these sentences with reflexive pronouns.

1 The people in our street haven't got much
money, so they have to do a lot of things for
....

2 Mr Taggart at Number 10 is 85 and he still
cooks and cleans for ....

3 The Archers next door never take their car
to a garage. They service it ....

4 Mr and Mrs Potter at Number 13 decorated
their whole house ....

5 Mrs Wheatcroft at Number 11 is 84. She lives
by .... and she seems to look
after .... very well.

6 We're lucky. We've got a big garden, so we eat
a lot of fresh vegetables. We grow them all
....

7 And I've got a good sewing-machine, so I
make .... a lot of clothes.

66 Someone, something, somewhere, anyone, anything, anywhere, etc.

Paul and Beth stopped at a small petrol station in Scotland. No-one came to serve them. They couldn't see anyone. 'Somebody must be here, because they've left the office door open. Perhaps there's someone in the office. Go and see, Beth. If you find anybody, tell them we want some petrol.' Beth knocked, but nobody answered. She went in, but she couldn't see anybody. 'Is anybody there?' No-one answered. Then she saw a notice. **If nobody's here, we're closed**, it said.

Step 1 | Someone/somebody, anyone/anybody, no-one/nobody

- *Someone/somebody* both mean the same, as do *anyone/anybody, no-one/nobody*. *They couldn't see **anyone**. = They couldn't see **anybody**.*

- *Someone, anyone, no-one* are used with a verb in the singular. *Perhaps there**'s someone** in the office. If **nobody's** here, we're closed.*
  BUT we use *they, them, their* when we refer to *someone*, etc. ***Somebody** must be here, because **they**'ve left the door open. If you find **anybody**, tell **them** we want some petrol.*

- We usually use *someone* in affirmative sentences and *anyone* in questions and negative sentences. ***Somebody must** be here. **Is anybody** there? She **couldn't** see **anybody**.*
  BUT we can use *anyone* in affirmative sentences. It means 'it doesn't matter who'. *If you **find anybody**, tell them we want some petrol.*

- *No-one* is used with a verb in the affirmative. ***No-one came** to serve them.*

CHECK QUESTIONS 1 ▶ **Put in *someone (-body), anyone (-body), no-one (-body)*.**
1 Was there ... at the petrol station?   2 ... had left the office door open.
3 Beth didn't find ... in the office.   4 When she called, ... answered.

Step 2 | Something, anything, nothing

At lunchtime, Paul and Beth stopped at a café. Paul wasn't hungry.
'Paul, are you going to eat anything?'
'No, there's nothing I like on the menu. I won't have anything.'
'But you must eat something. You've eaten nothing all day.'
'Oh, all right. I'll have something like a sandwich. What about you? Are you going to have something hot?'
'Yes, I'm starving. I could eat anything!'

- *Something, anything, nothing* follow the same rules as *someone, anyone, no-one*. (See Step 1.)

- Note that we can use *anything* in affirmative sentences, where it means 'it doesn't matter what'. *I **could** eat **anything**!*

- Note that *something* (like *someone* and *somewhere*) can also be used in polite questions, offers or suggestions. *Are you going to have **something** hot?*

Put in *something, anything* or *nothing*.
1 Paul doesn't want ...   2 Is there ... he likes on the menu?
3 He's eaten ... all day.   4 He wants ... light.

Step 3 | *Somewhere, anywhere, nowhere*

> The next morning Paul and Beth were deciding what to do.
> 'Where shall we go this morning?'
> 'I don't mind. We can go anywhere you like.'
> 'Shall we go somewhere by the sea?'
> 'OK. Where's the map? Have you seen it anywhere?'
> 'It must be somewhere in our room.'
> 'No, it isn't there. And it's nowhere in the car. I can't find it anywhere.'

- *Somewhere* also follows the same rules as *someone, anyone, no-one.* (See Step 1.)
- Note that *somewhere* (NOT anywhere) is used in suggestions. (See Step 2.)
  *Shall we go **somewhere** by the sea?*
- *Anywhere* can be used in affirmative sentences. It means 'it doesn't matter where'.
  *We **can** go **anywhere** you like.*

Put in *somewhere, anywhere* or *nowhere*.
1 Beth wants to go ... by the sea.
2 Paul hasn't seen the map ...   3 It's ... in their room.

Step 4 | *Something*, etc. + infinitive or adjective

> Paul and Beth are in Inverness, They're looking at the tourists' guide.
> 'Nothing to do today? You want somewhere nice to go? Somewhere
> different? Come to Inverness. There's nowhere more beautiful in
> Scotland. There's something interesting for all the family. Buy
> something special at the Castle Souvenir Shop. Have something to eat
> at Craigie's 5-star restaurant. You won't find anything better in
> Scotland! And you might meet somebody famous! If you need more
> information, you'll find someone to help you at the Tourist Office.'

After *someone, something, somewhere,* etc. we often use:

- an infinitive. *Nothing **to do**? You'll always find someone **to help** you.*
- an adjective or an adjective + an infinitive.
  *Somewhere **different**? something **interesting** somewhere **nice to go***

Paul and Beth didn't enjoy Inverness. Put in *anything, anybody* or *nobody*.
1 They didn't meet ... famous at Craigie's.
2 They couldn't buy ... special at the Castle. It was closed.
3 And there was ... to help them at the Tourist Office.

1 1 anyone (-body) 2 someone (-body)
3 anyone (-body) 4 no-one (-body)
2 1 anything 2 anything 3 nothing 4 something

3 1 somewhere 2 anywhere 3 nowhere
4 1 anyone (-body) 2 anything
3 no-one (-body)

Practice

> - We use *someone (-body)*, *something*, *somewhere* in affirmative sentences and in polite requests, offers and suggestions.
>   *I saw someone. Can someone help me, please?*
> - We use *anyone (-body)*, *anything*, *anywhere* in negative sentences and questions, and when they mean 'it doesn't matter who, which or where'.
>   *I can't see it anywhere. Can you see anything? Sit down anywhere.*
> - *No-one (nobody)*, *nothing*, *nowhere* are used with a verb in the affirmative. *Nobody came.*
> - All of them are used with a verb in the singular. *Somebody is at the door.*
>   All can be followed by an infinitive or an adjective.
>   *I want something to eat. Did you meet anybody interesting?*

1 Complete this conversation, using *someone (-body)*, *anyone (-body)*, *something*, *anything*, *nothing*.

'Is (1) .... hungry?'

'Yes, I am. Is there (2) .... to eat?'

'There are some eggs and some tuna fish. No, wait a minute. (3) .... has eaten the eggs. Do you want some tuna sandwiches?'

'No, I don't like (4) .... with fish. Is there (5) ....else?'

'No, there's (6) .... Would you like to go and buy (7) .... from the shop?'

'Yes. OK. Shall I get you (8) .... too?'

2 You are at the station. You have missed the last train home. Put in *someone (-body)*, *anyone (-body)*, *no-one(-body)*, *something*, *somewhere*, *nowhere*.

1 You can't phone because .... 's using the phone.

2 You're hungry. You want .... to eat.

3 You don't know .... who lives near the station.

4 You want to ask .... to lend you the money for a taxi, but there's .... around.

5 You want to sleep .... tonight, but there's .... to sleep.

3 You are in a jeweller's shop. Put in *something*, *anything* with one of these adjectives: *smaller, cheaper, expensive, nice*.

'It's my girlfriend's birthday tomorrow. I want to buy (1) .... for her. I can't afford (2) ....'

'What about this bracelet?'

'It looks too big for her. I need (3) .... , I think.'

'This is a smaller one. It's £55.'

'£55! That's expensive.'

'Shall I show you (4) .... ?'

4 Imagine a place where you can do what you like. Make sentences using *anyone (-body)*, *anything*, *anywhere*.
Example: It doesn't matter what you do.
You can do anything.

1 It doesn't matter where you go.

   ....

2 It doesn't matter what you eat.

   ....

3 It doesn't matter who you talk to.

   ....

4 It doesn't matter what you wear.

   ....

5 It doesn't matter where you park your car.

   ....

Possessive forms: *The man's children, the door of the room, a friend of mine*

The multi-millionaire, Mr Barney Varley, is dead. A maid found Mr Varley's body at his luxury flat in London. The dog's lead was tied round Mr Varley's hands, but the dog had disappeared. The millionaire's children, Anna and Seth, weren't with him. Anna and Seth's mother, Mrs Fay Varley, is in hospital suffering from shock. The children's grandmother, Mrs Ena Varley, is now looking after them. The police are refusing to answer reporters' questions.

Step 1 | Main uses of the apostrophe: *'s* and *s'*

- We use *'s* to show that something belongs to someone, or that something is associated with someone. We use it with singular nouns (people and animals).
  Mr Varley's body **the dog's** lead
- With plural nouns, we add an apostrophe after the final *s*.
  *The police are refusing to answer **reporters'** questions.*
- With plural nouns without a final *s* (*men, women*, etc.) we use *'s*.
  *the **children's** grandmother*
- With two or more names, we put *'s* after the last name.
  Anna and Seth's mother
- *'s* is pronounced /s/ after *c, f, k, p, ph, t, th: Seth's* /seθs/,
  /z/ after all other consonants: *The dog's* /dɒgz/ *lead*,
  /ɪz/ after *ch, s, sh: The boss's* /ˈbɒsɪz/ *daughter.*

CHECK QUESTIONS 1 | **Answer the questions.**
1 What was found round Mr Varley's hands?
2 Who is Mrs Fay Varley? She's ... wife.
3 Who is Mrs Ena Varley? She's ... grandmother.

Step 2 | Other uses of *'s* or *s'*

Today's newspapers all report Mr Varley's death. He was the chairman of Britain's biggest company and one of the country's richest men. The company's employees were shocked by his death. He had just returned from three weeks' holiday in Greece. The night before his death he stayed at his brother's in north London. It seems he went to the chemist's to buy some aspirin. He didn't have his own car; he was driving his wife's.

We can use the *'s* or *s'* form:

- on its own, when it isn't necessary to repeat a noun.
  *He didn't have his own car; he was driving **his wife's**.*
- on its own, when we talk about someone's home or a shop.
  *He stayed at **his brother's**.* (= at his brother's house or flat)
  *He went to **the chemist's**.* (= the chemist's shop)

- with organisations or groups of people (company, government, etc.).
  The company's *employees were shocked.*
Here, we can also use the noun + *of* + noun construction.
  The employees of the company *were shocked.* (See Step 3.)
- with places/countries.
  the country's *richest men.* ***Britain's*** *biggest company*
- with expressions of time (*today, Monday, a month*, etc.).
  today's *newspapers* ***three weeks'*** *holiday in Greece*

CHECK QUESTIONS 2 **Answer the questions.**
1 What's special about Mr Varley's company?
2 Who was shocked by his death?
3 Did Mr Varley stay at his own flat the night before his death?   No, he stayed ...
4 Whose car was Mr Varley driving?
5 Why had he been to Greece?   For ...

Step 3 | When we use noun + *of* + noun or noun + noun

Mr Varley's body was found in the kitchen of his London flat. The
kitchen window was open. There was a glove on the table. The maid
described to reporters the horror of the scene. The car keys and one of
Mr Varley's three cars were missing. The maid is the wife of the man
who looks after Mr Varley's cars. She hasn't seen her husband for two
days.

- When we talk about things, rather than people or animals, we usually use noun + *of* + noun rather than *'s/s'* to say that something belongs to something, or that something is associated with something.
  *the kitchen **of** his flat.* (NOT *his flat's kitchen*)
  *the horror **of** the scene.* (NOT *the scene's horror*)
- We can often simplify noun + *of* + noun and use just noun + noun.
  *the **car keys*** (You can also say: 'the keys of the car')
  *the **kitchen window*** (NOT *the window of the kitchen*)
Sometimes both constructions are possible (see *car keys* above), but not always. There's no clear rule that tells you when you can or can't use the noun + noun construction. If necessary, use a good dictionary.
- When the noun is accompanied by a descriptive phrase or clause, we must use *of* (and not *'s*).
  *She's **the wife of the man who looks after Mr Varley's cars***.
We can't say 'She's the man's wife who looks after Mr Varley's cars' because it isn't clear who looks after the cars.

CHECK QUESTIONS 3 **Complete the sentences.**
1 The police want to find (owner/glove).
2 They want to find (husband/the maid who works for Mr Varley).
3 They also want to find (keys/car).

Ralph Digby knew Mr Varley well. 'Barney Varley was a friend of mine. We played tennis together. I've still got a tennis racket of his. He lent it to me the last time we played. My son, Alex, is a friend of his daughter's.'

● *A friend*, etc. *of* can be followed by a possessive pronoun *mine, yours, hers*, etc. (see Unit 68) or by *'s*.

    *a tennis racket of **his***   *a friend of **mine***
    *a friend of **his daughter's***

We use *a friend*, etc. + *of* when we want to describe something by saying who it belongs to, or someone by saying who they're associated with.

CHECK QUESTIONS 4   **Answer the questions.**
1 Did Ralph Digby know Barney Varley well? Yes, he was ...
2 Does his son Alex know Mr Varley's daughter well? Yes, he's ...

Practice

> - We use 's for people and animals in the singular: *the man's dog   the dog's lead*
> And for plural nouns without a final *s*: *the women's changing room   the children's bedrooms*
> - We add an apostrophe after the final *s* of other plural nouns: *his parents' house*
> - We use noun + *of* + noun for things: *the title of the book   the front of the house*
> - We often use noun + noun: *the bathroom door   the team manager*

1 **A friend is helping you after a party. He is asking you who various things belong to.**
Example: Whose is this red sweater? (Jenny)
It's Jenny's.

1 Whose is this coat? (Jill)

....

2 Whose are these CDs? (Tom and Maggy)

....

3 Whose is this bottle of whisky? (my parents)

....

4 And what about this old sock? (the dog)

....

2 **Rewrite the following text, using 's with the items in italics.**

1 The weather *yesterday* was awful.

....

2 It was as bad as the storms *last year*.

....

3 I'm going to watch the television news *this evening* to see what has happened.

....

4 The weather forecast *for tomorrow* isn't very good.

....

3 **Here is a description of Lily Finch. Use the 's or s' forms or the noun + of + noun construction to complete the sentences.**

1 She doesn't like her name. 'Lily' is (her mother/name) .... Her father chose it because it's (the name/his favourite flower) ....

2 Lily likes reading (women/magazines) .... and listening to (the music/a new heavy metal band)

....

3 She doesn't like (England/terrible weather)

.... ; she prefers (the sunshine/southern Europe) ....

....

Every year she has (a month/holiday)

.... in Portugal.

4 She plays badminton for (a local girls/team)

.... She's (the team/best player) ....

5 (Her parents/house) .... is in the country, but she spends a lot of time at her (boyfriend) .... He's got a flat in London.

4 **I had a terrible day! Replace the words in italics with a noun + noun construction.**
Example: I opened the bathroom door and broke the *handle of the door*. *the door handle*

1 I broke *the window in the bedroom*.

....

2 I lost *the key of my garage*.

....

3 And I lost *the photos of my holiday*.

....

4 *The aerial of my car radio* was broken by vandals. ....

5 **Complete this dialogue, using *a friend of mine, a friend of my sister's*, etc.**
'Who's Jack Lynch? Is he (1 friend/you)

.... ?'
'No, he's (2 friend/my parents) ....

.... My mother teaches art at the local college. He's (3 student/she) ....

.... He's a very good artist. I've got (4 painting/he) ....
I'll show it to you.'

68

Possessive adjectives and pronouns: *my, mine*, etc. *My own Whose?*

Helen has just got married. All her family have come to the wedding. At the party afterwards she's telling a friend who the different people are.

'That old lady's my grandmother. She's 91, but she's very independent. She still lives on her own. The girl by the window is Maggy. She's got her own computer company. And that's her brother, Jack. They're my cousins. The man standing next to them is their father.'
'So, he's your uncle.'
'Yes.'
'How old are your cousins?'
'Jack's 17, and Maggy's 25.'
'What about the couple by the door?'
'They're our neighbours. They're quite rich. They've got their own swimming pool.'
'Is that their dog?'
'Yes. Have you seen its legs? It's only got three!'

Step 1 | Possessive adjectives: *my, your*, etc.

I	**my**	*I like **my** brother.*
You	**your**	*Do you like **your** uncle?*
He	**his**	*Does he like **his** sisters?*
She	**her**	*She doesn't like **her** father.*
It	**its**	*The dog likes **its** food.*
We	**our**	*We like **our** neighbours.*
You	**your**	*Do you both like **your** parents?*
They	**their**	*They like **their** grandmother.*

● Possessive adjectives are always followed by a noun, either singular or plural. The form of the possessive adjective is the same before a singular or plural noun.
   my grandmother   my cousins
   your uncle   your cousins

● We use possessive adjectives to make it clear that one person or thing belongs to another, or is associated with another.

● We use the possessive adjective *its* when the possessor is an animal or a thing. Don't confuse it with *it's* (= it is OR it has).
   *Have you seen **its** legs? **It's** (= **it has**) only got three!*

● We use a possessive adjective + *own* when we say that something belongs completely to someone.
   *She's got **her own** computer company.*
   *They've got **their own** swimming pool.*

● Note the expressions *on my own, on his own, on their own*, etc.
   *She still lives **on her own**.* (= She lives alone.)

CHECK QUESTIONS 1 **Look at the text above and complete the sentences using the correct possessive adjective. Use *own* where necessary.**
1 Jack: 'Maggy's ... sister.' 2 Helen: 'Jack and Maggy are ... cousins.'
3 'Is Helen ... granddaughter?' Grandmother: 'Yes, she is.'
4 'What a strange dog! What's ... name?' '... name's Tripod.'
5 Maggy's got ... computer company. 6 She doesn't live with anyone. She lives ...

Step 2 | Possessive pronouns: *mine, yours*, etc.   *Whose?*

It's late. One of the guests at the wedding wants to leave, but he can't move his car because another car is in the way. He's talking to another man.
'Whose car is this? Is it yours?'
'No, it isn't mine. Mine's a Ford.'
'What about Daniel? Is it his?'
'No, it isn't his. His is a Volkswagen.'
'What about the neighbours? Is it theirs?'
'No, they haven't brought theirs.'
'I'll ask Janet. Perhaps it's hers.'
'No, it isn't hers. She hasn't got a car.'
'Ah, here are Jack and Maggy. I'll ask them. Hi, you two! Do you know whose car this is? Is it yours?'
'No, it isn't ours. I don't know whose it is.'

I	**mine**	*This car belongs to me. It's **mine**.*
You	**yours**	*Does this car belong to you? Is it **yours**?*
He	**his**	*This car belongs to him. It's **his**.*
She	**hers**	*This car doesn't belong to her. It isn't **hers**.*
It (no possessive pronoun)		
We	**ours**	*This car belongs to us. It's **ours**.*
You	**yours**	*Does this car belong to you two? Is it **yours**?*
They	**theirs**	*This car belongs to them. It's **theirs**.*

- We use possessive pronouns on their own without a noun. We use them when it isn't necessary to repeat a noun (singular or plural).
    *Whose car is this? Is it **yours**?*
(The speaker doesn't need to say 'Is it your car?' His first question has already made it clear that he's talking about a car.)
Note: There isn't a possessive pronoun for *it*.

- We use the question word *Whose* to ask who something belongs to. There are two ways to ask the same question.
    ***Whose** car is this?* (= Who does this car belong to?)
    ***Whose** is this car?* (= Who does this car belong to?)
We use *Whose* without a noun when we don't need to repeat the noun.
    ***Whose** is this?*
    (When the speaker asks this question, it's clear he's pointing at the car.)
Note how we say that we don't know who something belongs to:
    I don't know whose it is.
OR plural: *I don't know whose they are.*

CHECK QUESTIONS 2

Answer the questions, using a possessive pronoun.
1 Does the car belong to the other man? No, it isn't ...
2 Does the car belong to Janet? No, it isn't ...
3 Does the car belong to the neighbours? No, ...
4 'Who does this car belong to?' Ask this question in another way.

ANSWERS TO
CHECK QUESTIONS
1, 2 AND 3

1 1 my 2 my 3 your 4 its Its 5 her own
6 on her own

2 1 No, it isn't his. 2 No, it isn't hers. 3 No, it isn't theirs. 4 Whose car is this? OR Whose is this car?

Practice

- Possessive adjectives (*my, your, his*, etc.) have the same form before a singular or a plural noun.
- Possessive pronouns (*mine, yours, his, hers*, etc.) are used on their own without a noun.
- We use the question word *Whose* to ask who something belongs to.

1 **Nobody can play tennis today. Put in the correct possessive adjective or pronoun.**

1 I can't play tennis because I've forgotten .... tennis shoes.

2 And Jessica can't play, because she's forgotten .... too.

3 Andy can't play because he's broken .... arm.

4 Rachel and Amanda can't play because they've forgotten .... rackets.

5 And Jilly and Laura have lost .... !

6 Clare's at home. She's looking after her cat. It's broken .... leg.

7 'Can you play, Lee? Or have you forgotten .... racket?'

2 **Complete the sentences, using *my, your, his*, etc. + *own*.**
At the moment I'm staying with my uncle and aunt in California. Their life-style is amazing.

1 They've got (private beach)

....

2 The house has got (swimming-pool)

....

3 I've got (bathroom) ....

4 My cousin Dean plays the guitar, and he's got (recording studio) ....

....

5 His sister Elena has got (horses) ....

.... , and each horse has got (stable)

....

6 My uncle and aunt grow (oranges and lemons) ....

3 **Rewrite this dialogue using the question word *Whose* and possessive pronouns (*mine, yours, his, hers*, etc.).**
Example: Who does this CD player belong to?
Whose is this CD player?
Does it belong to you, Tim? *Is it yours, Tim?*

'Who does this Walkman belong to?'

(1) ....
'Does it belong to you, Sebastian?'

(2) ....
'No, it doesn't belong to me.'

(3) ....
'What about Molly? Does it belong to her?'

(4) ....
'I don't think so. But Andy's got one like that. So, it probably belongs to him.'

(5) ....

4 **Replace the words in italics, using possessive pronouns (*mine, yours, his, hers, ours*, etc.) to avoid repetition of nouns.**

In the office there are some tomato sandwiches on top of the computer.

'Whose tomato sandwiches are these? Are they *your tomato sandwiches*, Ellen?' (1) ....

'No, they aren't *my tomato sandwiches*.

(2) .... I don't like tomatoes.'

'Well, whose are they? What about Laura? Are they *her tomato sandwiches*?' (3) ....

'No, they aren't *her tomato sandwiches*.

(4) .... She has lunch in the canteen.'

'Well, what about the office cleaners? Are they *their tomato sandwiches*?' (5) ....

'No, I don't think they're *their tomato sandwiches*.' (6) ....

'Well, I'm hungry, so now they're *my tomato sandwiches*.' (7) ....

69

> Sophie's buying clothes. She's talking to a shop assistant.
> 'I'm looking for a T-shirt with long sleeves. Have you got one?'
> 'What colour do you want?'
> 'Have you got a blue one?'
> 'I don't think so. ... I've got a green one.'
> 'No, I really wanted a blue one.'

Step 1 | *One = a/an* + noun

- We use *one* when we don't want to repeat a singular noun. We already know what the noun is.
  *Have you got **one**?*
  (Sophie doesn't need to repeat 'a T-shirt with long sleeves'.)

- When we add an adjective, we use *a/an* + adjective + *one*.
  *Have you got **a blue one**?*

CHECK QUESTIONS 1 ▸ **Replace a word in each of these sentences with *one*.**
1 Sophie wants a T-shirt, but they haven't got a T-shirt she likes.
2 There's a green T-shirt, but Sophie wants a blue T-shirt.

Step 2 | *The one/the ones   Which one(s)*, etc.

> 'How much are these jeans?'
> 'Which ones do you mean? The blue ones?'
> 'No, these black ones.'
> 'Ah, those are £39.99.'
> 'And how much is that red skirt?'
> 'Which one? Do you mean the one with pockets?'
> 'Yes.'
> 'Er, that one's £45.99. The green one without pockets is £39.00.'

- When we compare or select things and don't want to repeat the noun, we use *one/ones* with *the, this, that, which*.
  *Do you mean **the one** with pockets?*
  (The shop assistant doesn't need to repeat 'the red skirt'.)
  ***Which ones** do you mean?*
  (She doesn't need to repeat 'jeans'.)

- Note that we don't usually use *ones* after the plural forms *these* and *those*. We say *these* rather than *these ones*.
  But if *these* and *those* are followed by an adjective we use *ones*.
  *Ah, **those** are £39.99.   **These** black **ones**.*

Rewrite these sentences so that the noun is not repeated. Use *one* or *ones* where necessary.
1 Sophie wants some jeans; she likes the black jeans.
2 She prefers the red skirt to the green skirt.
3 Those jeans are £50.00, but these jeans are a lot cheaper.

Step 3 | When you can't use *one/ones*

> Sophie doesn't earn much money, and she spends the money she earns on clothes.
> It's Saturday morning. She's going shopping in town. It's raining. She can't find her umbrella.
> 'Mum! I can't find my umbrella. I can see yours, but I can't find mine.'
> 'OK. You can take mine.'
> Sophie wants some new shoes, so she's come into town to buy some. She wants some red ones. She's seen a few that she likes, but there aren't any in her size. The trouble is, she's got quite big feet.

- We never use *one* to replace an uncountable noun (like *money, music, water,* etc.).
  *Sophie doesn't earn much money, and she spends **the money** she earns on clothes.* (NOT She spends the one she earns on clothes.)

- We don't use *one/ones* after the possessive adjectives *my, your,* etc. Instead, we use a possessive pronoun, *mine, yours,* etc. without *one/ones*.
  *I can see **yours**, but I can't find **mine**.* (NOT I can see your one, but I can't find my one.)

- We don't use *one/ones* after 'number' words like *some, any, a few, many, a lot, three, fifteen,* etc.
  *She's come into town to buy **some**.* (NOT some ones)
  *She's seen **a few** that she likes.* (NOT a few ones)
  *There aren't **any** in her size.* (NOT any ones)
  But if there's an adjective after these words, we must use *one/ones*.
  *She's looking for **some red ones**.* (NOT some red)

Rewrite these sentences so that the noun is not repeated.
1 Sophie can see her mother's umbrella, but she can't find her umbrella.
2 Sophie wants to buy some shoes, but she can't find any shoes in her size.
3 She doesn't really need any more shoes, but she's going to buy some shoes.
4 She doesn't want black shoes; she's looking for some red shoes.
5 Most girls don't have big feet, but her feet are big.

---

1 1 but they haven't got one she likes. 2 but Sophie wants a blue one.
2 1 she likes the black ones. 2 to the green one. 3 but these are a lot cheaper.

3 1 but she can't find hers. 2 but she can't find any in her size. 3 but she's going to buy some. 4 she's looking for some red ones. 5 but hers are big.

Practice

We use *one* to replace a singular noun and *ones* to replace a plural noun.

Singular	**Plural**
the (blue) one	*the (blue) ones*
a blue one	*some blue ones*
this/that one	*these/those*
Which one ?	*Which ones?*

1 Change words in the second sentence to avoid repetition.

1 My socks have all got holes in them. I must buy some new socks.

....

2 There are some nice socks over here. Which socks do you like?

....

3 I like these blue socks. I don't like those socks.

....

4 You need a new jacket too. Which jacket do you like?

....

5 That jacket. The jacket with the big buttons.

....

6 That jacket's too expensive. Try this green jacket on.

....

2 Complete this dialogue in a fruit and vegetable shop.

'A kilo of potatoes, please.'

'Which (1) .... ?'

'The new (2) .... , please. And can I have a melon?'

'Which (3) .... would you like?'

'That (4) .... , please.'

'Anything else?'

'Yes can I have some apples, please?'

'The green (5) .... or the red (6) .... ?'

'Half a kilo of the red (7) .... , please.'

'Is that all?'

'Yes. Can I have a box to put them in, please?'

'Is this (8) .... big enough?'

'Yes, that (9) ....'s fine.'

3 Sarah is on holiday. She has found that one of her friends is staying in the same place but at a different hotel. Rewrite her letter home. To avoid repetition, use *one/ones* or other pronouns to replace nouns where necessary.

'There are a lot of hotels here. Lorna's staying in a hotel right by the sea. My hotel is in the town. It's a lot smaller than her hotel. Her hotel has got a swimming pool, but my hotel hasn't got a swimming pool. There are lots of cafés. We often go to a café that has really good pizzas. There are a lot of German and American tourists here; there are a few tourists from France, but there aren't many tourists from England. There are some lovely beaches. We like the beaches on the south side of the island. Our favourite beach is only 500 metres from the town.'

....

....

....

....

....

....

....

....

....

....

....

....

....

....

....

....

70

Martin Paxman is rich. He had rich parents who left him a fortune when they died. He lives in a big house in the town of Modbury. But that isn't his only home. He also owns a farm in a neighbouring village.

Nowadays the rich sometimes feel embarrassed when they see the homeless on the streets and when they read about the unemployed in the newspapers.

But Martin isn't ashamed. His life is good. He rarely gets ill. He's never alone. He just thinks he's been lucky and he's glad to be alive.

| **Step 1** | Adjectives used before a noun or not   Adjectives as nouns |

- Adjectives are used to describe things or people. They're the same before singular and plural nouns. Most adjectives can be used after a verb and before a noun.

  *Martin Paxman **is rich***. (used after the verb *be*)
  *He had **rich parents***. (used before a noun - *parents*)

- The following adjectives aren't normally used before a noun:
  afraid, alive, alone, apart, ashamed, asleep, awake, aware, glad, ill, pleased, ready, sure, unable, upset, well.
  *Martin isn't **ashamed***. (You can't say 'an ashamed person')
  *He rarely gets **ill***. (You can't say 'an ill person')

- Some adjectives aren't normally used alone after a verb. The most common are:
  eventual, existing, countless, indoor, main, maximum, neighbouring, occasional, only, outdoor, principal.
  *It isn't his **only home***. (You can't say 'The home is only')
  *a **neighbouring village***. (NOT The village is neighbouring)

- Sometimes when we talk about a group of people in general, we can use *the* + adjective as a noun. *The* + adjective is followed by a plural verb.

  ***The rich** sometimes **feel** embarrassed*. (= rich people)
  *when they see **the homeless*** (= homeless people)
  *when they read about **the unemployed***. (= unemployed people)
  Some common examples of adjectives used as nouns are:
  the blind, the dead, the deaf, the disabled, the elderly, the English, the Spanish, etc.,
  the handicapped, the homeless, the injured, the old, the poor, the underprivileged, the unemployed, the young.

CHECK QUESTIONS 1 **Complete the sentences, using each of these adjectives once: *alone, lonely, glad, happy.***
1 Martin's got lots of friends. He certainly isn't a ... person.
2 He's always ... when his friends come to see him.
3 He really enjoys life. He's a very ... man.
4 Martin isn't ... in the house tonight. Jessica's with him.

Martin's 25 years old. He's a pleasant young man. He's honest and generous. His girlfriend Jessica is a beautiful slim dark-haired American girl who likes wearing long black silk dresses and expensive silver jewellery. She's lively, warm and intelligent.
Last week Martin bought himself a big new wooden bed. It's 2.5 m long and 3 m wide. The mattress is 75 cm thick. He also bought a red and gold duvet cover to go on the bed. He wanted a long bed because he's nearly 2 m tall. But now he doesn't know where he'll be sleeping in a few weeks' time. This morning he had some sudden worrying news. The bank where he keeps all his money is having serious financial problems and is closing down!

- When we use more than one adjective, we put the adjective that gives our opinion before the adjective that gives factual information.
    *He's a **pleasant** young man.* (NOT a young pleasant man)
Martin's pleasant = an opinion.   Martin's young = a fact.

- Adjectives usually go in a particular order:

1	2	3	4	5	6	7
(opinion)	**(size)**	**(shape)**	**(age)**	**(colour)**	**(origin)**	**(material/type)**
a	*big*		*new*			*wooden* *bed*
a beautiful		*slim*		*dark-haired*	*American*	*girl*
	long			*black*		*silk* *dresses*
serious						*financial* *problems*

- Two adjectives together are often joined by *and*:
when there are two colour adjectives.
    *He also bought a **red and gold** duvet cover to go on the bed.*
when there are two adjectives alone after a link verb.
    *He's always **pleasant and generous**.*

- When there are three adjectives alone after a link verb, we usually put a comma after the first, and *and* between the last two.
    *She's **lively, warm and intelligent**.*

- When we give measurements, we put the adjectives *deep, high, long, old, tall, thick, wide* after measurement nouns.
    *Martin's **25 years old**.   He's nearly **2 m tall**.*
    *The bed's **2.5 m long** and **3 m wide**.*
    *The mattress is **75 cm thick**.*
Note: We don't say 'I'm 65 kilos heavy.' We say 'I'm 65 kilos in weight.'

CHECK QUESTIONS 2   **Put the adjectives in the best order. Add *and* where necessary.**
1 That (tall/young/nice) man is Martin Paxman.
2 He's got a (blue/grey) Mercedes.
3 His girlfriend's got (round/big/brown) eyes.
4 She's about (tall/1m 60).

ANSWERS TO
CHECK QUESTIONS
1 AND 2

1 1 lonely 2 glad OR happy 3 happy 4 alone
2 1 That nice tall young man 2 a blue and grey Mercedes 3 big round brown eyes 4 She's about 1m 60 tall.

Practice

Some adjectives can't be used before a noun: *asleep, ill, afraid, well*, etc.
We put 'opinion' adjectives before 'fact' adjectives: *A fantastic new car.*
We put 'fact' adjectives in this order: *size shape age colour origin material/type.*
Some adjectives are used as nouns: *the old, the rich, the unemployed, the Spanish*, etc.
Two adjectives alone after a link verb are joined by *and*: *I'm tired and hungry.*
Three adjectives alone after a link verb: *I'm tired, hungry and thirsty.*
Two colour adjectives are joined by *and*: *My dress is red and green.*
Measurements: *The swimming pool's 3m deep. The tower's 20m high.*

1 Choose the right answer (A or B) to these general knowledge questions. Look for the correct use of the adjective.

1 What's a somnambulist? ....
   A Someone who walks around when they're asleep. B An asleep person who walks around.
2 What do we call activities like mountain-climbing, skiing and sailing? ....
   A Activities that are outdoor. B Outdoor activities.
3 If someone is very sad and is crying, how are they feeling? ....
   A They're upset people. B They're upset.
4 How many stars are there in the universe? ....
   A The number's countless. B A countless number.
5 What's a sanatorium? ....
   A It's a place where people who are ill are treated. B It's a place where ill people are treated.

2 An estate agent is describing a house to a client. Are the adjectives in the right order? Write *Yes*, or rewrite the sentence, using the correct order. Add *and* if necessary.

1 It's an old lovely 18th century house.
   ....
2 It was built by an English famous architect.
   ....
   ....
3 It's at the end of a narrow country long lane.
   ....
   ....
4 It's near to a little pretty village.
   ....
5 It's got a lovely large garden.
   ....

6 And there are two beautiful old stables.
   ....
7 The kitchen is modern, well-equipped.
   ....
8 The bedrooms are painted green white.
   ....
   ....
9 There's an old stone interesting fireplace in the living room.
   ....
   ....
10 The house is solid, well-maintained and reasonably-priced.
   ....
   ....

3 Look at these drawings and write what the measurements are.

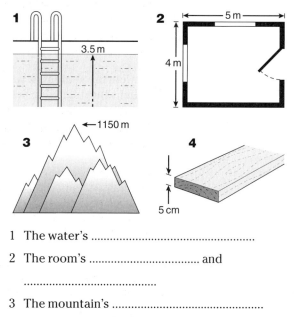

1 The water's ....
2 The room's .... and
   ....
3 The mountain's ....
4 The piece of wood is ....

229

Here are the results of a survey of the differences between men and women in Britain.

- Women are cleaner than men. 60% of women, but only 42% of men, have a bath or a shower every day. The cleanest women (7%) have a bath or a shower twice a day!
- Men are faster drivers than women. On motorways they're faster by 17 k.p.h., in town by 11 k.p.h.
- On average, adult men are taller than women (by 5 cm), because they usually have longer legs. The tallest man in the world was Robert Wadlow. He was 2m 72! The tallest woman (Zeng Jinlian) was 2m 48!
- A man's brain is bigger than a woman's, but Neanderthal man's brain was bigger than modern man's.

Step 1 | Uses of the comparative and superlative

We often compare people and things; we say how they are similar or different.

- If there are two things or people or two groups of things or people, we use the comparative.

  A man's brain is **bigger** than a woman's.
  Women are **cleaner** than men.

- If there are three or more people or things, we often use the superlative.

  The **tallest** man in the world was Robert Wadlow.

- We generally use *the* with the superlative. Sometimes *the* isn't used in informal speech. But we must use *the* if the superlative begins the sentence.

  Women who have a bath twice a day are *(the)* **cleanest**.
  The cleanest women have a bath twice a day.

- The comparative is often followed by *than*.

  A man's brain is **bigger than** a woman's.
  Women are **cleaner than** men.

CHECK QUESTIONS 1 **Complete the sentences with a comparative or a superlative.**
1 What's the difference between men and women drivers? Men are ... . (fast)
2 Young men between 17 and 20 are ... drivers. (fast).
3 Modern man's brain is ... than Neanderthal man's. (small)

Step 2 | Comparative and superlative forms: short adjectives

We form the comparative by adding -er to the adjective, and the superlative by adding -est.

	Comparative	**Superlative**
clean	cleaner	(the) cleanest
fast	faster	(the) fastest
tall	taller	(the) tallest
long	longer	(the) longest

Note the spelling changes in adjectives like these. (See also Step 3.)

big	bi**gg**er	(the) bi**gg**est
fat	fa**tt**er	(the) fa**tt**est
large	larg**er**	(the) larg**est**
dry	dr**ier**	(the) dr**iest**

CHECK QUESTIONS 2 **Write the missing forms.**
1 old   ...   the oldest
2 ...   cleaner   ...
3 wet   ...   ...
4 ...   nicer   ...

Step 3 | Adjectives with two syllables

- Men have dirtier hair than women. On average, women wash their hair twice a week, men only once.
- Women are more honest than men. 46% of men say they often do the cooking. 32% of women agree.
- Married men are healthier than unmarried men. The healthiest people are unmarried women!
- Women are more afraid of spiders than men: 69% of women, 16% of men. Women between 20 and 40 are the most afraid.

- We usually form the comparative and superlative of adjectives with two syllables ending in -y, -le, -er, -ow like this:

dirty	dirtier	(the) dirtiest
simple	simpler	(the) simplest
clever	cleverer	(the) cleverest
narrow	narrower	(the) narrowest

- We form the comparative and superlative of other two-syllable adjectives with more and (the) most.

honest	more honest	(the) most honest
afraid	more afraid	(the) most afraid

CHECK QUESTIONS 3 **Write the missing forms.**
1 ...   healthier   the healthiest
2 easy   ...   ...
3 ...   more careful   ...
4 modern   ...   ...

Step 4 | Long adjectives

> - Men are more interested in sport than women. 30% of men talk about it often, but only 5% of women.
> - Woman are more romantic than men. 62% of women keep old love letters, and only 22% of men.
> - Women are more religious than men. 8% go to church regularly, and 6% of men. Women over 65 are the most religious.
> - Men are more untidy than women. Only 18% of men hang up their clothes at night, compared to 37% of women. Boys between ten and eighteen are the most untidy.

- We usually form the comparative and superlative of long adjectives (with three syllables or more) with *more* and *(the) most*.

interested	more interested	(the) most interested
romantic	more romantic	(the) most romantic
religious	more religious	(the) most religious

- With adjectives that have a negative form beginning with *un-* (e.g. *tidy - untidy*), we can form the comparative and superlative using either *-er/-est* or *more/(the) most*.

untidy	untidier/more untidy	(the) untidiest/most untidy
unhappy	unhappier/more unhappy	(the) unhappiest/most unhappy
unhealthy	unhealthier/more unhealthy	(the) unhealthiest/most unhealthy

CHECK QUESTIONS 4 — **Write the missing forms.**
1 intelligent ... ...
2 ... more dangerous ...
3 ... ... the most interesting

Step 5 | Irregular comparatives and superlatives

> - 52% of men pass the driving test first time, but only 39% of women. But does this mean they're better drivers than women? In fact the best drivers (and the safest drivers) are women between 30 and 40. The worst drivers are young men between 18 and 25, because they're the most dangerous.

- A few adjectives have irregular comparative and superlative forms.

good	better	(the) best
bad	worse	(the) worst
old	older/elder	(the) oldest/(the) eldest
far	farther/further	(the) farthest/(the) furthest

- We use *elder, the eldest* only when we talk about members of a family, in phrases like:

   my **elder** brother   my **eldest** sister

We don't use *elder + than*. We can't say: 'He's elder than his brother.'

- *Farther* and *further* refer to distance. *Further* can also mean 'additional'.
  *Liverpool's 10 miles away. Manchester's **farther/further**.*
  *Have you got any **further** questions?*

CHECK QUESTIONS 5 **Complete the answers using *better, worse, the best, the worst.***
  1 Are men better drivers than women? No, they're ...
  2 Are men between 18 and 25 the best drivers? No, they're ...
  3 Are women between 30 and 40 the worst drivers? No, they're ...
  4 Do men think they're worse drivers than women. No, they think they're ...

Step 6 | The comparison of adverbs

- In general women drive better and more carefully than men. They have 25% fewer accidents. They drive most carefully when they have children in the car.
- Women get up earlier than men and go to bed later. (Six minutes earlier in the morning and ten minutes later at night.)
- Women work harder than men in the home. Women aged between 45 and 60 work the hardest. (They spend 2. 25 hours a day on housework.)

- We form the comparative and superlative of most adverbs with *more* and *most*.
  carefully   more carefully   (the) most carefully
  *They drive **most carefully** when they have children in the car.*

- There are some irregular adverbs:
  well/better/(the) best   badly/worse/(the) worst
  far/farther (further)/the farthest (the furthest)
  *Women drive **better** than men.*

- We form the comparative and superlative of the irregular adverbs *fast, soon, hard, high, near, long, late, early* with *-er* and *-est.*
  *Women get up **earlier** than men.*
  *Women work **harder** than men in the home.*

CHECK QUESTIONS 6 **Complete the sentences, using a comparative or a superlative.**
  1 Do women really drive ... than men? (well)
  2 Who gets up ... in your family? (early)
  3 Women drivers wait ... than men at traffic lights. (patient)
  4 In general men sleep ... than women. (long)

ANSWERS TO
CHECK QUESTIONS
1, 2, 3, 4, 5 AND 6

1 1 faster 2 the fastest 3 smaller
2 1 older 2 clean the cleanest 3 wetter the wettest 4 nice the nicest
3 1 healthy 2 easier the easiest 3 careful the most careful 4 more modern the most modern

4 1 more intelligent the most intelligent
  2 dangerous the most dangerous
  3 interesting more interesting
5 1 worse 2 the worst 3 the best 4 better
6 1 better 2 (the) earliest 3 more patiently 4 longer

Practice

	Comparative	**Superlative**
slow	slower	(the) slowest
dirty	dirtier	(the) dirtiest
stupid	more stupid	(the) most stupid
important	more important	(the) most important
carefully	more carefully	(the) most carefully

1 Compare Ben and Louise. Write comparative sentences, using the adjective given each time.

Ben	**Louise**
I'm 18.	I'm 19.
I've got one sister but no brothers.	I've got two brothers and a sister.
I weigh 79 kilos and I'm 1 metre 75.	I weigh 59 kilos and I'm 1 metre 72.
I'm not very good at tennis.	I'm a good tennis player.

Example: (young) *Ben is younger than Louise.*

1 (old)

....

2 (big/family)

....

3 (heavy)

....

4 (tall)

....

5 (good)

....

2 Why do British people go abroad for their holidays? Complete the sentences, using the information given.
Example: 76% (weather/good)
76% go abroad because the weather's better.

1 21% (hotels/comfortable)

....

2 5% (wine and cigarettes/cheap)

....

3 11% (sea/warm)

....

4 10% (beaches/clean)

....

5 23% (people/friendly)

....

6 15% (food/interesting)

....

7 10% (night-life/exciting)

....

8 12% (get a sun-tan/easily)

....

9 2% (bars stay open/late)

....

3 Write sentences about the planets, using a superlative.
Example: (Mercury/close/sun)
Mercury is the closest planet to the sun.

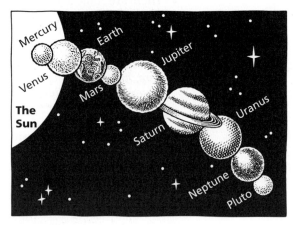

1 (Mars/near/Earth)

....

2 (Pluto/distant/from the sun)

....

3 (Venus/hot)

....

4 (Jupiter/big)

....

5 (Mercury/difficult to see)

....

Comparatives and superlatives (2)

You can now go from England to France by plane, by train through the Channel Tunnel ('Le Shuttle'), by ferry, or by hovercraft. The plane is four times as quick as the train, but a train ticket doesn't cost as much as a plane ticket. And nowadays going by train is just as comfortable as going by plane. The hovercraft is twice as fast as the ferry, but it isn't as fast as 'Le Shuttle'. The ferry costs about the same as the hovercraft, but the hovercraft doesn't have the same facilities as the ferry.

Step 1 | As ... as .../not as ... as ... + the same as ...

- We use *as ... as ...* to say that two things are the same or similar. *Just* adds emphasis.
  *Going by train is **just as comfortable as** going by plane.*

- We use *not as ... as ...* to say that two things are different.
  *A train ticket does**n't** cost **as much as** a plane ticket.*
  (= A plane ticket costs more than a train ticket.)
  *The hovercraft is**n't as fast as** 'Le Shuttle'.*
  (= 'Le Shuttle' is faster than the hovercraft.)

- We can use *twice, three times*, etc. to show the difference more precisely.
  *The hovercraft is **twice as fast as** the ferry.*

- We use *the same/not the same as ...* to say two things are or are not the same.
  *The ferry costs about **the same as** the hovercraft.*
  *The hovercraft does**n't** have **the same facilities as** the ferry.*

CHECK QUESTIONS 1   **Make complete sentences.**
1 The hovercraft/nearly as fast/'Le Shuttle'
2 A train ticket/cost as much/a plane ticket
3 Travelling by ferry/not the same/travelling by hovercraft

Step 2 | 'Double' comparatives: *bigger and bigger*

Every year more and more people travel from England to the continent. The cross-channel ferries are getting bigger and bigger. And they're becoming more and more luxurious.

- If something is increasing, we can use a comparative + *and* + a comparative.
  ***More and more** people travel from England.*
  *The ferries are getting **bigger and bigger**.*
  *They're becoming **more and more luxurious**.*

CHECK QUESTIONS 2   **Complete the sentences with a 'double' comparative form.**
1 Holidays on the continent are becoming ... (popular).
2 Nowadays ... English people travel abroad.
3 The English Channel is getting ... (busy).

| *The bigger the better*

> The ferry companies are building bigger ferries – the bigger the better.
> They think that the more comfortable the ferries are, the happier their
> passengers will be. But passengers want cheaper tickets – the cheaper
> the better. With the arrival of 'Le Shuttle', there's more competition.
> The more competition there is, the more quickly prices will come down.

- Note this construction: *the* + a comparative + *the better*.
  *The bigger **the better**. The cheaper **the better**.*

- When we want to talk about a change in one thing causing a change in another,
  we use *the* + a comparative followed by *the* + a different comparative.
  ***The more comfortable** the ferries are, **the happier** their passengers will be.*
  ***The more competition** there is, **the more quickly** prices will come down.*

CHECK QUESTIONS 3 **Complete the sentences, using comparatives.**
1 ... the ferries are, ... they are. (big/comfortable)
2 ... they are, ... people will use them. (cheap/more)
3 Prices must come down soon. ... ... ! (soon/good)

Step 4 | *More/(the) most, less/(the) least, etc.*

> * What's the least expensive way to cross the Channel? By ferry. At the
>   moment it's less expensive than 'Le Shuttle'.
> * Which crossing takes the most time? The ferry. Which crossing takes
>   the least time? 'Le Shuttle'.
> * Ferries can carry the most trucks. They can carry more foot passengers
>   than 'Le Shuttle'. 'Le Shuttle' takes less freight and fewer cars than the
>   ferry. The hovercraft takes the fewest foot passengers.
> * Most business travellers go by plane, although it costs the most.

●	*less/the least*	+	**adjective**	
The ferry's	less		*expensive*	*than the train.*
the	least		*expensive*	*way to cross the Channel.*
●	*more/the most*	+	**plural/uncountable noun**	
They carry	more		*foot passengers.*	
Which takes	the most		*time?*	
●	*less/the least*	+	**uncountable noun**	
It takes	less		*freight*	*than the ferry.*
Which takes	the least		*time?*	
●	*fewer/the fewest*	+	**plural noun**	
It takes	fewer		*cars*	*than the ferry.*
It takes	the fewest		*foot passengers.*	

- Note that *most* isn't always a superlative. It can be used (without *the*) with the
  meaning *nearly all.* ***Most** business travellers go by plane.*

CHECK QUESTIONS 4 **Use a comparative or a superlative.**
1 The ferry is ... expensive way to cross the Channel.
2 The hovercraft takes ... time than the ferry to cross the Channel.
3 The hovercraft carries ... passengers than the ferry.
4 The ferry carries ... freight and ... cars than 'Le Shuttle'.

Step 5 | *Slightly, a bit, much, a lot*, etc. + a comparative

> Cross the Channel on a P&O ferry! Our new ferries are now far more luxurious. They're also a bit faster than they were. There's a lot more space for the children to play. And we offer you far more entertainment. There's a casino and a cinema on board. We're now much bigger and much better! And we're slightly cheaper too!

- We can use *slightly, a bit, a little, much, far, a lot* before a comparative to say how different things or people are.
  *And we're **slightly cheaper** too!*
  (*Slightly, a bit, a little* have approximately the same meaning.)
  *Our new ferries are now **far more luxurious**.*
  (*Much, far, a lot* have approximately the same meaning.)

CHECK QUESTIONS 5 ▶ **Add the word in brackets to the sentences.**
1 P&O think their new ferries are more luxurious. (far)
2 Their ferries are bigger now. (a lot) 3 They say they're cheaper. (a little)

Step 6 | The superlative + *in* or *of* or a relative clause

> *Travel by 'Le Shuttle' through the longest railway tunnel in Europe!
> The most exciting of all the channel crossings!
> *Travel with P&O - the biggest ferry company in Britain!
> *Sail on 'Stena Europe', the newest ferry in the Stena fleet!
> *You'll have the best holiday of your life when you cross the Channel with 'Sealink'! The most experienced of all the ferry companies.
> *The smoothest Channel crossing you'll ever have! Why not fly to France with British Airways? It'll be the best decision you've ever made.

- After superlatives we can use phrases with *in* or *of*. We use *in* with the names of places and with words like *class, school, team, family, fleet*, etc.
  *the longest railway tunnel **in** Europe   the newest ferry **in** the Stena fleet*
  *the most exciting **of** all the Channel crossings*

- We can also use a relative clause.
  *The smoothest crossing (that) **you'll ever have**.*
  *The best decision (that) **you've ever made**.*

CHECK QUESTIONS 6 ▶ **Complete the sentences.**
1 Which is the longest railway tunnel ... the world?
2 Dover is the busiest ... all the channel ports.
3 Which is the biggest ferry company ... Europe?
4 If you fly to France, it'll be the smoothest Channel crossing that ... !

ANSWERS TO
CHECK QUESTIONS
1, 2, 3, 4, 5 AND 6

1 1 The hovercraft is nearly as fast as "Le Shuttle". 2 A train ticket doesn't cost as much as a plane ticket. 3 Travelling by ferry isn't the same as travelling by hovercraft.
2 1 more and more popular 2 more and more 3 busier and busier
3 1 The bigger the more comfortable 2 The cheaper the more 3 The sooner the better!
4 1 the least 2 less 3 fewer 4 more more
5 1 far more luxurious 2 a lot bigger 3 a little cheaper
6 1 in 2 of 3 in 4 you'll ever have OR you've ever had

Practice

- X is as fast as Y.   X is the same as Y.   Y isn't as fast as Z.
- The company's profits are getting smaller and smaller.   I like fast cars - the faster the better!
- I've got more confidence than Mike.   I know more people than him.
  He's got less money than me.   He's got fewer friends than me.
- She got the most correct answers in the exam.   She made the fewest mistakes.
  Which question was the least difficult?

---

1 Make sentences, using the correct comparative.

Example: Pears/not/expensive/mangoes
Pears aren't as expensive as mangoes.

1 Bananas/not as cheap/apples.

   ....

2 Bananas/twice/expensive/pears.

   ....

3 Mangoes/three times/expensive/apples.

   ....

4 Grapes/same price/bananas.

   ....

5 Apples/just/expensive/pears.

   ....

2 Complete these sentences with 'double' comparatives.

1 I'm getting (impatient) ....

2 It's getting (late) ....

3 .... we leave ....

   (soon/good)

4 .... we get there,

   .... we are to get good seats.

   (early/likely)

3 This bar graph shows which foreign countries Americans go to on holiday (in millions).

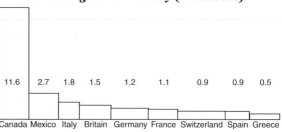

Complete the sentences with *the same, more/the most, less/the least, fewer/the fewest.*

1 .... number of people go to Switzerland and Spain.

2 .... Americans go to Britain than to Italy.

3 .... popular country is Greece.

4 .... Americans go to Canada than to any other country.

5 France is .... popular with American tourists than Germany.

6 Of all the European countries, Italy attracts

   .... American tourists.

7 Greece attracts .... American tourists.

4 Complete the sentences using the word or phrase in the bracket + a comparative.

1 English is (far + easy) ....
   to learn than Chinese.

2 Chinese is (a lot + difficult) ....

   .... to write than English.

3 English is a (much + international) ....

   .... language than Chinese.

4 But Chinese is spoken by (slightly ...) ....

   .... people than English.

73 Adjectives ending in *-ed* and *-ing*: *interested/interesting*

Two people are watching television.
'This programme's boring. Can we change channels?'
'No, it's interesting.'
'Well, I'm bored with it. I'm not interested in the destruction of the Brazilian rainforests. I mean, it isn't exactly fascinating, is it? I just find it depressing. Can't we watch something more exciting? There's a game-show on ITV.'
'I'm surprised at you! You only want to watch rubbish.'
'Why's that surprising? I'm tired when I get home.'
'You're so boring! Why don't you just go to bed?'

Step 1 | Use of adjectives ending in *-ing*

- We use these adjectives to describe what something, or someone, is like.
  *This programme's **boring**. No, it's **interesting**.*
  *You're so **boring**! I just find it **depressing**.*

CHECK QUESTIONS 1 ▷ **Choose the best word to complete these sentences:** *amusing, depressing, surprising.*
1 Programmes about the destruction of the environment are often ...
2 It's ... how many programmes about the environment they have on TV.
3 The film was very ... . We laughed a lot.

Step 2 | Use of adjectives ending in *-ed*

- We use these adjectives to describe how we feel.
  *Well, I'm **bored**. I'm not **interested**.*
  *I'm **surprised** at you. I'm **tired**.*

- The most common adjectives with *-ed* and *-ing* endings are:
  amazed/amazing amused/amusing annoyed/annoying astonished/astonishing bored/boring confused/confusing depressed/depressing disappointed/disappointing disgusted/disgusting embarrassed/embarrassing excited/exciting fascinated/fascinating frightened/frightening interested/interesting shocked/shocking surprised/surprising tired/tiring worried/worrying

CHECK QUESTIONS 2 ▷ **Choose the correct word.**
1 I think game-shows are very ... (amused/amusing)
2 I'm .... that you like them. (surprised/surprising)
3 I think they're ... (bored/boring)

ANSWERS TO
CHECK QUESTIONS
1 AND 2

1 1 depressing 2 surprising 3 amusing
2 1 amusing 2 surprised 3 boring

Practice

> - Adjectives which end in *-ing* describe what something, or someone, is like.
> - Adjectives which end in *-ed* describe how someone feels.
>   I'm **bored** because the subject's **boring**.
>   I'm **interested** because the subject's **interesting**.

1 **Complete this account of a motor race, using the correct forms of the adjectives. The speaker is talking to a friend.**

'The race was (1 excited/exciting) .... at the beginning. I was (2 amazed/amazing) .... when all those cars crashed at the first corner. After that it got a bit (3 bored/boring) .... when Maretti was thirty seconds ahead. But then he crashed into a barrier. It looked quite (4 frightened/frightening) .... The (5 amazed/amazing) .... thing was, he just got out of the car and walked away! He looked pretty (6 disgusted/disgusting) .... with himself.
Er, are you listening to me? You aren't (7 bored/boring) .... are you? I know you aren't really (8 interested/interesting) .... in motor racing.'

2 **Complete this dialogue with the correct form of the adjectives.**

'This weather's (1) .... ! I get really (2) .... when it just rains all day like this. (depressed/depressing)'
'You're too easily (3) .... , that's your problem. You find everything (4) .... after a few minutes. (bored/boring)'
'That isn't true. I'm simply not (5) .... in sitting here all day, doing nothing. I need to do something (6) .... (interested/interesting)'
'You're (7) .... ! I'm

(8) .... that you can't just relax. (amazed/amazing)'
'I don't want to relax! Aren't you (9) .... about how quickly your life is passing? I find it really (10) .... sometimes. Oh, look. It's stopped raining. Come on, let's go for a walk. (worried/worrying)'
'No, I'm too (11) .... (tired/tiring)'

3 **Complete the text with the correct form of the adjectives.**

We took off from Sydney, Australia. I thought it was going to be a very long and (1 tired/tiring)................................. flight back to London. I wasn't really (2 interested/interesting) .... in the film they were showing. It was a comedy. The other passengers found it (3 amused/amusing) ...., but I didn't. I was too (4 tired/tiring) .... Two hours after we'd left Sydney I was (5 surprised/surprising) .... when we turned round and started to fly back! The flight attendants didn't seem (6 worried/worrying) ...., and I was too (7 embarrassed/embarrassing) .... to ask what was wrong. We flew lower and lower. It was (8 amazed/amazing) ....
I could see sharks in the sea below us, which was a bit (9 worried/worrying) .... ! When we landed, fire engines and ambulances followed us down the runway! I don't think I've ever been so (10 frightened/frightening) .... in my life.

> Laura was Spanish. Matthew was English. He was extremely interested in cricket. She wasn't. She thought it was an absolutely stupid game. He asked her rather nervously if she'd like to go and see a match between England and Australia. She answered politely that she knew nothing about cricket. Matthew said that he could easily explain the rules to her. Unfortunately she couldn't think of another excuse, so she said yes, but she didn't say it terribly enthusiastically.
>
> The next day, at the match, Matthew explained the rules to Laura very carefully. She listened patiently, but she didn't really understand a thing!

Step 1 | Use of adverbs of manner, adverbs of degree, sentence adverbs

- We use an adverb of manner to describe how someone does something. The adverb modifies the verb. It tells us more about the verb. It answers the question *How?*

  *She answered **politely**.* (How did she answer? Politely.)
  *She listened **patiently**.* (How did she listen ? Patiently.)

- Remember, an adjective describes someone or something. It tells us more about a noun (a person, place or thing).

  *Laura was **polite**.* (*Polite* tells us more about Laura.)

  Note: After the verbs *look, feel, sound, smell, taste* we use an adjective, not an adverb. *She sounds polite.* (See Unit 33.)

- Adverbs of degree (*extremely, very*, etc.) can modify an adjective.

verb	+	**adverb**	+	**adjective**
He was		*extremely*		*interested.*
It was an		*absolutely*		*stupid game.*

  They can also modify another adverb.

verb	+	**adverb**	+	**adverb**
He explained the rules		*very*		*carefully.*
She didn't say it		*terribly*		*enthusiastically.*

- Sentence adverbs like *unfortunately, fortunately, actually, clearly, perhaps* modify a whole clause.

  ***Unfortunately** she couldn't think of another excuse.*

 What are the adverbs here?

Laura wasn't really interested in cricket; she thought it was a silly game, but clearly Matthew wanted her to go, so she reluctantly said yes.

Step 2 | Forms of the adverbs of manner

- To form an adverb of manner we normally add *-ly* to the adjective.

adjective	**adverb**
patient	*patiently*
polite	*politely*

- But, note these spelling changes:

easy	*easily* (y > i after a consonant.)
careful	*carefully* (l > ll)
terrible	*terribly* (le > ly)
enthusiastic	*enthusiastically* (ic > ically)

CHECK QUESTIONS 2 **Form adverbs from these adjectives.**

1 rude   2 noisy   3 horrible   4 automatic   5 quick

Step 3 | *Well, nearly, hard/hardly, late/lately*

> It was a good match. The ground was nearly full - there were hardly any empty seats. England hadn't been playing well lately, but they were playing very well today. Laura tried hard to concentrate, but she could hardly keep her eyes open and once or twice she nearly went to sleep. Then she had an idea. 'Matthew, can we go now? I'm not well. I've got a really bad headache. And I've just remembered that I've got an English lesson at 4.45 and I don't want to arrive late.'

- Note: Adjective: *good* > Adverb: *well* (NOT goodly).
  *It was a **good** match. England were playing very **well**.*
- We can also use *well* as an adjective meaning 'in good health'.
  *I'm not **well**. (= I'm ill.)*
- Note the meaning of *nearly*.
  *The ground was **nearly** full.* (= almost full)
  *She **nearly** went to sleep.*
  (= She didn't go to sleep, but she almost went to sleep.)
- Note the difference between the adverbs *hard* and *hardly* and *late* and *lately*.
  *She tried **hard** to concentrate.* (= She made a lot of effort.)
  *She could **hardly** keep her eyes open.*
  (= She could almost not keep her eyes open.)
  *There were **hardly** any empty seats.* (= There were almost no empty seats.)
  *She didn't want to arrive **late**.* (late = the opposite of *early*)
  *They hadn't been playing well **lately**.* (lately = recently)
- See also: *high* (= a long way above something) and *highly* (= very).
  *The ball went **high** into the air.*
  *Cricket is a **highly** popular sport in Australia.*
  and: *free* (= without paying) and *freely* (= with no restrictions).
    *Some people got into the ground **free**.*
    *You don't have to stay in your seat; you can move around **freely**.*

CHECK QUESTIONS 3 **Choose the correct word.**

1 Matthew has been out with Laura several times (late/lately) ...
2 But he doesn't know her very (good/well) ...
3 He used to have a girlfriend called Anna, but he (hard/hardly) ... sees her now.
4 Matthew and Laura didn't arrive (late/lately) ... at the match.

Step 4 | Adjectives and adverbs with the same form

Matthew didn't want to leave the match early. He wanted to watch it right to the end. Laura wanted to go straight home. He had to think fast - what was he going to do? He found some aspirin in his pocket. 'You don't need to go to your English lesson. You've been working too hard, that's why you've got a headache. Here, take some aspirin quick. We won't stay long, I promise. Just another two hours.'

● The words *early, fast, late, high, low, right, wrong, free, hard, long, straight* can be used as adjectives and adverbs.
*Matthew didn't want to leave **early**. (adverb)*
*Laura wanted to catch an **early** train. (adjective)*
*He wanted to watch the match **right** to the end. (= exactly: adverb)*
*For him it wasn't the **right** time to leave. (= correct: adjective)*
*Laura wanted to go **straight** home. (= directly: adverb)*
*Laura had long, **straight** hair. (adjective)*
*Matthew had to think **fast**. (= quickly: adverb)*
*Cricket isn't a very **fast** game. (adjective)*
*You've been working too **hard**. (adverb)*
*Cricket's a **hard** game to understand. (adjective)*
*We won't stay **long**, I promise. (= for a long time: adverb)*
*For Laura it was a **long** day. (adjective)*

● Note that in informal English we often use the adjective forms *cheap, quick, slow, loud* as adverbs:
*Take some aspirin **quick**! (= quickly)*
*Don't talk so **loud**! I'm trying to watch the game. (= loudly)*
*Matthew got the tickets **cheap**. (= cheaply)*
*Go **slow**! (= slowly)*

CHECK QUESTIONS 4 **Choose the right word to complete the sentences. Use *straight, long, early, hard*.**
1 Matthew thought ... for a moment.
2 Laura wanted to leave ...
3 She wanted to go ... back to her flat.
4 They'd stayed at the match too ...

Step 5 | Position of adverbs of manner/degree, and sentence adverbs

Laura looked at Matthew angrily. He sadly realised that he had no choice. Clearly he had to leave the match early. She certainly wouldn't wait till the end. He got up slowly. He could hardly take his eyes off the game. At least England had played well. He picked up his jacket impatiently. He nearly changed his mind, but then he said sadly: 'Let's go. I'll probably come again tomorrow. Fortunately the match goes on for another four days!'

- Note that we can't put an adverb between a verb and its object. We can't say:
He could take **hardly** his eyes off the game.
OR: He picked up **impatiently** his jacket.

- There are three normal positions for adverbs:
front position (at the beginning of a clause).
  Clearly he had to leave the match early.
mid-position (before the main verb, or between an auxiliary verb and the main verb).
  *He **nearly** changed his mind.   I'll **probably** come again tomorrow.*
end position (after the main verb, at the end of the clause).
  *Laura looked at him **angrily**.   He picked up his jacket **impatiently**.*

- Adverbs of manner normally go in mid-position or end position.
  *He picked up his jacket **impatiently**. (end position)*
OR *He **impatiently** picked up his jacket. (mid-position)*
BUT they go in end position when we want to emphasise the adverb.
  *Laura looked at him **angrily**. (We want to emphasise her anger.)*
  *He got up **slowly**. (We want to emphasise the way he got up.)*

- Sentence adverbs like *fortunately, unfortunately, clearly, actually, perhaps* usually come in front position.
  Fortunately the match goes on for another four days.
BUT the sentence adverbs *probably, certainly, definitely* don't come in front position. We usually put them in mid-position.
  *I'll **probably** come tomorrow.*

- Note that in negative sentences with the contracted form *-n't* we put *certainly, definitely, probably, simply* before the auxiliary.
  *She **certainly** wouldn't wait till the end.*

- We put the adverbs of degree *nearly, almost, hardly* in mid-position.
  *He could **hardly** take his eyes off the game.*

- We put the adverbs *well* and *badly* in end position.
  *At least England had played **well**. (NOT England had well played.)*
Note: It is not always possible to give precise rules about the position of adverbs in the sentence. But if you follow the rules in this Step you will not be wrong.

CHECK QUESTIONS 5 **Put in the adverbs.**
1 Laura wasn't interested in cricket. (clearly)
2 Matthew had explained the rules to her. (patiently)
3 She didn't want to stay at the match. (definitely)
4 She'd fallen asleep once or twice. (nearly)

ANSWERS TO
CHECK QUESTIONS
1, 2, 3, 4 AND 5

1 1 really 2 clearly 3 reluctantly
2 1 rudely 2 noisily 3 horribly 4 automatically
   5 quickly
3 1 lately 2 well 3 hardly 4 late
4 1 hard 2 early 3 straight 4 long

5 1 Clearly Laura wasn't interested in cricket. OR
   Laura clearly wasn't interested 2 Matthew had
   patiently explained the rules to her. OR
   Matthew had explained the rules to her
   patiently. 3 She definitely didn't want to stay
   at the match.
   4 She'd nearly fallen asleep once or twice.

Practice

Adverbs of manner:	How?	*politely, badly, well*, etc.
Adverbs of degree:	How much?	*extremely, very, completely*, etc.
Sentence adverbs:		*perhaps, fortunately, probably*, etc.

1 Complete this newspaper story by choosing the correct word each time.

Gary Webster of Dudley, near Birmingham was 17. After only four driving lessons he was (1 certain/certainly) .... that he was ready to take the driving test. 'I'm a (2 good/well) .... driver,' he (3 confident/confidently) .... told his friends. 'I'll pass the test (4 easy/easily) ....' He arrived at the Test Centre and (5 careful/carefully) .... parked his car. He was (6 slight/slightly) .... nervous, but still quite (7 confident/confidently) .... He waited for a few minutes, then he (8 impatient/impatiently) .... sounded his horn. The examiner came out (9 quick/quickly) .... and (10 angry/angrily) .... told Gary that he'd (11 definite/definitely) .... failed his driving test, because it was (12 illegal/illegally) .... to sound your horn while you were parked.

2 James is in his last year at school. He wants to go to university to study Maths. Choose the right word to complete the questions the university interviewer asked him.

1 Do you want to go .... from school to university? (direct/directly/straight)

2 Do you work .... ? (hard/hardly)

3 Do you work .... under pressure? (good/well)

4 Do you ever arrive .... for lessons? (late/lately)

5 What kind of books have you been reading ....? (late/lately)

6 How .... are you at Maths? (good/well)

7 Are you a .... student? (serious/seriously) Are you .... motivated? (high/highly)

8 Would you say your mind works .... or slowly? (quick/fast)

9 Are you .... (nervous/nervously), because you've .... answered any of my questions? (hard/hardly)

10 Well, we've .... finished. Have you got any questions? (near/nearly)

3 Kate is describing two people she works with. Put the adverb(s) in brackets in the correct position in the sentence.

1 I don't know Robert. (well)

....

2 He never speaks to anyone. (unfortunately)

....

3 He's just shy. (perhaps, terribly)

....

4 Sharon's different. (completely)

....

5 She's the laziest person I know. (probably)

....

....

6 She won't get promotion. (definitely) ....

....

7 She's been taking a lot of time off work (lately) ....

....

8 The manger has sacked her twice this year. (nearly) ....

....

9 She's a very nice girl. (actually)

....

> Some foreign visitors were asked: 'What do you like best about Britain?'
> - The fact that people always say 'please'. They're very rarely rude.
> - The old people. They're friendly and they often call you 'Love' or 'Dear'.
> - The television. There's always something good to watch every evening.
> - Carpets in pubs! In Greece you hardly ever find a carpet on the floor in a bar. But there are usually carpets in English pubs.
> - British gardens! They're beautiful. Do we usually have gardens in the USA? Yes, we normally do. But we don't usually have so many flowers. I've never seen so many lovely flowers.
> - The weather! Every summer in Turkey it's always hot and dry, and we don't normally have any rain. Here in Britain it's generally warm. Sometimes it rains, of course. And occasionally I miss the sun. But it doesn't rain every day, and British weather is always interesting!

Step 1 | Adverbs of frequency: *often, always, sometimes*, etc.

- We use adverbs of frequency when we say how often something happens. The most common are:

  100%   always
             usually/normally/generally
             often/frequently
             sometimes/occasionally
             rarely/seldom
             hardly ever
    0%   never

  People **always** say please.   We don't **normally** have rain.
  I've **never** seen so many lovely flowers.

- *Frequently* = *often*. But *often* is more common.
  Seldom = *rarely*. But *rarely* is more common.
  Usually, normally, generally all mean the same, but *usually* is the most common.
  Occasionally and *sometimes* mean approximately the same, but *sometimes* is more common.

  Note: It is not always possible to give precise rules about the position of adverbs in the sentence. But if you follow the rules in Steps 2 and 3 you will not be wrong.

CHECK QUESTIONS 1

1 How often do you find carpets in Greek bars?
2 How often do British people use the word 'please'?
3 How often can you find an interesting programme on British TV?

- Adverbs of frequency normally come in mid-position.
They come before a main verb.

	adverb	+	main verb	
People	*always*		*say*	*'please'.*
They	*often*		*call*	*you 'Love' or 'Dear'.*

They come between an auxiliary and the main verb.

auxiliary	+	adverb	+	main verb	
I've		*never*		*seen*	*so many lovely flowers.*
We don't		*normally*		*have*	*any rain.*

- BUT adverbs of frequency come after the verb *be*.

	be	+	adverb	
Their answers were			*often*	*different.*
	There's (is)		*always*	*something good to watch.*

- In questions and in short answers, adverbs of frequency come just before the main verb.

	adverb	+	main verb	
Do we	*usually*		*have*	*gardens in the States?*
Yes, we	*normally*		*do.*	

In questions with the verb *to be* these adverbs come after the verb *be*. But in short answers they come before.

be	+		adverb	
Is	*there*		*usually*	*a carpet on the floor?*
Are	*old people*		*always*	*friendly? – They usually are.*

- We usually put the adverbs *sometimes, occasionally, often, usually, generally, normally* in mid-position.
   *It **sometimes** rains, of course.   I **occasionally** miss the sun.*
But we can put them in front or end position to emphasise them.
   ***Sometimes** it rains, of course.   **Occasionally** I miss the sun.*
   *Does it rain **often**? – It rains **occasionally**.*

- Note that we don't usually put the adverbs *always, never, rarely, seldom, hardly ever* in front position. We can't say: 'Always people say 'please'.'
(BUT we must put *always* and *never* before an imperative: 'Never forget to say 'please'!')

- Adverb phrases like *every day, every year, every evening*, etc. usually come in end position. But they can also come in front position if you want to emphasise them.
   *There's something good to watch on TV **every evening**.*
   ***Every evening** there's something good to watch.*
These phrases are never used in mid-position.

CHECK QUESTIONS 2 **Which sentences are correct?**
1 I've visited often Britain.
2 I don't usually come in the winter.
3 British gardens normally have lots of flowers in them.
4 It rains in Turkey hardly ever in the summer.

- The postal service is the best thing about Britain. If I post a letter today, it'll almost certainly arrive tomorrow. The letters I send very rarely arrive late.
- Clean air! Nowadays most English people have stopped smoking. Now you can go into restaurants and offices and breathe clean air.
- Car drivers usually stop at pedestrian crossings here. But it's different in France. There, drivers very rarely stop.

- Adverbs of time answer the question 'When?' The most common are: *again, now, then, recently, once, nowadays, suddenly, immediately, finally, afterwards, today, tomorrow, yesterday, late, early.*
  + adverb phrases like: *on Monday/last week/next summer,* etc.
  We usually put them in end position, at the end of a clause.
    *If I post a letter **today**, it'll almost certainly arrive **tomorrow**.*

- *Now, then, recently, once, nowadays, suddenly, finally, afterwards, tomorrow, yesterday* and the adverb phrases above can also go in front position for emphasis.
    ***Nowadays** most English people have stopped smoking.*

- Adverbs of definite time like *yesterday, tomorrow, last week,* etc. don't go in mid-position, but they can go in front position for emphasis.
    *I posted a letter **yesterday**.   **Yesterday** I posted a letter.*
  NOT I yesterday posted a letter. (mid-position)

- *Now, then, recently* and *once* can come in front, mid or end position.
    ***Now** you can go into offices and breathe clean air.*
    *You can **now** go into offices and breathe clean air.*
    *You can go into offices and breathe clean air **now**.*

CHECK QUESTIONS 3a **Which sentences are correct?**
1 Nowadays very few English people smoke.
2 I went into a restaurant last week and no-one was smoking.
3 I posted yesterday a letter and it today arrived.

- Adverbs of place answer the question 'Where?'. They include words like *here, there, nearby, opposite, upstairs,* etc. and phrases like *in Britain, at home,* etc.
  These adverbs normally go in end position.
    *Car drivers usually stop at pedestrian crossings **here**.   But it's different **in France**.*
  But they can come in front position for emphasis:
    ***There**, drivers very rarely stop.*

- Note that if there are several adverbs in a sentence, the normal word order is:

	degree	+	**manner**	+	**place**	+	**time**
It rained	*very*		*heavily*		*in London*		*yesterday.*

CHECK QUESTIONS 3b **Which sentences are correct?**
1 I arrived in Britain yesterday.
2 I like Britain and I here come every year.
3 Next summer I'm coming here again.

ANSWERS TO CHECK QUESTIONS 1, 2 AND 3
1 1 Hardly ever OR Rarely/Seldom. 2 Frequently OR Often. 3 Always
2 2, 3
3a 1, 2
3b 1, 3

Practice

1 Look at these definitions. Choose the correct alternative (a, b or c).

1 An intelligent person:
   a) Someone who agrees always with you.
   b) Someone who always agrees with you.
   c) Someone always who agrees with you.
   ....

2 A friend:
   a) A person who dislikes usually the same people as you do.
   b) A person who dislikes the same people usually as you do.
   c) A person who usually dislikes the same people as you do.
   ....

3 The horizon:
   a) The line that always has disappeared when you get there.
   b) The line that has always disappeared when you get there.
   c) The line that has disappeared always when you get there.
   ....

4 A gentleman:
   a) A man who would never hit a woman with her glasses on.
   b) A man who would hit a woman never with her glasses on.
   c) A man who would hit never a woman with her glasses on.
   ....

5 A sightseer:
   a) Someone who goes frequently inside churches when he's on holiday, but who goes hardly ever to church when he's at home.
   b) Someone who goes inside churches when he's on holiday frequently, but who goes to church when he's at home hardly ever.
   c) Someone who frequently goes inside churches when he's on holiday, but who hardly ever goes to church when he's at home.
   ....

6 A tourist:
   a) A person who complains always because the country he's visiting is never exactly the same as his own.
   b) A person who always complains because never the country he's visiting is exactly the same as his own.
   c) A person who always complains because the country he's visiting is never exactly the same as his own.
   ....

2 How to write a love story! Put the words in brackets in the best place in the sentences. Mark the position of the adverb.

Example:
Love stories are the same. (always)
*Love stories are * the same.*

Love stories are always the same. The girl's name is Lucy (1 often). She's been in love before (2 never). She meets Mark (3 at a party). He asks her: 'Can I give you a lift (4 somewhere)?' He phones her (5 the next day). After that they are apart (6 hardly ever). But then another woman appears (7 always). She's very attractive (8 usually). And her name's Miranda (9 generally). Lucy sees them together (10 in town). She phones him (11 later) at his flat. He isn't (12 there). She tries (13 again). She can't believe (14 really) that it's all finished. She locks herself (15 in her room). She's terribly unhappy (16 at first). But then Mark realises that he doesn't love Miranda (17 really). And he returns to Lucy (18 for ever).

76

Adverbs of degree:
quite, fairly, pretty, rather   So, such

> Now it's time for the weather forecast here on Radio 5. There'll be quite a big change in the weather today. Most of the country will be quite cold, with temperatures between 5° and 8°. Winds from the south east will be fairly strong. In the north it'll be a fairly wet day, and it's likely to rain quite heavily on the north west coast.

Step 1 | *Quite, pretty, fairly*

- We use the words *quite, pretty* and *fairly* to change the strength of an adjective or an adverb.

Hot   35°
Quite, pretty hot   28°
Fairly hot   25°

> *It'll be **pretty cold**. (adverb + adjective)*
> *It's likely to rain **quite heavily**. (adverb + adverb)*

- *Pretty* usually means the same as *quite* but it's more informal. *Fairly* isn't as strong as *pretty* or *quite*.

- Note that if we stress the words *quite, pretty* and *fairly* and not the adjective which follows, we make the adjective less strong.

> *It'll be quite **cold**. (= 4° perhaps)*
> *It'll be **quite** cold. (= not as cold as 4°, perhaps 8°)*

- We often use *quite* before an adjective + noun.

	quite	+	**a/an**	+	**adjective**	+	**noun**
There'll be	quite		a		big		change in the weather.
It'll be	quite		a		dry		day.

But with *fairly* and *pretty* the word order is different.

	a/an	+	**fairly/pretty**	+	**adjective**	+	**noun**
It'll be	a		fairly		wet		day.

CHECK QUESTIONS 1 ▸ **Put in *quite, fairly* or *pretty*.**
1 It'll be ... cold tomorrow, about 8°.
2 Thursday will be ... a fine day.
3 It'll also be a ... windy day.

Step 2 | Other uses of *quite*

> The weather in the south will be quite different. In the south it'll be quite a dry day, with quite a few sunny periods and only one or two showers. But it'll be pretty cold with temperatures never higher than 7°. Winter hasn't quite finished yet, I'm afraid, although I must say I quite enjoy cold, clear days like today.

- *Quite* can also mean 'completely' or 'absolutely' when we use it with some adjectives. The most common are: *alone, amazing, brilliant, certain, different, dreadful, extraordinary, right, sure, terrible, true, unnecessary, useless, wrong*.
    The weather in the south will be **quite different**.
    (= **completely** different from the weather in the north)
- We can also use *quite* (but not *pretty* or *fairly*) with these verbs: *agree, enjoy, finish, forget, like, understand*.
  Quite sometimes means 'a little/moderately'.
    although I **quite enjoy** cold, clear days (= enjoy a little)
  It can also mean 'absolutely/completely'.
    The winter hasn't **quite finished** yet.   (= hasn't completely finished)
- Note the expression *quite a few* which means 'quite a lot of'.
    with **quite a few** sunny periods

CHECK QUESTIONS 2 **Complete these sentences with *quite, pretty* or *fairly*.**
1 The weather this winter has been ... extraordinary, hasn't it?
2 Yes, I ... agree. We've had ... a lot of sunshine.

Step 3 | Rather

> Now the forecast for tomorrow. It'll be rather cold and wet, I'm afraid, in the north. But the weather will be rather better in the south. In fact, it'll be rather a warm day for the time of year, the kind of day I rather like, with temperatures reaching 14°.

- When we use *rather*, it usually gives the adjective a negative meaning.
    It's **rather** warm today. (= too warm, not pleasant)
    It's **quite** warm today. (= pleasantly warm)
- But we can also use *rather* when a positive adjective is surprising.
    It'll be **rather** a **warm** day for the time of year.
    (= This is surprising. It's not normally warm at this time of year.)
- We can use *rather* (NOT *quite, fairly* or *pretty*) before comparatives.
    The weather will be **rather better** in the south.
- *Rather* can come before or after *a/an*.
    It'll be **rather a** warm day for the time of year.
  OR It'll be **a rather** warm day for the time of year.
- *Rather* can also be used with certain verbs like *enjoy, hope, like, think*. It means 'moderately' or 'to some degree'.
    the kind of day I **rather like**

CHECK QUESTIONS 3 **Can you add 'rather' to these sentences?**
1 The weather tomorrow will be ... good.
2 It ... rains in the north of England.
3 It's been ... a wet month.

251

And finally the forecast for Friday. It won't be such a cold day in the north, and it won't be so wet. People up there will be glad to hear this because they've had such bad weather and such low temperatures recently. In fact on the north west coast they've had such a lot of rain that many houses have been flooded. It's rained for so long in Barrow that some old people haven't left their homes for days. But the rain hasn't been such a problem in other parts of the region.

- We use *such* before a noun (countable or uncountable) or an adjective + noun. *Such* emphasises the noun or the adjective + noun that follows. Note the word order:

	such +	*a/an* +	adjective +	noun
It hasn't been	*such*	*a*		*problem.*
It won't be	*such*	*a*	*cold*	*day.*
...	*such*		*low*	*temperatures*
They've had	*such*		*bad*	*weather.*

- We can use *such* before *a lot of* (but NOT before *much* and *many*).
  *They've had **such a lot** of rain.*

- We use *so* before an adjective without a noun, or before an adverb.
  *It won't be **so wet**.* (adjective)
  *It's rained for **so long**.* (adverb)

- We can use *so* and *such* + a *that* clause when we talk about a result.
  *It's rained for **so long (that)** some people haven't left their homes.*
  *They've had **such a lot of rain (that)** many houses have been flooded.*
  Note: We often leave out *that*.

- We use *so* (NOT *such*) with *many* and *much*. (See Unit 60.)

CHECK QUESTIONS 4

Put in *so* or *such*.
1 The north of England hasn't had ... a lot of rain for months.
2 The wind was ... strong that trees were blown down.
3 In the east of England they haven't had ... much rain.

Practice

	with adjective	with adverb	with verb	with comparative
quite:	*quite slow*	*quite slowly*	*I quite agree*	X
rather:	*rather slow*	*rather slowly*	*I rather like*	*rather better*
fairly/pretty:	*fairly/pretty slow*	*fairly/pretty slowly*	X	X

so + adjective on its own: *I'm so hungry.*
so + *much/many* + (adjective) + noun: *so many interesting people*
such + *a/an* (+ adjective) + noun: *such a good film*
such (+ adjective) + plural noun: *such difficult questions*
such (+ adjective) + uncountable noun: *such terrible weather*
such + *a lot of* (+ adjective) + noun: *such a lot of empty seats*

1 **Complete this school report, using *quite* + a positive adjective and *rather* + a negative adjective.**

Science: Katherine is (1) .... good at Physics but her Chemistry is (2) .... weak.

French: Katherine's pronunciation is (3) .... poor but her writing is (4) .... a lot better.

English: She writes (5) .... interesting essays but her spelling is still (6) .... bad.

History: She finds History (7) .... difficult although she is obviously (8) .... intelligent.

2 **Complete this dialogue, using *quite, rather, fairly* or *pretty*. It is sometimes possible to use more than one of these words.**

'I'm reading (1) .... a good book at the moment. It's about the history of the railways in Britain.'

'It sounds (2) .... boring to me.'

'No, in fact it's (3) .... interesting. There's (4) .... a lot about social history which I (5) .... enjoy. I haven't (6) .... finished it yet. I can lend it to you when I've finished. I think you'd (7) .... enjoy it. But I'm afraid it's (8) .... a long book. Do you want to borrow it?'

'No, it's (9) .... all right thanks. I'm reading a (10) .... more interesting book at the moment.'

3 **Complete the following text, using *such* or *so*.**

Truck driver Ed Johnson from Red Oak, Texas, felt (1) .... ill he went to the Glenwood hospital in Fort Worth. Doctors there decided he was (2) .... a difficult case they needed to consult a heart specialist from Dallas. He told Mr Johnson it wasn't (3) .... a serious problem after all and he only needed a minor heart operation. Two weeks later Mr Johnson was feeling (4) .... much better the doctors decided he could go home. He thanked the nurses for being (5) .... kind and went to the desk to ask for the bill. There they told him that he'd spent (6) .... a long time in hospital and he'd had (7) .... a lot of tests, that the bill came to $27,964. Mr Johnson was (8) .... shocked he dropped dead of a heart attack.

253

77

Adverbs of degree: *a lot, a bit, much,* etc.
More, most, better, best, etc.

The American Marianne Rich is only 16, but she's already a tennis star. 'I started playing when I was 5. My father helped me a little, but then I got my own tennis coach when I was 6. I played a lot between the ages of 7 and 14 - at least four hours a day. Life wasn't easy. I didn't like it very much. I was getting a bit bored with tennis. And I didn't see my friends much. Last year I injured my back. It hurt so much I had to go into hospital. For six months after the injury I couldn't play as much, and at last I could relax a bit. I enjoyed that very much, and after those six months I felt a lot stronger and very much happier. And I started to play much more positively.'

Step 1 | *A lot, much,* etc. used alone or before an adjective or adverb

- We can use *a lot, a little, a bit, much, very much, so much, as much* on their own, as adverbs. They tell us something more about the verb.
  *My father **helped** me **a little**.*
  (**How much** did your father help you? He helped me **a little**.)

- We normally put them after the main verb and its object.

	main verb	+	**object**	+	**adverb**
My father	*helped*		*me*		*a little.*
I	*didn't like*		*it*		*very much.*
I	*didn't see*		*my friends*		*much.*

- Note that we can use *very much* in positive or negative sentences. But we can only use *much* on its own (without *very*) in negative sentences.
  *I enjoyed that **very much**.* (NOT I enjoyed that much.)
  *I didn't like it **very much**. I didn't see my friends **much**.*

- We often use *a lot, a bit, a little, much, very much, so much* before a comparative adjective or adverb.
  *I felt **a lot stronger** and **very much happier**.*
  *I started to play **much more positively**.*
  Note: *Much* + adjective or adverb can be used in positive sentences.
  A bit and *a little* (but not *a lot, much, very much, so much*) can also be used with an adjective not in the comparative form.
  *I was getting **a bit bored** with tennis.*

- *A lot* means the same as *very much*. *A bit* means the same as *a little* but it's less formal and is used more often.

CHECK QUESTIONS 1 **Add the words in brackets to the sentences.**
1 Marianne didn't like practising. (very much)
2 When she was in hospital, her friends didn't visit her. (much)
3 She sometimes feels tired (a bit).
4 But generally she feels happier now. (a lot)

Step 2 | *More, most, better, best, etc. used alone as adverbs*

'Nowadays I practise less, perhaps only fourteen hours a week. I haven't got time to practise, because I travel a lot more. I play in tournaments all over the world. I like Wimbledon most. I love the grass courts there. I play best on grass. It's strange, but the tournament I like least is the American Open at Flushing Meadow. I always play worst there. I don't know why. Perhaps I'll do better this year.'

- The comparative forms *more, less, better, worse* and the superlative forms *most, least, best, worst* can be used on their own, as adverbs of degree. We usually put them after the main verb and its object.
  *Nowadays I practise **less**.*
  (= I don't practise as much as I used to.)
  *the tournament I like **least***
  (= I prefer all the other tournaments.)
  *I like Wimbledon **most**. (= Wimbledon is my favourite.)*
  *I always play **worst** there.*
  (= I play better at all the other tournaments.)
- We can use *a lot, a bit, much, very much, so much* before *more, less, better, worse.*
  *I travel **a lot more** now.* OR *I travel **much more** now.*
  Note that we can use *much* in positive sentences as well as in negative sentences, when it comes before *more, less, better, worse.*
- *Most, least, best, worst* can also be used with adjectives formed from the past participle of verbs.
  *Wimbledon is **the best known** tennis tournament in the world.*
  *Marianne is **the most photographed** tennis player in the USA.*

CHECK QUESTIONS 2 **Rewrite the sentences, using *less, least* and *worse*.**
1 She doesn't practise as much now. She practises ...
2 She prefers all the other tournaments to the American Open. She likes ...
3 She played two sets against the Wimbledon champion. She played better in the first set than in the second. She played ...

ANSWERS TO
CHECK QUESTIONS
1 AND 2
1 1 Marianne didn't like practising very much.
2 ... her friends didn't visit her much.
3 She sometimes feels a bit tired.
4 But generally she feels a lot happier now.

2 1 She practises less now. 2 She likes the American Open least. 3 She played worse in the second set than in the first.

Practice

> I **watch** television **a lot**.   English is **a lot easier** to learn than Japanese.
> I **don't** watch videos **much**.   I feel **much happier** today.
> I watch television **less** than I used to.
> I like the wildlife programmes **best**.
> He talks to everybody, but he talks to me **least**.
> I speak Spanish **worse** than my wife.

1 **Complete the dialogue, using *a lot, a bit, much, very much, so much, as much*.**

'Do you go to the cinema (1) .... ?'

'I don't go (2) .... as I used to.'

'Why's that?'

'The cinema's (3) .... expensive now. I usually hire a video instead. I hired the video of 'Redemption' the other night. I liked it (4) .... I watched it three times!'

'Have you read any good books lately?'

'No. I don't usually read (5) .... But a friend gave me a book on astrology for Christmas. I enjoyed that (6) ....'

'Do you believe in astrology?'

'Not (7) .... as my mother! She always reads her horoscope. But I must admit I was feeling (8) .... depressed when I started reading it. When I'd finished, I felt (9) .... happier that I went to the library and got another book on astrology.'

2 **Jack is in the restaurant. All the people round him are talking. He can hear bits of different conversations. Complete the dialogues, using *more, most, less, least, better, best, worse, worst*.**

A: Do you fancy a coffee?

B: No thanks. I used to drink it a lot, but I drink it a lot (1) .... now. It keeps me awake. I always sleep (2) .... if I don't have coffee.

C: What's your favourite music? What do you listen to (3) .... nowadays?

D: I listen to country and western (4) .... than any other kind of music.

E: I like your sweater. Is it new?

F: Yes. I'm glad you like it, because my wife doesn't. She says I'm the (5) .... dressed man she knows.

G: Did you watch the match last night?

H: Yes. Leeds played badly, didn't they? They played (6) .... than I've ever seen them play.

I: I'm trying to choose a dress for Martha's wedding. I'll show you the catalogue. Look. Which one do you like (7) ....?

J: I like the blue one (8) .... It's nicer than all the others.

I: Oh, I like that one (9) .... Blue just isn't my colour.

78

Still, yet
Any more/any longer/no longer

> Bill Myers is 82, but he still acts like a 50-year-old. He still plays tennis. He still drives a car. He's still interested in women and he's got a 'girlfriend' called Doris, who's 79. He asked her to marry him five years ago. He's still waiting for her answer!

Step 1 | *Still* in affirmative sentences and questions

- We use *still* (= up to now) to talk about an action or a situation that is continuing longer than we expected.
  *He **still** plays tennis.* (We don't expect an 82-year-old to play tennis.)

- In affirmative sentences we put *still* after the verb *be*, before a main verb on its own, and between an auxiliary and the main verb. In questions we put *still* after the verb *be* and after the auxiliary.

the verb *be*	+	*still*		
He's		still interested in women.		
Is he		still interested in women?		

auxiliary	+	*still*	+	main verb
He		still		plays tennis.
Does he		still		play tennis?
He's		still		waiting for her answer!
Is he		still		waiting for her answer?

CHECK QUESTIONS 1 **Put *still* into these sentences.**
1 Bill's interested in tennis.
2 He's got a 'girlfriend'.
3 Doris is his 'girlfriend'.

Step 2 | *Still* and *yet* in negative sentences

> Bill lost his glasses last night. His daughter's phoning him:
> 'Have you found your glasses yet?'
> 'No, I've looked everywhere in the house, but I still haven't found them. Of course they may be in the car. I haven't looked there yet.'
> 'Have you phoned the optician's?'
> 'I can't read the number in the phone book, so I haven't phoned them yet.'
> 'How's Doris?'
> 'She's fine. She's coming to see me this morning, but she hasn't arrived yet.'
> 'Has she said "yes" yet?'
> 'No, she still hasn't given me an answer.'

- We use *yet* (= 'up to now') in negative sentences and in questions when we talk about something that hasn't happened, but that we expect to happen in the future. We normally put *yet* at the end of the sentence or clause. (See also Unit 8.)

     *She hasn't arrived **yet**. Has Doris said 'yes' **yet**?*

- In negative sentences, if we want to emphasise that something hasn't happened up to now, we use *still*, not *yet*.

     *Bill hasn't found his glasses **yet**. He's looked everywhere but he **still** hasn't found them.* (He hasn't found them, even after looking everywhere.)

  Here, we put *still* before the auxiliary (*hasn't, doesn't*, etc.).

CHECK QUESTIONS 2 **Put in *yet* or *still*.**
1 Doris hasn't said 'yes' to Bill ...   2 She ... hasn't answered him.
3 Bill lost his glasses last night and he's ... looking for them.
4 He hasn't phoned the optician's ...

Step 3 | *Any more, any longer, no longer*

> Things have changed for Bill. He and Doris don't see each other any more. Three weeks ago he told her: 'Doris, if you can't decide, I can't wait any longer.' He sees her occasionally in town, but they no longer speak to each other, and Doris doesn't visit him any more.
> At first Bill missed Doris, but he doesn't miss her any more and he's no longer lonely. Two months ago he met Gladys, who's 81, in the club. He's no longer got a girlfriend. He's got a wife! He married Gladys yesterday!

- We use *any more* and *any longer* in negative sentences to say that a past situation has now finished. We put them at the end of the sentence. *Any more* is more common than *any longer*.

     *They don't see each other **any more**. (OR **any longer**)*
     *I can't wait **any longer**. (OR **any more**)*

- We can use a positive verb + *no longer* instead of a negative verb + *any more/any longer*. *No longer* isn't used as often as *any more/any longer* and is more formal.

     *They **no longer speak** to each other.*
     (= They don't speak to each other any more.)
     *He **no longer** misses Doris. (= He doesn't miss Doris any more.)*

- We put *no longer* after the verb *be*, before a main verb on its own, and between an auxiliary and the main verb.

the verb *be*	+	***no longer***		
He's		*no longer*		*lonely.*
auxiliary	+	***no longer***	+	**main verb**
They		*no longer*		*speak to each other.*
He's (has)		*no longer*		*got a girlfriend.*

CHECK QUESTIONS 3 **Put *any more/any longer* or *no longer* in these sentences.**
1 Bill speaks to Doris.   2 They aren't going to get married.
3 Bill couldn't wait for an answer.   4 Doris visits him.

ANSWERS TO
CHECK QUESTIONS
1, 2 AND 3

1 1 Bill's still interested in tennis.   2 He's still got a girlfriend.   3 Doris is still his girlfriend.
2 1 yet 2 still 3 still 4 yet

3 1 Bill no longer speaks to Doris.   2 They aren't going to get married any more/any longer.
3 Bill couldn't wait any longer for an answer. OR Bill couldn't wait for an answer any longer/any more.   4 Doris no longer visits him.

Practice

- *Still* in affirmative sentences and questions = A continuing situation.
  *He **still** smokes. Does he **still** smoke?*
- *Still* in negative sentences = We're surprised that the situation has continued for so long.
  *He's smoked for 20 years, and he **still** hasn't stopped.*
- *Yet* in negative sentences and questions = Something that hasn't happened, but we expect it to happen in the future.
  *He hasn't stopped smoking **yet**.*
- *Any more/any longer* with a negative verb = *no longer* with a positive verb.

---

1 Some British people do not want Britain to be in the European Union. Add *still* to each of these sentences. Put a mark * to show its position.

1 Britain has been in the European Union for years, but some British people don't like the idea.
2 They're worried about being part of Europe.
3 They want to keep their national identity.
4 The EU has been good for Britain, but they don't see the advantages.
5 They're hoping that Britain will soon leave the Union.

2 Molly has just met someone who lived in her village when they were children. She is asking her friend about the village. Write her questions, using *still*.

When Molly was a child ...
1 Jack Lynch owned the village shop. 2 there was a fish and chip shop. 3 the Taylors were living in Church Street. 4 people had picnics by the river. 5 old Mrs Stamp was alive. 6 the village had a big party on New Year's Eve.

Example:
1 *Does Jack Lynch still own the village shop?*

2 ....
   ....
3 ....
   ....
4 ....
   ....
5 ....
   ....
6 ....
   ....

3 Complete the text, using *yet, still* or *any more/any longer* or *no longer*.

Alex Hamilton has travelled a lot. He's been all over the world, but there are (1) .... some places he hasn't been to. He hasn't been to the Arctic (2) .... And although he knows Europe quite well, he (3) .... hasn't been to Germany. He used to go to Turkey a lot, but he (4) .... goes there in summer because it's too hot for him. When he was young he used to take a tent with him and go camping, but he doesn't do that (5) .... He says he's getting too old. He's 81. He (6) .... goes somewhere every year, but he doesn't know where he's going this year (7) .... He (8) .... hasn't decided. An Australian friend has invited him to go to Sydney, but he doesn't enjoy long flights (9) .... , so he doesn't want to go. One day he wants to write a book about his travels. But he hasn't written it (10) .... , and the problem is that he can (11) .... remember a lot of his journeys. His memory isn't very good (12) .... He hasn't replied to his Australian friend's invitation (13) .... He's lost his address. He's looked everywhere for it, but he (14) .... can't find it.

79

This is part of a speech given at a political meeting.
'This government has been in power for a very long time. In fact they've been in power for too long. They've made too many mistakes and wasted too much money. But they're much too proud to admit it or they're too stupid to realise it. It's too easy for ministers to say "Be patient. Things are getting better." We've heard that far too many times. It's too late for them to say that now ...'

Step 1 | *Too*

- *Too* means 'more than is necessary'. It doesn't mean the same as *very*. *Too* always has a negative meaning. *Very* is neutral. It can have a positive or negative meaning, depending on the word that follows. We can say *very good* or *very bad*.

  *This government has been in power for a **very long** time.*
  (*a very long time* = a simple fact)
  *In fact they've been in power for **too long**.*
  (*too long* = a criticism, a negative comment)

- We often use *too* before an adjective or an adverb.
  *They're **too proud** to admit it.* (adjective)
  *The government has been in power for **too long**.* (adverb)

- Note the use of *too* in this construction:

	too +	**adjective/adverb** +	*(for* + object) +	**infinitive**
They're	*too*	*stupid*		*to realise it.*
It's	*too*	*easy*	*for ministers*	*to say.*
It's	*too*	*late*	*for them*	*to say.*

- We also use *too many* + a countable noun and *too much* + an uncountable noun. (See also Unit 63.)
  *They've made **too many mistakes**.* (countable noun)
  *They've wasted **too much money**.* (uncountable noun)

- We can put the words *much, far, a little, a lot, a bit* before *too*.
  ***far too** many times*   *they're **much too** proud*

CHECK QUESTIONS 1 **Put in *too*+ one of these words: *many* (x 2), *much, easy, long*.**
1 15 years in power is ... for any government.
2 Some people think governments have ... power.
3 And it's ... for them to say things will get better.
4 ... ministers have made ... mistakes.

'... The country's in a mess. Some people don't have enough to eat. There's never enough money for schools or hospitals. But there's always enough for motorways and nuclear submarines. This government has been in power for long enough. Even some of its supporters are honest enough to admit it. Government ministers say, "Give us more time." It's easy enough for them to say that. But they've had enough time. They've had enough opportunities. And now we've heard enough of their promises. The people of this country have had enough of this government!'

- *Enough* means 'a sufficient number or amount'. It normally comes before a noun (countable or uncountable).

  They've had **enough opportunities**. (= a sufficient number)
  They've had **enough time**. (= a sufficient amount)

- *Enough* comes after an adjective or adverb.

  It's **easy enough** for them to say that.
  This government has been in power for **long enough**.

- We use *enough* + noun.

  There's never **enough money**. (NOT enough of money)

  But, we use **enough** + *of* before pronouns (*him, them*, etc.) or words like *the, this, my*, etc. + a noun.

  And now we've heard **enough of their** promises.
  The people of this country have had **enough of this** government.

- *Enough* can be used on its own when the noun is understood.

  There's always **enough** for motorways. (= enough money)

- Note the use of *enough* in these constructions:

	adjective +	***enough*** +	**infinitive with *to***
Its supporters are	*honest*	*enough*	*to admit it.*

	adjective +	***enough*** +	***for*** +	**object** +	**infinitive with to**
It's	*easy*	*enough*	*for*	*them*	*to say that.*

	enough +	**(noun)** +	**infinitive with *to***
They've had	*enough*	*time*	*to improve the situation.*
They don't have	*enough*		*to eat.*

CHECK QUESTIONS 2 **Add *enough* to these sentences.**

1 It's easy for ministers to make promises.
2 They don't understand the country's problems well.
3 There aren't hospitals or schools.
4 There's always money to build more roads.

Rewrite the sentences, using *enough of*.

5 We don't want this government any more. We've had ...
6 We don't want to see their failed policies any more. We've seen ...

ANSWERS TO CHECK QUESTIONS 1 AND 2

1 1 too long 2 too much 3 too easy
4 Too many too many

2 1 It's easy enough 2 well enough 3 enough hospitals or schools 4 enough money
5 We've had enough of this government.
6 We've seen enough of their failed policies.

Practice

> *Too* comes before an adjective: *Too difficult*
> *Too much/too many*: *Too much wine   Too many cars*
> *Too* + adjective + (*for* + object) + infinitive: *It's too expensive for us to buy.*
> *Enough* comes after an adjective or an adverb, before a noun: *Easy enough   Enough money*
> *Enough* + noun + (*for* + object) + infinitive: *There's enough money for us to buy a pizza.*

1 Carla and Simon went to a new restaurant last night but it was not good. Complete these sentences with *too* or *enough* + the adjectives in brackets.

Carla: We couldn't hear what we were saying. It was (1 noisy) ....

Simon: There weren't many things on the menu. It wasn't (2 varied) ....

Carla: We waited a long time for the menu. The service was (3 slow) ....

Simon: And then the food didn't arrive for over half an hour. We had to wait (4 long) ....

Carla: I like my food hot. My steak definitely wasn't (5 hot) ....

Simon: And the bill came to over £40 each. It was (6 expensive) ....

2 Two people are walking home after a football match. Complete the dialogue with *enough* and the words in brackets.

'The defence is (1 good) .... but the rest of the team isn't.'

'No, they're definitely not playing (2 well) .... and they're not scoring (3 goals) .... They'll have to buy some new players.'

'But they haven't got (4 money) .... because not (5 people) .... come to watch them play.'

'The city's (6 big) .... to have a good football team but the people aren't (7 interested) .... in football.'

3 Judy wants to buy a car. But she is not sure which one she wants. Complete the dialogue, using *too* or *enough* + these adjectives: *dark, hard, small, comfortable, old, expensive, cheap, big* (x 2).

'How about this Volkswagen?'

'No, the boot isn't (1) ....
I couldn't get much luggage in there. And the

back seat's (2) .... You couldn't get three people in there.'

'This Renault might suit you.'

'No, I don't like the colour I'm afraid. It's (3) .... I prefer light colours.'

'How about this BMW?'

'Yes, I like that. But it's (4) .... I can't afford a BMW.'

'Well I'm sure this Opel's (5) .... for you. It's only £4,500. Try sitting in it.'

'Um, I don't think it's (6) .... These seats are very hard.'

'Try this Citroen then. These seats certainly aren't (7) ....'

'No, you're right, the seats are fine. But it's (8) .... It'd be very difficult to park.'

'This Ford's much smaller.'

'No, it's (9).............................. . A 1992 car might give me a lot of trouble.'

'Well, I'm very sorry. I haven't got any other cars I can show you.'

4 These two parents have an 18-year-old son who is causing them problems. Rewrite the sentences, using *too* + adjective + (*for* + object) + infinitive OR adjective + *enough* + (*for* + object) + infinitive.

Example: He's lazy. He won't get up in the morning. *He's too lazy to get up in the morning.*

1 He's quite old now. He can't go back to school. ....

....

2 He's not very independent. He can't live on his own. ....

....

3 He's very difficult. We can't control him.

....

4 He was offered a job but it wasn't very interesting. He didn't accept it. ....

....

80

Time prepositions: *in, at, on*

In the 1930s a lot of people tried to break flying records. At that time Douglas Corrigan was a young pilot, and in 1938 he decided to try to fly solo, non-stop across the USA. He planned to leave early in the morning, and on the morning of Monday July 16th, 1938, at dawn, Corrigan took off from an airport near New York, exactly on time. He expected to land in California in about twenty-three hours, just in time to celebrate his birthday on July 17th. In the summer there are usually clear skies over the USA, but in July that year the weather was bad and Corrigan had to fly in thick cloud. At 16.20 on Tuesday afternoon, at the end of a heroic flight, he landed - in Ireland, not California! He'd made the flight in twenty-eight hours, but he'd flown east, not west! After the flight he was always called Douglas 'Wrong Way' Corrigan!

Step 1 | *In* before periods of time

We use *in* with periods of time:

- parts of the day: early **in** the morning, **in** the afternoon, **in** the evening
- months: **in** July, **in** October
- seasons: **in** (the) summer, **in** (the) autumn, **in** (the) winter, **in** (the) spring
- years: **in** 1938, **in** 1995, **in** 2001
- decades and centuries: **in** the 1930s, **in** the 21st century
- *In* can mean 'during or within a period of time'.
  He'd made the flight **in** twenty-eight hours.
In can also mean 'at the end of a period of time'.
  He expected to land in California **in** about 23 hours.
- Note that the phrase *in time* means 'early enough for something' or 'not too late for something'.
  just **in time** to celebrate his birthday on July 17th

CHECK QUESTIONS 1 **Answer the questions.**
1 When did a lot of people try to break flying records?
2 In which year did Corrigan make his famous flight?
3 In which month?

Step 2 | *On* before days/dates

We use *on* before particular days or particular dates:

- days: **on** Monday, **on** Tuesday, **on** his birthday, **on** Christmas Day
- dates: **on** July 17th, **on** November 2nd
- with parts of days/dates: **on** Tuesday afternoon, **on** Friday evening, **on** the morning of Monday, July 16th
- Note that the phrase *on time* means 'at exactly the right time'.
  Corrigan left exactly **on time**.

Put *in* or *on* before these words and phrases.
1 Monday morning   2 Tuesday   3 July 16th   4 1938

Step 3 | *At* before exact times

We use *at*:

- with clock times: ***at** 16.20, **at** six o'clock*
But we don't normally use *at* in questions like:
***What time** did he leave New York?*
(*At what time did he leave New York?* is very formal.)

- with single words meaning a time of day.
***at** dawn, **at** midday, **at** lunchtime, **at** night*

- with *beginning, start, end.*
***at the end** of a heroic flight   **at the beginning** of the flight*

- with the words *time, moment.*
***at that time** he was a young pilot   **at the moment** (= now)*

- with public holidays and festivals.
***at** Christmas* (BUT ***on** Christmas Day*)
***at** Easter* (BUT ***on** Easter Sunday*. See Step 2 above.)
***at** the weekend* ('on the weekend' in American English.)

Put *in* or *on* or *at* before these words and phrases.
1 10.15   2 dawn   3 the winter   4 1911   5 the start of the flight   6 breakfast

Step 4 | When not to use *in, on* or *at*

- We don't use *in, on* or *at* before the words *every, next, this, last* and *tomorrow, yesterday.*
*Corrigan's making his flight **next Monday**.* (NOT on next Monday)
*He thinks about his flight **every day**.* (NOT on every day)
*He left New York **this morning**.* (NOT on this morning)
*He hopes to arrive in California **tomorrow morning**.*
(NOT on tomorrow morning)
*He landed in Ireland **last Tuesday**.* (NOT on last Tuesday)

Put *in, on* or *at* or no word at all before these words and phrases.
1 every evening   2 the evening   3 yesterday evening   4 this evening
5 tomorrow evening   6 the evening of July 16th   7 next Christmas
8 three o'clock in the morning

---

1 1 In the 1930s. 2 In 1938. 3 In July.
2 1 on Monday morning 2 on Tuesday
3 on July 16th 4 in 1938
3 1 at 10.15 2 at dawn 3 in the winter
4 in 1911 5 at the start of the flight
6 at breakfast

4 1 every evening 2 in the evening 3 yesterday
evening 4 this evening 5 tomorrow evening
6 on the evening of July 16th 7 next
Christmas 8 at three o'clock in the morning

Practice

> **in**: *in the evening, in July, in 1938, in the summer, in three weeks, in time*
> **on**: *on Monday, on my birthday, on July 16th, on Friday morning, on the morning of May 3rd, on time*
> **at**: *at 6.30, at midday, at Christmas, at the beginning, at the moment*

1 **Complete the dialogue with *in, on, at* or no word at all.**

'I want a return flight from London to Barcelona
(1) ..on.... August 6th, please.'

'That's (2) ..on.. Friday, isn't it? Do you want to
leave (3) ..in..... the morning?'

'No, (4) .....in.... the afternoon, please.'

'All right. I'll be with you (5) ...at.... a moment.
(Pause) Yes, there's a flight (6) ...at... 14.35.'

'That's fine.'

'And when do you want to return?'

'(7) ..on... Sunday evening.'

'There's only one flight (8) ...in.... the evening
and that's (9) ..at..... 18.15. But (10) ....at... the
moment there are no seats on that flight, I'm
afraid. It's often difficult to get seats
(11) ....in..... July and August. (12) ...in..... the
winter it isn't a problem. Could you fly back
(13) .... the next morning?'

'Yes, if there's a flight (14) ...at..... dawn! I've got
a meeting in London (15) ...at..... midday.'

'Well, there's a British Airways flight (16) ..at...
8.50 which gets into London (17) .at....... 10.15.'

'Good. If the flight's (18) ..on..... time I could just
get to my meeting (19) ...on..... time.'

2 **Complete this telephone conversation with *in, on, at* or no word at all.**

'Hello.'

'Hi. This is Jason We met (1) .... last
Saturday, remember?'

'Yes, I remember.'

'Are you doing anything (2) .....in.. this evening?'

'Yes, I'm going out. In fact I'm busy (3) ....
every evening this week.'

'Are you free (4) ..at.... the weekend?'

'I'm very busy, I'm afraid. (5) ....on.... Saturday
morning I'm going shopping and then
(6) ...in..... the afternoon I'm playing in a
volleyball match.'

'What are you doing (7) ....in..... the evening?'

'You mean (8) ...on..... Saturday evening?'

'Yes.'

'I'm not sure. That's (9) .... four days, and
I'm never sure what I'll be doing (10) ....
four days' time.'

'Well, I'll call for you (11) ..at....... about 8 o'clock
(12) .on...... Saturday evening.'

'Yes, all right. Why not?'

3 **Complete this text about Jimi Hendrix using *in, on, at* or no word at all.**

(1) ....in.... the 1960s Jimi Hendrix was a rock
superstar. He was born (2) ....in 1945 in
Seattle, USA. (3) ....at..... the middle of the 60s he
formed his own band - the Jimi Hendrix
Experience. (4) ....in..... July, 1967 he had his first
big hit with the song 'Hey Joe'. He was the star
of the Woodstock Festival (5) ...in..... the
summer of 1969. He died of a drug overdose
(6) ...on... May 16th, 1970. (7) .... the time he
was building a big new recording studio in New
York. (8) .... the moment it seems that Jimi
Hendrix will still be influencing rock music
(9) .... the 21st century.

There was an article in the Daily Mail recently about the number of homeless people in Britain.
Jason Mitchell lives in a tent in the park in the middle of a square in London. He sleeps in a sleeping bag. He hasn't slept in a bed since he was in hospital last year. His dog sleeps with him in a corner of the tent. He used to live in the country, but it's easier to find food in the city. He finds food in the waste bins in the street, outside restaurants. But when he's got some money in his pocket, he eats in cheap cafés.

Step 1 | *In*

- In general, we use *in* when we talk about an enclosed space that is surrounded on all sides.
  *He lives **in a tent**.   He sleeps **in a sleeping bag**.*

- We use it with buildings and areas surrounded by walls, etc.
  in** cheap **cafés**   **in** the **park**   **in** a **square**   **in** the **street

- with larger areas like cities, states, countries, continents.
  ***in** the **city**   **in** the **country**   **in** London   **in** Britain*

- with words that describe the relative position of something.
  ***in the middle of** the square   **in a corner of** the tent*
  ***in the south of** England*

- with words like *hospital, church, school.*
  *He was **in hospital** last year.*

- with newspapers and magazines.
  *an article **in** the **Daily Mail***

CHECK QUESTIONS 1 **Add *in* where necessary.**
1 There are lots of homeless people Britain, especially London.
2 You read about them every day the newspapers.
3 Jason doesn't live a house. He lives a tent.

Step 2 | *On*

Alexander Berrisford, an international art dealer, lives on the top floor of an apartment building on the north bank of the River Thames.
There are Persian rugs on the floor of his apartment and valuable paintings on the walls.
Alexander often sits on his balcony. On the left he can see Tower Bridge and on the right Westminster Bridge. On the other side of the river he can see the National Theatre.
He's got two other homes – a castle on an island on the west coast of Scotland, and a villa on a lake on the border between Italy and Austria.
He does most of his work on the phone and on his computer. He's quite famous. He's often on television and this morning his photograph was on the front page of the newspapers.

- In general, we use *on* when we talk about a horizontal or vertical surface.
  on** the **floor ***on** the front **page*** ***on** the **walls***

- We use it with any kind of line.
  ***on** the north **bank** of the River Thames*
  ***on** the **border** between Italy and Austria*
  ***on** the west **coast** of Scotland*

- with machines.
  on** the **phone ***on** his **computer*** ***on** television*

- with the positions *right* and *left* and the word *side*.
  on** the **right ***on** the **left*** ***on** the other **side** of the river*

CHECK QUESTIONS 2 **Add *on* where necessary.**
1 Alexander's apartment's the top floor.
2 He's quite famous and he's often the radio and television.
3 His castle's the north coast of the island.

> The Perring family also live in London, at 89, Elm Road, Balham. Alan Perring works at the garage near his house. Carol Perring works at the newsagent's at the end of the road. Their two children are at the local primary school. They meet their friends at the children's playground at the bottom of the hill.
> At the front of the Perrings' house there's a small garden. At the back, there's a bigger garden.
> The Perrings spend most evenings at home. But sometimes they meet their friends at the Ten Pin Bowling at the corner of the street. And Alan sometimes sees his friends at a football match on Saturday.

- In general, we use *at* when we talk about a particular point.
  *The playground's **at** the bottom of the hill.*
  *The Ten Pin Bowling's **at** the end of their road.*
  ***At** the back of the house there's a garden.*

- We use *at* with a building when we're thinking about what normally happens there, and not about the building itself.
  *Alan works **at** the garage.   Carol works **at** the newsagent's.*
  Compare: 'There's a dog in the newsagent's.' (= inside the four walls of the shop.)
  Compare also:
  *The Perrings live **in** Balham.* (= surrounded by houses, etc.)
  *The train stops **at** Balham.* (= a point on the railway line.)

- Note that we say *at the corner of the street* (a point) but *in the corner of the room* (a place surrounded on all sides).

- We use *at* with social activities:
  *Alan Perring sometimes sees his friends **at** a football match.*
  *I'll meet you **at** the theatre/**at** the cinema/**at** the party.*

- Note these expressions: *at home, at work, at school.*
  *The Perrings spend most evenings **at home**.   Alan doesn't have lunch **at work**.*

- With addresses, we use *at* if we give the house number.
  *They live **in** Elm Road.* BUT *They live **at** 89, Elm Road.*
  (In American English we say 'They live **on** Elm Road.')

CHECK QUESTIONS 3 **Add *at* or *in* where necessary.**
1 There's a Ten Pin Bowling Balham, the corner of Elm Road.
2 During the day, the Perrings' children are school.
3 The children have got friends who live 16, Elm Road.

1 1 in Britain in London 2 in the newspapers   3 on the north coast
    3 in a house in a tent
2 1 on the top floor 2 on the radio on television
3 1 in Balham at the corner 2 at school
    3 at 16, Elm Road.

Practice

1 Complete the description of the picture, using *in*, *on* or *at*.

(1) *on* the picture Sarah Bell is (2) *at* work. She's sitting (3) *at* her desk (4) *in* her office. She's (5) *on* the phone. She's got a pen (6) *in* her hand. There's a plant (7) *on* the right of her desk. (8) *In* the middle of her desk there's a computer. There's a graph (9) *on* the screen. There's a report (10) *on* her desk. (11) *at* the top of the page there's the headline 'Sales Figures'. There's a calendar (12) *on* the wall. There are several files (13) *on* the shelf behind her. Her bag's (14) *on* the floor. Her coat's hanging (15) *on* the door. (16) *In* the open drawer of the filing cabinet there are several files. There's a book (17) *on* top of the filing cabinet.

2 Complete the following description, using *in*, *on* or *at*.

Holbeton is a small village (1) ...... the River Erme (2) ...... the south west of England. Many people who live (3) ...... the village go to work (4) ...... Plymouth, which is ten miles away. A few people work (5) ...... home and do all their work (6) ...... computer.

The owner of most of the land (7) ...... the area lives (8) ...... a large house (9) ...... the top of the hill.

Most of the young people of Holbeton meet (10) ...... the war memorial (11) ...... the centre of the village. The older teenagers meet (12) ...... a small room (13) ...... the back of the local pub. There isn't much for them to do (14) ...... Holbeton.

Kevin Sloman, who lives (15) ...... 28, Vicarage Road, said: 'I've lived (16) ...... Holbeton all my life. I spent five years (17) ...... the primary school (18) ...... the village. Now I go to school (19) ...... Ivybridge, which is seven miles away. No trains stop (20) ...... Holbeton now. They've closed the station, so we can't get into Plymouth easily. The village is OK for people who want to spend a holiday (21) ...... the country or (22) ...... the beach. But it's different if you have to spend twelve months of the year here!'

Prepositions of place: *under, opposite*, etc.

I wanted to live outside London and I was looking for a flat in Richmond. The estate agent took me to see one. The flat was opposite a church, near Richmond Park. It was above a Chinese restaurant. We stood on the pavement in front of the restaurant. It was raining so I held a newspaper over my head. The entrance to the flat was round the side of the restaurant. I asked the agent where I could park my car. He said there was a parking place behind the restaurant.
'Now, would you like to see inside the flat?' he asked me.

Step 1 | *Outside, inside, behind, in front of, above, over, near, round, opposite*

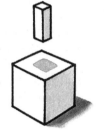

It was **above** a restaurant.

I held a newspaper **over** my head.

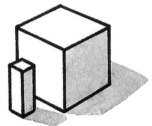

in front of the restaurant

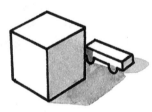

a parking place **behind** the restaurant

I wanted to live **outside** London.

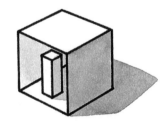

Would you like to see **inside** the flat?

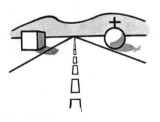

It was **opposite** a church

near Richmond Park.

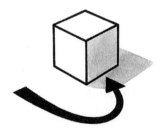

The entrance was **round** the side of the restaurant.

- *Above* and *over* usually have the same meaning: 'higher than'.
  *The flat was **above** (OR **over**) a restaurant.*
  But *over* can sometimes mean 'covering'.
  *I held a newspaper **over** my head.*
- We use *inside* rather than *in* to emphasise the interior of an enclosed space.
  *A flat **in** Richmond. Would you like to see **inside** the flat?*

CHECK QUESTIONS 1 **Complete the sentences with prepositions.**
1 Richmond is ... London.
2 The flat was ... a restaurant.
3 It was ... Richmond Park.
4 She could park her car ... the restaurant.

Step 2 | *Among, between, under, below, on top of, next to, beside, by*

There were four rooms in the flat. The bathroom was between the bedroom and the living room. The kitchen was next to the living room. In the living room there was a table and two chairs under an old sheet. 'All included in the price!' the agent said. The flat was by the Thames, on top of a hill, and there was a lovely view. I stood beside the estate agent at the living room window. I could see Richmond Park below us. There were some deer among the trees in the park. And I could see the river between the trees. Suddenly we heard a loud crash below us and people shouting in Chinese. 'Have you got any other flats?' I said.

*a table and two chairs **under** an old sheet*

*I could see the park **below** us.*

*some deer **among** the trees*

*I could see the river **between** the trees.*

271

*The flat was **on top of** a hill.*

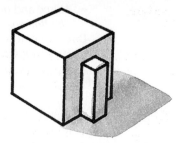

*The kitchen was **next to** the living room.*

*The flat was **by** the Thames.*

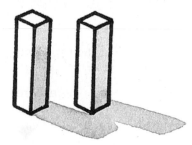

*I stood **beside** the agent.*

- *Below* and *under* often have the same meaning: 'lower than'.
  *The restaurant kitchen was **below** (OR **under**) the living room.*
But we use *below* and not *under* when we mean 'lower than', but not necessarily 'directly under':
  *I could see the park **below** us.* (NOT vertically under them)
We use *under* when we mean 'covered by'.
  *There was a table **under** an old sheet.* (The sheet covered it.)

- *Among* and *between* don't mean the same. We say something or someone is *between* two or more things when we see these things as separate objects.
  *I could see the river **between** the trees.*
  (She could see it in the space that separated one tree from another.)
We say that something is *among* a group of things or people when it's surrounded by them. We don't see these things or people separately.
  *There were some deer **among** the trees.*
  (The deer were in the middle of the trees.)

- *By*, *next to* and *beside* all mean 'very close to'. Compare:
  *The flat was **by** the Thames.* (= very close to the river)
  *The flat was **near** the Thames.* (= close to - further away than *by*)

CHECK QUESTIONS 2 **Complete the sentences with prepositions.**
1 The agent stood ... her and showed her the view.
2 They could see Richmond Park ... them, because they were ... a hill.
3 There were some children playing ... the trees in the park.

ANSWERS TO
CHECK QUESTIONS
1 AND 2
1 1 outside 2 above/over 3 near 4 behind
2 1 beside/next to 2 below on top of
  3 among

272

Practice

1 Look at this picture of a hotel lobby and complete the sentences with prepositions. Choose from:
outside, among, behind, opposite, by, between, in front of, above, next to.

1 There are two girls *behind* .... the reception desk.

2 There's a big sign *above* .... their heads saying Reception.

3 There are several people *in front of* .... the desk.

4 *among* .... these people there's a young boy.

5 *oppo* .... the reception desk there's a bar.

6 *between* .... the stairs and the lift there's a telephone box.

7 There's a woman *outside* .... the telephone box, waiting to use the phone.

8 There's a suitcase on the floor *next to* .... her.

9 Two people are waiting *by* .... the lift.

2 Look at this picture of a living room. Complete the sentences with prepositions. Choose from:
near, round, over, under, below, on top of, beside.

1 There's a lamp .... the television.

2 There's a dog .... the table.

3 The dog's got a collar .... his neck.

4 There's a girl sitting .... an old woman on the sofa.

5 There's a picture on the wall, ... the fire.

6 .... the picture there's a shelf with a clock on it.

7 There's a bookcase .... the window.

Yesterday Miss Ada Jenkins of Cardiff tried for half an hour to catch her cat Floss to give it some medicine. But it ran away from her. It ran out of the kitchen, up the stairs, round and round the bedroom, down the stairs again, in and out of the living room, from the living room into the kitchen and finally into the back garden. She chased it round the garden pond. Then the cat climbed up a tree and couldn't get down. So Miss Jenkins went to the phone and rang the Fire Brigade. Ten minutes later they arrived. The firefighters took a ladder off the fire engine. They then carried it through the hall and the kitchen and into the back garden.

Step 1 | *Up, down, round, into, out of, off, through, to, from*

*The cat ran **away from** her.*

*It ran **out of** the kitchen*

***up** the stairs*

***down** the stairs*

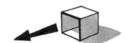

***from** the living room*

***into** the back garden*

***round** the garden pond.*

*She went **to** the phone.*

*They took a ladder **off** the fire engine.*

*They carried it **through** the hall.*

- We can join some of these prepositions with *and*:
round **and** round, up **and** down, in **and** out of, on **and** off, to **and** from

***round and round** the bedroom*

***in and out of** the living-room*

CHECK QUESTIONS 1 **Complete the sentences with prepositions of movement.**
1 Miss Jenkins followed the cat ... the stairs and ... the bedroom.
2 The cat ran ... the house and ... the garden.
3 The firefighters had to carry the ladder ... the hall and the kitchen because they couldn't get ... the side of the house.

One of the firefighters climbed up the tree, then along a branch towards the cat. Floss moved onto another branch! But twenty minutes later the firefighter climbed down with Floss in his arms. Just as the fire engine was leaving, Floss ran past Miss Jenkins and jumped over the garden fence. The cat then ran across the road and under the wheels of the fire engine. Unfortunately, the driver couldn't stop in time.

along a branch

towards the cat

onto a branch

The cat ran ***past*** Miss Jenkins

and jumped ***over*** the garden fence.

The cat ran ***across*** the road

and ***under*** the wheels of the fire engine.

CHECK QUESTIONS 2

Complete the sentences with prepositions of movement.
1 The firefighter climbed up the ladder … the cat.
2 They walked … the road to their fire engine parked on the other side.
3 They put their ladder back … the fire engine.

Practice

1 Look at the numbered diagrams and complete the text, using prepositions of movement.

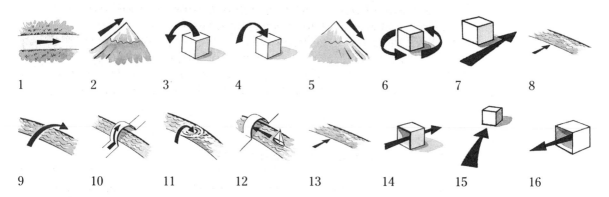

Martin went for a ride on his mountain bike. He rode (1) .... a path until he came to a very steep hill. He started to ride (2) .... the hill, but soon he had to get (3) .... his bike and walk. At the top of the hill he got back (4) .... his bike and rode (5) .... the other side. He then went (6) .... a big lake. He rode (7) .... an old castle by the side of the lake. He then came (8) .... the river. He couldn't get (9) .... the river at this point. Fortunately there was a bridge a few hundred metres away, and he rode (10) .... the bridge. He was hot, so he decided to have a swim. He dived (11) .... the river, swam (12) .... the bridge a couple of times and then swam back (13) .... the place where he'd left his bike. He continued his ride. He went (14) .... a tunnel. It was long and dark and he rode carefully (15) .... the light he could see at the end. When he came (16) .... the tunnel, he found it was raining, so he rode quickly home.

2 Complete these sentences, using the following prepositions: *up, down, round, into, out of, towards, onto, past, over, under.*

1 In tennis you have to hit the ball .... the net, but you mustn't hit the ball .... the court.

2 In football you have to get the ball .... the goalkeeper and then .... the horizontal bar and .... the net.

3 In skiing you use a ski lift to go .... the mountain and then you ski .... the mountain as fast as possible.

4 In motor racing you have to drive .... a circuit or track.

5 In golf you hit the ball .... a flag and then .... a hole.

6 In judo you try to get the other person .... the floor.

> Every year students at Bristol University have a competition to see who can travel the furthest in 24 hours, without spending any money on transport. Last year the winner was Danny Green.
> 'I couldn't travel by air or by rail, because you need a ticket to go by plane or by train and we weren't allowed to spend any money on transport. You can't usually travel free on a plane or on a train, so the only solution was to go by road and to get a lift in a car or a truck.'

Step 1 | Go by air, by train, etc. on a bus/in a car

- To talk about different ways of travelling we use *by* + *air, rail, road, sea* and + *train, bus, coach, car, plane, boat, taxi,* etc. with the verbs *go, come, travel.*
  I couldn't travel by air or by rail.   You need a ticket to go by plane or by train.

- We use *on* with different kinds of public transport: *on a train, a plane, a boat, a ferry, a hovercraft, a tram, a bus, a coach.* (But we also use *on* with *a bike, a motorbike, a horse.*)
  We use *in* with other forms of transport: *in a car, a truck, a taxi, a small boat* or *plane.*
  You can't travel free on a plane or on a train.   to get a lift in a car or a truck

CHECK QUESTIONS 1 | **Put in prepositions.**
1 Danny knew he couldn't go ... air or ... rail.
2 He couldn't go ... a bus or ... a coach, because that cost money.
3 He had to go ... road, ... a car or ... a truck.

Step 2 | Get into/out of a car,   on/off a train   Go into/out of a building
Arrive in a town/a country   Arrive at a place

> Danny continued: 'I did the first two kilometres of my trip on foot – I went out of the university building and into the first shop I could find to buy some food. Then I walked to the beginning of the motorway. I got into the first car that stopped for me. The driver was going to London. We got to London at 2.15. I got out of the car, and my next lift was even better - a motorcyclist. I got on his motorbike and I arrived in Folkestone, on the south coast, at 4.30. When I got off the motorbike, I walked for a bit and arrived at the Shuttle Terminal ten minutes later. Now I needed to get to France as quickly as possible. I had to get on a train and through the Channel Tunnel – without paying!'

- Note that we say *on foot* and not 'by foot'.
  I did the first two kilometres on foot. (= I walked.)

- We use *out of* and *into* when we're talking about buildings or rooms.
  I went out of the university building and into the first shop I could find.

- We say *to get into* (OR *in*) */out of* a car, a taxi, a truck, etc.
  *I **got into** (OR **in**) the first car that stopped for me.*
  *I got **out of** the car, and my next lift was even better.*
- We say *to get on/off* a train, a bus, a plane, a boat, a bike, a motorbike.
  *I got **on** his motorbike.   I got **off** the motorbike and walked for a bit.*
- We say *to get to* a town or a country.
  *We got **to** London at 2.15.   Now I needed to get **to** France.*
- But we say *to arrive in* a town or a country.
  *I arrived **in** Folkestone at 4.30.   When will he arrive **in** France?*
  And we say *to arrive at* a place.
  *I arrived **at** the Shuttle Terminal ten minutes later.*
  (See also *In, on, at,* Unit 81.)

CHECK QUESTIONS 2 **Put in prepositions.**
1 He got ... the car and they got ... London two hours later.
2 When he arrived ... Folkestone he got ... the motorbike.
3 He soon arrived ... the Shuttle Terminal.

Step 3 | *Go to* a place, a town or a country   *Go/get home*

'At the terminal I found a car driver who had room for another passenger. We arrived in France half an hour later! My next lift was in a French truck. I told the driver I wanted to go to the south of France. Fortunately, the driver had been to England several times and he spoke English. He said he'd also been to Scandinavia, to Russia, to Italy and to Greece. He took me to Paris. I'd never been to Paris before. In fact I'd never been to France. Next, a woman in a big Mercedes took me all the way to the south coast. We got there just before 12 o'clock the next day. I went to the post office and posted a card to prove where I was after 24 hours - Marseille, 1,411 kilometres from Bristol! And it hadn't cost me a penny! Now it was time to go home again. But I didn't have to get home in 24 hours!'

- We say *to go to* a place, a town, a country, a continent.
  *The truck driver had been **to** England several times.*
  *I told him I wanted to go **to** the south of France.*
  *I'd never been **to** Paris before.   I went **to** the post office.*
- Note that we don't use a preposition before the word *home* with verbs like *go, get, come, arrive, leave.*
  *I wanted to **go home**.   I didn't have to **get home** in 24 hours.*

CHECK QUESTIONS 3 **Complete the sentences, using prepositions where necessary.**
1 Had the truck driver been ... Scandinavia?
2 Had he been ... Greece?
3 After 24 hours Danny was ... Marseille.
4 He didn't know how to get ... home.

ANSWERS TO
CHECK QUESTIONS
1, 2 AND 3

1 1 by by 2 on on 3 by in in
2 1 into to 2 in off 3 at
3 1 to 2 to 3 in 4 –

Practice

go **by** car, train, etc.	go **in** a car, **on** a train	go **by** road, rail, etc.
go **to** London/France	go **into/out of** a building, a room	go home
get **on/off** a bus	get **into/out of** a car	
get **to** London/France	arrive **in** London/France	arrive **at** a place
I've been **to** London/France.		

1 **Complete the text, using prepositions where necessary.**

Last summer we went on holiday (1) .... Greece. We'd never been (2) .... Greece before. We left (3) .... home in Birmingham at midday and went (4) .... taxi (5) .... the station. We got (6) .... the station only two minutes before the train left. We then went (7) .... train to Gatwick Airport. We had our lunch (8) .... the train. We arrived (9) .... the airport at 17.15, three hours before our plane left. Eventually we took off and flew (10) .... Athens. We arrived (11) .... Athens at 4 o'clock in the morning. From there we went (12) .... bus (13) .... the port of Piraeus. An hour later we got (14) .... a ferry. We couldn't sleep (15) .... the ferry because it was too crowded. When we finally got (16) .... the island of Naxos we got (17) .... a very old taxi. The driver said he couldn't take us all the way (18) .... our hotel because it was at the top of a very steep hill. We had to do the last 100 metres of our journey (19) .... foot! We finally arrived (20) .... our hotel, more than 24 hours after we'd left (21) .... home. We were more than ready for our holiday!

2 **Complete the dialogue, using prepositions where necessary.**

'Yes, sir. Can I help you?'

'I want to get from London (1) .... Brussels as cheaply as possible.'

'Well, if you go (2) .... rail, it'll cost you £155 return.'

'And if I leave at about midday, when will I arrive (3) .... Brussels?'

'At 16.15.'

'And if I go (4) .... air?'

'If you go (5) .... plane, it'll cost you £190 and you'll get (6) .... Brussels at 14.30.'

'And what about going (7) .... car?'

'Well, if you went (8) .... your own car, you'd have to drive (9) .... Dover. Then when you arrived (10) .... Dover you'd have to go (11) .... the Ferry Terminal and get (12) .... a ferry that goes (13) .... Ostend. When you got (14) .... the ferry in Ostend, you'd take the motorway (15) .... Brussels. It would take much longer (16) .... car.'

'But how much would it cost?'

'£79. But then you'd have to eat (17) .... the boat and that costs quite a lot. The food (18) .... the plane is free. And, if you went (19) .... road, you'd have to buy petrol. I'd go (20) .... the train if I were you. It isn't too expensive and it's very comfortable.'

The British have had the metric system for nearly 30 years. Some of them use it for two or three weeks a year when they go on holiday to continental Europe. But most of them still don't understand litres, kilometres and kilograms. In the 1970s, when the system was first introduced, they'd used pints and gallons, miles and pounds for a long time, and they didn't want to change. One old man said: 'When I was young, I lived in France for a year, but I couldn't understand kilometres and kilograms. I've used miles and pounds all my life. I can't change now. I'll go on using them for the rest of my life.'

Step 1 | Time preposition *for*

- We use *for* to answer the question 'How long?'
For is usually followed by a period of time, often a number of hours, days, weeks, months, years, etc.
> The British have had the metric system **for nearly 30 years**.
> I lived in France **for a year**.

- *For* can be used with past, present and future tenses.
Present simple: They **use it for** two or three weeks a year.
Present perfect: I've **used** miles and pounds **for** sixty years.
Past perfect: They'**d used** pints and gallons **for** a long time.
Past simple: I **lived** in France **for** a year.
Future: I'**ll go on** using them **for** the rest of my life!

- We don't use *for* with expressions like: *all morning, all day, all evening, all year, all my life*, etc.
> I've used miles **all my life**. (NOT for all my life)

CHECK QUESTIONS 1 | **Use *for* in your answers.**
1 How long have the British had the metric system?
2 How long did the old man live in France?
3 How long will he continue to use the word 'gallon'?

Step 2 | *Since*

The British have had the metric system since the 1970s, and ever since then they've been unhappy about it. The old man said: 'It's a long time since I was in France. When I was there I always asked for "a litre" of beer. But then I came back to England, and I haven't used the word "litre" since. Of course, young people in Britain have used the metric system since they started school, so it's not a problem for them.'

- We use *since* + a point in time to say when something started:
> The British have had the metric system **since the 1970s**.

OR (with a negative verb) to say when something stopped.
*The old man hasn't lived in France **since 1952**.*

- *Since* is often followed by a subject + a verb to show the point in time.
  *Young people have used it **since they started school**.*

- We usually use *since* with the present perfect.
  *The British have had the metric system **since** 1971.*

- We use *ever since* when we want to emphasise that something has continued without stopping for a period of time.
  ***Ever since** then the British have been unhappy about it.*

- *Since* and *ever since* can be used on their own.
  *I haven't used the word 'litre' **since**.*

- Note these common expressions with *since*.
  ***It's a long time since** I was in France.*
  ***How long is it since** the old man lived in France?*

(For *since* see also Units 8 and 90.)

CHECK QUESTIONS 2 **Answer these questions, using *since*.**
1 How long have the British had the metric system?
2 When did the old man last use the word 'litre'? He hasn't used it ...

Step 3 | *Ago*

The Americans started to introduce the metric system a long time ago, in 1785, when they changed 'pounds, shillings' and 'pence' to 'dollars' and 'cents'. Twenty years ago the American government announced plans to introduce more of the metric system. A few days ago an American senator asked: 'How long ago did we decide to make the change? Twenty years ago! And what has changed since then? Nothing!'

- We use *ago* to say when something happened in the past.
  ***Twenty years ago** the American government announced plans.*
  (Twenty years ago = twenty years before now.)

- We put *ago* after the expression of time.
  *twenty years **ago**   a few days **ago*** (NOT ago twenty years)

- We use *ago* with the past simple (and sometimes with the past continuous). But we don't use it with the present perfect.
  ***A few days ago** an American senator asked.*
  (We can't say: 'A few days ago an American senator has asked.')

- Note these question forms:
  ***How long ago** did we decide to make the change?*
  ***How many years ago** did they introduce 'dollars' and 'cents'?*

CHECK QUESTIONS 3 **Use *ago* in your answers.**
1 When did the US government first plan to introduce the metric system?
2 When did the senator talk about the metric system?
3 How long ago did the USA change to 'dollars' and 'cents'?

ANSWERS TO
CHECK QUESTIONS
1, 2 AND 3

1 1 For nearly thirty years. 2 For a year.
3 For the rest of his life.

2 1 Since the 1970s 2 since he lived in France.

3 1 Twenty years ago. 2 A few days ago.
3 A long time ago. OR Years ago.

Practice

1 This man is homeless and depressed. Rewrite the sentences using the present perfect + *for*.
Example: It's five years since I had a new pair of shoes. *I haven't had a new pair of shoes for five years.*

1 It's a week since I had a good meal.

....

2 It's a year since I had a job.

....

3 It's years since I last saw my family.

....

4 It's a long time since I had a hot bath.

....

5 It's ages since I slept in a comfortable bed.

....

2 Complete this dialogue with *for* or *since*.
'I haven't seen you (1) .... ages.'
'I know. Not (2) .... we left school.'
'What have you been doing (3) .... then?'
'I've been at college (4) .... three years. How about you?'
'I went to Australia (5) .... six months and then to America (6) .... two years.'
'And what have you been doing (7) .... you came back?'
'I've been looking for a job (8) .... the last three months.'
'I've been looking for a job, too. But I've been looking (9) .... the last year!'

3 Complete the text with *for, since* or *ago*.
Fifty years (1) .... in Britain 68% of adults smoked and they went on smoking (2) .... the next twenty years. But then, about thirty years (3) ...., doctors started telling them it was dangerous, and ever (4) .... then the number of adults who smoke has fallen. The strange thing is that

(5) .... 1993 the number of young people who smoke has increased.

4 Four views of Oxford. Complete each one with *for, since* or *ago*.
'I'm a student at the university. I came to Oxford a year (1) .... and I'll be here (2) .... two more years. It's a beautiful place to live (3) .... three years, but it isn't the real world.' *(Robert Watkins)*
'I've lived in Oxford (4) .... over twenty years, (5) .... I left school in fact. (6) .... most of that time I've worked in the car factory at Cowley. Oxford has changed a lot (7) .... I first moved here. Nowadays it's full of tourists and (8) .... three months every summer you can't move!' *(Tony Slater)*
'I'm a foreign student from Spain and I'm in Oxford (9) .... eight weeks because I want to learn English. I arrived a month (10) .... and (11) .... then my English has improved a lot. A week (12) .... I went to London and stayed there (13) .... two days. But I definitely prefer Oxford.' *(Laura Menendez)*
'I'm a nurse in Oxford. I started work here eighteen months (14) .... and I love it. But it's difficult to find accommodation. I looked for a flat (15) .... over a month. I found a very small flat and stayed there (16) .... six months. Then, a year (17) .... , I moved into a house with some friends, and (18) .... then I've been much happier.' *(Zoe Jones)*

86 | *For, during, while*

> For a long time Mr and Mrs Fuller had wanted to go on holiday abroad. In March 1995 they decided to go camping in France. For three months they planned their trip. Then on July 10th they arrived in France. For ten days they had a nice time, but then, one morning, their car broke down. They'd had the car for years and it had never broken down before. They sat in the car for ages, waiting for someone to stop and help them.

Step 1 | *For*

- *For* answers the question 'How long?' (See Unit 85.)
  ***For three months** they planned their trip.*
  (NOT During three months they planned their trip.)
  ***For ten days** they had a nice time.*
  (NOT During ten days they had a nice time.)

- Note these common expressions with *for*:
  for hours, for days, for weeks, for months, for years, for ages.
  ***For a long time** they'd wanted to go on holiday abroad.*
  *They sat in the car **for ages**.*
  We don't use *during* in these expressions.

CHECK QUESTIONS 1 ▸ **Answer these questions, using *for*.**
1 How long had the Fullers wanted to go on holiday abroad?
2 How long had they had their car?
3 How long did they wait for help?

Step 2 | *During*

> At last a car stopped. The driver was English. His name was Brian Walters. During the conversation he told Mr and Mrs Fuller that he always spent two months in France during the summer, and during his holidays he'd learnt to speak French well. He phoned several garages for them. But it was Saturday and most garages were only open during the week. At last a mechanic arrived. He said he couldn't work on the car during the weekend and it would probably take a week to repair it!

- *During* doesn't mean the same as *for*.
  For answers the question 'How long?'
  During answers the question 'When? In what period of time?'

- We use *during* before a fixed period of time (*the day, the week*, etc.).
  *Most garages were only open **during the week**.*
  We don't use *during* with a number of days or weeks, etc.
  *The mechanic said he needed the car **for a week**. (= 1 week)*
  (NOT during a week)

- We use *during* before some form of activity.
  during* his *holidays*   *during* the *conversation
- Note that when we say that something happens inside a particular period of time, we can use either *during* or *in*.
  *He spent two months in France **during/in** the summer.*

CHECK QUESTIONS 2 **Choose *for* or *during*.**
1 The Fullers stayed at the first camp site (for/during) a week.
2 (For/During) the day they swam in the pool and sunbathed.
3 (For/During) their stay in France it only rained once.

Step 3 | *While*

> While the mechanic was talking to Mr Walters, Mr and Mrs Fuller discussed their problem. Mrs Fuller had to get back to England because she started work in two days. While they were trying to decide what to do, Mr Walters offered to take her to Paris to catch a train to Boulogne where she could get the ferry to England. 'Don't worry,' said Mr Fuller, 'While Brian's driving you to Paris, I'll look after the car and find a hotel.'
> Mr Walters and Mrs Fuller arrived at the station in Paris. While she was getting her luggage out of the car, Mr Walters asked, in French, which platform the Boulogne train left from. Ten minutes later Mrs Fuller was on the train. While thinking how lucky she'd been to meet Mr Walters, she discovered, during a conversation with the woman in the next seat, that she was on a non-stop train to Bologna in Italy!

- *While* is a conjunction. It is followed by a subject + a verb.
  During is a preposition. It is followed by a noun.
    ***while* the mechanic *was talking* to Mr Walters ...**
    ***during* a *conversation* with the woman in the next seat ...**
- We often use *while* + the past continuous followed by a verb in the past simple.
    ***while* they *were trying* to decide, Mr Walters **offered** to take ...**
  (For the past continuous, see Unit 6.)
- When *while* is used in a future sentence, it's followed by a verb in the present and not *will*. (See Unit 87.)
    ***While* Brian *is driving* you to Paris, I'll look after the car.**
- We can use the *-ing* form of a verb after *while*.
    ***while* *thinking* how lucky she'd been to meet Mr Walters ...**

CHECK QUESTIONS 3 **Choose the right word to complete the sentences.**
1 Mrs Fuller waited (for/during/while) Mr Walters asked about the train.
2 (For/During/While) she was waiting, she thought how lucky she was.
3 (For/During/While) a conversation on the train she discovered where it was going.
4 (For/During/While) a few minutes she couldn't believe what the woman had said.

ANSWERS TO CHECK QUESTIONS 1, 2 AND 3

1 1 For a long time. 2 For years. 3 For ages.
2 1 for a week 2 During the day 3 During their stay in France

3 1 while Mr Walters asked about the train.
2 While she was waiting 3 During a conversation on the train 4 For a few minutes

Practice

For answers the question 'How long?' *I went to Spain for two weeks.*
During answers the question 'When? In what period?' *He died during the night.*
During + noun *during the night*
While + subject + verb *while we were waiting*

1 **Put these words and phrases into three columns:** *three days, 1994, we were there, an hour, a long time, the lesson, his lifetime, we've got time, a week, the week, I'm young, ages, I was on holiday, the meal, the band was playing.*

For	During	While
....	....	....
....	....	....
....	....	....
....	....	....
....	....	

2 **Ben is jealous of his girlfriend, Amy. Complete the dialogue with *for* or *during*.**

Ben: You told me to phone you (1) .... the evening. But you were out when I phoned.

Amy: That's strange. Oh, I remember, I went out (2) .... half an hour.

Ben: You mean you went out (3) .... the whole evening!

Amy: No, I didn't. I went out (4) .... a couple of hours.

Ben: And where were you (5) .... that time?

Amy: I went to a party, but (6) .... the party I felt ill, so I came home.

Ben: And who was with you (7) .... the evening?

Amy: Stop interrogating me! You've been like this (8) .... ages. You always want to know what I 'm doing, (9) .... the day and (10) .... the night!

3 **Complete this text, using *for, during* or *while*.**

Elvis Presley worked as a truck driver (1) .... three years before making his first record in 1954. (2) .... 1956 he made four records and all were No. 1 hits. He then went into the army (3) .... two years. (4) .... he was in the army, he continued to make records. (5) .... the nine years that followed he made thirty films. (6) .... he was making these films, he was also making records. In 1969 he gave his first live concert in Las Vegas. He continued to give concerts (7) .... eight years until he died of a drug overdose in 1977.

4 **Complete this text with *for, during* or *while*.**

For your summer holiday why not come to Burnham Sands Holiday Camp? (1) .... two weeks you can just enjoy yourself (2) .... other people do all the work! (3) .... you're here you can take part in all sorts of activities. (4) .... the day there are sports like volleyball, tennis and swimming. And (5) .... your stay there'll be variety shows, ballroom dancing and discos every night.

Prices (6) .... May and June start at £310 (7) .... two weeks.

When, as soon as, etc. in future sentences

> Four young people are talking about their future.
> Simon: When I leave school, I'm going to train to be a teacher. Then, after I've qualified, I'll probably teach English abroad.
> Beth: I'm going to buy a car when I've saved enough money. Then I'm going to get married as soon as I find the right man. I don't want to be alone when I'm older. But I don't want to get married before I'm 30.
> Shanti: I don't want to settle down until I've travelled a lot. Once I've done that, I'll probably get married.
> Harry: Jobs are difficult to find. I might be 25 by the time I get a job! I don't know what I want to do. I'll decide while I'm at college.

Step 1 | *When,* etc. + a present tense or the present perfect

When we talk about the future, we use either a present tense (normally the present simple) or the present perfect after the link words *when, as soon as, once, after, before, while, by the time, until (till).* We don't use *will.*

When clause (present) + Main clause (future)
When I leave school,   *I'm going to train as a teacher.* (NOT When I will leave)
When clause (present perfect) + Main clause (future)
After I've qualified,   *I'll probably teach.* (NOT After I will have qualified)
Note: When we use *when* as a question word, it can be followed by *will* or *going to.*

CHECK QUESTIONS 1 **Answer these questions.**
1 When's Beth going to get married? ... the right man.
2 Is she going to get married when she's 25? No, she ... 30.
3 When will Harry decide about his future?

Step 2 | The simple present or the present perfect?

- It's often possible to use either the simple present or the present perfect after *when, as soon as,* etc. without changing the meaning.
  *I'm going to get married **as soon as I find/I've found** the right man.*

- BUT when it's important to make it clear that one action will be finished before the second one starts, we must use the present perfect.
  *I don't want to settle down **until I've travelled** a lot.*

(Shanti can't say *until I travel.* She can't settle down while she's travelling! So she uses the present perfect. She'll finish travelling, and then she'll settle down.)

CHECK QUESTIONS 2 **Is it essential to use the present perfect in these sentences? Yes, or no?**
1 Shanti: Once I've done that, I'll probably get married.
2 Beth: I'm going to buy a car when I've saved enough money.

ANSWERS TO
CHECK QUESTIONS
1 AND 2

1 1 As soon as she finds the right man. 2 She isn't going to get married before she's 30.

3 While he's at college.
2 1 Yes. 2 Yes.

Practice

> **When clause (present simple or present perfect)** + **Main clause (will/going to)**
>   *As soon as the programme finishes,*   *I'll go to bed.*
> OR *As soon as the programme has finished,*   *I'll go to bed.*
> We must use the present perfect after *when, as soon as,* etc. when it's essential to show clearly that
>   the first action will be completed before the second starts.
> **When clause (present perfect)** +   **Main clause (will/going to)**
> *When I've written the letter,*   *I'll show it to you.*

1 **Martha is going to Paris. She is at London airport with her mother. Complete the dialogue with the correct forms of the verbs.**

'You'll phone me when you (1 get) ....

there, won't you?'

'Yes, mum. I'll phone you as soon as I (2 arrive)

.... in Paris.'

'It'll be three o'clock by the time I (3 get)

.... home, so don't ring before three.'

'No, mum.'

'Don't forget to write to me while you

(4 be) .... away.'

'No, mum. Stop worrying!'

'Shall we have a cup of coffee before you

(5 go) .... ?'

'No thanks, mum. You don't need to wait. I'm

perfectly all right.'

'No, I'll wait till they (6 call) ....

your flight.'

2 **Martha is writing to her mother from Paris. Put in the correct forms of the verbs.**

I've taken some super photos. I'll send you

some of them as soon as they (1 be) ....

developed. We went to a great party last night,

but today I've got a really bad headache. But

don't worry. I'll feel better once I (2 have)

.... a good night's sleep. We're

going to Versailles and Eurodisney next week.

I'll wait until we (3 be) .... there

before I write again. It's lunchtime now, so I'll

post this after we (4 have) ....

lunch.

3 **Someone is giving you directions to 39, Mill Street. Match the two parts of each sentence. Then mark your route on the map.**

1 Go straight on here,   a) you'll see a church
2 When you get to the   ahead of you.
   traffic lights,   b) you'll see Mill Street
3 As soon as you've   on the right.
   turned left,   c) turn left.
4 Just before you get   d) you'll find number 39
   to the church,   on the left.
5 After you've gone   e) until you come to
   about 100 metres,   some traffic lights.

   1 ...   2 ...   3 ...   4 ...   5 ...

4 **Adam's party has just finished. The house is in a mess. His parents are coming back tomorrow evening. Complete each sentence with the correct form of the verb.**

1 I'll make the beds as soon as I (get up)

   .... tomorrow.

2 Then before I (go) .... to

   college, I'll hoover the carpets.

3 As soon as I (get back) ....

   from college, I'll buy some food before the

   shops (close) ....

4 Once I (do) .... that, I'll try to

   repair the CD player.

5 When I (finish) .... the

   housework, I'll make the dinner.

6 Then I'll sit and wait till they (get)

   .... home.

88 | *By, by the time, till/until*

> Zoe and her boyfriend Ben are arranging to meet.
> Ben: Can you be ready by 8.30?
> Zoe: No, not by then. By the time I've had a bath it'll be quarter to nine. I could be ready by nine though.

Step 1 | *By, by the time*

- *By* here is a preposition of time. It means 'not later than'.
  *Can you be ready **by** 8.30?* (= Can you be ready at 8.30 or before, but not later?)
  *I could be ready **by** nine.* (= at 9 o'clock or earlier, but not later)
  By is usually followed by a time or date (*5.15, June 1st*, etc.)

- *By the time (that)* is a linking phrase. It's always followed by a verb.
  ***By the time** I've had a bath it'll be quarter to nine.*
  (= not later than the moment she finishes her bath)

CHECK QUESTIONS 1   **Put in *by* or *by the time*.**
1 I can't be ready ... 8.30.   2 But we must be there ... 9.
3 ... we've finished this phone call it'll be 7 o'clock.

Step 2 | *Till/Until*

> Ben arrived at 8.55. But he had to wait until Zoe was ready, until 9.15.
> Zoe: I'm sorry I'm late. I had to work till 7.15 and we didn't eat till 8 o'clock. Then I had to wait till my sister had finished in the bathroom. And by then it was quarter to nine ...

- We use *till* or *until* when we talk about an activity or a situation which continues and then stops at a particular time.
  *I had to work **till** 7.15.* (= She was working before 7.15 and stopped at 7.15.)
  *Ben had to wait **until** 9.15.* (= He was waiting before 9.15 and stopped at 9.15.)

- *Till* is short for *until*. *Till* is more common in informal English.

- *Until* and *till* can be link words or prepositions.
  *He had to wait **until Zoe was ready**.* (link word + a clause)
  *We didn't eat **till 8 o'clock**.* (preposition)

- *By* = not later than that time. *Until* = up to that time.
  *Zoe wasn't ready **by** nine.* (= She wasn't ready at or before 9.)
  *Zoe wasn't ready **till** 9.15.* (= She was ready at 9.15 but not before.)

CHECK QUESTIONS 2   **Put in *by*, *by the time* or *till/until*.**
1 I didn't get home ... 7.45.   2 My sister was in the bathroom ... 8.45.
3 ... we'd had dinner, it was 8.30.   4 I've got to be home ... 12.

ANSWERS TO
CHECK QUESTIONS
1 AND 2

1   1 by   2 by   3 By the time
2   1 till/until   2 till/until   3 By the time   4 by

Practice

- *By* + time/date, etc. = at or 'not later than'.
  I'll be home by 11 o'clock.
- *By the time (that)* + verb = at or 'not later than the time something happens'.
  I'll be home by the time you arrive.
- *Till/until* + a time or event = an activity or situation continues and then stops at that time.
  I worked till 6.30.   We waited till the bus came.

---

1 **Helen Fisher is speaking to a travel agent. Complete the dialogue, using *by*, *by the time* or *until/till*.**

Helen Fisher: I must be in Los Angeles

(1) .... 3 o'clock on Thursday afternoon.

Travel Agent: There's an 11.00 flight from Heathrow but it doesn't get into LA

(2) .... 3.15. Is that too late?

Helen Fisher: Yes, I'm afraid it is. My meeting will have started (3) .... I arrive.

Travel agent: There's an earlier flight at 9.55. That would get you to LA (4) .... 2.20.

Helen Fisher: That's fine. And 9.55 isn't too early in the morning.

Travel agent: But don't forget you must be at the airport (5) .... 7.55.

Helen Fisher: 2 hours before?! That means I'd have to leave home (6) .... 6.00 at the latest if I'm going to drive to the airport. I reckon if I get there (7) .... 8.45, I'll have plenty of time.

Travel agent: But (8) .... you've parked and got a bus to the terminal, the plane might have left.

Helen Fisher: But if I get there at 7.55, I'll have to wait for ages (9) .... my flight's called.

Travel agent: And if you miss your flight, you may have to wait (10) .... the next day for another flight!

Helen Fisher: OK then. I'll stay in bed

(11) .... 6.00 and leave home

(12) .... 6.30. Then I'll be at the airport (13) .... 7.30.

2 **Complete this newspaper report, using *by*, *by the time* or *till/until*.**

TWO KILLED IN LATE NIGHT CRASH

Two men lay unconscious in the road last night (1) .... a motorist found them at 11.00. (2) .... the motorist had telephoned for an ambulance, it was 11.15. They promised that an ambulance would be at the scene of the accident (3) .... 11.30 at the latest. The motorist said he would stay with the injured men (4) .... the ambulance arrived. In fact the ambulance didn't get there (5) .... 11.50. And (6) .... it arrived, one man was dead. The other man was also dead (7) .... the ambulance got him to hospital.

---

3 **Some people are giving their opinions about the future. Complete the sentences, using *by*, *by the time* or *till/until*.**

1 I think we'll be able to cross the Atlantic in less than two hours .... the year 2020.

2 They'll have found a cure for cancer .... the middle of the 21st century.

3 .... I go to bed tonight 2,000 more children will have died of starvation.

4 We won't solve the problem of famine .... we've stopped the world's population growing.

5 .... my children are 50 there'll probably be cities on the Moon.

6 Pollution in the cities will get worse .... they develop an electric car that really works.

Sue goes out to work all day. Then she comes home to her family and has to start work again.
'It's like this every day. I work like a slave at the factory and then I come home and the house is like a pig-sty. Other women like me come home and the dinner's cooked and the house is tidy. I wanted to be something exciting, like an air-hostess. But I just do boring things, like making beds and feeding the family. It's like having two full-time jobs, but this one's unpaid!'

Step 1 | *Like*

- Note the two meanings of the preposition *like*:

A We use *like* when we compare one thing or person with another. *Like* usually means 'similar to' or 'in the same way as'.

  *The house is **like** a pig-sty.* (NOT as a pig-sty)
  *I work **like** a slave.* (NOT as a slave)

B *Like* can also be used when we mean 'for example'.

  *I just do boring things, **like** making beds.* (NOT as making)
  *I wanted to be something exciting, **like** an air-hostess.*

- *Like* is a preposition. We use it before a noun, a pronoun or the *-ing* form of a verb.

  *I work **like a slave**.* (*like* + noun)
  *other women **like me*** (*like* + an object pronoun)
  *It's **like this** every day.* (*like* + a demonstrative)
  *It's **like having** two jobs.* (*like* + the *-ing* form of a verb)

CHECK QUESTIONS 1 ▷ **Find examples in the text of *like*. Which have meaning A and which have meaning B?**

Step 2 | *As* and *as if/as though*

Sue's angry again. 'Darren! Your clothes are all over the floor again, just as I expected. Now, do as I say! Put them away! Jessie, I'm not your servant. Will you please tidy your room! You all act as if you're guests in a hotel. And you treat me as though I was a hotel maid! As my friend Meg said, I do far too much for you.'

- We use *as* (= 'in the same way') before a subject + a verb. We don't normally use *like* here. (But see the note on informal English and American English below.)

  *Do **as I say**!* (NOT Do like I say.)
  *Your clothes are all over the floor again, just **as I expected**.*

- *As if* and *as though* both mean the same. We use them before a subject + a verb to say that two things are similar.

  *You act **as if** (OR **as though**) you're guests in a hotel.*

- We sometimes use a past tense form after *as if/as though* when we're talking about the present:

  *You treat me as though I **was** (OR were) a hotel maid.*

  We use the past tense form (*was*) here to show how unreal the idea is. (Sue isn't a hotel maid.) We can also use *were* to emphasise this unreality.

- But if the speaker thinks that something is real, he or she can use the present tense.

  *You act as if you**'re** guests in a hotel.*

  (Sue really thinks they behave like guests at a hotel!)

- In informal English, we often use *like* instead of *as, as if/as though*. *Like* is often used here in American English too.

  ***like** my friend Meg said* (= As my friend Meg said)

  *You all act **like** you're guests in a hotel.* (= as if you're guests)

- We often use *as if/as though* with a verb of perception (*look, feel, seem*, etc.) See Unit 33.

CHECK QUESTIONS 2 **Put in *as* or *as if*.**
1 Sue wants Darren to do ... she says.
2 Jessie acts ... her mother is her servant.
3 They treat the house ... it's a hotel.

Step 3 | *Like* or *as*?

> Sue works as a machinist during the day. In the evenings and at weekends she works as a mother and a housekeeper. She says she works like a slave, and her family treat the house like a hotel. When she has time she reads romantic novels. She uses them as an escape from reality.

- *As* can be used as a preposition followed by a noun. But it doesn't have the same meaning as *like* + a noun. We use *as* to say what someone or something really is. We use *like* to compare things or people:

  *During the day she works **as** a machinist.* (She is a machinist.)

  *Her family treat the house **like** a hotel.* (The house isn't a hotel.)

- We also use *as* when we talk about the role or function of something.

  *She uses them **as** an escape from reality.*

CHECK QUESTIONS 3 **Put in *like* or *as*.**
1 Is their house a hotel? No, but they treat it ... a hotel.
2 Sue works in a factory ... a machinist.

ANSWERS TO
CHECK QUESTIONS
1, 2 AND 3

1 Meaning A: It's like this. I work like a slave. The house is like a pig-sty. Other women like me. It's like having two full-time jobs.
Meaning B: like an air-hostess. like making beds.

2 1 as 2 as if 3 as if
3 1 like 2 as

Practice

> Like + a noun/pronoun/-ing form He drinks **like** a fish. It's **like being** on holiday.
> As + a subject + a verb OR + a noun **As** I thought, she can't come. He works **as** a barman.
> As if/as though + a subject + a verb You talk to me **as if** I was a child.

---

1 **Complete the text with *like* or *as*.**

Katie Fox works part-time (1) .... a hotel receptionist. But she looks (2) .... a model. And in fact she works (3) .... a model for a small cosmetics firm once or twice a month. They sell things (4) .... lipstick, mascara and eye-liner. It isn't a really glamorous job, (5) .... being a model for Yves Saint-Laurent. But, as the man who acts (6) .... her agent often tells her, you have to start somewhere. And (7) .... a model she earns more in a day than she earns in a week (8) .... a hotel receptionist.

2 **The people who work in this office have got a new manager and they do not like him. Complete the sentences with *as if/as though* + a subject + *was/were*.**
Example: *He behaves as though he was/were the owner of the company.* OR *He behaves as if he was/were the owner of the company.*

1 When he talks, he shouts .... we .... all in the next room.

2 He acts .... we .... all his servants.

3 He talks to us .... we .... children.

4 He talks .... he .... an expert on everything.

5 He makes decisions .... he .... the only person in the company.

3 **Complete the dialogue with *like* or *as*.**

Rachel Bryson works (1) .... a freelance journalist, but she's just had her first baby. She's talking to her friend Anna.

'People say he looks (2) .... his mother.'

'No. I think he looks (3) .... his father.'

'It's changed my life completely, just (4) .... everybody said it would. But (5) .... a fool, I didn't believe them. I just don't have time to do anything. When the baby's asleep I can do a few jobs, (6) .... the washing-up. But (7) .... my mum says, your life is never the same again.'

4 **Matthew is 17. He has just passed his driving test. Complete the dialogue between Matthew and his father with *as* or *like* or *as if/as though*.**

'Can I borrow the car, dad?'

'No. It's dark and it's raining. It's not (1) .... driving on a dry road in daylight.'

'You talk (2) .... I was still a learner. I'm not. I've passed my test.'

'But, (3) .... your driving teacher said, you've still got a lot to learn. And I'm sure you drive (4) .... a Formula 1 driver when I'm not in the car.'

'No, I don't. I drive (5) .... you – slowly and carefully!'

'I'm sorry, Matthew, but, (6) .... I said before, the answer's "no".'

'Why do you still treat me (7) .... a child? I'm 17.'

'Well, you should behave a bit more (8) .... an adult. Why don't you pay for something occasionally, (9) .... a few litres of petrol?'

'Because I spend my money on more important things.'

'(10) .... what?'

'(11) .... clothes and things. Oh, let me take the car, dad. It's not (12) .... I borrow it every evening.'

'Oh, all right.'

Although, though, even though
In spite of Because, since, so

Although Britain isn't a very important country, the English language is very important all over the world. Nearly 400 million people speak English as their first language. English isn't the most widely used language in the world though. Mandarin (Northern Chinese) is spoken by 580 million people. But, in spite of being the most widely-used language, it isn't spoken by many people outside China. Even though there are about 800,000 words in English, many English speakers only use about 5,000. Learning a foreign language is difficult, but, in spite of the difficulty, more and more people are starting to learn English every year. They can try to learn 800,000 words if they want to, though they only need to know about 2,000 to speak English quite well!

Step 1 | *Although, though, even though* and *in spite of*

- We use the link words *although, though, even though* to join two parts of a sentence. We use them to contrast two statements.
  Although Britain isn't a very important country, the English language is very important all over the world.
  (Contrast: Britain isn't important BUT the English language is.)

- We use *even though* when the contrast is particularly strong.
  Even though there are about 800,000 words in English, many English speakers only use about 5,000.
  (big contrast: 800,000 > 5,000)

- We can use *though* instead of *although*.
  They can try to learn 800,000 words, though they only need to know about 2,000.

- We can use *though* (NOT *although*) at the end of a sentence.
  It isn't the most widely-used language in the world though.
  (= But it isn't the most widely-used language in the world.)

- *In spite of* is usually followed by a noun, a pronoun or the *-ing* form of a verb.
  In spite of the difficulty, more and more people are starting to learn English every year.
  (= although it's difficult, more and more people ...)
  In spite of being the most widely used language, it isn't spoken by many people outside China.
  (= although it's the most widely-used language)

- We can also use the expression *in spite of the fact that*.
  In spite of the fact that it's the most widely used language, it isn't spoken by many people outside China.

CHECK QUESTIONS 1 ▷ **Rewrite the sentences using *although* and *though*.**
1 In spite of the fact that I'm not very good at languages, I want to learn English.
2 English isn't easy to learn, in spite of being a very useful language. English isn't ...
3 But thousands of people learn it. Thousands ...

Step 2 | *Because, since* and *so*

> Many people from Europe and South America go to the USA because they need to do business there. And, since they have to speak to Americans, they have to learn English.
> English is important because it's the language of business and science. As 75% of all business letters in the world are written in English, it's easy to see why business people want to learn it.
> English is used for air and sea communications, so airline pilots and ships' officers have to learn it too.
> But the importance of English is a problem for many British and American people. They think everybody in the world should speak English, so they refuse to learn any foreign languages!

- We use the link words *because, since* and *as* when we want to say why we do something or why something happens.
  We normally use *because* to give the reason, and the *because* clause usually comes at the end.
  We normally use *since* and *as* when the reason is already known. *Since* and *as* mean the same.
  > *Many people from Europe and South America go to the USA **because** they need to do business there.*
  > *And **since** (OR **as**) they have to speak to Americans, they have to learn English.*
- We use the link word *so* to talk about the result of an action or situation.
  > *They think everybody in the world should speak English, **so** they refuse to learn any foreign languages!*

(For other link words see Units 40, 87 and 88.)

CHECK QUESTIONS 2 **Make single sentences, using *because, since* or *so*.**
1 Air communications are in English. Airline pilots must learn it.
2 Many people in Europe want to work abroad. They have to learn a foreign language.
3 Many British and American people won't learn foreign languages. They think everybody should speak English.

---

1 1 Although I'm not very good at languages, I want to learn English. 2 English isn't easy to learn although/though it's a very useful language. 3 Thousands of people learn it though.

2 1 Since/As air communications are in English, airline pilots must learn it. OR Air communications are in English, so airline pilots must learn it. 2 Many people in Europe want to work abroad, so they have to learn a foreign language. 3 Many British and American people won't learn foreign languages because they think everybody should speak English.

Practice

> I went to the concert, **although/though** I didn't have a ticket.   I went **in spite of** the bad weather.
> I didn't want Joe to come. He came **though**.   I went **in spite of feeling** ill.
> I went out **even though** I was feeling ill.   I went **in spite of the fact that** I was ill.
> **Since/As** I couldn't get a ticket I came home.   I went to bed **because** I wasn't feeling well.
> I was feeling terrible, **so** I phoned the doctor.

1 This evening Andy Pole is tired and bored. Make single sentences. Choose a second clause from the list and use *although* to join the two clauses:
he'd already had one in the morning
there was nothing interesting on
he didn't want to read
he usually goes to bed at 11 p.m.

1 He picked up a book

....

2 He switched on the television

....

3 He had a bath

....

4 ....

.... he went to bed at 9.30 p.m.

2 Complete the sentences, using *although* or (where it seems better) *even though*.

(1) .... I really dislike Michael Bates, I always smile at him and say 'Hello'. He was on the bus yesterday, (2) .... he usually walks to college. I smiled at him, but (3) .... he looked straight at me, he didn't smile back. (4) .... I'm not a nervous person, I felt a bit worried when he sat behind me. (5) .... I could hear him breathing I couldn't see him. I suddenly stood up. (6) .... the bus was moving quite fast, I jumped off and walked the rest of the way to college. I'll have to catch the same bus tomorrow (7) .... Michael Bates will probably be on it again.

3 Rewrite the sentences, using *in spite of* + (*not*) *-ing*.

1 Although he's 90, Jim Lake is still active.

....

2 He still does his own shopping although he lives a long way from the shops.

....

....

3 He still goes to watch his football team although he can't see very well.

....

....

4 Make sentences about people's hobbies with *though* at the end.
Example: Sebastian plays the cello. (not be/in an orchestra). *He's not in an orchestra though.*

1 Jay doesn't like playing sport. (be/a good chess player)

....

2 Tariq keeps snakes. (not like/spiders)

....

3 Beth collects stamps. (not have/valuable ones)

....

5 Complete the text with *because, since* or *so*.
Bryn Wallis was hungry (1) .... he went into a café. They didn't have any hot-dogs (2) .... he had a cheeseburger. He hadn't had anything to eat that day (3) .... he'd had a lot of work to do, and he knew he wouldn't have time for dinner (4) .... he was going to the cinema at 7 p.m. (5) .... he was going to miss his dinner, he decided to have a second cheeseburger. Now he was thirsty, (6) .... he ordered a large milk-shake. It was now 6 p.m., (7) .... he left the café to catch his bus. As he got onto the bus, he heard a shout. The owner of the café was running after him (8) .... he'd forgotten to pay.

Bernard Thomas is from Cariacou, a small island which is part of the West Indies. He's come to Britain to live with a cousin who's got a house in Leeds. His cousin's telling him about the people who live in his street.
'You must meet Betty.'
'Who's Betty?'
'She's the one who looks like Margaret Thatcher.'
'Who's Margaret Thatcher?'
'She's the woman who was Prime Minister in the 80s. Betty's very patriotic. She's got a doorbell which plays the National Anthem when you press it! And then there's Tom Marchant.'
'Who's Tom Marchant?'
'He's the guy that used to play football for Manchester United. He's the one who lives at number 23, the house that's painted red and white.'

Step 1 | *Who/that* for people *Which/that* for things

- *He's come to live with a cousin **who's got a flat in Leeds**.*
who's got a flat in Leeds is a relative clause. A relative clause identifies a person or a thing. The clause *who's got a flat in Leeds* identifies the cousin.

- We use the relative pronoun *who* for people, and *which* for things.
***She's the one who** looks like Margaret Thatcher.*
***a doorbell which** plays the National Anthem*

- BUT we often use *that* instead of *who* and *which*.
***She's the one that** looks like Margaret Thatcher.*
***a doorbell that** plays the National Anthem*
*He's the guy **that** (OR **who**) used to play football for Manchester United.*
*the house **that's** (OR **which is**) painted red and white*
With people, we use *who* more often than *that*.
With things we use *that* more often than *which*.
Note: Sometimes we must use *who* and *which*, not *that*. (See Unit 93 Step 1.)

CHECK QUESTIONS 1 **Put in a relative pronoun.**
1 Bernard's the man ... has just arrived from Cariacou.
2 Cariacou's an island ... is north of the South American coast.
3 Bernard's got a brother ... lives in Leeds.
4 His brother lives in a house ... was built in the 1920s.

Step 2 | *Who, which, that* as objects, and *whom*

Bernard's cousin Irvin has lived in England for fifteen years.
'I like the job that I've got. I can live quite well on the money I earn. The people who I know at work are very friendly. I'd like to get married, but most of the women I meet have already got a husband! I really liked a girl I met in a pub the other day, but she was married. There's one thing which I don't like in England. The weather! I miss the Caribbean sun.'

- *Who, which, that* can be the subject of the relative clause.
  *She's the woman **who** was Prime Minister.* (She was Prime Minister.)
  We can't leave out *who, which, that* here.

- *Who, which, that* can also be the object of the relative clause.
  *I like the job **that** I've got.* (I've got *the job*.)
  *The people **who** I know at work are very friendly.* (I know *the people*.)
  *There's one thing **which** I don't like in England.* (I don't like *one thing*.)
  When *who, which, that* are the object, we can leave them out. We usually leave them out in informal spoken English. We prefer to say:
  I like the job I've got. The people I know at work are friendly.
  There's one thing I don't like in England.

- We can use *whom* when the object is a person.
  *The people **whom** I know at work are very friendly.*
  But *whom* is very formal and rarely used in conversation. We usually leave out the pronoun, or we use *who* instead.
  the people (who) I know

CHECK QUESTIONS 2 **Which relative pronouns are left out?**
1 The women Irvin meets are usually married.
2 The thing Irvin misses is the Caribbean sun.

Step 3 | Prepositions in relative clauses: *The man I spoke to.*

> Irvin's making plans for Bernard. 'I'll take you to the club I go to. And you must meet the friends I play football with. We must find you a job too. The company I work for is looking for a truck driver. I'll ask Gary Miller about it. He's the man I spoke to last night in the club. We could ask Tom Marchant too. You know, the man I told you about. He owns a sports shop. He might have a job you can apply for.'

- When we use verbs followed by a preposition, the preposition usually comes at the end of a relative clause.

(I go to a club.)	*I'll take you to the club I go **to**.*
(I play football with friends.)	*You must meet the friends I play football **with**.*
(I work for a company.)	*The company I work **for**.*

- In very formal English we can put the preposition before *whom* or *which*.
  *He's the man **to whom** I spoke last night in the club.*
  *He might have a job **for which** you can apply.*
  But in conversation we prefer to say:
  *He's the man **I spoke to** last night in the club.*
  *He might have a job **you can apply for**.*

CHECK QUESTIONS 3 **Make relative clauses ending with a preposition.**
1 (Irvin works for a company.) Britex is the company ...
2 (They're looking for a truck driver.) Bernard might be the man ...

ANSWERS TO
CHECK QUESTIONS
1, 2 AND 3

1 1 who (preferable to *that*) 2 that/which
3 who (preferable to *that*) 4 that/which
2 1 that/who   2 that/which

3 1 Britex is the company he works for.
2 Bernard might be the man they're looking for.

Practice

- We use *who* for people: *I'm the person* **who** *phoned you.*
  And *which* for things: *Is this the bus* **which** *goes to the town centre?*
  We often use *that* for both *who* and *which*.
  I'm the person **that** *phoned you. Is this the bus* **that** *goes to the town centre?*
- *Who, that, which* are usually left out when they are the object of the relative clause.
  *He's the man (***that/who***) I saw at the station.   These are the photos (***that/which***) I took on holiday.*
- A preposition comes at the end of the relative clause: (*I go to church.*) *This is the church I go to.*

---

1 **Look at the information and write sentences with *who*. Use the information given.**
Example: Albert Einstein (scientist). *He was the scientist who created the theory of relativity.*

- He helped to make India independent from Britain.   • He conquered the Inca Empire of Peru in 1532.   • She discovered radium.
- He painted the roof of the Sistine Chapel in Rome.

1 Leonardo da Vinci. (artist)

....

....

2 Gandhi (Indian leader)

....

....

3 Marie Curie (scientist)

....

....

4 Francisco Pizarro (soldier)

....

....

2 **Complete the text, using *who, which* or *that* and put – if no relative pronoun is necessary.**

The film (1) .... I saw last night wasn't very good. It was about a woman (2) .... could see into the future. Her name was Petra. She lived in a house (3) .... was full of strange objects – pieces of rock (4) .... came from the Moon, dinosaur bones (5) .... she'd found in the Arizona desert and beautiful pieces of crystal (6) .... had been found in the Andes. The people (7) .... came to see her wanted to know about their future. One day a young man (8) .... felt he had no future came to see her. He was the kind of man (9) .... Petra found very attractive. The things (10) .... she told him really surprised him. She said he was going to get married in two months' time. Marriage was something (11) .... he'd never wanted. She said the woman (12) .... he would marry was beautiful and intelligent. He was mystified and came to see Petra every day. He really enjoyed the time (13) .... he spent with her. He realised that she was the only woman (14) .... could make him happy. After two months they got married! What a surprise!

3 **Mark is showing his friends the video of a holiday he had in India. Make sentences, using a relative clause.**
Example: I went with this girl. *This is the girl I went with.*

1 We stayed with this family in Bombay.

....

2 We went on this train to Goa.

....

3 We stayed at this hotel in Goa.

....

4 We sat on this beach every day.

....

5 We ate at this restaurant every evening.

....

6 I had a ride on this elephant.

....

7 We spent a lot of time with these Indian friends.

....

8 We flew back on this plane.

....

92

The relative pronouns *where, whose, what*

Helen Gore's 17. She's left school but she hasn't got a job. She's bored. 'The town where I live hasn't got anything for young people. We need a club where we can go and meet friends. Somewhere where we can play music and have a drink. It's boring here. I want to leave. I want to go where I can get a job. I want to live where I can have more fun.'

Step 1 | *Where* in relative clauses

- We use the relative pronoun *where* to describe places:
  *the town **where** I live* ('where I live' describes the town)
  *We need a club **where** we can go and meet friends.*

- We can also use *where* without identifying the place it describes.
  *I want to go **where** I can get a job.*
  *I want to live **where** I can have more fun.*
  Here, *where* = to a place/in a place where.

- Sometimes we can leave out *where* and add a preposition to the verb.
  *the town **where** I live* OR *the town I live **in***

CHECK QUESTIONS 1 · **Rewrite the sentences, using *where*.**
1 The town *Helen lives in* is boring.
2 She wants to be *in a place where* it's possible to find a job.

Step 2 | *Whose* in relative clauses

'I don't like living in a town where people are always talking about their neighbours. When they see someone in the street they say: 'She's the woman whose husband ran off with the doctor's wife. He's the man whose daughter the police arrested for selling drugs. He lives in the house whose curtains are always drawn. He's the owner of a company whose workers are very badly paid, and so on and so on.' They're only interested in other people's lives.'

- We often use the possessive word *whose* in relative clauses. It's always followed by a noun. It can be the subject or object of the verb. It can't be left out.
  *the woman **whose husband** ran off with the doctor's wife*
  (Subject: **Her husband** ran off with the doctor's wife.)
  *the man **whose daughter** the police arrested* (Object: The police arrested **her**.)

- We use *whose* mostly for people.
  *the man **whose** daughter the police arrested*
  But it can also be used for things.
  *the house **whose** curtains are always drawn*
  *a company **whose** workers are very badly paid*

- Don't confuse: *whose* and *who's* (=*who is* or *who has*)
  *That's the man **who's** (= who is) the manager of the supermarket.*

Make a single sentence, using *whose*.
1 She's the woman. Her dog attacked the postman.
2 He's the man. I saw his young son drinking whisky in the pub.
3 She owns the house. Its garden looks like a jungle.

Step 3 | *What* in relative clauses

'This town's dead. That's what I think. And that's what worries me. I'm going to leave soon. I can't find what I want here. What I'd really like to do is live in London. I can do everything I want there. But I haven't got enough money. What I need is a job. But what's difficult is finding one.'

- The relative pronoun *what* means 'the thing(s) that'. It can be used as the subject or object of a verb.
   *I can't find **what** I want here.* (Object = the things that I want)
   *that's **what** worries me* (Subject: = the thing that worries me)

- We can start a sentence with *what* if we want to emphasise something.
   ***What** I'd really like to do is live in London.*
   (= I'd like to live in London. That's the important thing.)
   ***What** I need is a job.* (= I need a job. That's the important thing.)
   ***What**'s difficult is finding a job.* (= Finding a job is the most difficult thing.)

- Note that we don't use *what* after *everything* and *all*. (See Unit 61 Step 1.)
   *I can do **everything I want** there.*
   (NOT *everything what I want*)

Rewrite the sentences, using *what*.
1 The town can't give her the things she needs.
2 The thing she wants to do is go to London.
3 The thing that's difficult is that she hasn't got enough money.

---

1 1 The town where Helen lives is boring.
2 She wants to be where it's easy to find a job.
2 1 She's the woman whose dog attacked the postman. 2 He's the man whose young son I saw drinking whisky in the pub. 3 She owns the house whose garden looks like a jungle.

3 1 The town can't give her what she needs.
2 What she wants to do is go to London.
3 What's difficult is that she hasn't got enough money.

Practice

> • *This is the house **where** I used to live.* (= the house in which I used to live)
> *This is **where** I used to live.* (= the place where I used to live)
> • *That's the girl **whose** brother plays in a rock band.* (Her brother plays in a rock band.)
> *That's the girl **whose** brother I know.* (I know her brother.)
> *This is the country **whose** population is growing the fastest.* (Its population is growing the fastest.)
> • *What = 'the thing(s) that'*
> *Nobody saw **what** happened.   I don't like **what** he said.   **What** you need is a holiday.*

1 Peter Rigg is showing his son round the village he used to live in when he was young. Rewrite the sentences, using *where*.
Example: I lived in this house for fifteen years.
This is the house where I lived for fifteen years.

1 I used to play football in this field.

....

2 I worked in this shop for two years.

....

3 We used to play tennis here.

....

4 My old friend Tom lived in this house.

....

5 I learnt to swim in this river.

....

....

2 Alan Owen is reading the local newspaper. He is asking his wife who certain people are. Give her answers, using *whose*.

Mike Rowe's got a sister who works for the UN.
Jane Bell's mother won $100,000 in the Lottery.
Nicky Bland's house was burnt down last week.
The Owens met Anna Thorpe's brother at the cinema last night.
They went to Jack Birch's 50th birthday party two years ago.

Example: Who's Mike Rowe? *He's the man whose sister works for the UN.*

1 Who's Jane Bell? She's the girl ....

....

2 Who's Nicky Bland? He's the man ....

....

3 Who's Anna Thorpe? She's the woman ....

....

4 Who's Jack Birch? He's the one ....

....

3 A detective is interviewing Mark Knott about a crime that took place on Thursday evening. Complete the sentences, using *what* or *that* or – if no word is necessary.

Detective: Tell me again (1) .... happened on Thursday.

Mark: I've told you everything (2) .... I know. I was at home all day.

Detective: That isn't (3) .... you said a moment ago.

Mark: Well, I stayed in the house all evening. That's all (4) .... I can say. I can tell you (5) .... I watched on television. I can describe all the programmes (6) .... I watched.

Detective: But you can't prove it, can you? Listen! We simply want the truth.

4 Here are the views of three different people on politics in Britain. Rewrite the sentences, using *What* at the beginning to give more emphasis to what they say.
Example: This country needs a new government.
What this country needs is a new government!

1 I'd like to see more women in Parliament.

....

....

2 It annoys me that rich people don't pay enough tax.

....

....

3 It surprises me that people don't complain more.

....

....

Defining and non-defining relative clauses

Jack Rimmer and his wife are looking at the boats in the marina at Portsmouth.

'Look! That's the man who's planning to sail round the world. And that's the boat he built himself, the one that's painted red and white. And the other man must be the man he's going with.'

Later that evening they heard this report on the local radio:

'Our reporter was at the marina this morning. He met 75-year-old Alan Weeks, who's planning to sail round the world. He also spoke to 73-year-old Gerry Banks, who Alan's going with. Alan's boat, which he built himself, is called *Morning Star*. *Morning Star*, which took Alan five years to build, is a 15-metre catamaran ...'

Step 1 | Non-defining relative clauses

● There are two types of relative clause, defining (or identifying) and non-defining.

Defining:

*That's the man **who's planning to sail round the world**.*

Here, the relative clause identifies 'the man'. It tells us which man the speaker's talking about.

Non-defining:

*He met 75-year-old Alan Weeks, **who's planning to sail round the world**.*

Here, the man is already identified ('75-year-old Alan Weeks') so the relative clause doesn't identify him. It simply gives us extra information about him.

● Note that in written English we put a comma (,) before a non-defining relative clause. If it's in the middle of a sentence we put a comma after it as well.

*'Morning Star', **which took Alan five years to build**, is a 15-metre catamaran.*

We don't put a comma before a defining relative clause.

That's the man who's planning to sail round the world.

● In defining relative clauses we can leave out *who, which* and *that* when they're objects. (See Unit 91.)

the man he's going with

(= the man who (OR that) he's going with)

the boat he built himself

(= the boat that (OR which) he built himself.)

But in non-defining relative clauses we can't leave out *who* and *which*.

*He spoke to Gerry Banks, **who** Alan's going with.*

*Alan's boat, **which** he built himself, is called 'Morning Star'.*

● We don't use *that* in non-defining relative clauses. We can't say: Alan's boat, that he built himself, is called 'Morning Star'.

CHECK QUESTIONS 1

Put commas (,) where necessary.

1 Jack Rimmer saw the man who's going to sail round the world.
2 Alan Weeks is sailing with Gerry Banks who's a friend of his.
3 The boat that he built is called 'Morning Star'.
4 He's sailing from Portsmouth which is on the south coast of England.

Step 2 | *Where/whose/which* in non-defining relative clauses

> The news report continued:
> 'Alan and Gerry, whose lifelong ambition has been to sail round the world, leave tomorrow. By this time next year they hope to be back in Portsmouth, where they're sure to receive a hero's welcome. Their trip is sponsored by Barclay's Bank, who Alan used to work for. The bank have sent Alan a card, which they've written a good luck message on. Alan and Gerry are going to be away for a long time, which will be difficult for their families. But Marjory Weeks, Alan's wife, said last night: "They're both doing something they've always wanted to do, which is marvellous." '

- We can also use *where* and *whose* in non-defining relative clauses .
  *Alan and Gerry, **whose lifelong ambition has been to sail round the world**, leave tomorrow.*
  *By this time next year they hope to be back in Portsmouth, **where they're sure to receive a hero's welcome**.*

- In formal English we can use *whom* and *which* after a preposition in a non-defining relative clause.
  *Their trip is sponsored by Barclay's Bank, **for whom** Alan used to work.*
  *The bank have sent a card, **on which** they've written a message.*
  But in informal English we normally say:
  *Their trip is sponsored by Barclay's Bank, **who** Alan used to work **for**.*
  *The bank have sent a card, **which** they've written a message **on**.*

- *Which* can refer to a whole clause.
  *They're going to be away for a long time, **which** will be difficult for their families.*
  *They're both doing something they've always wanted to do, **which** is marvellous.*
  Note: We use *which* here, NOT *what*.

CHECK QUESTIONS 2 **Make single sentences, using relative clauses.**
1 That's Alan Weeks. I spoke to him this morning.
2 That's his boat 'Morning Star'. He's going to sail round the world on it.
3 The two men are over 70. This is amazing.

ANSWERS TO CHECK QUESTIONS 1 AND 2

1 1 Jack Rimmer saw the man who's going to sail round the world. 2 Alan Weeks is sailing with Gerry Banks, who's a friend of his. 3 The boat that he built is called 'Morning Star'. 4 He's sailing from Portsmouth, which is on the south coast of England.

2 1 That's Alan Weeks, who I spoke to this morning. OR (formal) That's Alan Weeks, to whom I spoke this morning. 2 That's his boat *Morning Star*, which he's going to sail round the world on. OR (formal) That's his boat *Morning Star*, on which he's going to sail round the world. 3 The two men are over 70, which is amazing.

Practice

- Defining relative clause: *He's the man who looks like the Prime Minister.*
- Non-defining relative clause: *That's my friend Tony, who looks like the Prime Minister.*
- We must use *who, which, whose, where* in non-identifying relative clauses. We can't leave out *who* or *which*. We can't use *that.*
- We use commas (,) with non-identifying relative clauses.
- *Which* (NOT *what*) can refer to a whole clause: *He hasn't eaten anything today, which is worrying.*

---

1 Make complete sentences, using the sentences in brackets as non-identifying relative clauses. Put commas (,) where necessary.

George Thompson (1 He lives on a boat on the River Thames.) is 100 years old today. He keeps his boat at Richmond. (2 It's on a very beautiful part of the river.) George (3 His wife died ten years ago.) lives alone with two dogs and a cat. But he's got a lot of friends in Richmond. (4 They look after him well.) His boat (5 It was built in the 1920s.) is a very comfortable home. Every day he walks into Richmond. (6 He does his shopping and meets his friends there.) Today he's having a big birthday party. (7 All his friends and family are coming to it.)

1 *George Thompson, who lives on a boat on the River Thames, is 100 years old today.*

2 ....
....

3 ....
....

4 ....
....

5 ....
....

6 ....
....

7 ....
....

2 Write *Defining* or *Non-defining* after the relative clauses. Add commas (,) where necessary.

'I know that girl. Look! The one who's standing at the bar.' (1) ....

'Yes, it's Melanie Rigg who sings with "The Machine".' (2) ....

'Do you mean the rock group that was on television last night?' (3) ....

'Yes. She lives in Henley which is about two miles from here. (4) .... She's got a house that was built in the sixteenth century. (5) .... She's got her own recording studio which is in the garden. (6) .... She's also got a house in California where she spends six months of the year.' (7) ....

'Who's the guy she's talking to?' (8) ....

'That's Gary Trench whose brother's the drummer with "The Machine".' (9) ....

'Have you got a piece of paper I can write on? (10) .... I'm going to get her autograph.'

3 Choose items from the list and make single sentences, using the relative pronoun *which.* Don't forget the comma (,).
● *This was 20 minutes after the beginning of the match.* ● *This meant I arrived late.* ● *He refused to do it.* ● *This took me another ten minutes.* ● *He wasn't allowed to do it.* ● *That was very expensive.* ● *That made me very angry.*

1 I paid £50 for a ticket for the match.
I paid £50 for a ticket for the match, which was very expensive.
2 When I left home there were traffic jams everywhere
....
3 When I arrived, I found a man sitting in my seat
....
4 He didn't want to move
....
5 I asked him to show me his ticket
....
6 I went to find a policeman.
....
7 I finally sat down at 3 o'clock
....

> A woman coming out of the Midland Bank in Tonbridge High Street was attacked this morning by two people carrying knives. Mrs Amy Hyde of Church Street, Tonbridge lost a handbag containing £35 in the attack. There were several people walking past the bank at the time. A man selling newspapers tried to help Mrs Hyde, but the attackers stabbed him repeatedly before escaping in a car waiting at the end of the street. The man injured in the attack has since died in hospital. A knife found on the pavement is thought to be the weapon used in the attack. There was a price ticket attached to the knife.
>
> The police are looking for a man in his 20s with jeans and a baseball cap, and a young woman with long blond hair and a silver ring in her nose. They were driving a blue Ford Escort with a broken side window. Anyone who saw the incident should contact the police on 0371 668453.

Step 1 | *-ing* clauses

- We can use a clause with the *-ing* form of a verb to say what someone or something is doing or was doing.

    *A woman **coming out** of the Midland Bank*
    (= who was coming out)
    *She was attacked by two people **carrying** knives.*
    (= who were carrying)

    We can also use it to describe a situation that exists or existed.

    *a handbag **containing** £35* (= that contained)

    The *-ing* form is often used with *There is/are/was/were*.

    ***There were** several people **walking** past the bank at the time.*

- Note that these clauses are similar to relative clauses, but we must use a full relative clause for a completed action in the past.

    *Anyone **who saw the incident***
    (NOT *Anyone seeing the incident*)

CHECK QUESTIONS 1

Make single sentences, using the *-ing* form.

1 A woman was attacked this morning. She was doing her shopping.
2 A young man stole her handbag. He was wearing a baseball cap.
3 He also stole a silver bracelet. It belonged to the woman.
4 There was a man near the bank. He was selling newspapers.

Step 2 | Clauses beginning with a past participle

- We can also use a clause beginning with a past participle (*injured, used, found,* etc.). This type of clause has a passive meaning.

  The man **injured** in the attack has since died. (= who was injured)

  A knife **found** on the pavement is thought to be the weapon **used** in the attack.
  (= that was found; that was used)

- A past participle is often used after *There is/are/was/were.*

  There was a price ticket **attached** to the knife.

CHECK QUESTIONS 2 · **Make single sentences, using a past participle.**

1 They escaped in a car. It was parked at the end of the street.
2 The woman is Mrs Amy Hyde. She was attacked by the thieves.
3 The money hasn't been found. It was stolen from Mrs Hyde.

Step 3 | *With* used to identify people and things

- We can use a noun + *with* to describe the physical features or possessions of someone or something.

  a man in his 20s **with jeans and a baseball cap**
  (= who was wearing jeans and a baseball cap)

  a young woman **with long blond hair and a silver ring in her nose**
  (= who had long blond hair and a silver ring in her nose)

  a blue Ford Escort **with a broken side window**
  (= that had a broken side window)

CHECK QUESTIONS 3 · **Make single sentences, using *with*.**

1 A man attacked Mrs Hyde. He had short dark hair.
2 Later the police found an empty handbag. It had blood on it.
3 A boy was walking past the bank at the time of the attack. He had a dog.

ANSWERS TO
CHECK QUESTIONS
1, 2 AND 3

1 1 A woman doing her shopping was attacked this morning. 2 A young man wearing a baseball cap stole her handbag. 3 He also stole a silver bracelet belonging to the woman. 4 There was a man near the bank selling newspapers.

2 1 They escaped in a car parked at the end of the street. 2 The woman attacked by the thieves is Mrs Amy Hyde. 3 The money stolen from Mrs Hyde hasn't been found.

3 1 A man with short dark hair attacked Mrs Hyde. 2 Later the police found an empty handbag with blood on it. 3 A boy with a dog was walking past the bank at the time of the attack.

306

Practice

- Clauses with *-ing*:
*I found someone **trying to steal my car**.* (= who was trying to steal my car)
***There's** a man at the door **asking** to see you.*
- Clauses with a past participle (a passive meaning):
*Many of the cars **made in British factories** are Japanese.* (= that are made in British factories)
***There was** a parking ticket **stuck** on the car window.*

---

1 **Heavy rain has caused serious flooding in the Orlando area of Florida. Rewrite the two sentences as one, using the *-ing* form of a verb.**
Example: Travellers have been told they can't get into the city. They're arriving at Orlando Airport. *Travellers arriving at Orlando Airport have been told they can't get into the city.*

1 This morning the road was blocked by floodwater. The road connects Orlando to the coast.

....

....

2 A woman had to abandon her car and walk home. She was taking her children to school.

....

....

3 A train fell into the river below when a bridge collapsed. It was carrying 73 passengers.

....

....

4 A car was swept into the river. It belonged to the mayor of Orlando.

....

....

2 **Rewrite the two sentences as one sentence, using a past participle.**
Example: Four fishermen are still missing. They've been lost for 12 hours off the coast of Scotland. *Four fishermen lost for 12 hours off the coast of Scotland are still missing.*

1 A life-raft was empty. It was found at the scene.

....

....

2 A helicopter is still searching the area. It was called from Lossiemouth.

....

....

3 Last week another Scottish fishing boat sank in the same area. It was hit by a submarine.

....

....

4 There have been three fishing boats. They've been hit by submarines this year.

....

....

3 **Complete the text, using an *-ing* form, a past participle or the word *with*. Use each of these verbs once:** *play, live, make, build, grow, buy, spend, be married, study, teach.*

Rowan Greaves comes from a big family.

They're all very different. He's got a sister

(1) .... three children (2) .... in

Australia and (3) .... to an Australian

farmer. She's the one (4) .... blond hair

and blue eyes. He's got another sister

(5) .... English in Tokyo. She's the one

(6) .... dark hair and brown eyes. He's

got a brother (7) .... professional

football in Italy. He lives in a luxury house

(8) .... on the shore of Lake Maggiore.

He's got another brother (9) .... Chinese

medicine in Beijing. He lives a simple life. He

only eats food (10) .... organically. And

he goes everywhere on a bicycle (11) ....

for £2 at a Beijing market. Rowan lives in

London. He works for an electronics company

(12) .... computers. His friends at work

think he's lucky when he tells them about his

holidays (13) .... in China, Italy, Australia

and Japan.

307

In formal, written English there are very few grammatical differences between British and American English. But in informal, spoken English there are a number of differences. The following are the most important.

American English	**British English**

Nouns

● Collective nouns like *team, family* and *crowd* are normally singular in American English, but usually plural in British English.

*England **is** playing Italy tomorrow.*	*England **are** playing Italy tomorrow.*
*The team **was** good.*	*The team **were** good.*
*The crowd **is** getting angry.*	*The crowd **are** getting angry.*

Verbs

● In American English the verb *have* is used more often than the verb *have got*. In British English *have got* is more common.

*They **have** two children.*	*They**'ve got** two children.*
***Do you have** a car?*	***Have you got** a car?*
*I **don't have** any money.*	*I **haven't got** any money.*

● In American English *gotten* is often used as the past participle of the verb *get*.

*Your tennis has **gotten** better since we last played.*	*Your tennis has **got** better since we last played.*

● In American English *should* is used in offers and suggestions where *shall* is used in British English.

***Should** I post that letter for you?*	***Shall** I post that letter for you?*
***Should** we go for a walk?*	***Shall** we go for a walk?*

● In American English the past simple is often used for an action that has just happened. It is also frequently used with *just, already, yet, ever* and *never*. In British English the present perfect is used.

*I **won** the lottery!*	*I**'ve won** the lottery!*
***Did you hear** the news?*	***Have you heard** the news?*
*I **just ate**.*	*I**'ve just eaten**.*
*He **already went**.*	*He**'s already gone**.*
*I **didn't finish yet**.*	*I **haven't finished yet**.*
*That's the biggest fish I **ever saw**.*	*That's the biggest fish I**'ve ever seen**.*

● Question tags are much less common in American English than British English.

*This is yours, **right**?*	*This is yours, **isn't it**?*
*You understand, **OK**?*	*You understand, **don't you**?*

Adverbs

● In informal American English the *-ly* ending to adverbs of manner is often omitted. Similarly the *-ly* ending is often omitted from the adverb *really*.

*He drove **slow**.*	*He drove **slowly**.*
*She looks **real** pretty.*	*She looks **really** pretty.*

American English	British English

Prepositions

- Note the use of the following prepositions in American and British English:

American English	British English
He sees her **on** weekends.	He sees her **at** weekends.
She's the best player **on** the team.	She's the best player **in** the team.
It's 8 minutes **after** 2.	It's 8 minutes **past** 2.
We stayed from May **through** July.	We stayed from May **to** July.
I looked **out** the window.	I looked **out of** the window.
Let's stay home.	Let's stay **at** home.
Will you write me?	Will you write **to** me?
They're starting Monday.	They're starting **on** Monday.
I met **with** an old friend yesterday.	I met an old friend yesterday.
They protested the war.	They protested **against** the war.
I can't see **around** the corner.	I can't see **round** the corner.
She walked **toward** me.	She walked **towards** me.
I haven't seen him **in** ten days.	I haven't seen him **for** ten days.

Other differences

American English	British English
My mother is in **the** hospital.	My mother is in hospital.
My brother plays guitar.	My brother plays **the** guitar.
It looks **like** it's going to rain.	It looks **as if** it's going to rain.
(On the telephone) Hello. Is **this** Helen?	Hello. Is **that** Helen?

Spelling differences

American English	British English
traveling, canceled, etc.	travelling, cancelled, etc.
center, theater, meter, etc.	centre, theatre, metre, etc.
color, labor, favorite, etc.	colour, labour, favourite, etc.
dialog, catalog, etc.	dialogue, catalogue, etc.
program	programme
practice (verb and noun)	practise (verb), practice (noun)
defense, offense, etc.	defence, offence, etc.
tire	tyre

We often use contractions or short forms in spoken English and in informal written English. We use an apostrophe to replace the missing letters. The most common contractions are:

I'm	=	I am	I've	=	I have	I'll	=	I shall OR will
You're	=	You are	You've	=	You have	You'll	=	You will
He's	=	He is	He's	=	He has	He'll	=	He will
She's	=	She is	She's	=	She has	She'll	=	She will
It's	=	It is	It's	=	It has	It'll	=	It will
We're	=	We are	We've	=	We have	We'll	=	We shall OR will
You're	=	You are	You've	=	You have	You'll	=	You will
They're	=	They are	They've	=	They have	They'll	=	They will

I'd	=	I had OR should OR would
You'd	=	You had OR would
He'd	=	He had OR would
She'd	=	She had OR would
It'd	=	It had OR would
We'd	=	We had OR should OR would
You'd	=	You had OR would
They'd	=	They had OR would

- *Not* is often shortened to *n't*.
  isn't = is not don't = do not haven't = have not can't = cannot
  won't = will not shan't = shall not, etc.

- Note the following alternative negative contractions:
  You aren't/You're not He isn't/He's not She isn't/She's not
  It isn't/It's not We aren't/We're not They aren't/They're not

- We use contractions or short forms after:
  Personal pronouns: *I've, They're*, etc.

Nouns:	*My mother's 38. = My mother is 38.*
	The manager's got a new office = The manager has got a new office.
Question words:	*What's your address? = What is your address?*
	Who've you invited? = Who have you invited?
here/there/that:	*Here's your pen. = Here is your pen.*
	There's a man outside. = There is a man outside.
	That's enough. = That is enough.

- Note that *-'s* can be a contraction of *is* or *has.*
  He's English. = He is English. He's got an English car. = He has got an English car.

- *It's = It is* OR *It has*
  Its = a possessive adjective. *The dog has lost its ball.*

- *Let's go! = Let us go!*

- *-'d* can be a contraction of *had* or *would*.
  They'd won = They had won   They'd have won = They would have won.

- We can't use short forms when a verb is stressed, as in short answers.
  'Have you got a pen?' 'Yes, I have.' (NOT Yes, I've.)
  'Is she Spanish?' 'Yes, she is.' (NOT Yes, she's.)

A, e, i, o and *u* are vowels.
All the other letters (*b, c, d, f,* etc.) are consonants.

Doubling a final consonant: *stop - stopped - stopping; careful > carefully*

The final consonant of a word is doubled:
- if it comes after a single vowel.
- if the final syllable is stressed.

stop > stopped
*be**gin** > begi**nn**ing*

The final consonant is not doubled:
- if it comes after two vowels.
- if the word ends in two consonants.
- if the final consonant is -*y* or -*w*.

clean > cleaned
sing > singing
play > playing
slow > slowed

- if the word has more than one syllable but the final consonant is not stressed.

ópen > opened

- But if a word ends in -*l* in British English, the -*l* is doubled even if the final syllable is not stressed.

trável > travelled
cáreful > carefully

This is not true in American English.

travel > traveled

Words ending in -*y*: *try > tries*

If the ending -*s* is added to a word which ends in a consonant + -*y*, the -*y* changes to -*ie*.

city > cities
factory > factories
try > tries

If the endings -*ed, -er, -est* or -*ly* are added to a word which ends in a consonant + -*y*, the -*y* changes to -*i*.

worry > worried
happy > happier
silly > silliest

But if there is a vowel before the final -*y*, the -*y* does not change to -*ie*.

boy > boys
key > keys
play > played
grey > greyer

Note that -*y* does not change to -*i* before -*ing*.
But note the exceptions:

carry > carrying
say > said, pay > paid

Words ending in -*e*: *take > taking, tie > ties*

If a word ends in a consonant + -*e*, the -*e* is omitted before the endings -*ed, -ing, -er* and -*est*.

like > liked
live > living
white > whiter
nice > nicest

But the -*e* is not omitted before -*s*.
And if the word ends in -*ee*, the final -*e* is not omitted.
Note that if a word ends in -*ie*, the -*ie* changes to -*y* before -*ing*.

make > makes
see > seeing

die > dying
lie > lying

If an adjective ends in -*le*, the -*le* ending changes to -*ly* to form the adverb.

comfortable > *comfortably*
simple > *simply*

Words which add -e before -s: *kiss* > *kisses, do* > *does*

If a word ends in -*s*, -*ss*, -*x*, -*sh* or -*ch* we put an extra -*e* before:

- the -*s* in noun plurals.

bus > *buses*
glass > *glasses*
box > *boxes*
dish > *dishes*
church > *churches*

- the -*s* in the present simple, 3rd person singular.

push > *pushes*
pass > *passes*

Note also verbs ending in -*o*.

I do > *he does*
I go > *she goes*

- Some nouns ending in -*o* add -*es* in the plural.

potato > *potatoes*
hero > *heroes*

But most nouns ending in -*o* have the plural ending -*s*.

photo > *photos*
kilo > *kilos*

The plural of nouns which end in -*f* or -*fe*: *knife* > *knives*

Many nouns which end in -*f* or -*fe* add -*ves* in the plural.

half > *halves*
wife > *wives*

-*ie* or -*ei*?

-*ie* and -*ei* are both pronounced /iː/.
We normally write -*ie*.
But after -*c* we write -*ei*.

believe   niece   thief
receive   ceiling

Capital letters

Note that we use capital letters with:

- months
- days
- nationalities, languages
- festivals

January, August
Monday, Wednesday
English, Spanish
Christmas, Easter

4   Phrasal verbs

(For the use of phrasal verbs, see Unit 32.)

to break down	My car **broke down** and I had to walk home.
to break off	The United States has **broken off** diplomatic relations with Cuba.
to break up	Andy and Gemma have **broken up**; Gemma wants a divorce.
to bring up	My father **brought** me **up**; my mother died when I was very young.
to burn down	His house **burned down** last week and he lost everything.
to call in	I'll **call in** to see Joanna on my way home this evening.
to carry on	The party **carried on** till 3 a.m.
to carry out	$100,000 has been stolen. The police are **carrying out** an investigation.
to catch up	Don't wait for me. I'll **catch** you **up**.
to clear up	a) The weather's **clearing up**. b) Your bedroom's in a mess. **Clear** it **up**!
to close down	The factory has **closed down** so I've lost my job.
to come back	I've been to Greece. I **came back** yesterday.
to come off	a) The button's **come off**. b) If my plan **comes off**, I'll be living in Hawaii next year.
to come out	a) What time can you **come out** tonight? b) His new book **comes out** tomorrow.
to come round	He **came round** to see me yesterday.
to cross out	You haven't spelt the address correctly. **Cross** it **out** and write it again.
to cut down	a) They've **cut** all the trees **down**. b) **Cut down** your smoking. You must smoke less.
to cut off	They **cut off** his electricity because he hadn't paid his bill.
to cut out	They didn't show the whole film on TV. They **cut out** the violent scenes.
to do up	I've bought an old house in the country; I'm going to **do it up**.
to drop in	**Drop in** and see me any time. You don't need to phone first.
to fall through	My plans to go to New York have **fallen through**. I haven't got enough money.
to fill in	Can you **fill in** this form, please, and sign your name at the bottom.
to find out	I don't know where he lives, but I'll **find out** and tell you his address.
to get away	The police ran after the thief, but he **got away**.
to get back	We leave at 7 a.m. and we **get back** at 6 this evening. (= come back)
to get on	She's **getting on** very well at college. Her results are good.
to get through	I'm trying to phone her, but I can't **get through**. The line's engaged.
to get up	I **get up** at 7 every morning.
to give away	I didn't want my old bike any more, so I **gave** it **away**.
to give back	I lent him some CDs, but he hasn't **given** them **back** yet.
to give in	The police questioned him for three hours, until he **gave in** and admitted to the crime.
to give out	Can you **give** the books **out**? Give one to each member of the class.
to give up	I **gave up** the piano two years ago. I play the guitar now.
to go away	a) **Go away!** I don't want to talk to you. b) I'm **going away** for a week. (= for a holiday)
to go on	The meeting **went on** for three hours.
to go out	a) Gary **went out** at 7 and I haven't seen him since then. b) The lights suddenly **went out**.
to go up	The price of petrol has **gone up** again.
to grow up	My 12-year-old son wants to be an architect when he **grows up**.
to hand in	When I arrived at the hotel I had to **hand in** my passport.
to hand over	A man with a gun went into the bank and asked them to **hand over** all the money.
to hold up	I'm sorry I'm late. The traffic **held** me **up**.
to keep on	My children **keep on** asking me to stop smoking.
to keep out	They built a fence round the camp to **keep out** the wild animals.
to knock down	a) They've **knocked down** the old church. b) She was **knocked down** by a car.
to leave out	You don't have to say 'The car that I bought'. You can leave 'that' **out**.
to let in	Mrs Reeves is at the door. Can you **let** her **in**, please?
to let off	I thought the traffic warden was going to give me a parking ticket, but she **let** me **off**.
to look round	I thought I heard someone behind me, so I **looked round**.
to look up	a) They all **looked up** when I came into the room. b) **Look up** the new words in a dictionary.
to make up	He's very inventive. He **makes up** stories to tell his children.
to pay back	I lent him £50, but he hasn't **paid** me **back** yet.

to pick up	a) *I've dropped my pen. Can you **pick** it **up** for me?* b) *I'll **pick** you **up** at the airport at 8.*
to put away	***Put** your books **away**. Don't leave them on the table.*
to put down	***Put** that vase **down**. You might drop it.*
to put off	a) *They've **put** the match **off** till next Saturday.* b) *I didn't buy it. The price **put** me **off**.*
to put on	a) ***Put** a coat **on**. It's cold outside.* b) *He **put** the radio **on** to listen to the news.*
to put out	*The fire brigade came and **put** the fire **out**.*
to put through (telephone)	*Do you want to speak to Mrs Hill? I'll **put** you **through** to her office.*
to put up	a) *The hotels are full. I'll **put** you **up** for the night.* b) *They've **put up** the price of beer again.*
to see off	*When he left for Australia, his whole family came to the airport to **see** him **off**.*
to set out	*If we **set out** early, we should get to London by eleven o'clock.*
to set up	*The Japanese have **set up** a new computer company in England.*
to settle down	***Settle down**, everybody, and listen. I want to talk to you.*
to show off	*Jack's always **showing off**. He loves being the centre of attention.*
to stay up	*I **stayed up** very late. I didn't go to bed till 2 a.m.*
to switch off	***Switch** the television **off**. I don't want to watch it any more.*
to switch on	***Switch** the lights **on**. I can't see a thing.*
to take down	*I want to paint your bedroom, so you'll have to **take** all your posters **down**.*
to take off	a) *The plane **took off** at 11.30.* b) *It was hot, so I **took** my sweater **off**.*
to take over	a) *I'll **take over** the driving if you're tired.* b) *A US company has **taken over** our firm.*
to take up	a) *It's too big. It **takes up** too much room.* b) ***Take up** yoga, if you want to be healthy.*
to talk over	*I can't decide now. I'll have to **talk** it **over** with my wife first.*
to think over	*You don't have to tell me now. Why don't you **think** it **over** and tell me tomorrow?*
to throw away	*Don't **throw** that old painting **away**. It might be valuable.*
to try on	*I like this blue sweater. Can I **try** it **on**?*
to try out	*I've just bought a new surfboard. I'm going to **try** it **out** this afternoon.*
to turn down	a) *I applied for a job, but they **turned** me **down**.* b) ***Turn** the radio **down**. It's too loud.*
to turn off	*Don't forget to **turn** the lights **off** before you go to bed. (= switch/put off)*
to turn on	***Turn** the television **on**. There's a good film on. (= switch/put on)*
to turn out	*I didn't like my new teacher at first, but she **turned out** to be very nice.*
to turn over	***Turn** the steak **over**. It's done on that side.*
to turn up	a) *He was late. He **turned up** at 7 o'clock.* b) ***Turn** the TV **up**. I can't hear it.*
to wear off	*His tooth was painful when the anaesthetic **wore off**.*
to wear out	*He walked across India. He **wore out** five pairs of shoes!*
to wipe out	*The poisonous gas **wiped out** the whole village. Everyone was killed.*
to work out	*285 x 46? Give me the calculator. I can't **work** it **out** in my head.*

Phrasal-prepositional verbs

to be up to	a) *The job's too difficult for Anna. She **isn't up to** it.*
	b) *I can't help you any more. It**'s up to** you now.*
to catch up with	*I'm not ready yet. Why don't you leave now and I'll **catch up with** you.*
to come up to	*I was standing on the corner when a man **came up to** me and asked me the way to the station.*
to fall out with	*Gemma's **fallen out with** her boyfriend. They don't speak to each other any more.*
to get on with	a) *'Do you **get on with** your parents?' 'No. We argue a lot.'*
	b) *I can't talk to you for long, because I must **get on with** my work.*
to go off with	*Jack's father left his wife and **went off with** another woman when Jack was six.*
to keep up with	a) *Don't walk so fast! I can't **keep up with** you.*
	b) *Danny always reads the local newspaper. He likes to **keep up with** all the local news.*
to look forward to	*I'm **looking forward to** seeing my girlfriend tomorrow. I haven't seen her for three weeks.*
to look out for	*Zoe said she might be in town this morning. We must **look out for** her.*
to put up with	*My neighbours play loud music all night. I can't **put up with** the noise any more. I'm going to tell the police.*
to run out of	*I **ran out of** petrol in town this morning, and I had to push the car to a garage.*

5 Adjectives with prepositions

(For adjectives + preposition + the *-ing* form of a verb, see Unit 50.)

- bad, brilliant, good, hopeless, useless AT
*He's very **good at** chess, but he's **useless at** ball games.*
- amazed, surprised, shocked AT/BY
*I was really **surprised at** (OR **by**) her reaction. She was furious!*

- excited, upset, worried ABOUT
*I'm really **excited about** the holiday. She's **upset about** her mother's death. Don't be **worried about** me!*
- disappointed, happy, pleased ABOUT (a situation) (See WITH.)
*He's got a new job. He's very **pleased about** it, but his wife isn't **happy about** moving house.*
- angry, annoyed, cross ABOUT (something)/WITH (someone)
*Someone stole her car; she's very **annoyed about** it. My father's very **angry about** my exam results.*
*Please don't get **angry with** me. She's very **cross with** her brother because he broke her Walkman.*
- sorry ABOUT/FOR
*I'm **sorry about** the broken vase. I'll buy you another one.*
*I feel **sorry for** Jenny. She's had a very hard life.*

- difficult, easy, essential, important, impossible FOR
*It's **difficult for** people to find jobs. It's **impossible for** me to come because I haven't got a car.*
- famous, late, responsible FOR
*'What's Shakespeare **famous for**?' 'He's **famous for** the plays he wrote.'*
*There was a traffic jam, so I was **late for** work and the children were **late for** school.*
*I broke the lamp, but I'm not **responsible for** the broken window.*

- different FROM (*different TO* is possible, but it is considered less 'correct')
*I can't use this disk because your computer is **different from** mine.*

- interested, involved IN
*Mark's very **interested in** photography. Gemma was **involved in** a serious road accident last week.*

- careless, clever, good, kind, nice, sensible, silly, stupid, unreasonable, wrong OF
*It was **good of** you to come. It was **stupid of** the man to drive at 110 k.p.h. through the village.*
- afraid, ashamed, aware, fond, frightened, jealous, proud, scared, tired OF
*Mrs White's very **proud of** her children. I'm **scared of** heights. She's **ashamed of** what she did.*
- full, short, capable OF
*The room's **full of** people. He's just won a million pounds, so he'll never be **short of** money.*
*Maria lost all her matches this year. She's **capable of** better results.*

- keen ON *She loves volleyball and she's very **keen on** tennis too.*

- cruel, good, kind, nice, rude, unkind TO
*The nurses were very **good to** me. Don't be **rude to** your mother!*
- engaged, married TO
*'Is Rick **married to** Anna?' 'No , he's only **engaged to** her.'*
- related, similar TO
*Your sweater's **similar to** the one I bought. 'Are you **related to** him?' 'Yes, he's my cousin.'*

- bored, fed up WITH
*I'm **bored with** my job and I'm **fed up with** the people I work with.*
- disappointed, pleased, satisfied WITH (a person, a thing)
*The players are **disappointed** with their performance, and the manager isn't **pleased with** them.*

(For verbs + preposition + the *-ing* form, see Unit 50.)

agree with	*Yes, you're right. I **agree with** you.*
apologise for	*I **apologised for** my mistake.*
apply for	*He **applied for** the job, but he didn't get it.*
approve of	*Her parents don't **approve of** her boyfriend.*
argue with	*Don't **argue with** me! Do as I tell you!*
ask for	*Can you **ask for** another bottle of wine?*
believe in	*Do you **believe in** ghosts?*
belong to	*'Whose is this umbrella?' 'It **belongs to** Jack.'*
care about	*He doesn't **care about** his family. They aren't important to him.*
care for	*Old Mrs White lives alone. She needs help. She hasn't got anyone to **care for** her.*
complain about	*The music at the party was a bit loud. The neighbours **complained about** the noise.*
complain to /about	*My hotel room was dirty. I **complained to** the manager **about** it.*
concentrate on	*I don't like carphones. You can't **concentrate on** your driving if you're using a phone.*
consist of	*The United Kingdom **consists of** England, Scotland, Wales and Northern Ireland.*
decide on	*They could buy a new car or have an expensive holiday. They **decided on** a new car.*
depend on	*'Can we go to the beach tomorrow?' 'I don't know. It **depends on** the weather.'*
die of	*Both my parents **died of** cancer.*
dream about	*I had a strange dream last night. I **dreamt about** my birth.*
happen to	*What's **happened to** Jenny? I haven't seen her all day.*
hear about	*Have you **heard about** James? He was in a car accident yesterday.*
hear from	*She went to Australia a year ago. I haven't **heard from** her since. She hasn't written.*
hear of	*'Have you **heard of** a restaurant called 'The Hotpot'?' 'No, I've never **heard of** it.'*
hope for	*Daniel said he'd contact me today. I'm **hoping for** a telephone call this morning.*
laugh at	*When I dyed my hair green, everybody **laughed at** me. They thought I looked ridiculous.*
listen to	*Don't turn the radio off. I'm **listening to** the news.*
live on	*He isn't very healthy. He **lives on** junk food.*
look after	*I can't come out tonight. I've got to **look after** my baby brother.*
look at	*'What are you **looking at**?' 'I'm **looking at** that man with the dog.'*
look for	*'What are you **looking for**?' 'I'm **looking for** my credit card. I can't find it anywhere.'*
pay for	*'I've only got £5.' 'Don't worry. I'll **pay for** the tickets.'*
refer to	*The newspaper report **refers to** a bank robbery in London on Tuesday.*
rely on	*Emily will be here on time. You can **rely on** her. She's never late.*
run into	*I had an accident in my car. I **ran into** a lorry. (OR I **crashed into** a lorry.)*
search for	*The police are **searching for** two men who robbed a bank.*
shout at	*He **shouts at** me when he gets angry.*
shout to	*I saw Henry in the High Street. I **shouted to** him, but he didn't hear me.*
suffer from	*He **suffers from** high blood pressure.*
talk about	*I met Nick in town. He was **talking about** his new job.*
talk to	*Have you got a minute? I'd like to **talk to** you.*
think about	*'You look worried. What are you **thinking about**?' 'I'm **thinking about** my exams.'*
think of	*'What do you **think of** Emma's new boyfriend?' 'He seems quite nice.'*
wait for	*I'll see you at about 8. I'll **wait for** you outside the restaurant.*
write to	*Don't forget to **write to** me when you're on holiday.*

Note that the following verbs are not followed by a preposition:

approach	*We were **approaching** London when the train suddenly stopped.*
enter	*Suddenly a policeman **entered** the room.*
expect	*I don't think the hotel will be full. We don't **expect** many people in October.*
phone	*I'll **phone** you when I get to the airport.*
reach	*It was about 7.30 when we **reached** London.*

Infinitive	Past simple	Past participle
be	was	been
beat	beat	beaten
become	became	become
begin	began	begun
bend	bent	bent
bet	bet	bet
bite	bit	bitten
bleed	bled	bled
blow	blew	blown
break	broke	broken
bring	brought	brought
build	built	built
burn	burnt (burned)	burnt (burned)
burst	burst	burst
buy	bought	bought
catch	caught	caught
choose	chose	chosen
come	came	come
cost	cost	cost
cut	cut	cut
dig	dug	dug
do	did	done
draw	drew	drawn
dream	dreamt (dreamed)	dreamt (dreamed)
drink	drank	drunk
drive	drove	driven
eat	ate	eaten
fall	fell	fallen
feed	fed	fed
feel	felt	felt
fight	fought	fought
find	found	found
fly	flew	flown
forbid	forbade	forbidden
forget	forgot	forgotten
forgive	forgave	forgiven
freeze	froze	frozen
get	got	got (AE gotten)
give	gave	given
go	went	gone
grow	grew	grown
hang	hung	hung
have	had	had
hear	heard	heard
hide	hid	hidden
hit	hit	hit
hold	held	held
hurt	hurt	hurt
keep	kept	kept
kneel	knelt (kneeled)	knelt (kneeled)
know	knew	known
lay	laid	laid
lead	led	led
lean	leant (leaned)	leant (leaned)
learn	learnt (learned)	learnt (learned)
leave	left	left
lend	lent	lent
let	let	let
lie	lay	lain
light	lit	lit

Infinitive	Past simple	Past participle
lose	lost	lost
make	made	made
mean	meant	meant
meet	met	met
pay	paid	paid
put	put	put
read	read	read
ride	rode	ridden
ring	rang	rung
rise	rose	risen
run	ran	run
say	said	said
see	saw	seen
seek	sought	sought
sell	sold	sold
send	sent	sent
set	set	set
shake	shook	shaken
shine	shone	shone
shoot	shot	shot
show	showed	shown (showed)
shrink	shrank	shrunk
shut	shut	shut
sing	sang	sung
sink	sank	sunk
sit	sat	sat
sleep	slept	slept
slide	slid	slid
smell	smelt (smelled)	smelt (smelled)
speak	spoke	spoken
spell	spelt (spelled)	spelt (spelled)
spend	spent	spent
spin	spun	spun
spit	spat	spat
split	split	split
spread	spread	spread
spring	sprang	sprung
stand	stood	stood
steal	stole	stolen
stick	stuck	stuck
sting	stung	stung
strike	struck	struck
swear	swore	sworn
sweep	swept	swept
swim	swam	swum
swing	swung	swung
take	took	taken
teach	taught	taught
tear	tore	torn
tell	told	told
think	thought	thought
throw	threw	thrown
tread	trod	trodden
understand	understood	understood
wake	woke	woken
wear	wore	worn
weep	wept	wept
win	won	won
write	wrote	written

ADJECTIVE: A word which describes a noun or a pronoun.
An old woman.   The house was big.   It's difficult.

ADVERB: A word which adds information about a verb, an adjective or another adverb.
She spoke loudly.   He's very tall.   They walked extremely slowly.

ADVERB OF DEGREE: A word which tells us 'how much' or 'to what extent'.   *She was very thin.*
The exam was fairly easy.   It's too expensive.

ADVERB OF FREQUENCY: A word which tells us 'how often'.   *It never rains.   They often argue.*
She usually comes late.

ADVERB OF MANNER: A word which tells us 'how' or 'in what way'.
They work slowly.   She played well.

ADVERB PARTICLE: A word like *on, away, up* used as part of a verb.
Turn off the light.   Throw away the rubbish.

AFFIRMATIVE: *I like coffee* is an **affirmative** (or **positive**) sentence.
I don't like coffee is a **negative** sentence.

AGENT: The person or thing which does the action in a passive sentence.
The dog was attacked by the cat.

APOSTROPHE: The apostrophe (') has two uses:
a) It shows that a letter has been left out.
It's cold. = It is cold.   b) It shows possession.
Jack's sister.   The government's policy.

ARTICLE: *A/an* are the indefinite articles.
A car. An answer.
The is the definite article.   *The problem.*

AUXILIARY VERBS: The verbs *to be, to have, to do* which help to form some of the tenses (and question forms) of other verbs.
He is coming.   They have gone.   Do you know him?
See also **MODALS**.

CAPITAL LETTER: If we write the word 'danger' in **capital letters**, we write DANGER.

CARDINAL NUMBERS: *One (1), fifteen (15), six hundred and five (605)*, etc. are cardinal numbers.
See also **ORDINAL NUMBERS**

CLAUSE: A clause is a part of a sentence. It has a subject and a verb. In the sentence *He lost because he played badly* there are two clauses, *He lost* and *because he played badly*.
See also **MAIN CLAUSE**.

COLLECTIVE NOUN: A noun that refers to a group of people or things.
A team, a family, a fleet, a committee.

COMPARATIVE: *Younger* and *more difficult* are the comparative forms of the adjectives *young* and *difficult.   You're younger than me.*

CONDITIONAL: A clause that starts with *if* or *unless* (or similar words).
If it rains, I won't play.   I won't go unless you come too.

CONJUNCTION: Link words like *and, but, because, when* that join two clauses.
He ran because he was late, but he missed the train.

CONSONANT: All the letters of the alphabet are **consonants**, except for *a, e, i, o, u*, which are **vowels**.

CONTINUOUS TENSES: The tenses (sometimes called **progressive** tenses) which have a form of the verb *be + -ing.*
I'm coming. (**Present continuous**).
They were waiting. (**Past continuous**) etc.

CONTRACTED FORM: The contracted or short form of a verb. See Appendix 2.   *I'm sorry.* (= *I am sorry.*)   *She can't swim.* (= *She cannot swim.*) etc.

COUNTABLE NOUNS: Nouns that are the names of things or people that we can count. They have a singular and a plural form.   *A girl > three girls*
The problem > many problems, etc.

DEFINING RELATIVE CLAUSE: A relative clause that defines or clearly identifies a noun.
There's the dog that bit me.
I don't know the people who live at number 16.
See also **NON-DEFINING RELATIVE CLAUSE**.

DEFINITE ARTICLE: See **ARTICLE**.

DEMONSTRATIVE ADJECTIVE: The demonstrative adjectives are *this, that, these* and *those.*
I like these trousers, but I don't like that shirt.

DEMONSTRATIVE PRONOUN: The demonstrative pronouns are *this, that, these* and *those.*
This is my pen.   Those are nice.

DIRECT OBJECT: A verb can be followed by a **direct object** and/or an **indirect object**. In the sentence *He sent me a postcard* the **direct object** is *a postcard*, the **indirect object** is *me.*

DIRECT SPEECH: The exact words somebody speaks. *'I'm tired'* is **direct speech**. *She said she was tired* is **indirect** or **reported speech**.

EMPHATIC PRONOUNS: The emphatic pronouns *myself, himself, ourselves*, etc. emphasise the subjects *I, he, we*, etc.   *They built the house themselves.*

ENDING: The last part of a word as in *speaks, coming, badly, finished, cities*, etc.

EXCLAMATION: Something we say suddenly, usually because we are surprised. *What!   I don't believe it! Oh, no!* are all exclamations followed by an exclamation mark (!).

FORMAL: *Good morning. How are you?* is **formal**.
Hi, how's it going? is **informal**.

GERUND: The *-ing* form of a verb when it is used as a noun.
Smoking is forbidden.   I'm afraid of flying.

IMPERATIVE: A form of the verb which is the same as the infinitive without *to*. We use the imperative to give orders or instructions.   *Walk, don't run.*

INDEFINITE ARTICLE: See **ARTICLE**.

INDIRECT OBJECT: See **DIRECT OBJECT**.

INDIRECT SPEECH: See **REPORTED SPEECH**.

INFINITIVE: The basic form of the verb. *To go, to sleep, to remember* are infinitives.

INFORMAL: See **FORMAL**.

-ING FORM: A verb with the **-ing** ending. It can be a gerund: *Smoking is forbidden*, or a present participle: *There's a woman waiting outside.*

IRREGULAR VERBS: Verbs like *go* and *see* are irregular. (*go - went - gone; see - saw - seen*) They do not have the same *-ed* endings as most other (regular) verbs. *He came in and sat down.* (NOT *He comed in and sitted down.*) See Appendix 7.

LINK WORD: See **CONJUNCTION**.

MAIN CLAUSE: In the sentence *The phone rang while I was having a bath*, 'The phone rang' is the main clause, the more important clause.
The clause 'while I was having a bath' is a sub-clause (subordinate clause). The sub-clause usually begins with a conjunction.

MODALS: Modal verbs (or modal auxiliaries) are verbs like *can, should, may, must,* etc. which we use to express feelings or opinions rather than facts.
*You **must** listen. He **may** die. They **shouldn't** go.*

NEGATIVE: See AFFIRMATIVE.

NON-DEFINING RELATIVE CLAUSE: A non-defining relative clause gives extra, but not essential information.
*The plane, **which was a TriStar**, crashed near Paris.*
See also DEFINING RELATIVE CLAUSE.

NOUN: The name of a person, place, thing, etc. *chair, cinema, fear, death* are all nouns.

OBJECT: See DIRECT OBJECT.

OBJECT PRONOUN: *Me, him, her, us, them* are object pronouns. *He kissed **her**.*

ORDINAL NUMBERS: *First, second, twentieth,* etc. are ordinal numbers. They are often shortened to *1st, 2nd, 20th,* etc. See CARDINAL NUMBERS.

PARTICIPLES: *Going* and *went* are the present and past participles of the verb *to go.*

PASSIVE: In a passive sentence the subject of the verb is the person or thing that is affected by the action. *A thief stole his bike* is an active sentence. *His bike **was stolen*** is **passive**.

PAST CONTINUOUS: *She was crying* and *They were arguing* are examples of the past continuous.

PAST PARTICIPLE: Regular verbs have a past participle with the *-ed* ending.
*He has **finished**. Ten people have been **killed**.*
Some past participles are irregular.
*They've already **left**. The money has been **found**.*

PAST PERFECT: *They had gone* and *The film had started* are examples of the past perfect.

PAST PERFECT CONTINUOUS: *She had been waiting* and *It had been snowing* are examples of the past perfect continuous.

PAST SIMPLE: *It rained, We left* and *She didn't come* are examples of the past simple.

PERCEPTION: The verbs of perception are *to see, to hear, to feel, to taste, to smell,* etc. We use our eyes, ears, etc. to perceive things.

PERSON: The first **person** singular is *I*, the second **person** singular is *you,* etc.

PERSONAL PRONOUNS: The personal subject pronouns are *I, you, he, she, it, we, you, they.* The personal object pronouns are *me, you, him, her, it, us, you, them. **He** married **her**.*

PHRASAL VERB: A verb with two (or sometimes three) parts (verb + adverb or verb + adverb + preposition).
*He **turned on** the light. I **got up** at 7.00.*
*We **ran out of** petrol.*

PHRASE: A group of words which we use together but which is not a clause or sentence.
*I waited **for a long time**.*

POSSESSIVES: Possessive adjectives are *my, your, his, her, its, our, their.*
*What's **your** name? **My** name's Simon.*
Possessive pronouns are *mine, yours, his, hers, its, ours, theirs. This isn't **mine**. Is it **yours**?*

PREPOSITION: A word like *in, on, through* placed before a noun or pronoun.
*They're **at** home. He was **with** her.*

PRESENT CONTINUOUS: *It's raining, They're coming* and *You aren't listening* are examples of the present continuous.

PRESENT PARTICIPLE: The *-ing* form of the verb when it is used as an adjective or an adverb. *A **falling** tree. A **crying** baby. She ran out **screaming**.*

PRESENT PERFECT CONTINUOUS: *I've been working* and *You haven't been listening* are examples of the present perfect continuous.

PRESENT PERFECT SIMPLE: *They've arrived, She's finished* and *I haven't forgotten* are examples of the present perfect simple.

PRESENT SIMPLE: *She smokes* and *They don't understand* are examples of the present simple.

PROGRESSIVE: See CONTINUOUS.

PRONOUN: A word used in place of a noun.
*That's my brother. **He's** got his girlfriend with **him**.*
(**He** and **him** are pronouns referring to *my brother*.)

QUESTION TAGS: Short questions at the end of a sentence. *It's hot, **isn't it**? You haven't finished, **have you**? They didn't win, **did they**?*

REFLEXIVE PRONOUN: A pronoun ending in *-self* or *-selves* which is used to show that the action is directed back to the subject.
*I cut **myself**. They hurt **themselves**.*

REGULAR: If a verb, for example, is regular it has the same form as most other verbs. The verbs *talk, stop* and *look* are **regular**. The **regular** noun plural ending is *-s: boys, problems*. See also IRREGULAR.

RELATIVE CLAUSE: A clause that describes or qualifies a person or thing. See also DEFINING RELATIVE CLAUSES.
*The car **which he bought** was cheap.*
*The woman **who I spoke to** was very helpful.*

RELATIVE PRONOUN: The pronoun which we use to introduce a relative clause. *Who, which, whose* and *that* are **relative pronouns**.

REPORTED SPEECH: *'I'm married'* is in **direct speech**. We can report what she said using **reported** (or **indirect speech**).
She said she was married.

SENTENCE: A group of words which together form a statement (*The taxi has arrived.*), a question (*Are you ready?*), an exclamation (*What terrible weather!*) or an order (*Get out!*). A sentence begins with a capital letter and ends with a full stop (.), a question mark (?) or an exclamation mark (!).

SHORT ANSWER: Answers formed with *Yes* or *No* + an auxiliary verb or a modal.
*'Have you eaten?' – '**No, I haven't.**'*
*'Can you come?' – '**Yes, I can.**'*

STATEMENT: A sentence that simply gives information (not a question or an order).
The house is on fire. He speaks English.

STRESS: To give emphasis to a syllable or a word, we put stress on it. We say it with more force. In the word *agree* the stress is on the second syllable.

SUB-CLAUSE: See MAIN CLAUSE.

SUBJECT: In the sentences ***The man** took the money* and ***They** won the match,* the subjects are *The man* and *They*.

SUPERLATIVE: *The tallest man The most expensive shoes.* **Tallest** and **most expensive** are the superlative forms of the adjectives *tall* and *expensive*.

SYLLABLE: Part of a word. ***Man*** has one syllable, ***woman*** has two syllables, ***intelligent*** has four syllables (in-tell-i-gent).

TENSE: A verb form which tells us when something happens, the time of an action.
He's coming. (present) He came. (past)
He's going to come. (future)

UNCOUNTABLE NOUNS: Nouns that are the names of things that cannot be counted, that do not have a plural form. *Water, air, information, music, beauty,* etc.

VERB: A verb expresses an action (*to throw*), an attitude (*to love*) or a state (*to be*).

VOWEL: See CONSONANT.

Index

The numbers in the index refer to **pages**, not units.

a/an 184–185
 a/an and *the* 177
a bit (adverb) 254
able (*be able to*) 79–80
above 270–271
across 275
active/passive 53–54
adjectives
 adjectives ending in *-ing* and
  -ed (*boring/bored*) 239
 adjectives not used before a
  noun 227
 adjectives used only before
  a noun 227
 order of adjectives 228
 adjectives used as nouns
  (*the poor*) 227
 adjectives + infinitive
  (*easy to remember*) 143–144
 adjective + *for* +
  noun/pronoun + infinitive:
  It isn't easy for me to say
  143–144
 adjective + *of* +
  noun/pronoun + infinitive:
  It's nice of you to come 144
 comparatives (*bigger, more
  expensive*) 230–233, 235–237
 superlatives (*the biggest, the
  most expensive*) 230–233,
  236–237
 adjectives with prepositions
  (*afraid of*) 315
admit (+ *-ing*) 146
adverbs
 adverbs of manner
  (*slowly*) 241–244
 adverbs of degree
  (*extremely*) 241, 243–244
 adverbs of frequency
  (*often*) 246–247
 adverbs of time and place
  (*today, here*) 248
 sentence adverbs
  (*Unfortunately ...*) 241, 244
 quite, fairly, pretty, rather
  250–251
 so, such 252

a lot, a little, a bit, much, etc.
 254–255
 comparatives
  (*more slowly*) 233
 more, less, better, worse 255
 superlatives
  (*the most carefully*) 233
 most, least, best, worst 255
 too/enough 260–261
 *any more, any longer,
  no longer* 258
 still, yet 257–258
 position of adverbs 243–244,
  247, 248
advice (uncountable) 192
advise + object + infinitive:
 He advised me to stay 140
 in reported speech 174
a few
 only with countable nouns
  (*a few cars*) 190–191
 a few and *a little* 195
afraid of 315
 afraid of doing 148
 I'm afraid so/not 72
after
 in future sentences +
  simple present or present
  perfect 286
 after + *-ing* 148
ago 281
 ago with past simple 32–33
 How long ago did you decide?
  281
 *How many years ago did you
  start?* 281
agree
 + infinitive with *to* 136
 agree to + passive infinitive:
 He agreed to be photographed
  54
a little (adverb: *We talked a
 little*) 254
all/everything/everybody
 (everyone) 200
 all day, morning, week, etc.
  34, 202
 all/every/each 200–202

all of 204
all + preposition (*all over the
 floor*) 202
all/whole 201–202
 position of *all* 205
along 275
a lot (of) 194
 a lot (adverb: *He smokes a
  lot*) 254
already with the present
 perfect 27, 33
although/though 293
always 13, 246–247
 with present continuous:
  You're always complaining!
  10–11
amazed at/by 315
 amazed/amazing 239
American English 308–309
among 271–272
an 184–185
 a/an and *the* 177
angry about/with 315
annoyed about/with 315
 annoyed/annoying 239
any
 any (*of*) 204
 any and *some* 197–198
 any and *no* 197
 any used in affirmative
  sentences: *Choose any book
  you like* 198
any more/any longer 258
anyone (anybody)/anything/
 anywhere 214–215
apologise for 175
apostrophe *s* ('s),
 ***s* apostrophe (s')** (*The man's
  name/The parents' bedroom*)
  217–218
arrange + infinitive with *to*
 136
arrive in/arrive at 277–278
articles (See: *a/an/the*)
as
 (preposition) 290–291
 as/like 291
 as/since (reason) 294

as (good) as (in comparative sentences) 235
as if/as though 106, 290–291
as long as 127–128
ask
  ask in reported speech 173–174
  ask where/what, etc. + infinitive 138, 173
  ask for 174, 316
as much (adverb) 254
as soon as in future sentences + present simple or present perfect 286
astonished/astonishing 239
at (time) 264
  at (place) 268
auxiliary verbs used alone 75–77
aware *of* 315

be used to 112
bear (*I can't bear waiting*) 151
because 294
bed (*in bed/to bed*) 178
been to/gone to 30
before
  with the present perfect 28
  in future sentences + simple present or present perfect 286
  before + *-ing* 148
begin (*doing/to do*) 164
behind 270
belong (to) 316
below 271–272
beside 271–272
best
  (adjective) 232–233
  best (adverb) 255
better
  (adjective) 232–233
  better (adverb) 255
  had better (*I'd better go now*) 96
between 271–272
bored/boring 239
  bored with 315
both
  (*the*) + noun 205
  both of 205

both ... and ... 205
  position of *both* 205
bread (uncountable) 192
business (countable and uncountable) 192
by
  preposition of place (*by the window*) 271–272
  preposition of time (*by lunchtime*) 288
  by with the passive 54
  by/until 288
  by car/by bus etc. 178, 277
  by + *-ing* 148
by myself/himself/ themselves, etc. 211
by the time 288
  in future sentences + simple present or present perfect 286

can
  for ability (*I can ski*) 79
  for offers (*Can I help you?*) 83
  for permission (*You can use my car*) 82–83
  in requests (*Can I use the phone?*) 82
can't
  can't bear 151–152
  can't stand 151
  can't help 151–152
  can't have done 90
  can't for deductions (*It can't be true*) 89
capable *of* 315
church (*church/the church*) 180
clauses with *-ing* **or a past participle** 305–306
clever of someone to do something 144, 315
college (*college/the college*) 180
come
  come (+ *-ing*) (*Do you want to come sailing?*) 146
  come and see etc. 137–138
comparatives
  (*bigger, more quickly*) 230–233

irregular forms (*better, worse*) 232–233
adverb forms (*more quickly*) 233
  as (*good*) *as* ... 235
  the same as ... 235
  bigger and bigger 235
  the cheaper the better 236
  more, less, fewer + noun 236
  much bigger, slightly cheaper, etc. 237
complain to/about 316
concentrate on 316
conditional sentences (*if* sentences) 120–122, 124–125
confused/confusing 239
consist of 316
continue doing/to do 164
contractions (short forms) 310
corner in/at 266, 268
could
  for ability 80
  for permission 82–83
  for present and future possibility 92
  in requests 82
could have for past possibilty 93
countable and uncountable nouns 190–192
countries, continents 179
court (*court/the court*) 180
cross about/with 315

damage (uncountable) 192
dare 137
decide
  + infinitive with *to* 136
  decide where to go, etc. 138
definite article (*the*) 177, 180, 182
demonstratives (*this, these*, etc.) 207–208
deny (+ *-ing*) 146
depend on 316
depressed/depressing 239
deserve to 136

did/didn't
in past simple questions and
negatives 20
in question tags 66
die of 316
different from/to 315
difficult for 315
direct object 117–118
disappointed
+ infinitive 143
disappointed with/about 315
disappointed/disappointing
239
discover *how to fly,* etc. 138
discuss *where to go,* etc. 138
disgusted/disgusting 239
dislike (+ *-ing*) 146
do/does/don't/doesn't
in present simple questions
and negatives 7
in question tags 66
as auxiliary verb used alone
76
down (preposition) 274
dream
dream of + *-ing* 149
dream about 316
during/for 283–284

each/every/all 200–201
each of 201
only with countable nouns
191
each other/ourselves/
yourselves/themselves 212
early (adjective and adverb)
243
easy for 315
either
+ noun 205
either ... or 205
either of 205
elder/eldest 232
embarrassed/embarrassing
239
emphatic pronouns (*I did it
myself*) 212
engaged to 315
enjoy + *-ing* 146
enough 261
even though 293

ever (with the present perfect)
28
ever since 280–281
every/all/each 200–202
every only with countable
nouns 191
everybody (everyone)/all 200
everything/all 200
excited *about* 315
excited/exciting 239
exclamations (*What a mess!*)
184, 190
expect
+ infinitive with *to* 136
+ passive infinitive (*He
expected to be chosen*) 54
I expect so/I don't expect so 72
She's expected to win 56
explain what to do 138

fail + infinitive with *to* 136
fairly 250–251
famous for 315
fancy (+ *-ing*) 146
far (*far bigger, far too much*)
237, 260
fast (adjective and adverb)
243
fed up with 315
feel
feel like 105
feel + adjective 105
feel as if/as though 106
I feel/I'm feeling 14
few
(*very*) *few* 195
few and *little* 195
few and *a few* 195
fewer, the fewest 236
finish (+ *-ing*) 146
first (*It's the first time I've ...*)
30
fond of 315
for/since 280–281
for/during 283–284
for with the past simple 34
for with the present perfect
34, 36–37
for + indirect object 118
forget doing/to do 165–166
forget what to do, etc. 138

forgive someone for doing
something 149
free
(adjective and adverb) 243
free/freely (adverbs) 242
frequently 246–247
frightened of 315
frightened/frightening 239
from 274
full of 315
furniture (uncountable) 192
further 232–233
future
present tenses for the future
11, 16, 286
going to/will 48
will/won't/shan't 45–46
when and *if* sentences 120
future continuous
(*will be doing*) 50–51
future perfect
(*will have* done) 51
future continuous and future
perfect for present time 51
future passive 53

generally 246–247
geographical names with and
without *the* 179
gerund *see -ing*
get
something done 60
get someone to do something
140
get used to 111
get in/out of/on/off 277–278
give (passive: *He was given
£100*) 58
go
+ *-ing* (*Shall we go shopping?*)
146
go and see, etc. 137–138
going to 16
going to/will 48
was/were going to 48
gone to/been to 30
good
good at/to 315
*good of someone to do
something* 144, 315
good and *well* 242

it's no good + *-ing* 152
go on doing/to do 165
go to (a place) 278

had
I had done – past perfect simple 42–43
I had been doing – past perfect continuous 43
had to 85
had better 96
hair (countable and uncountable) 192
half (of) 204
happen + infinitive with *to* 136
happy about/with 315
hard/hardly (adverbs) 242
hardly ever 246–247
hate
hate doing/to do 157
would hate to do 158
would hate to have done 159
have/has
have for actions 100
I have/He has finished (present perfect simple) 25
I have been working (present perfect continuous) 36–37
I have written or *I have been writing* 39–40
have and *have got* 99–100
have (got) to and *must* 85–87
don't have to or *mustn't* 87
have something done 60
having (done) 154–155
hear of/about/from 316
help
+ infinitive with or without *to* 137
can't help 152
her, hers 221–222
high
(adjective and adverb) 243
high/highly (adverbs) 242
his 221–222
home
at home 178
go/get home 278
hope
I hope so/I hope not 72
hope + infinitive with *to* 136

hope+ passive infinitive (*I hope to be chosen*) 54
hospital
(*hospital/the hospital*) 180
how long? 40, 280–281
how long is it since ... ? 281
how long ago did you decide? 281
how long + present perfect 40
how many + present perfect 40
how much/how many? 194
hundred(s) 187

***if* sentences**
1st and 2nd conditional sentences 120–122
3rd conditional 124–125
if or *when* 120
if and *in case* 128
if/whether 173
if in reported questions 173
if only 130–131
imagine (+ *-ing*) 146
impossible for 315
in (preposition)
in (time) 263
in (place) 266
in time and *on time* 263
in case 128
indirect object 117–118
infinitive
verb + infinitive 136–137
infinitive after a question word 138
verb + object + infinitive 140
make and *let* + infinitive (without *to*) 140–141
verbs followed by the infinitive or *-ing* 164–166
infinitive of purpose (*He phoned to ask her out*) 133–134
adjective + infinitive 143–144
information (uncountable) 192
in front of 270
-ing
verb + *-ing* 146

verbs followed by *-ing* or the infinitive 164–166
prepositions + *-ing* 148–149
in spite of being ill ... 293
verb + preposition + *-ing* 148–149
it's like having two jobs 290
be/get used to + *-ing* 111–112
-ing clauses 154–155, 305
-ing in passive constructions:
He hates being watched 56
in order to 133
inside (preposition) 270–271
insist on + *-ing* 149
in spite of 293
in spite of the fact that ... 293
intend (*doing/to do*) 164
interested/interesting 239
interested in 315
into 274
into/out of a car 277–278
invite + object + infinitive with *to* 140
involved in 315
irregular verbs 18–19, 317
its (possessive) 221
it's no good/it's no use + *-ing* 152
it's said that ... 57
it's worth + *-ing* 152

jealous of 315
just with the present perfect 27, 33

keen on 315
keep (on) + *-ing* 313
kind to 315
kind of someone to do something 315
know how to, etc. 138
He's known to be dishonest 56
It's known that she's rich 57

late
(adjective and adverb) 243
late/lately (adverbs) 242
late for 315
laugh (*at*) 316
learn how to 138

least
  (*the*) *least* + adjective/noun
    236
  least (adverb) 255
less
  with uncountable nouns 191,
    236
  less (adverb) 255
let + object + infinitive
  without *to* 140–141
like doing/to do 157–158
  would like (*to do*) 158
  would like to have done 159
like (preposition) 290
  like/as 291
listen (to) 316
little
  (*very*) *little* 195
  a little and *a few* 195
  (*very*) *little* and *a little* 191
  a little (adverb) 254
live (on) 316
long + infinitive with *to* 136
look
  He looks/He's looking 14
  look as if/as though 106
  look forward to 314
  look + adjective 105
  look at/for/after 316
  look like 105
lot (*a lot/lots*) 194
love doing/to do 157
  would love to do 158
  would love to have done 159
luggage (uncountable) 192

make + object + infinitive
  without *to* 140–141
manage + infinitive with *to* 136
many 194
married to 315
may
  for present or future
    possibility 92
  may have for past possibility
    93
  may as well 93
  may for offers 83
  may for permission 82–83
  may in requests 82
mean + infinitive with *to* 136

might
  for present or future
    possibility 92
  might have done for
    past possibility 93
  might as well 93
  might in *if* sentences 120
mind + *-ing*
  *don't mind doing/would you
    mind doing?* 147
mine 222
miss (+ *-ing*) 146
modal verbs
  can, could 79
  can't and *must* for
    deductions 89
  may 82–83, 92
  *may have, might have,
    could have* 93
  might 92
  must, mustn't 85–87
  ought to, ought to have 95–97
  should, should have 95–97
  will 45–46, 48
  would 82–83, 109, 121–122
  modal verbs in passive
    constructions 54
  modal verbs in reported
    speech 169–170
more
  in comparatives 231–233
  more, the most + noun 236
  more (adverb) 255
most
  + plural or uncountable noun
    204
  most of 204
  most in superlatives 231–233
  the most + noun 236
  most (adverb) 255
much 194–195
  much (adverb) 254
must
  must/mustn't 85–87
  must and *can't* for
    deductions 89
  must and *have to* 85–87
  mustn't/don't have to 87
  must have done 90
my 221
myself/ourselves, etc.

  (reflexive/emphatic
    pronouns) 210–212

near (preposition) 270
nearly 242
need 114–115
  need doing/to do 165
needn't 114–115
  needn't have done and
    didn't need to do 115
negative questions 63
neither
  + noun 205
  neither of 205
  neither … nor 205
  neither am I, neither do I, etc.
    73
never 246–247
  never with the present simple
    13
  never with the present
    perfect 28
  never used to 108
news (uncountable) 192
next to 271–272
nice to 315
  *nice of someone to do
    something* 315
no
  no and *none* 197
  no and *any* 197
no longer 258
**non-defining relative
  clauses** 302-303
none 197
  none of 204
no-one (nobody)/nothing/
  nowhere 214
nor am I, nor do I, etc. 73
normally 246-247
nothing/something/anything
  214–215
nouns
  (countable and uncountable)
    190–192
  abstract (*love, peace*, etc.)
    182
  collective (*family, government*,
    etc.) 188
  compound (*credit card*, etc.)
    187

The numbers in the index refer to **pages**, not units.

plural forms 187,
(with *the* or not) 182
singular or plural? 188
uncountable (with *the* or not)
182
nowhere 215

objects (direct and indirect)
117–118
occasionally 246–247
of and *-'s* (possession)
218–219
off (preposition) 274
offer
in passive sentences 58
offer + infinitive with *to* 136
often 13, 246–247
on (preposition)
on a bus/in a car 277
on/off a train 277–278
on (time) 263–264
on (place) 267
on time and *in time* 263
once in future sentences +
simple present or present
perfect 286
one, ones
(*a blue one, the ones in the
shop*) 224–225
Which one/Which ones? 224
one another (= each other)
212
onto 275
on top of 271–272
opposite 270
ought to/should 95–96
ought to have done 97
our, ours 221–222
ourselves/each other 212
out of 274, 277–278
outside (preposition) 270
over 270–271, 275
own
(*my own car*) 221
on my own/on her own, etc.
221

passive
passive: main uses 53–54
passive infinitive (*be done*)
54

passive *-ing* form 56
passive with *know, say*, etc.
56–57
it's said/thought/known/ etc.
that ... 57
*he was given/sent/*etc. 58
past (preposition) 275
past continuous
(*was/were doing*) 22–23
past continuous/past simple
23
past continuous passive 53
past perfect
(*had done*) 42–43
past perfect/past simple
42–43
past perfect after *if* 124–125
past perfect after *wish* 131
past perfect passive 53
past perfect continuous
(*had been doing*) 43
past simple
(*I saw*) 18–20
past simple and past
continuous 23
past simple or present
perfect 32–34
past simple and past perfect
42–43
past simple passive 53
people 187–188
persuade someone to do
something 140
phrasal verbs (*wake up, turn
on*, etc.) 102–103, 313–314
plan + infinitive with *to* 136
pleased
+ infinitive 143
pleased with/about 315
plenty (of) 194
plural nouns 187–188
point *there's no point* (*in*) + *-ing*
152
police (plural noun) 188
possessive adjectives and
pronouns (*my, mine*, etc.)
221–222
possessive forms 's, s' (*the
man's hat/my parents' house*)
217
noun + *of* + noun

(*the title of the book*) 218
noun + noun (*the kitchen
door*) 218
a friend of mine/of my father's
219
practise + *-ing* 146
prefer doing/to do 161
would prefer to do 161–162
would prefer to have done
162
prepare + infinitive with *to*
136
prepositions
of place (*under, over*, etc.)
270–272
of movement (*up, down*, etc.)
274–275
for travel/transport (*at, by, in,
on, off*, etc.) 277–278
at/on/in (time) 263–264
at/on/in (place) 266–268
by with the passive 54
preposition + *-ing* 148–149
prepositions in relative
clauses 297
adjective + preposition + *-ing*
(*tired of waiting*) 148–149
verbs with prepositions 316
present continuous
(*I am doing*) 9–11
present continuous with
always 11
present continuous and
present simple 6, 13
present continuous for the
future 11, 16
present continuous
passive 53
verbs not used in present
continuous 10
present perfect simple (*I have
done*) 25
present perfect simple with
already, just, yet 27
present perfect simple with
ever, never, before 28
present perfect continuous
(*I have been doing*) 36–37
present perfect simple and
continuous 39–40

present perfect with *for* and
since 33, 34
present perfect continuous
with *for* and *since* 36–37
present perfect and past
simple 32–34
present perfect after a
superlative 30
present perfect after *the
first/second time that* ... 30
present perfect with *today,
this morning*, etc. 30
present perfect passive 53
present simple
(*I do*) 6–7
present simple and present
continuous 13–14
present simple for the future
16
present simple passive 53
presume so/not 72
pretend + infinitive with *to*
136
pretty (adverb) 250
prevent someone from doing
something 149
prison (*prison/the prison*) 180
probably (position) 243–244
progress (uncountable) 192
promise
(in reported speech) 174–175
promise + infinitive with *to*
136
proud of 315
prove + infinitive with *to* 136
provided/providing that
127–128
purpose infinitive of purpose
133–134

questions 62–63
questions with *Do/does* 7, 62
questions with *Did* 20, 62
questions with *Who, Which,
How*, etc. 63, 69–70
negative questions 63
Do you know what/who...? 70
reported questions 173
short reply questions (*I don't
like it – Don't you?*) 77
question tags 65–67

quite 250–251

rarely 246–247
rather
would rather do 162
would rather you did 162
would rather have done 162
*rather cold, rather a warm
day* 251
realise not used in
continuous tenses 14
recently with present perfect
33
reckon (*I reckon so*) 72
reflexive pronouns
(*myself, herself, themselves*,
etc.) 210–211
by myself, by yourself, etc. 211
adjective + preposition +
reflexive pronoun: *angry
with myself* 211
refuse + infinitive with *to* 136
regret (*doing/to do*) 166
related to 315
relative clauses 296–297,
299–300
non-defining relative clauses
302–303
rely on 316
remember
remember (*doing/to do*) 166
remember who/where, etc.
+ infinitive 138
remind someone to do
something 140
report in passive
constructions (*It is reported
that* ...) 57
reported speech 168–171,
173–175
reported questions 173
reported commands,
requests, advice 174
reporting verbs (*agree, offer,
suggest*, etc.) 174–175
responsible for 315
risk + -*ing* 146
round (preposition) 270, 274
rude to 315

's (apostrophe s) 217–218

same *the same as* ... 235
satisfied with 315
say
(and *tell* in reported speech)
168
It's said that ... 57
He's said to be very ill 56–57
scared of 315
school (*school/the school*) 180
search for 316
see not used in present
continuous 10
seem
seem as if/as though 106
seem + infinitive with *to* 136
seem + adjective 105
seem like 105
seem so/not 72
sensible (*of someone to
do something*) 315
several only with countable
nouns 191
shall/shan't 45–46
Shall I/Shall we? 45–45
shocked at/by 315
shocked/shocking 239
short of 315
short forms (*I'm, you've,
didn't*, etc.) 310
short reply questions 77
should/ought to 95–96
should have done 97
shout at/to 316
show
in passive constructions 58
Show me how to do it 138
silly (*of someone to do
something*) 315
similar to 315
since
(time) 280–281
ever since 280–281
with present perfect 33, 36
since and *for* 280
How long is it since ... ? 281
It's a long time since ... 281
since/as (reason) 294
smell
smell + adjective 105
smell like 105

so
so am I, so do I, etc. 73
I think so, I hope so, etc. 72
so + adjective + *that* 252
so/such 252
so (result) 294
so as not to + infinitive 134
some 204
some of 204
some and *any* 197
some with countable nouns
185
some used in questions 198
something/someone
(somebody) 214
*something to do/something
different* 215
sometimes 13, 246–247
somewhere/anywhere/
nowhere 215
so much/so many 195
so much (adverb) 254
sorry about/for 315
so that/so (purpose) 134
sound
sound + adjective 105
sound as if/as though 106
sound like 105
spelling rules 311–312
spite (*in spite of*) 293
stand (*can't stand*) 151–152
start doing/to do 164
still/yet 33, 257–258
stop doing/to do 165
stop someone (from) + -ing
149
stupid (*of someone to do
something*) 315
succeed (in) + *-ing* 149
such/so 252
suffer from 316
suggest + *-ing* 146
superlatives
(*the biggest, the most
expensive*) 230–233, 236–237
irregular forms 232
adverb forms 233
the most, the least, the fewest
+ noun 236
*the biggest in the world, the
biggest I've seen* 237

suppose
I suppose so/I suppose not 72
supposed (*He's supposed to ...*)
57–58
surprised
+ infinitive 143
surprised at/by 315
surprised/surprising 239
suspect so/not 72
swear + infinitive with *to* 136

tags (question tags) 65–67
talk (*about doing something*)
149
taste
taste + adjective 105
taste like 105
teach
in passive sentences 58
Teach me how to do it 138
tell/say 168
tell someone to do something
140
tell someone what to do 138
tend + infinitive with *to* 136
than after comparatives
230–233
that/this/these/those 207
that in relative clauses
296–297
the 177–180, 182
the and *a/an* 177
the + adjective (*the rich*) 179
the + nationality words 179
eggs/the eggs, etc. 182
school/the school, etc. 180
the with geographical
names 179
the with streets, buildings,
etc. 179
the sooner the better 236
their, theirs 221–222
themselves/each other 212
there's no point (-ing) 152
these/those/this/that 207–208
think
I think so/I don't think so 72
think about doing something
149
think of/about 316
this/that/these/those 207–208

this morning, etc.
with present perfect 30, 33
with past simple 34
those/these,/this/that 207–208
though 293
as though 290–291
even though 293
threaten + infinitive with *to*
136
through (preposition) 274
till (see *until*)
time
it's the first time I've ... 30
on time and *in time* 263
tired of 315
tired/tiring 239
to (preposition) 274
to + *-ing* (*I'm looking forward
to seeing you*) 149
to/for + indirect object
117–118
today
with present perfect 30, 33
with present perfect or past
simple 34
too (*too big, too late*) 260
too much/too many 195, 260
towards 275
transport (uncountable) 192
travel (countable and
uncountable) 192
try doing/to do 166

uncountable nouns 190–192
without *a/an* 185
under 271–275
understand
what to do, etc. 138
not used in continuous
tenses 10
He's understood to be in Africa
56
It's understood that ... 57
university (*university/the
university*) 180
unkind to 315
unless 127
until/till 288
in future sentences + simple
present or present perfect
286
until/by 288

The numbers in the index refer to **pages**, not units.

up (preposition) 274
upset about 315
use (*it's no use -ing*) 152
used to do 108–109
  be/get used to 111–112
usually 246–247

verbs
  with prepositions 316
  verb + -ing (*I enjoy dancing*)
    146
  verb + preposition + -ing
    (*I've given up smoking*)
    148–149
  verb + question word
    + infinitive (*I asked how to
    get there*) 138
  verb + infinitive with *to*
    (*I hope to see him*) 136
  verb + infinitive with *to*
    or -*ing* 164–166
  verb + object + infinitive
    (*I want you to come*) 140–141
  verb + indirect object
    + direct object (*I sent him a
    letter*) 117
  verbs not used in continuous
    tenses 10, 14, 37, 40
  irregular verbs 317
very much (adverb) 254

wait for 316
want
  + object + infinitive with *to*
    141
  want to + passive infinitive
    (*I want to be loved*) 54
warn
  in reported speech 174
  *warn someone (not) to do
    something* 140
was/were 18
  was/were doing 22–23
  was/were going to 48
  was or *were* in *if* sentences
    122
weather (uncountable) 192
well (adverb) 242
what
  what in exclamations 184,
    190

What in questions 63, 69–70
what in relative clauses 300
when
  when in future sentences 286
  when + simple present or
    present perfect 286
  when or *if* 120
where
  Where in questions 63
  where in relative clauses
    299, 303
whether in reported questions
  173
which
  Which in questions 69–70
  which in relative clauses
    296–297, 302–303
  Which one(s)?/Which of ...? 70
while 284
  in future sentences +
    simple present 286
who
  Who in questions 63, 69
  who in relative clauses
    296–297, 302
whole 201
  *the whole day, morning, week,
    etc.* 202
whom
  whom in relative clauses 297
  whom after a preposition
    (*The man to whom I gave
    it ...*) 297, 303
whose
  Whose in questions 222
  whose in relative clauses
    299, 303
why in negative questions
  (*Why don't you have a
  holiday?*) 63
will/won't 45–46
  will in requests 46
  will or *going to* 48
  future continuous (*will be
    doing*) 50
  future perfect (*will have
    done*) 51
  will in the passive 53–54
wish 130–131
with (in identifying phrases)
  306

without + -*ing* 148
won't 45–46
  won't in refusals 46
word order
  in questions 62
  Do you know who he is? 70
  reported questions 173
  order of adjectives 228
  position of adverbs 243–244,
    247–248, 250, 254–255
  with phrasal verbs (*Turn on
    the radio/Turn the radio
    on/Turn it on*) 103
work
  (countable and uncountable)
    192
  at work/to work 178
worried
  worried (about) 315
  worried/worrying 239
worse
  worse (adjective) 232–233
  worse (adverb) 255
worst
  (the) worst (adjective)
    232–233
  worst (adverb) 255
worth (*it's worth -ing*) 152
would
  in requests 82
  would like + infinitive 158
  would like in offers/
    invitations 83
  *would like/love/prefer
    + object + infinitive* 141
  would rather 162
  would for regular actions in
    the past 109
  would (have) in *if* sentences
    121–122, 124
  wish ... would 130
write to 316
wrong (*of someone to do
  something*) 315

yesterday with past simple
  32–33
yet/still 257–258
  yet + present perfect 27, 33
your, yours 221–222
yourselves/each other 212

Answers to Practice Exercises

Unit 1

1 1 get up 2 gets up 3 watch 4 watches 5 cries 6 go 7 washes goes out 8 gets

2 1 Spain belongs to the European Union.
2 Russia and Switzerland don't belong to the EU.
3 They don't drive on the right in Britain.
4 You see a lot of Japanese cars in Europe.
5 Britain doesn't have a president.
6 The US president doesn't live in New York.
7 They speak Spanish in Argentina.
8 They don't speak Spanish in Brazil.

3 1 Do you speak English? 2 Where do you come from?
3 What does that mean? 4 It means 'beautiful city'.
5 How much does a cola cost?
6 Does this machine take German money?
7 No, it doesn't.

4 1 Do you watch much TV? – Yes, I do. OR No, I don't.
2 Does TV in your country have many American programmes? – Yes, it does. OR No, it doesn't.
3 Do you and your friends play much sport?
– Yes, we do. OR No, we don't.
4 Does the place where you live have a sports centre? – Yes, it does. OR No, it doesn't.

Unit 2

1 1 B 2 A 3 D 4 A 5 B 6 C 7 B 8 C 9 A 10 B

2 1 Who's speaking? 2 are you phoning 3 I'm staying
4 The sun's shining 5 I'm having 6 you don't seem
7 do you know 8 are you phoning 9 I want
10 I understand 11 do you want 12 I just wish
13 you're enjoying 14 I don't care 15 I'm trying
16 I'm getting up 17 you don't mind 18 I'm going back

3 1 we're flying 2 we're crossing 3 is blowing
4 is slowing 5 I don't think 6 is 7 the sun's shining
8 is 9 you're enjoying 10 are (OR is) looking after you

Unit 3

1 1 makes/make are/'re are/'re building 2 produce
are/'re producing 3 are buying are becoming get
are 4 pay stay rises 5 make are expanding

2 1 What are you doing? 2 I'm writing 3 What's she
doing 4 Is she 5 she's spending 6 What's she doing
7 Is she 8 she's working 9 How much do they pay
10 They give 11 she gets

3 1 Do you know 2 who's wearing 3 I know 4 I don't
remember 5 I think 6 I'm not 7 She's talking
8 I think 9 he likes 10 he's being 11 What do you
mean 12 Does he realise 13 her boyfriend's
standing 14 I don't think 15 he knows

Unit 4

1 1 I'm going to the cinema. 2 I'm going to Andy's party.
3 I'm meeting my mum at the bus-station.
4 I'm having a Spanish lesson. 5 I'm playing tennis
with Jack. 6 I'm not doing anything.

2 1 The plane leaves at 10.15.
2 We stop in Antigua for an hour.
3 The flight takes 9½ hours.
4 We arrive in Grenada at quarter to four, local time.

3 1 I'm going 2 are giving/is giving 3 I'm going
4 We aren't/We're not going 5 leaves 6 stops
7 arrives 8 we're taking 9 starts 10 leaves
11 get back

Unit 5

1 1 were 2 was 3 weren't 4 weren't 5 were
6 wasn't 7 was 8 weren't 9 were 10 wasn't

2 1 Did you like the food? 2 When did you arrive back?
3 Where did you stay? 4 How often did it rain?
5 Did you hire a car?
6 How much Greek did you learn?

3 1 cost 2 didn't 3 paid 4 wore 5 went 6 were
7 felt 8 came 9 broke

4 1 went 2 gave 3 said 4 read 5 didn't have 6 put
7 hid 8 ran 9 got 10 were 11 had

Unit 6

1 1 At 9.25 he was going to the airport.
2 At 10.15 he was sitting in the departure lounge.
3 At 10.55 he was walking to Gate 36.
4 At 11.15 he was waiting (for the plane) to take off.
5 At 12.00 he was flying to Paris.

2 1 finished rang 2 was listening phoned
3 turned rang 4 were trying suggested
5 came drove 6 were using arrived
7 bought were waiting 8 were playing started
9 stopped started 10 stopped went on

3 1 stopped 2 arrested 3 was standing 4 told
5 was driving 6 saw 7 was wearing 8 said
9 wasn't doing 10 was only trying

Unit 7

1 1 They've taken 2 's (has) gone 3 They've made
4 They've thrown 5 I haven't phoned the police.

2 1 Have you found the passports? – Yes, I have.
2 Where have you put the tickets and the travellers' cheques? – I've put them in my bag.
3 Have you left the key with the neighbours? – Yes, I have.
4 Have you given the neighbours our holiday address? – No, I haven't.
5 Have you packed our snorkels and masks? – Yes, I have.

3 1 He hasn't changed. 2 He's left 3 They've moved
4 She's had 5 I've finished 6 I've applied 7 I haven't had

4 1 There's been
2 The US President has flown
3 The European Parliament has/have voted
4 Two British women have climbed
5 Rescuers haven't found
6 Strong winds have damaged

Unit 8

1 1 They've built a lot more houses. 2 The population has increased to 5,000. 3 The railway station has closed. 4 They've cut down the trees in the square. 5 But the people haven't changed. They're still very friendly.

2 1 I've just cleaned the carpets. 2 I haven't mended it yet. 3 I haven't turned the water on yet. 4 I've just made some. 5 I haven't finished the living room yet.

3 1 I've already given you £70 this month. 2 You haven't done it yet. 3 You've already lost it. 4 You haven't rung him yet.

4 1 Yes, I've never been in a Rolls Royce before. 2 Wow! I've never had a gold watch before. 3 Yes, I've never stayed at the Ritz before. 4 Yes, please. I've never drunk real champagne before. 5 Oh no! I've never been on television before.

Unit 9

1 1 I haven't seen her this morning. 2 She's only come twice this week. 3 She's had ten days off this month. 4 She's missed two months' work this year. 5 Has she phoned this morning?

2 1 Where's (has) he gone? 2 Where have they been? 3 Where's (has) he gone? 4 Where have you been?

3 1 gone 2 been 3 gone 4 gone

4 1 you've had 2 I've flown 3 you haven't been 4 Have you been 5 I've had 6 you've eaten 7 I haven't eaten

5 1 it's the most interesting book I've read. 2 I think it's the worst film he's made. 3 it was the most exciting game I've watched

Unit 10

1 1e 2c 3f 4a 5b 6d

2 1 What's happened? 2 There's (has) been 3 What happened 4 ran 5 swerved 6 hit 7 When did it happen 8 Has anyone called 9 have arrived 10 They've probably called 11 we've had 12 wasn't

3 1A 2A 3B 4B 5A 6B 7A 8A 9A 10B 11A 12A

Unit 11

1 1 have been going out 2 They've been planning 3 They've been looking for 4 they've been saving up 5 James has been doing 6 he's been working 7 she's been making 8 she hasn't been feeling well 9 She's been going 10 James has been worrying 11 he hasn't been sleeping 12 they've been feeling

2 1 She's been working hard. 2 He hasn't been feeling well all day. 3 He's been playing football. 4 She's been buying clothes. 5 He's been watching television all evening. 6 It's been raining all day.

3 2 How long have you been playing in professional tournaments? 3 How long have you been living in Monaco? 4 How long have you been doing yoga? 5 How long have you been travelling?

Unit 12

1 1 She's been sunbathing 2 The sun has been shining 3 She hasn't had 4 She's been reading 5 She's only read 6 she's been watching who's been surfing

7 he's only fallen off 8 He's looked he's smiled 9 she's been hoping he hasn't come 10 Kerry has always wanted

2 1 How long have you been living in England? 2 How long have you been a circus acrobat? 3 How many times have you fallen off the trapeze? 4 How many books have you written? 5 How long have you been learning English? 6 How long have you been married to Tessa?

Unit 13

1 1 hadn't spoken 2 hadn't sat 3 hadn't drunk 4 hadn't eaten 5 hadn't driven

2 1 When we'd parked our car, we went to the check-in desk. 2 Once they'd weighed our suitcases, they gave us our boarding passes. 3 After we'd shown our passports at immigration, we went to the café in the departure lounge. 4 We got on the plane after we'd handed in our boarding passes. 5 As soon as we'd found our seats, we sat down and fastened our seat-belts. 6 We didn't unfasten our seat-belts until the plane had taken off.

3 1 As soon as the alarm clock rang, I woke up. 2 When I'd got dressed, I went downstairs. 3 After I'd had breakfast, I cleaned my teeth. 4 When I looked at my watch, I realised I was late. 5 When I arrived at the bus stop, I remembered it was Sunday.

4 1 they'd been jogging 2 she'd been playing 3 he'd been drinking 4 she'd been studying

Unit 14

1 A6 B5 C1 D3 E2 F4 G7

2 1 Will 2 will 3 won't 4 won't/shan't 5 Will? 6 I'll 7 Will 8 I'll 9 I'll 10 won't 11 won't/shan't

3 1 I'll make them. 2 I'll go and buy some. 3 I'll read (tell) them a story. 4 I'll take him. 5 I'll look after them.

4 1 Shall I open a window? 2 Shall I put/turn the radio on? 3 Shall we stop at the next service station? 4 Shall I drive?

Unit 15

1 1 Will you come 2 I won't be 3 I'll be 4 What are you going to do 5 I'm going to see 6 When will you be 7 I'll be 8 what are you going to do 9 I'll phone 10 I'll see

2 1 I'll take 2 I'll be 3 Will that be 4 I'll pick you up 5 What are you going to buy 6 I'm going to buy 7 I'm going to get 8 That'll be 9 I'm not going to buy 10 will be 11 I'm going to borrow 12 I'll see

3 1 She's going to jump (off the bridge). 2 He's going to drop the plates. 3 The boat's going to sink. 4 They're going to play tennis. 5 The rope's going to break.

Unit 16

1 1 I'll be listening to flamenco music.
2 The sun will be shining. 3 It won't be raining.
4 I won't be working.
5 I won't be sitting in this boring office.
2 1 I'll have finished my exams. 2 I'll have left home.
3 I'll be living in my own flat. 4 I'll have got a job.
5 I'll be earning a lot of money.
6 I'll be going out every night.
3 1 he'll have walked 2 He'll have passed through
3 He'll have eaten 4 He'll have drunk
5 He'll have used 6 He won't have seen
4 1 She'll be working in the garden.
2 And she'll have forgotten to put the answering
machine on.
3 Or she'll be watching TV.
4 And she won't have heard the telephone.
5 Or she'll be having a bath.

Unit 17

1 1 A new hospital has been built.
2 A new shopping centre is being built.
3 It'll be finished next October.
4 The town hall was knocked down last week.
5 A new one is going to be built soon.
2 1 was born 2 was taken 3 were nearly killed 4 were
forbidden 5 was used 6 was lent 7 is now installed
3 1 has just been sent 2 was given 3 is shocked
4 hasn't been painted 5 are covered 6 he's (is) woken
up 7 He's (is) allowed 8 will be let out 9 he'll be kept in
4 1 I don't want to be told what to do.
2 I'd like to be listened to.
3 I should have been given more freedom.
4 I ought to have been allowed to be more independent.

Unit 18

1 1 She enjoyed being taken to the cinema to see her
films.
2 She didn't like being asked how old she was.
3 She hated being seen when she wasn't wearing any
make-up.
4 She was afraid of being forgotten when she was
dead.
2 1 At first nobody was said to have been killed.
2 But now 250 people are thought to have died in the
earthquake.
3 The death toll is expected to rise.
4 Three coastal villages are reported to have
disappeared completely.
3 1 British people are supposed to be careful drivers.
2 When you drive in Britain, you're supposed to wear
a seat belt.
3 You aren't/You're not supposed to drink and drive.
4 You aren't/You're not supposed to park on the
pavement.
4 1 Nurses aren't paid much money.
2 They are being offered a 1% pay rise (by the
government).
3 They've been promised a further rise next year (by
the Minister).
4 They might be given a 2% rise then.
5 The Minister has been sent a letter (by the nurses).
OR A letter has been sent to the Minister.

Unit 19

1 1 I had my watch repaired. 2 I had my hair cut.
3 I had my shoes mended. 4 I had my teeth checked.
5 We had a burglar alarm installed.
6 We had stronger locks fitted to the doors.
7 I had my passport renewed.
8 We had two new tyres fitted to our car.
2 1 He had his pockets searched. 2 He had his hair cut.
3 He had his blood tested. 4 He had his photo taken.
5 He also had his cigarettes stolen.
6 Then he had his nose broken.
7 he had one of his teeth knocked out in a fight.
3 1 I'm having it done. 2 I had them painted.
3 I'm going to have it repaired. 4 I had it fitted.
5 I'm going to have it built.
4 1 She has her hair done 2 She has her apartment
cleaned 3 She also has her apartment redecorated
4 She has all her clothes specially made 5 She has
her body and her face massaged 6 She has the
sheets on her bed changed 7 She has breakfast
brought to her

Unit 20

1 1 Have you ever seen a ghost?
2 Were/Weren't you afraid? 3 Can you describe it?
4 Did you know her? 5 Did the ghost speak to you?
6 Have you seen it again?
7 Would you like to see it again?
2 1 Where do you come from?
2 Why have you come to England?
3 When did you arrive?
4 What do you do in Tokyo?
5 How long are you staying in England?
6 Who do you know in England?
3 1 Wasn't the weather very good?
2 Didn't you take your credit card?
3 Didn't you get a new one?

Unit 21

1 1 isn't it? 2 is it? 3 wasn't it? 4 has it? 5 isn't it?
6 doesn't it? 7 wasn't there? 8 have they?
9 did they? 10 won't it?
2 1c 2e 3d 4g 5f 6a 7b
3 1 will you?/would you?/can you?/could you?
2 isn't there? 3 isn't it? 4 doesn't it? 5 won't it?
6 didn't you? 7 have we? 8 could you? 9 can't you?
10 aren't I? 11 shall we?

Unit 22

1 1 Who did you invite 2 Who invited him? 3 who
brought him 4 Who did Rick bring? 5 what
happened 6 What did he throw? 7 what did Sam do
2 1 What 2 Which 3 Which 4 What 5 Which 6 what
7 Which 8 which
3 1 Do you know where I can find a chemist's?
2 Could you tell me how I get there?
3 Do you know where the town hall is?
4 Have you any idea what time they close?
5 Do you know if they are (they're) open now?

Unit 23

1 1 I think so.   2 I believe so.   3 No, I don't expect so./I expect not.   4 No, I'm afraid not.   5 Yes, I suppose so.   6 No, I don't think so.   7 No, I don't suppose so./No, I suppose not.   8 I'm afraid so.

2 1 So did I.   2 Neither/Nor did I.   3 Nor/Neither do I.   4 So am I.   5 Neither/Nor do I.   6 So would I.   7 So do I.   8 Neither/Nor have I.   9 Neither/Nor can I.

Unit 24

1 1 can't   2 isn't   3 doesn't   4 isn't   5 won't   6 might   7 does   8 hasn't   9 did   10 didn't

2 1 I might have (done).   2 somebody must have (done)   3 I would have (done)   4 I might (do).   5 I haven't (done) yet   6 I will (do)

3 1 Are you?   2 Has she?   3 Haven't you?   4 Is it?   5 Did she?   6 Do they?   7 Will you?

Unit 25

1 1 can   2 he'll be able to   3 be able to   4 can't   5 can't   6 I haven't been able to   7 I'll be able to   8 I won't be able to

2 1 could   2 could   3 couldn't   4 could   5 could   6 could   7 could   8 couldn't   9 couldn't

3 1 Were you able to   2 couldn't/wasn't able to   3 was able to   4 Were you able to   5 could   6 couldn't/wasn't able to   7 couldn't/wasn't able to   8 couldn't/weren't able to   9 were able to   10 couldn't/wasn't able to   11 was able to

Unit 26

1 1 Can I/Could I/May I open the window?   2 Yes, you can/may.   3 Can I/Could I/May I give you my homework next week?   4 No, you can't.   5 Can I/Could I/May I give it to you tomorrow?   6 Yes, you can/may.   7 Can I/Could I/May I go outside for a moment?   8 Yes, you can/may.   9 Would you like me to explain   10 Yes, I would.   11 Can I/Could I/May I borrow your calculator?   12 you can't   13 Would you like to borrow mine?

2 1 Would you/Could you/Can you   2 Can you/Could you/Would you   3 Can I/Could I/May I   4 Can you/Could you/Would you   5 Can I/Could I/May I   6 you can't   7 Can you/Could you/Would you   8 Can I/Could I/May I   9 can you/could you/would you   10 Would you/Could you/Can you   11 Can I/Could I/May I   12 Yes, you can/may.

Unit 27

1 1 d   2 c   3 b   4 a

2 1 You mustn't smoke.   2 You must stop.   3 You don't have to make an appointment.   4 You mustn't talk./You mustn't make any noise.   5 You don't have to pay (for an eye-test).   6 You must fasten your seat-belt.

3
You must/you have to	You mustn't	You don't have to
B, E, I	C, D, G	A, F, H

4 1 You don't have to   2 You must   3 You don't have to   4 You mustn't   5 You must   6 You don't have to

Unit 28

1 1 She must be very popular.   2 She must like animals.   3 She must be a very good player.   4 She can't be very interested in current affairs.   5 She can't be looking forward to it.   6 She must be feeling depressed.

2 1 must have spent   2 can't have spent   3 must have fallen   4 can't have fallen   5 must still be   6 must have taken   7 can't have been   8 can't just disappear   9 must have taken

3 1 can't have got   2 must have gone   3 can't have gone   4 must have gone   5 must have been buying   6 must have been   7 can't have been   8 must have made   9 can't have been wearing   10 can't have been

Unit 29

1 1 She may not/might not be feeling well.   2 She may/might/could be worrying about her exams.   3 She may/might/could need help.   4 She may not/might not want to talk to anybody.

2 1 She may have/might have/could have stayed late at work.   2 Or she may not have/might not have heard the phone.   3 She may have been/might have been/could have been having a bath.   4 She may not have/might not have wanted to talk to him.   5 She may have/might have/could have forgotten about the arrangement.

3 1 could have/might have   2 might have/could have   3 couldn't have   4 might have/could have   5 might not have   6 couldn't have   7 might not have   8 might have/could have   9 couldn't have   10 couldn't have

4 1 We may as well walk. OR We might as well walk.   2 We may as well have a drink. OR We might as well have a drink.   3 You may as well buy the green one. OR You might as well buy the green one.   4 We may as well go home. OR We might as well go home.

Unit 30

1 1 Yes.   2 Yes.   3 No.   4 No.   5 Yes.

2 1 He should be/ought to be more interested.   2 He shouldn't/oughtn't to go out so often.   3 He shouldn't be/oughtn't to be watching TV.   4 He should be/ought to be studying.

3 1 He shouldn't have/oughtn't to have bought a flat like that.   2 He shouldn't have/oughtn't to have had so many holidays.   3 He should have/ought to have paid at least a bit of tax.   4 He should have/ought to have spent more time with them.   5 He should have/ought to have been more responsible.

4 1 You'd better not move him.   2 We'd better phone the police.   3 We'd better put a coat over him.   4 We'd better stop the traffic.

Unit 31

1 1 I've got 2 has got 3 I've got 4 How long have you had it? 5 I've had 6 you've got 7 has got 8 Have you got time 9 I haven't 10 have

2 1 Yes. 2 Yes. 3 Yes. 4 No. 5 No. 6 Yes. 7 Yes. 8 No. 9 No. 10 No. 11 No. 12 No. 13 Yes. 14 No. 15 No. 16 No. 17 No.

3 1 I've got 2 he's got 3 He's got 4 I haven't 5 I've got 6 He's got 7 he's got 8 I haven't got 9 He and his family have 10 I had 11 We're having 12 have 13 his wife's having

Unit 32

1 1 got back 2 rang me up 3 call in 4 found out 5 paid back 6 go on 7 hold on 8 put it off 9 carried on (OR went on) 10 work out 11 turned me down

2 1 get on with 2 switch the television on 3 turn it down 4 come round 5 go away 6 throws it away 7 look forward to 8 get up 9 wakes up 10 go on 11 put up with

3 1a 2b 3a 4a OR 4b 5a 6a OR 6b 7b 8a OR 8b

Unit 33

1 1 Martha seems nervous. 2 Adam looks tired. 3 Joanne sounds angry. 4 Simon doesn't look well.

2 1 It smells like perfume.
2 It looks like a jewellery box.
3 It looks like me when I was a baby.
4 It sounds like Elvis Presley.
5 It feels like real hair.

3 1 of 2 like 3 of 4 like 5 like

4 1 as if/as though (informal: like) 3 like 5 as if/as though (informal: like) 7 as if/as though (informal: like) 9 as if/as though (informal: like) 10 as if/as though (informal: like) 11 like

Unit 34

1 1 He used to play football. Now he watches it on television.
2 He used to stay up till 12.00. Now he goes to bed at 9.30.
2 He used to ride a motorbike. Now he drives a car.
4 He didn't use to wear glasses. Now he wears glasses all the time.

2 1 Gemma used to go out with Paul, but now she goes out with Ben.
2 Paul used to go out a lot, but now he stays in in the evening.
3 Gemma used to be in love with Paul, but now she feels nothing for him.
4 Paul didn't use to think about her, but now he misses her a lot.

3 1 Which team did you use to play for?
2 How much did you use to earn?
3 Did you use to be a good player? – I used to be the best.
4 Where did you use to live? – I used to live in a big house.
5 What kind of car did you use to have?
6 How many friends did you use to have? – I used to have hundreds.

Unit 35

1 1 He isn't used to travelling to work.
2 He isn't used to starting work at 8.30.
3 He isn't used to wearing a suit and tie.
4 He isn't used to sitting at a desk all day.
5 He isn't used to working nine hours a day.
6 He isn't used to having money to spend.

2 1 get used to 2 we soon got used to 3 we were already used to driving 4 get used to 5 We weren't used to 6 we were used to 7 get used to 8 we still aren't used to 9 I'm not used to seeing 10 we'll never get used to having

3 1 I was used to sharing 2 I was used to doing 3 I'm not used to living 4 get used to 5 get used to having 6 I'm used to cooking 7 I'm still not used to waking up 8 I'll never get used to

Unit 36

1 1 What do you need 2 We need 3 we need to win 4 I need to buy 5 do you need? 6 I don't need 7 we don't need 8 I don't need

2 1 You needn't have waited up for me.
2 But you needn't have worried.
3 But you needn't have rung her.
4 You needn't have phoned the police.
5 You needn't have given me the money.

3 1 he didn't need to get up early. 2 He didn't need to get there so he didn't need to worry 3 He needn't have taken 4 he didn't need to read 5 He needn't have looked at them 6 he didn't need to worry

Unit 37

1 1 She gave her husband a new car.
2 And she bought her daughter some new clothes.
3 Did she give them anything?
4 she booked them a holiday in Thailand.
5 She bought a new computer for her brother.
6 And she got some flowers for all her neighbours.
7 and she gave the rest to charity.
8 She sent £3,000 to Save the Children.
9 and she gave £2,000 to the Red Cross.
10 She didn't give me anything.
11 She just showed me the £50,000 cheque!

2 1 for 2 to 3 for 4 for 5 for 6 to 7 for 8 for 9 for

Unit 38

1 1 go 2 there'll be 3 it'll be 4 go 5 won't be 6 will be 7 take 8 it'll take 9 we'll be able 10 it'll be 11 it'll cost 12 won't see

2 1 had I'd be able 2 I'd find were 3 I'd be had 4 I was/were I'd go 5 wouldn't be understood

3 1 want 2 were/was 3 I'd spend 4 went 5 I'd have to 6 would you go 7 you didn't have to 8 you'd be able to 9 I'll write 10 like 11 stayed 12 I'd have to 13 wouldn't be 14 gave 15 you'd be able to

Unit 39

1 1 I'd known 2 I'd have made/I would've made
   3 I'd have phoned/I would've phoned 4 I'd had
   5 I'd phoned 6 it wouldn't have been
   7 what would you have done 8 I hadn't been
   9 I'd have gone/I would've gone 10 I'd stayed
   11 I'd have gone/I would have gone
2 1 If she hadn't been wearing her seat-belt, she might
     have been killed.
   2 If the lorry's brakes had been working, the driver
     could have stopped in time.
   3 Rosie wouldn't be in hospital now if she'd taken
     her normal route to work.
   4 If the lorry driver hadn't been looking at his map,
     he would have seen Rosie's car.
   5 The lorry might have exploded if the fire brigade
     hadn't arrived and put out the fire.
3 1 If he'd taken his car, he wouldn't have got to work
     on time.
   2 If he hadn't checked the figures, he wouldn't have
     found the mistake.
   3 If he'd chosen the chicken, he would've had food
     poisoning.
   4 If he hadn't had his umbrella with him, he would
     have got wet.
   5 If the newsagent hadn't persuaded him to buy a
     lottery ticket, he wouldn't have won £500.

Unit 40

1 1 Unless we stop polluting the sea, we'll kill
     everything that lives in it.
   2 Unless we forget about economic growth, we'll use
     up all the earth's natural resources.
   3 Unless we act now, there won't be a future for our
     grandchildren.
   4 But we can't change the world unless we change
     ourselves.
   5 Unless people cooperate with each other, we'll
     destroy ourselves.
2 1 provided/providing/as long as 2 unless
   3 provided/providing/as long as 4 unless
   5 Provided/Providing/As long as 6 unless 7 unless
   8 provided/providing/as long as 9 unless
   10 provided/providing/as long as
3 1 We'd better reserve our seats on the train in case
     it's full.
   2 I'm going to insure the video camera in case it gets
     stolen.
   3 I gave the travel agent our telephone number this
     morning in case they needed (OR need) to contact us.
   4 I phoned the bank yesterday in case they'd (had)
     forgotten to get our travellers' cheques.

Unit 41

1 1 I wish you'd turn the volume down. 2 I wish you
   wouldn't make so much noise. 3 I wish I could break
   that guitar. 4 If only you'd try to understand.
   5 If only you'd practise somewhere else. 6 I wish
   parents wouldn't be so intolerant. 7 I really wish I
   could get my own flat.

2 1 I wish my computer had a CD ROM.
   2 If only my dad had a Mercedes.
   3 I wish I was/were going to the Caribbean this
     winter.
   4 If only there was/were a swimming pool in our
     garden.
   5 I wish I looked like a fashion model.
   6 I wish I didn't have ordinary light brown hair.
   7 I wish I didn't live in England.
   8 If only I lived in New York.
3 1 were 2 had ('d) invited 3 wasn't coming
   4 hadn't invited 5 wouldn't talk 6 hadn't said
   7 wouldn't be OR weren't 8 hadn't told 9 would ('d)
   stop 10 would ('d) try

Unit 42

1 1 On Monday she's going to the Indian Embassy to
     get a visa.
   2 On Tuesday she's going to the doctor's to have her
     vaccinations.
   3 On Wednesday she's going to the bookshop to buy
     a Hindi dictionary.
   4 On Thursday she's going to the camping shop to
     choose a tent.
   5 On Friday she's going to the travel agent's to book
     her ticket.
2 1 I need a map to plan my route.
   2 I'll take a compass to help me find my way.
   3 I need enough food to last for two days.
   4 I'll take some matches to light a fire.
3 1 He sets his alarm clock for 5 a.m. so as not to be
     late/so that he won't be (isn't) late.
   2 He puts the alarm clock near his bed so that he
     hears (can hear) it.
   3 He makes his sandwiches the night before so that
     he has ('ll have) more time in the morning.
   4 He listens to the weather forecast so that he knows
     ('ll know) what to wear.
   5 He doesn't make any noise so as not to wake/so that
     he won't (doesn't) wake the family.
   6 He shuts the front door carefully so as not to
     disturb/so that he won't (doesn't) disturb the
     neighbours.

Unit 43

1 1 hopes to go 2 asked to fill in 3 chosen to study
   Maths 4 happens to be 5 plan to do 6 help me (to)
   decide 7 train to become 8 tend not to find
   9 intend to work 10 manage to complete
2 1 afford to take 2 decided to steal 3 planned to
   drive 4 managed to get 5 attempted to start
   6 decided to leave 7 happened to go past 8 help
   them (to) start 9 pretended to be 10 decided to
   open 11 didn't dare (to) wait 12 managed to
   contact 13 didn't seem to be
3 1 how to translate 2 how to write 3 how to speak
   4 what to do 5 whether to take 6 what to do 7 how
   to spell 8 how to ask 9 how to use 10 what to say

Unit 44

1 1 She warned me not to leave anything valuable in my car.
2 She advised me to go to the police station.
3 I got the police officer to give me a written report of the theft.
4 I asked him to sign the report.
5 He reminded me to phone the ferry company to tell them I'd lost my passport.
6 He asked me to show him the police report.
7 He told me to get a new passport as soon as possible.
8 Then he allowed me to go through.

2 1 What do you want me to do? 2 I'd like you to translate this letter for me. 3 They want me to write it in Spanish. 4 I'd hate you to find that I'd made some terrible mistakes. 5 I'd prefer you to ask someone else. 6 They want me to reply by Friday 7 I'd like you to do it.

3 1 make their students wear a uniform. 2 don't let them smoke. 3 don't let their students leave the school 4 This makes some students very angry.

Unit 45

1 1 It's essential to have the right equipment.
2 It isn't/It's not safe to dive on your own.
3 It's important not to take any risks.
4 It's dangerous to stay under the water for too long.

2 1 It's hard to pronounce many English words.
2 It's difficult for me to understand some English people when they talk.
3 It's difficult not to make mistakes when you speak .
4 It isn't important to understand all the grammar.
5 It was very kind of him to give me extra lessons.

3 1 It was good of you to come. 2 It was kind of you to ask me. 3 That's a difficult question to answer.
4 It would be easy for me to say 5 it would be more honest of me to say 6 You must have been amazed to hear 7 I was surprised to hear 8 It's too early for me to say. 9 it would be nice to spend 10 it would be silly of me not to enjoy 11 it'll be hard to know 12 I'd be happy to help

Unit 46

1 1 Have you finished writing 2 I'll keep working
3 I can't imagine doing 4 I've never really considered stopping. 5 Do you mind being old? 6 I enjoy looking back 7 I miss talking to them. 8 I regret not giving up smoking 9 not learning how to use a computer.

2 1 being 2 being 3 buying 4 going 5 saying
6 answering 7 letting him go 8 asking

3 1 swimming 2 sailing 3 windsurfing 4 fishing
5 exploring 6 riding 7 sight-seeing 8 shopping
9 dancing

Unit 47

1 1 Last night I went to bed without setting my alarm clock.
2 After sleeping well for eight hours, I got up.
3 I left home without locking the door.
4 After sitting in a traffic jam, I arrived at work an hour late.
5 Before leaving work I was told I was going to lose my job.
6 After arriving home, I found my TV and video had been stolen.

2 1 tired of spending 2 interested in meeting
3 keen on swimming 4 cycling 5 fond of cooking
6 against spending 7 fed up with watching
8 afraid of showing 9 in meeting 10 forgetting
11 bad at remembering 12 good at remembering
13 how about sending 14 to hearing

3 1 I warned you last week against thinking you could win every match.
2 I'd like to congratulate Wayne on scoring a goal.
3 But I'm not just accusing Wayne of playing badly.
4 I blame the whole team for losing the game.

Unit 48

1 1 Would you mind not smoking?
2 Would you mind sitting down?
3 Would you mind putting your seat-belt on?
4 Would you mind not using your mobile phone?

2 1 I don't mind going.
2 I'm sure she won't mind me taking it.
3 She doesn't mind people using it.
4 Do you mind getting some butter too?

3 1 I can't stand drinking cold coffee.
2 I can't stand parents hitting their children.
OR I can't stand it when parents hit their children.
3 I can't stand being stopped by a customs officer.
4 I can't stand people smoking in a restaurant. OR
I can't stand it when people smoke in a restaurant.

4 1 I can't help liking her. 2 she can't help getting angry sometimes. 3 I couldn't help it 4 I couldn't help laughing.

5 1 There's no point trying to phone. OR It's no use/no good trying to phone.
2 There's no point shouting. OR It's no use/no good shouting. OR It isn't worth shouting.
3 There's no point getting angry. OR It's no use/no good getting angry. OR It isn't worth getting angry.
4 It's worth trying.

Unit 49

1 1 Two boys were standing on the stairs arguing.
2 A girl was sitting in the hall crying.
3 A boy was in the toilet feeling sick.
4 Three people were in the kitchen making themselves something to eat.

2 1 An old woman had been knocked over crossing the road.
2 A woman had burnt her hands trying to light a barbecue.
3 A man had cut himself sawing wood.

3 1 Having been to the cinema, we decided to go to a restaurant.
2 Having decided to have a Chinese meal, we went to the Mandarin restaurant.
3 Having looked at the menu, we ordered our food.
4 Having waited for half an hour for our food, we decided to leave.

4 1 Feeling very nervous, she's arrived at the examination room half an hour early.
2 Having chosen to do History at university, she wants to do well in this exam.
3 But having stayed up late last night, she's feeling very tired.
4 But being a very clever girl, she'll probably pass the exam.

Unit 50

1 1 He likes living/likes to live on his own.
2 He hates doing housework.
3 He doesn't enjoy washing up.
4 He doesn't like cooking/doesn't like to cook his own meals.
5 He doesn't like eating/doesn't like to eat healthy food.
6 He enjoys staying in bed.
7 He loves going/loves to go to the pub.
8 He loves writing/loves to write songs.
9 He loves going/loves to go to Hawaii.

2 1 She likes to clean it every weekend.
2 She always likes to get to work on time.
3 She likes to keep fit.
4 It likes to give them a bonus every year.
5 She likes to spend it carefully.

3 1 What sort of job would you like to get? 2 What would you like to be? 3 I'd like to work 4 I'd hate to spend 5 I'd like to meet her. 6 I'd like to have talked to her. 7 I'd like to have asked 8 Yes, I'd like to. (NOT Yes, I'd like.) 9 I'd hate to have done badly.

Unit 51

1 1 I'd rather have some coffee.
2 I'd rather sit on a chair.
3 I'd prefer to watch the news.
4 I'd rather go home.
5 I'd prefer to go now.

2 1 I'd prefer to go to Canada rather than the USA.
2 I'd prefer to go for two weeks rather than just one.
3 I'd rather stay in an apartment than a hotel.
4 I'd rather fly from Manchester than London.
5 I'd prefer to decide now rather than later.

3 1 I'd prefer to stay here. 2 I'd rather you went on your own. 3 I'd prefer you to wait a bit. 4 I'd prefer not to go to the same place twice. 5 I'd rather have gone to a sea-food restaurant. 6 I'd rather have gone somewhere quieter. 7 I'd rather you kept quiet

Unit 52

1 1 starts to cry OR starts crying 2 stop crying
3 goes on crying 4 try giving 5 try reading
6 need changing 7 need to do
8 Don't bother phoning OR to phone 9 to check
10 intend to stay OR intend staying 11 forget to lock

2 1 stopped to look at 2 tried to stop
3 remember getting 4 thinking 5 remember putting
6 forgotten to put 7 remember hearing
8 stopped reading 9 went on reading
10 remember seeing 11 need to examine

3 1 forget to send 2 forget going 3 remember doing
4 Remember to brush 5 need washing
6 remember to take 7 need to take
8 go on repeating 9 Try to phone 10 try leaving
11 stop to find 12 stop worrying

Unit 53

1 (Note: The doctor might be a woman, so you can write *she, her*, etc.)
The patient said she had a problem. She said she felt a pain in her right eye every time she drank a cup of tea. The doctor said he didn't think it was serious. He said he thought she should take the spoon out of the cup before she drank the tea.
(Note: The patient might be a woman, so you can write *she, her*, etc.)
The patient told the doctor she must (OR had to) help him. The doctor said she would if she could, but she didn't have much time that day, so it might not be possible. The patient said he had a terrible pain in his right leg. He said it had started two days before. The doctor said that was interesting. She said she wanted him to stand at the window and put his tongue out. The patient said that wouldn't stop the pain in his right leg. The doctor said (OR replied) it was going to help her, because she didn't like the man who lived opposite.

2 1 then 2 he would come round that day or the following day/the next day 3 he'd fix 4 that week 5 he'd redecorate 6 the following week 7 he'd checked 8 the month before 9 he'd had 10 a week before 11 had all been cleaned the day before/the previous day 12 had 13 could ring him that night at home.

Unit 54

1 The policeman asked him what his name was. He said it was Jason Cox. He asked him who the motorcycle belonged to. He said it belonged to him. He asked him if/whether he had a driving licence. He said he had. He asked if he could see it. (OR He asked to see it.) He said he didn't have it on him. (OR He said he hadn't got it on him.) The policeman asked him if he could bring it to Redland Police station the next day. (OR The policeman asked him to bring it to Redland Police station the following day.) He said he could. The policeman asked him if he knew his back light wasn't working. He said he didn't. The policeman said he must/had to fix it or walk home.

2 1 The doctor wanted to know what the problem was.
2 She asked if/whether he knew why he collapsed (OR he'd collapsed).
3 She asked him to roll up his sleeve. 4. She advised him to take a complete rest. 5 She suggested (that) he went away on holiday. 6 She warned him that if he didn't take it easy he might make himself seriously ill. 7 She reminded him (that) he wasn't a young man any more. 8 She told him to take the sleeping pills to help him sleep. 9 She insisted (that) he came and saw her again on Thursday (OR the following Thursday).

Unit 55

1 4 the 6 the 7 the 11 The 12 the 13 the 17 the
2 3 the 5 the 7 the 8 the 11 the 13 the 14 the
3 1 the 4 the 6 the 10 the 11 the 12 the 13 the
14 the 15 the 16 the
4 3 (the) 8 the 11 the 14 the

Unit 56

1 1 General 2 General 3 Particular 4 General
5 Particular 6 Particular 7 General 8 General
2 1 - the - 2 - - the - - 3 - - - the - 4 The -
5 - the
3 1 the 3 - the 6 the
4 1 Crime 2 The music 3 money 4 Marriage 5 drugs and sex 6 The respect 7 Young people

Unit 57

1

a:	an:
US citizen	empty glass
European country	honest answer
one-way street	Eastern European country
CD-player	untidy room
Chinese restaurant	unusual name
used car	international airport

2 2 an 3 an 4 a 5 a 6 an 7 a 8 a 10 an 12 an 15 an
16 an 17 a 18 an 20 an 21 a 22 an 23 an 24 a
25 a 26 a
3 1 a (some) 3 some 4 Some 6 some 7 some 10 a
12 (some) 13 (some) 14 a

Unit 58

1 1 mice 2 flies 3 mosquitoes 4 beaches 5 churches
6 photos 7 loaves 8 fruit 9 peaches 10 oranges
11 tomatoes 12 shelves 13 fish 14 buses 15 feet
16 wolves 17 people 18 families 19 men 20 wives
21 children 22 lives 23 centuries 24 countries
2 1 two parties 2 a lot of people 3 two women
4 my three children 5 Two men 6 his three wives
7 several oil companies 8 the many Arab countries
9 a few sandwiches 10 five or six glasses of wine
3 1 are 2 have got 3 are 4 are 5 stop 6 ask 7 avoid
8 are 9 is 10 is

Unit 59

1

Countable	Uncountable
potatoes	coffee
vegetables	salt
bananas	cooking oil
eggs	rice
mushrooms	toilet-paper
tomatoes	washing-powder
sausages	fruit
matches	milk
	toothpaste
	meat
	marmalade
	tea

2 1 There's 2 there isn't 3 There aren't 4 there are
5 there's 6 there's 7 There are 8 there isn't
9 there's
3 1 a bit of luck 2 accommodation 3 is 4 a 5 is
6 some 7 some 8 isn't 9 is 10 a problem 11 work
12 office equipment 13 an 14 is 15 help 16 a

Unit 60

1 1 a lot of tomatoes many peppers 2 too many
courgettes a lot 3 much celery many peas 4 so
much fruit a lot 5 so many apples a lot of cider
2 1 How much 2 much 3 a lot of time 4 many friends
5 lots 6 much television 7 a lot of 8 How many
9 many cinemas 10 too much trouble
3 1 We've got plenty of petrol.
2 There'll be plenty of room/plenty of spaces.
3 I've got plenty of money.
4 There are plenty of pubs/cafés/bars.
4 1 very little coffee 2 very few cooked vegetables
3 a little orange juice a few grapes 4 a little cheese
a few raw vegetables 5 a little rice a little wine
6 very little sugar very little fat very few snacks

Unit 61

1 b, e, c, a, f, d
2 1 no 2 any 3 no 4 any 5 No
3 1 any 2 none 3 any 4 no 5 any 6 some 7 some
8 some
4 1 any 2 any some 3 any 4 any 5 some any

Unit 62

1 1 Everybody/Everyone 2 everything 3 All 4 all
5 Everything 6 Everybody/Everyone
7 everybody/everyone

2 1 all the trees 2 every house 3 all the houses
4 each of them 5 they've all (each) written
6 Every time (Each time) 7 all the pollution
8 every/each new road

3 1 he drinks the whole bottle. 2 He buys a whole
case. 3 He watches the whole programme.
4 he takes a whole suitcase

4 1 all week/the whole week 2 every day
3 all morning/the whole morning
4 all afternoon/the whole afternoon 5 every half an
hour 6 all evening/the whole evening 7 every
Friday evening 8 every day 9 all year/the whole
year

Unit 63

1 1 Most British holidaymakers 2 Many of them
3 all of them 4 Some people 5 any of the people I
know 6 All of them 7 a few of my friends 8 All my
friends (Less common: All of my friends) 9 half the
time (Less common: half of the time) 10 half (of)
the time 11 most of the time 12 none of the things
13 any of them 14 Some of us 15 all the time (Less
common: all of the time)

2 1 both (of) these sweaters 2 Neither of them
3 either of them 4 either 5 both colours 6 Either
7 Either 8 neither of them

3 1 My girlfriend Sadie and I both like flying./Both my
girlfriend Sadie and I like flying.
2 At the time we were all having lunch.
3 The flight attendants were serving us all coffee.
4 We both stopped eating.
5 Then we both fastened our seat-belts.
6 The captain told us all to keep our seat-belts
fastened.
7 They had all stopped talking.
8 The flight attendants had all returned to their seats.
9 We both held hands.
10 Then the captain spoke to us all again.
11 We all cheered.

Unit 64

1 1 those 2 These 3 those 4 those 5 these 6 those
7 this 8 that 9 that 10 That

2 1 this 2 this 3 That 4 That 5 those 6 That
7 these 8 this

3 1 that 2 This 3 that 4 this 5 this 6 this 7 those
8 that 9 this 10 this 11 these

Unit 65

1 1 yourselves 2 ourselves 3 themselves 4 myself
5 himself 6 myself 7 themselves 8 herself
9 herself 10 itself 11 yourself 12 myself
13 themselves

2 1 each other 2 themselves 3 each other
4 themselves 5 each other 6 each other
7 yourself 8 yourself

3 1 themselves 2 himself 3 themselves 4 themselves
5 herself herself 6 ourselves 7 myself

Unit 66

1 1 anyone (-body) 2 anything 3 Someone (-body)
4 anything 5 anything 6 nothing 7 something
8 something

2 1 someone 2 something 3 anyone (-body)
4 someone (-body) no-one (-body)
5 somewhere nowhere

3 1 something nice 2 anything expensive
3 something smaller 4 something cheaper

4 1 You can go anywhere. 2 You can eat anything.
3 You can talk to anyone (-body). 4 You can wear
anything. 5 You can park your car anywhere.

Unit 67

1 1 It's Jill's. 2 They're Tom and Maggy's.
3 It's my parents'. 4 It's the dog's.

2 1 Yesterday's weather was awful.
2 It was as bad as last year's storms.
3 I'm going to watch this evening's television news.
4 Tomorrow's weather forecast isn't very good.

3 1 her mother's name the name of his favourite
flower. 2 women's magazines the music of a new
heavy metal band. 3 England's terrible weather the
sunshine of southern Europe OR southern Europe's
sunshine a month's holiday 4 a local girls' team
the team's best player. 5 Her parents' house at her
boyfriend's

4 1 the bedroom window 2 my garage key
3 my holiday photos 4 my car radio aerial

5 1 a friend of yours 2 a friend of my parents'
3 a student of hers 4 a painting of his

Unit 68

1 1 my 2 hers 3 his 4 their 5 theirs 6 its 7 your

2 1 their own private beach 2 its own swimming-pool
3 my own bathroom 4 his own recording studio
5 her own horses its own stable
6 their own oranges and lemons

3 1 Whose Walkman is this? OR Whose is this Walkman?
2 Is it yours, Sebastian? 3 No, it isn't mine.
4 Is it hers? 5 It's probably his.

4 1 Are they yours? 2 No, they aren't mine.
3 Are they hers? 4 No, they aren't hers.
5 Are they theirs? 6 No, I don't think they're theirs.
7 ... so now they're mine.

Unit 69

1 1 I must buy some new ones. 2 Which ones do you like? 3 I don't like those. 4 Which one do you like? 5 That one. The one with the big buttons. 6 That one's too expensive. Try this green one on.

2 1 Which ones? 2 The new ones 3 Which one? 4 That one 5 The green ones 6 the red ones 7 the red ones 8 this one 9 that one

3 There are a lot of hotels here. Lorna's staying in one right by the sea. Mine is in the town. It's a lot smaller than hers. Hers has got a swimming pool, but mine hasn't got one. There are lots of cafés. We often go to one that has really good pizzas. There are a lot of German and American tourists; there are a few from France, but there aren't many from England. There are some lovely beaches. We like the ones on the south side of the island. Our favourite one is only 500 metres from the town.

Unit 70

1 1 A 2 B 3 B 4 B 5 A

2 1 a lovely old 18th century house 2 by a famous English architect 3 a long narrow country lane 4 a pretty little village 5 Yes 6 Yes 7 modern and well-equipped 8 green and white 9 an interesting old stone fireplace 10 Yes

3 1 The water's 3.5m deep. 2 The room's 5m long and 4m wide. 3 The mountain's 1150m high. 4 The piece of wood is 5cm thick.

Unit 71

1 1 Louise is older than Ben. 2 Louise's family is bigger than Ben's. 3 Ben's heavier than Louise. 4 Ben's taller than Louise. 5 Louise is a better tennis player than Ben. OR Louise is better at tennis than Ben.

2 1 21% go abroad because the hotels are more comfortable.
2 5% go abroad because wine and cigarettes are cheaper.
3 11% go abroad because the sea's (is) warmer.
4 10% go abroad because the beaches are cleaner.
5 23% go abroad because the people are friendlier/more friendly.
6 15% go abroad because the food's (is) more interesting.
7 10% go abroad because the night-life is more exciting.
8 12% go abroad because they get a sun-tan more easily.
9 2% go abroad because the bars stay open later.

3 1 Mars is the nearest planet to Earth.
2 Pluto is the most distant planet from the sun.
3 Venus is the hottest planet.
4 Jupiter is the biggest planet.
5 Mercury is the most difficult planet to see.

Unit 72

1 1 Bananas aren't as cheap as apples.
2 Bananas are twice as expensive as pears.
3 Mangoes are three times as expensive as apples.
4 Grapes are the same price as bananas.
5 Apples are just as expensive as pears.

2 1 more and more impatient 2 later and later 3 The sooner the better 4 The earlier the more likely OR the likelier

3 1 The same 2 Fewer 3 The least 4 More 5 less 6 the most 7 the fewest

4 1 far easier 2 a lot more difficult 3 much more international 4 slightly more

Unit 73

1 1 exciting 2 amazed 3 boring 4 frightening 5 amazing 6 disgusted 7 bored 8 interested

2 1 depressing 2 depressed 3 bored 4 boring 5 interested 6 interesting 7 amazing 8 amazed 9 worried 10 worrying 11 tired

3 1 tiring 2 interested 3 amusing 4 tired 5 surprised 6 worried 7 embarrassed 8 amazing 9 worrying 10 frightened

Unit 74

1 1 certain 2 good 3 confidently 4 easily 5 carefully 6 slightly 7 confident 8 impatiently 9 quickly 10 angrily 11 definitely 12 illegal

2 1 directly OR straight 2 hard 3 well 4 late 5 lately 6 good 7 serious highly 8 fast 9 nervous hardly 10 nearly

3 1 I don't know Robert well.
2 Unfortunately he never speaks to anyone.
3 Perhaps he's just terribly shy.
4 Sharon's completely different.
5 She's probably the laziest person I know.
6 She definitely won't get promotion.
7 She's been taking a lot of time off work lately. OR Lately she's been taking a lot of time off work.
8 The manager has nearly sacked her twice this year.
9 Actually she's a very nice girl.

Unit 75

1 1 b 2 c 3 b 4 a 5 c 6 c

2 1 The girl's name is often Lucy. OR Often the girl's name is Lucy.
2 She's never been in love before.
3 She meets Mark at a party.
4 Can I give you a lift somewhere?
5 He phones her the next day. OR The next day he phones her.
6 After that they're hardly ever apart.
7 But then another woman always appears.
8 She's usually very attractive.
9 And her name's generally Miranda. OR And generally her name's Miranda.
10 Lucy sees them together in town. OR Lucy sees them in town together.
11 She phones him later at his flat. OR Later she phones him at his flat.
12 He isn't there.
13 She tries again.
14 She can't really believe OR She really can't believe
15 She locks herself in her room.
16 She's terribly unhappy at first. OR At first she's terribly unhappy.
17 ... he doesn't really love Miranda.
18 And he returns to Lucy for ever.

Unit 76

1 1 quite good 2 rather weak 3 rather poor
4 quite a lot better 5 quite interesting 6 rather bad
7 rather difficult 8 quite intelligent

2 1 quite/rather 2 pretty/fairly/rather
3 pretty/rather/quite 4 quite 5 quite/rather 6 quite
7 quite/rather 8 quite/rather 9 quite 10 rather

3 1 so 2 such 3 such 4 so 5 so 6 such 7 such 8 so

Unit 77

1 1 much/very much 2 as much 3 a bit 4 so much
5 much/very much 6 a lot/very much 7 as much
8 a bit 9 so much

2 1 less 2 better (possibly: best) 3 most 4 more
5 worst 6 worse 7 best (most) 8 best 9 least

Unit 78

1 1 Britain has been in the European Union for years,
but some British people still don't like the idea.
2 They're still worried about being part of Europe.
3 They still want to keep their national identity.
4 The EU has been good for Britain, but they still
don't see the advantages.
5 They're still hoping that Britain will soon leave the
Union.

2 2 Is there still a fish and chip shop?
3 Are the Taylors still living in Church Street?
4 Do people still have picnics by the river?
5 Is old Mrs Stamp still alive?
6 Does the village still have a big party on New Year's
Eve?

3 1 still 2 yet 3 still 4 no longer 5 any more/any
longer 6 still 7 yet 8 still 9 any more/any longer
10 yet 11 no longer 12 any more/any longer 13 yet
14 still

Unit 79

1 1 too noisy 2 varied enough 3 too slow 4 too long
5 hot enough 6 too expensive

2 1 good enough 2 well enough 3 enough goals
4 enough money 5 enough people 6 big enough
7 interested enough

3 1 big enough 2 too small 3 too dark 4 too
expensive 5 cheap enough 6 comfortable enough
7 too hard 8 too big 9 too old

4 1 He's too old to go back to school.
2 He isn't independent enough to live on his own.
3 He's too difficult for us to control.
4 It wasn't interesting enough for him to accept.

Unit 80

1 1 on 2 on 3 in 4 in 5 in 6 at 7 On 8 in 9 at 10 at
11 in 12 In 14 at 15 at 16 at 17 at 18 on 19 in

2 4 at 5 On 6 in 7 in 8 on 9 in 10 in 11 at 12 on

3 1 In 2 in 3 In 4 In 5 in 6 on 7 At 8 At 9 in

Unit 81

1 1 In 2 at 3 at 4 in 5 on 6 in 7 on 8 In 9 on 10 on
11 At 12 on 13 on 14 on 15 on 16 In 17 on

2 1 on 2 in 3 in 4 in 5 at 6 on 7 in 8 in 9 at 10 at
11 in 12 in 13 at 14 in 15 at 16 in 17 at 18 in
19 in 20 at 21 in 22 on OR at

Unit 82

1 1 behind 2 above 3 in front of 4 Among
5 Opposite 6 Between 7 outside 8 next to 9 by

2 1 on top of 2 under 3 round 4 beside 5 over
6 Below 7 near

Unit 83

1 1 along 2 up 3 off 4 onto 5 down 6 round 7 past
8 to 9 over 10 across 11 into 12 under 13 to
14 through 15 towards 16 out of

2 1 over out of 2 past under into 3 up down
4 round 5 towards into 6 onto

Unit 84

1 1 to 2 to 4 by 5 to 6 to 7 by 8 on 9 at 10 to
11 in 12 by 13 to 14 on 15 on 16 to 17 into 18 to
19 on 20 at

2 1 to 2 by 3 in 4 by 5 by 6 to 7 by 8 in 9 to
10 in 11 to 12 on 13 to 14 off 15 to 16 by 17 on
18 on 19 by 20 on

Unit 85

1 1 I haven't has a good meal for a week.
2 I haven't had a job for a year.
3 I haven't seen my family for years.
4 I haven't had a hot bath for a long time.
5 I haven't slept in a comfortable bed for ages.

2 1 for 2 since 3 since 4 for 5 for 6 for 7 since
8 for 9 for

3 1 ago 2 for 3 ago 4 since 5 since

4 1 ago 2 for 3 for 4 for 5 since 6 For 7 since 8 for
9 for 10 ago 11 since 12 ago 13 for 14 ago 15 for
16 for 17 ago 18 since

Unit 86

1

For	During	While
three days	1994	we were there
an hour	the lesson	we've got time
a long time	his lifetime	I'm young
a week	the week	I was on holiday
ages	the meal	the band was playing

2 1 during 2 for 3 for 4 for 5 during 6 during
7 during 8 for 9 during 10 during

3 1 for 2 During 3 for 4 While 5 During 6 While
7 for

4 1 For 2 while 3 While 4 During 5 during 6 during
7 for

Unit 87

1 1 get 2 arrive 3 get 4 are (you're) 5 go 6 call/have called

2 1 as soon as they've been developed 2 once I've had 3 until we've been 4 after we've had

3 1e 2c 3a 4b 5d

4 1 I get up 2 I go 3 I get back   the shops close 4 I've done 5 I've finished 6 they get

Unit 88

1 1 by 2 until/till 3 by the time 4 by 5 by 6 by 7 by 8 by the time 9 until/till 10 until/till 11 until/till 12 by 13 by

2 1 until/till 2 By the time 3 by 4 until/till 5 until/till 6 by the time 7 by the time

3 1 by 2 by 3 By the time 4 until/till 5 By the time 6 until/till

Unit 89

1 1 as 2 like 3 as 4 like 5 like 6 as 7 as 8 as

2 1 he shouts as if/as though we were all in the next room.
2 He acts as if/as though we were all his servants.
3 He talks to us as if/as though we were children.
4 He talks as if/as though he was/were an expert on everything.
5 as if/as though he was/were the only person in the company.

3 1 as 2 like 3 like 4 as (informal: like) 5 like 6 like 7 as (informal: like)

4 1 like 2 as if/as though 3 as 4 like 5 like 6 as 7 like 8 like 9 like 10 Like 11 Like 12 as if/as though

Unit 90

1 1 He picked up a book, although he didn't want to read.
2 He switched on the television, although there was nothing interesting on.
3 He had a bath, although he'd already had one in the morning.
4 Although he usually goes to bed at 11 p.m., he went to bed at 9.30 p.m.

2 1 Even though 2 although 3 even though 4 Although 5 Although 6 Even though 7 even though

3 1 In spite of being 90, Jim Lake is still active.
2 He still does his own shopping in spite of living a long way from the shops.
3 He still goes to watch his football team in spite of not being able to see very well.

4 1 He's a good chess player though.
2 He doesn't like spiders though.
3 She hasn't got any valuable ones though.

5 1 so 2 so 3 because 4 because 5 Since 6 so 7 so 8 because

Unit 91

1 1 Leonardo da Vinci was the artist who painted the roof of the Sistine Chapel in Rome.
2 Gandhi was the Indian leader who helped to make India independent from Britain.
3 Marie Curie was the scientist who discovered radium.
4 Francisco Pizarro was the soldier who conquered the Inca Empire of Peru in 1532.

2 (possible alternatives given in brackets) 1 – (that, which) 2 who 3 that (which) 4 that (which) 5 – (that, which) 6 that (which) 7 who (that) 8 who 9 – (that, who, whom) 10 – (that) 11 – (that) 12 – (that, who, whom) 13 – (that) 14 who (that)

3 1 This is the family we stayed with in Bombay.
2 This is the train we went on to Goa.
3 This is the hotel we stayed at in Goa.
4 This is the beach we sat on every day.
5 This is the restaurant we ate at every evening.
6 This is the elephant I had a ride on.
7 These are the Indian friends we spent a lot of time with.
8 This is the plane we flew back on.

Unit 92

1 1 This is the field where I used to play football.
2 This is the shop where I worked for two years.
3 This is where we used to play tennis.
4 This is the house where my old friend Tom lived.
5 This is the river where I learnt to swim.

2 1 She's the girl whose mother won £100,000 in the Lottery.
2 He's the man whose house was burnt down last week.
3 She's the woman whose brother we met in the cinema last night.
4 He's the one whose 50th birthday party we went to two years ago.

3 1 what 2 that/– 3 what 4 that/– 5 what 6 that/–

4 1 What I'd like to see is more women in Parliament!
2 What annoys me is that rich people don't pay enough tax!
3 What surprises me is that people don't complain more!

Unit 93

1 2 He keeps his boat at Richmond, which is on a very beautiful part of the river.
   3 George, whose wife died ten years ago, lives alone with two dogs and a cat.
   4 But he's got a lot of friends in Richmond, who look after him well.
   5 His boat, which was built in the 1920s, is a very comfortable home.
   6 Every day he walks into Richmond, where he does his shopping and meets his friends.
   7 Today he's having a big birthday party, which all his friends and family are coming to.

2 1 Defining. 2 Non-Defining. It's Melanie Rigg, who sings with 'The Machine'. 3 Defining.
   4 Non-Defining. She lives in Henley, which is about two miles from here. 5 Defining.
   6 Non-Defining. She's got her own recording studio, which is in the garden.
   7 Non-Defining. She's also got a house in California, where she spends six months of the year. 8 Defining.
   9 Non-Defining. That's Gary Trench, whose brother's the drummer with 'The Machine'. 10 Defining.

3 2 When I left home there were traffic jams everywhere, which meant I arrived late.
   3 When I arrived, I found a man sitting in my seat, which he wasn't allowed to do.
   4 He didn't want to move, which made me very angry.
   5 I asked him to show me his ticket, which he refused to do.
   6 I went to find a policeman, which took me another ten minutes.
   7 I finally sat down at 3 o'clock, which was 20 minutes after the beginning of the match.

Unit 94

1 1 This morning the road connecting Orlando to the coast was blocked by floodwater.
   2 A woman taking her children to school had to abandon her car and walk home.
   3 A train carrying 73 passengers fell into the river below when a bridge collapsed.
   4 A car belonging to the mayor of Orlando was swept into the river.

2 1 A life-raft found at the scene was empty.
   2 A helicopter called from Lossiemouth is still searching the area.
   3 Last week another Scottish fishing boat hit by a submarine sank in the same area.
   4 There have been three fishing boats hit by submarines this year.

3 1 with 2 living 3 married 4 with 5 teaching 6 with
   7 playing 8 built 9 studying 10 grown 11 bought
   12 making 13 spent

Richmond Publishing
19 Berghem Mews
Blythe Road
London W14 0HN

© David Bolton and Noel Goodey, 1996
Published by Richmond Publishing®
First published 1996

ISBN: 84-294-4430-0
Depósito legal: M-266-2000
Printed in Spain by
Huertas, S. A.

Design   Jonathan Barnard
Layout   Mike Cryer
Cover design La Pot

Illustrations
Kathy Baxendale, Greg Becker, Peter Cornwall,
Stephen Dew, Mark Duffin, Antonia Enthoven,
Clyde Pearson, Chris Rothero